WITHDRAWN

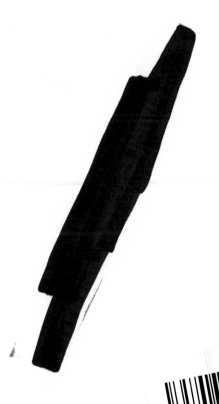

Christopher Durang

COMPLETE FULL-LENGTH PLAYS
1975–1995

Published by Smith and Kraus, Inc., PO Box 127, Lyme, NH 03768
Copyright ©1997 by Christopher Durang
Manufactured in the United States of America
Cover and Text Design by Julia Hill

ISBN 1-57525-017-9

Christopher Durang

COMPLETE FULL-LENGTH PLAYS

1975–1995

Contemporary Playwrights Series

SK
A Smith and Kraus Book

THE AUTHOR

Christopher Durang has had plays on and off Broadway including *The Nature and Purpose of the Universe; Titanic; A History of the American Film* (Tony nomination, Best Book of a Musical); *Sister Mary Ignatius Explains It All For You* (Obie Award, off-Broadway run 1981–1983); *Beyond Therapy; Baby with the Bathwater; The Marriage of Bette and Boo* (Obie Award, Dramatists Guild Hall Warriner Award); *Laughing Wild.* Recently an evening of six of his one acts called *Durang, Durang* premiered at Manhattan Theatre Club in 1994.

His plays have been presented extensively in regional theaters in America, and also abroad. He has had the pleasure of working on premiére productions at the Eugene O'Neill Playwrights Conference, the American Repertory Theatre, Arena Stage, Mark Taper Forum, Playwrights Horizons, and the Public Theatre, among others.

Durang has also been active in cabaret, having co-written and performed with Sigourney Weaver in their Brecht-Weill parody *Das Lusitania Songspiel* (both receiving Drama Desk nominations in musical performing); and later having performed his own satiric nightclub act *Chris Durang and Dawne,* first at the Criterion Center in New York, then at Caroline's Comedy Club, and in 1995 at the Bay Street Theatre in Sag Harbor and the Triad in Manhattan. He has been working with Donna McKechnie on her one-woman show, *Inside the Music.* And years ago at the Yale Cabaret, he co-wrote two cabaret pieces with Albert Innaurato, and one with Wendy Wasserstein.

He has also written several screenplays and teleplays: *The Nun Who Shot Liberty Valance* for Warner Brothers; *The House of Husbands* (co-authored with Wendy Wasserstein) for the Ladd Company; *The Adventures of Lola* for Tri-Star and director Herbert Ross; a sitcom, *Dysfunction—The TV Show,* again for Warner Brothers.

He is also an actor, sometimes performing in his own plays *(The Marriage of Bette and Boo,* ensemble acting Obie; *Laughing Wild* in New York and L.A.), sometimes in other people's plays (Wallace Shawn's *The Hotel Play,* Charles Schulman's *The Birthday Present* at the Young Playwright's Festival). He performed in the Stephen Sondheim revue *Putting It Together* with Julie Andrews at Manhattan Theatre Club. And he played a conservative Congressman in *Call Me Madam* with Tyne Daly in the City Center Encore Series. He can be heard on the CD's of both shows. And he's had supporting roles in the films *Secret of My Success, Mr. North, Penn and Teller Get Killed, The Butcher's Wife, Housesitter, Life with Mikey, The Cowboy Way.*

He has received a Guggenheim, a Rockefeller, the CBS Playwriting Fellowship, the Lecompte du Nouy Foundation grant, and the Kenyon Festival Theatre Playwriting Prize. In 1995 he won the prestigious three-year Lila Wallace Readers Digest Writers Award; as part of his grant, he is working with the Alcoholism Council Fellowship Center in New York, running a workshop for adult children of alcoholics.

Mr. Durang is a graduate of Harvard College and of Yale School of Drama; a member of the Dramatists Guild Council; and with Marsha Norman is the co-chair of the playwriting program at the Juilliard School Drama Division.

He wrote a new play on commission for Lincoln Center Theatre called *Sex and Longing,* which premiered in the fall of 1996, starring Sigourney Weaver.

CONTENTS

AUTHOR'S NOTE

This volume was prepared for reading the plays, not for producing them.

If you should end up wanting to produce any of the plays, I would ask that you be sure to get ahold of the acting edition versions of these plays, published by Samuel French or by Dramatists Play Service. (Samuel French publishes *A History of the American Film* and *Beyond Therapy;* Dramatists Play Service publishes the other five plays.)

In the acting editions, I include extensive author's notes geared to putting on the plays: suggestions and guidance about acting tone, about set, about common misunderstandings in the plays, sometimes about possible cuts.

This material is usually helpful to your production, and is my attempt to let you know my thoughts, as if I were present at your first rehearsal. The notes are meant to be suggestive, not meant to say there is only one way to do something; but if I've seen certain choices that seem to make something not work, why not let you know of that? Most people seem to like the notes.

I have not included these notes in this volume because they get too specific to be of interest to the general reader. (By the way, there are no additional notes for *The Vietnamization of New Jersey* but for the other six plays, there are.)

So if you do produce the plays, aside from your needing to get the performance rights from Samuel French or Dramatists Play Service, I hope you will also be sure to get the acting editions they publish, and not rely only on the texts in this book. Thanks.

INTRODUCTION

I have been reading and watching Christopher Durang's plays for over twenty-five years now, ever since he entered the playwriting program of the Yale School of Drama in the early seventies when I was the Dean. Chris was a member of a now legendary class, many of whose members not only performed, directed, and designed his work at the school and the Yale Rep, but were to be his regular collaborators for many years to come. He is a famously loyal friend, but also someone who is stimulated by talents compatible with his own.

In a sense, Chris set the tone for this witty and brilliant, sometimes acerbic, sometimes disaffected generation. I once described him as an angelic altar boy with poison leeching through his writing fingers, which was my way of saying how behind his shy and courteous demeanor lurked a literary Jack the Ripper. After rereading the seven full-length works in this volume, I realize that this characterization is only marginally true. There is a great deal of anger in his work, all right, often proceeding from genuine pain and wounded innocence. But except on rare occasions—when a demon leaps out of his skin and starts pitchforking some fatuous damned soul—Chris is much too kindhearted to go for the jugular.

It's probably more accurate to describe him as a Catholic lapsarian, troubled over the meaninglessness of life and heartsick over the absence of God—when he is not being dumbstruck by His malevolence and delinquency. Durang's surrogate Matt says it best in *The Marriage of Bette and Boo*: "I don't think God punishes people for specific things....I think He punishes people in general, for no reason." This has a Doestoyevskian ring, doesn't it? And I've always suspected Chris of being the reincarnation of Ivan Karamozov, assuming Ivan had been reborn in New Jersey, educated at Harvard, and forced to reach his liberal arts baccalaureate degree by wading knee deep through the swamps of American pop culture.

Does that sound too sober? I think so too. It certainly does little justice to Durang's anarchic sense of humor. So let me wash my brains, as Chris might say, and start again.

Christopher Durang's unwashed brain is an uneasy compound of Hollywood movies and sit-coms, Eugene Ionesco plays, and Monty Python skits. Like Ionesco, Durang certainly knows how many crimes are committed in the name of language. (I'm wild about the female analyst in *Beyond Therapy* who for the life of her can't remember the word for "Porpoise. Pompous. Pom Pom. Paparazzi. Polyester. Pollywog. Olley olley oxen free. Patient. I'm sorry, I mean patient.") It was Ionesco who told us that philology always leads to calamity. For Durang calamity is more often the result of stupidity. Don't his people sometimes remind you of John Cleese selling a half hour of "abuse" to Michael Palin? Sudden explosions of fury, followed by an overwhelming sense of relief, this seems to be the trademark behavior not only of the playwright's characters but of us who watch them. Perhaps of everybody.

Durang began his writing life as a parodist. In *The Idiots Karamazov* (co-authored with his classmate, Albert Inaurato), he turned his mocking eyes on the whole corpus of Russian and American literature, fashioning the revenge of an innocent undergraduate who, having had Doestoyevsky, Chekhov, Dickens, Anais Nin, Djuan Barnes, James Joyce, and Eugene O'Neill crammed down his throat for four years, regurgitated them in the form of demented Cliff Notes. The four Karamazov Brothers transform into the Three Sisters (with a touch of the four Marx Brothers), Aloysha turns into Pip, Constance Garnett into Miss Havisham, and Mrs. Karamazov becomes Mary Tyrone. It was the first full-length Durang I ever read, and it still makes me laugh out loud. Chris is kind enough to mention that I have always been a supporter of his work. Well, at least I recognized, though not everything was of equal merit, that all his work had special genius. And thank God I did! Otherwise I might have found myself in it. There is nothing that so damns a producer (or a critic) to the lowest circle of a satirist's hell than failing to recognize a genuine talent.

Pardon the note of nostalgia—this whole volume has been a trip into the past for me—but I shall never forget the two Yale productions of this play, both featuring the divine Meryl Streep, a wart on her nose, her eyes oozing gum, playing the "ancient translatrix" Constance Garnett, bane of all lovers of Russian literature. Brandishing her cane and fixing us all with a baleful scowl, she concluded the action by circling the stage in her wheelchair, screaming at the audience "Go home! GO HOME!" Lying in ruins on stage was the detritus of Western literature, having been jammed into some crazy blender that spewed it out as pulp and seeds.

It was assumed at this time that Durang's great talent was for satiric cabarets. And, indeed, in his next play, *The Vietnamization of New Jersey,* he ridiculed the anti-war plays of the age, particularly *Sticks and Bones* by the hugely gifted but (at the time) overly conscience-stricken David Rabe. The poster we made for the Yale production was a sardonic variant on the famous Norman Rockwell Thanksgiving dinner painting, this time featuring a family you wouldn't dare take home with you, much less share a drumstick with. Skewering right-wing warmongers and leftwing guiltmongers alike, like Lenny Bruce before him, Durang managed to make comedy out of the unthinkable and the unspeakable. The play showed a brave, outspoken generation beginning to find its voice—before political correctness shoved a big bone down its throat.

The History of the American Film was Durang's last dramatic parody. After this, he was to explore the more difficult terrain of his own life and his own family, without ever abandoning his almost Swiftian indignation. (His parody was now reserved for short plays and nightclub cabarets, many featuring his Yale contemporary Sigourney Weaver.) American Film, however, was the ultimate cabaret parody—a whirlwind tour through four decades of Hollywood shlock, featuring most of the movie characters who still haunt our dreams: Jimmy and Loretta, Hank and Bette, etc. These and other celluloid archetypes are encountered so frequently in so many guises—most hilariously as the ("'cause we're the People") Joad family in The Grapes of Wrath—that we come to realize they are always playing the same parts. Someone once advanced the theory that the mark of a really fine mind was the capacity to find not differences but rather similarities among several species or things. The History of American Film, like The Idiots Karamazov, proves it.

When I first read Beyond Therapy, Chris' most mainstream comedy, it disappointed me. I thought it no more than a cute meet. I missed the Durangian outrage. Either the play has deepened since, or I have. Indisputably Durang's wittiest and most lighthearted work, it also contains a hidden lode of fury and resentment. It's like a dose of laughing gas that doesn't quite manage to subdue the toothache. Psychoanalysis in particular gets the full impact of the dentist's drill, as the therapists prove to be more aggressive, and often more looney, than their patients. And this is Durang's first play, to my knowledge, to examine his complex feelings toward bisexuality, a theme to which he returns in Laughing Wild.

Durang's preoccupation with dead babies (they first appear in American Film) becomes an obsession in what is clearly his finest play to date, the thinly disguised autobiographical drama The Marriage of Bette and Boo. In this play, Durang reveals himself as another child of O'Neill, entering the action as a character (also as an actor) in much the same way O'Neill did in A Long Day's Journey and for much the same reasons. "Unless you go through all the genuine anger you feel, both justified and unjustified," Durang writes in his poignant introduction to the play, "the feelings of love that you do have will not have any legitimate base…Plus, eventually you will go crazy." *The Marriage of Bette and Boo* is an extremely touching tribute to a recently dead mother, to an alcoholic father, and to a son who has finally learned to forgive his family and himself.

Baby With the Bathwater, which also deals with dead or abused children, is another comedy about a dysfunctional family, an emphasis that led one of Durang's critics (Benedict Nightingale) to accuse him and other American dramatists of writing "diaper plays." (An even more overworked and wrong-headed epithet for Durang is "sophomoric".) But if Durang writes diaper plays, so did O'Neill, Odets, Miller, Albee, and Williams. Indeed, the quintessential American drama is and always has been a family drama—a work in which the writer lays his ghosts to rest at last, making peace with his past by exorcising the dead.

Laughing Wild is the last play in the volume and one of the strangest: two stream-of-consciousness monologues and a very bizarre dialogue in which the pair of speakers share each other's dreams. It features some of Durang's most experimental writing and free-floating connections (consider the character who sees his father in a baked potato, smears him with butter, and eats him!). And it contains an extremely eloquent diatribe against the paleocons who regard AIDS as a punishment for sexual deviation. Worth quoting from this play is one of Durang's most telling witticisms, characteristic in the way the playwright combines metaphysics with show business. Recoiling from an egotistical actor who blesses his Creator for an award as featured performer, the male speaker says: "God is silent on the Holocaust, but he involves himself in the Tony Awards? I don't think so."

Christopher Durang doesn't think so either, and this conflict between conventional wisdom and perceived reality continues to be a prime trigger of his anger. Another is the arrogance and muddle-headedness of us theatre critics, particularly Frank Rich, who had the distinction of panning many of the plays in this volume. Appended to *Laughing Wild* is Durang's wrenching description of how Rich, during his tenure as *The New York Times* drama critic, was strangulating the stage, if not disheartening the playwright. I know of many other distinguished dramatists at the time who felt the same way. But of course there is much more to be found here than a display of wounded feelings—namely, seven extremely fine plays, complete with eloquent introductions, that now have a permanent life in published form, impervious to critical abuse. They represent a brilliant and daring dramatic mind at work. And they make me very very proud.

Robert Brustein
American Repertory Theatre

The Idiots Karamazov

co-authored with Albert Innaurato

INTRODUCTION

The Idiots Karamazov was my first professional production as a playwright, presented at the Yale Repertory Theatre in New Haven, Connecticut in the fall of 1974.

It's a co-authored play, written with my playwright colleague, Albert Innaurato. (Albert went on to write *Benno Blimpie, Gemini, Coming of Age in Soho,* and *Gus and Al,* among many other fine plays.)

Albert and I were fellow playwriting students at Yale School of Drama, from 1971 to 1974. I remember our first reaction to one another was a bit suspicious—we both were raised Catholic and tended to bring nuns into our work; there was a little bit of a feeling of, is the school big enough for both of us? However, Albert has a riotous sense of humor, and many of his comments, even insulting ones, made me laugh. And so we became friends.

I had been a bit obsessed with Dostoevesky's *The Brothers Karamazov.* I read it my freshman year at college, and was taken with its saintly brother, the monk Alyosha, and his nihilistic intellectual brother, Ivan. All the surface melodrama of the plot is layered with feverish philosophical analysis; Ivan and Alyosha have many talks, asking how God can allow evil in the world.

Although while I was reading the book I had not yet seen the Hollywood movie version (starring Yul Brynner, William Shatner, and an endlessly grinning Maria Schell as Grushenka), I started to be amused by the total impossibility of filming the novel.

And so as a joke, I made an hour-long 8mm student film of *The Brothers Karamazov,* with printed titles for dialogue, starring myself as Alyosha, my friend Michale Bronski as Fr. Zossima, and various friends from New Jersey musical theatre as the rest of the cast. It was extremely jokey, and filled with parodies of foreign films. (The sensualist Dmitri runs into a worldly Anouk Aimee character, sporting a black eye as she did *La Dolce Vita;* Ivan's girl friend is a French Maoist who keeps shouting slogans at the camera, as in Godard's *La Chinoise;* Grushenka seduces Alyosha, and seems to turn into Mrs. Robinson from *The Graduate.*)

I showed Albert this film, and he became excited about the idea of his and my writing a "Karamazov" musical in the same crazy style. Albert had been hired by Silliman College (one of the undergraduate residence halls) at Yale College to direct a production for them; he was initially going to do *Hedda Gabbler,* but then decided that this idea would be more fun than Ibsen.

Our first version was totally insane. Albert directed and also played the narrator, the crazy "translatrix," Constance Garnett. (Constance Garnett seemingly translated every Russian novel in existence; and Albert and I both flashed on the idea of creating a made-up version of Ms. Garnett, who would talk to the audience and explain, and mix up, the plot.)

As Constance, Albert didn't dress in drag, though he did put a big garden party hat on his head, and talked and acted like Edith Evans. Indeed, we advertised the play around Yale as "*The Brothers Karamazov,* starring Dame Edith Evans." Then at every performance, we announced that Dame Edith had fallen and broken her hip, and that Albert would have to play the role.

The rest of the show was in a giddy, musical comedy style. I played Alyosha, and got to run about in a monk's robe, looking excited and innocent. A very funny undergraduate, Patrick Dillon, played a screaming queen of a Fr. Zossima, who seemed riveted by his eighteen-year-old altar boys. (There was a strange musical number where Fr. Zossima prepared for a bath, while his altar boys, dressed only in towels, sang a ditty about wintry weather. I can't imagine what the Silliman administration thought of this show; or rather, I can.)

Anais Nin, a comic obsession of Albert's, became a character in the play, who wanted to seduce Alyosha. Albert had met Anais Nin, and was amused by her preposterous focus on "sensitivity" and who was an artist. An obsession of mine, Mary Tyrone from *Long Day's Journey Into Night,* became Alyosha's mother.

A highlight of the show was Alyosha's fall from grace, made into a rock star by Anais, and singing the rock 'n' roll anthem, "Everything's Permitted." (In the novel, "everything's permitted" is Ivan's darkly philosophic reaction to his lack of belief in God.)

Except for me and Albert (who were grad students at the Drama School), all the performers were undergraduates. Ruth Nerken was a very funny Anais, Catherine Schreiber a loony, lyrical Mary Tyrone; and Ted Tally, who went on to be a respected playwright and to win an Oscar for his screenplay of *Silence of the Lambs,* was an amusingly tortured Ivan.

Howard Stein, the dean of playwriting at the Drama School, came to see the production, and seemed to love its craziness. He then brought it to the attention of Tom Haas, the head of the acting department at the Drama School, and Haas decided to schedule it for a full production the following year at the Drama School.

Playwriting students at the Drama School were not guaranteed productions of their work; and some went through the whole three-year program without receiving any.

Albert and I, both ambitious, had befriended directors in the school, and already had had one acts produced at the Yale Cabaret. (We also wrote and performed in our own anarchic cabaret shows, one called *I Don't Generally Like Poetry But Have You Read 'Trees'?* the other called *Gyp: The Life Story of Mitzi Gaynor,* with myself as Mitzi, and Albert as Mitzi's mother.)

The acting students, most very talented, were regularly assigned by Haas to full productions, usually of classic plays, very occasionally of student work; the student work chosen was usually rather serious. That Haas was interested in our crazy work was extremely surprising.

Haas was a bit of a terror. He had a wonderful eye for choosing acting talent; but he seemed to have this pattern of having favorite acting students for the first few months, and then inexplicably turning against them.

Albert and I were set to do rewrites for Haas. He wanted a lot more of Fr. Zossima's attraction for Alyosha; he wanted the ramifications of Constance translating what we were seeing worked out better (a good request; that aspect was haphazardly done in our first version); he wanted more texture to Alyosha's other brothers, Dmitri and Smerdyakov (whom Albert and I barely bothered to write).

For the production, Haas cast many of the Drama School's most talented actors, including Meryl Streep as Constance, Lizbeth Mackay as Anais, Franchelle Stewart Dorn as Grushenka, Linda Atkinson as Mary Tyrone, Dan Desmond as Fr. Zossima, Stephen Rowe as Ivan, Steven Nowicki as Alyosha, Alma Cuervo as Djuna. (Though Meryl had already fallen out of his favor; in a casting session with me and Albert, Haas said crankily, "Have you *ever* seen Meryl be good?" indicating he hadn't.)

Albert and I did not go to all the rehearsals; but when we did, we started to fear that the intense acting going on in our crazy play was seeming itself a little crazy. Fr. Zossima, for instance, is obsessed with feet, while Alyosha is turned off by them. ("How can there be a God, if there are feet?," Alyosha asks.) Haas and his actors were acting up a storm in these scenes, "investigating" them, finding their inner pain, their sexuality, etc., etc. The scenes were still funny, but they were on the brink of becoming endless and grotesque if they went one smidgen slower and got one degree more serious.

Then a few days later, we came back to rehearsals, and now the laugh lines were all cut. All of them. So there were no pay-offs, no signals from the author that we were having fun; what was left was only this eerie, sort of uncomfortable sexual scene between Zossima and Alyosha; and three pages that seemed to take ten minutes.

So Albert and I were very upset, and we had a meeting with Haas and said he had to put the laugh lines back in; that it was our names on the script, not his; and his version did not represent us. Haas was very angry, and indicated that he thought we were difficult and insane (the feeling was mutual, I guess), but he did put them back in.

But we were very worried about the production; the other scenes also seemed too serious, too portentous for the material.

Then Haas got pneumonia, and was out of rehearsal for about a week. His assistant, directing student Walt Jones, took over for the week; Walt had a good sense of humor, and was liked by his fellow students; and he lightened the tone of some of it, and added a lot of good staging for the musical numbers (that had previously been sort of ignored).

Then Haas got back, and the actors ran the play for him. During it, he squirmed in his seat, rolled his eyes, and during many scenes, snapped his fingers obsessively, indicating "faster! faster!" When the run-through was over, and the actors came out sheepishly to hear Haas's notes, Meryl spoke up bravely to her teacher and told him his snapping behavior in the run-through had been one of the most difficult, unpleasant experiences she'd ever been through in theatre. Haas nodded and said "uh huh," as if she'd said something pleasant but uninteresting; and then he proceeded with his notes.

Surprisingly, Albert and I liked and were in agreement with his notes, all of which had to do with wanting the pace to be faster, the tone to be lighter, etc., etc. (Of course, this isn't what he told anyone previously.)

The show played to the school a few days later, and was triumphantly good. Meryl was deeply hilarious (which I've seen her be on stage a number of times; she's yet to be so on film, her film roles are usually so realistic; her comic stuff on stage was always a bit stylized, out there). Lizbeth was beautiful, charming and dotty as Anais, Linda hilarious as hophead Mary Tyrone (suddenly turning into Katherine Hepburn at an appropriately climactic moment); they were all great.

Strangely, even though the rehearsal process was unpleasant and confusing, the outcome was first-rate; and I even thought that the early work Haas did of having the actors "investigate" the material and play it too seriously paid off ultimately. The trick was that the pace got cranked up to comedy pace, and the actors "lightened" their intentions, but did not throw the intentions out. Thus Mary Tyrone was truly concerned about Alyosha and truly felt guilt; it's just it was no longer pushed into heavy-handed seriousness. And Zossima still truly was turned on by Alyosha and was busy manipulating him, but it was no longer grotesque, it was now strange comedy.

So it was a confusing process. But it was an early lesson in the advantages of playing comedy with real psychology underneath. And I think the production was one of the very best I have ever seen.

Robert Brustein, dean of the Drama School and artistic director of the Yale Repertory Theatre, flipped for the play, and scheduled it for production on the Rep's main stage the following fall. This, for student playwrights, was like winning the lottery; it was rare that student work was chosen for the Rep.

Brustein was also scheduling a serious production of Dostovevsky's *The Possessed,* already presented in London to acclaim and directed by the distinguished Polish film director, Andrzej Wajda. So *Karamazov* would be in juxtaposition with that, which would be fascinating.

However, Haas was out. That spring, at a faculty meeting Haas suggested throwing Meryl Streep out of the school; Brustein thought Meryl was wonderful and, I'm told, Haas's suggestion sort of crystallized Brustein's opinion of Haas's craziness; and so he was let go instead.

Haas went on to run the Indiana Rep for several years; and then died, pretty young. Even the actors who didn't like him admitted that he was an inspiring, valuable teacher; and many of his productions (including *Karamazov*) were excellent. He was very talented; but also very odd, very difficult.

So obviously Haas was not asked to direct. Instead Brustein asked William Peters, a talented Yale directing graduate who specialized in comedy. Albert and I thought that sounded like a very good idea.

The Haas production featured many second year actors; and in the school, when the actor entered the third year, he was cast at Yale Rep itself—sometimes in spear-carrying roles, the more favored ones in good roles. So many of the cast from the Haas production, in their third year in the fall, would be used again.

Certainly, Meryl as Constance, the crazy octogenarian translator, was cast again. In a wheelchair, with a rat's nest of gray hair, with a putty nose turning her witch-like, Meryl's Constance was a complexly funny creation: Talking to the audience and explaining her life and mixing up all the Russian books she had translated, Meryl was cagey and unpredictable, sometimes lost in her memories, then suddenly sharp as a tack. Meryl has a real gift of creating characters that are totally separate from herself; and Constance was one of her best.

But the rest of the Rep casting was confusing. Kate McGregor-Stewart, a wonderful actress from my class, had been hired as a member of the company, and it was necessary to find her a role; and so Lizbeth Mackay's glamorous Anais was given to Kate, and Lizbeth took over the put-upon, drab role of Djuna. Stephen Rowe, who was so good as Ivan, was bumped for company member Charles Levin; and Rowe was given the smallish part of Smerdyakov.

Dan Desmond chose to leave school, and his role was given to Rep stalwart Jeremy Geidt.

I was cast as Alyosha. Talk about winning the lottery. I was enrolled in the playwriting program, but I kept acting in shows at the cabaret. Brustein had seen me in several of these, and he also heard me sing in the third-year acting class's annual show. (This was a yearly event from work in Elizabeth Parrish's singing class for actors; as someone who liked to sing, I asked to be allowed to take it along with the actors.)

Steven Nowicki, who had been excellent as Alyosha, nonetheless couldn't really sing; and Alyosha was written to become a rock star. So Brustein cast me. And then I was also given a small role, as a nihilistic student (who says "I think God should be shot!") in the Wajda production of *The Possessed*.

So I was thrilled to be cast as an actor, and to receive my Actors Equity card. To be paid to work in theatre was a heady feeling; I was very happy.

And I loved my role in *The Possessed,* and loved watching the exciting work of the other actors (Meryl, Christopher Lloyd, Alvin Epstein, the exciting Polish actress Elzbieta Czyzewska—whose accent and charismatic quirks Meryl later used for partial inspiration for Sophie in *Sophie's Choice*).

But over at *Karamazov* things were not going as smoothly. As authors, Albert and I had little experience with thinking through what a design should be; though a director should be expected to know. The Haas production had been done in the round, without walls, but with oriental rugs and samovars and potted palms. And Meryl as Constance could wheel herself around swiftly, and show up in the middle of the action in a flash; and sometimes the texture of the scene would be Meryl's reaction in the background to whatever scene she was "translating" and presenting to us, and then suddenly she'd be gone again.

When we all got on stage, we found that the walls of the set made it impossible for Meryl to even get on-stage with her wheelchair, let alone zip about. And what was worse, the stage was raked! So unless she kept her brake on constantly, Meryl's wheelchair would roll off the stage into the front row. This was not well thought out.

The makeshift solution was to carve a section out of the walls that Meryl could sit in and watch the action; so at least now we could see her, though she was stationary. But it lost the magic of Constance's weaving in and out, which stylistically was better.

And a more serious thing was happening. Even though Haas's over-seriousness worried me and Albert, eventually we credited his approach with creating this complicated tone, where the characters took their dilemmas seriously, and that made the madness of the lines and situations all the funnier.

Director Peters never saw the Haas production; and he was directing the play as a simple farce, with no psychological underpinnings whatsoever. And so the production was becoming unpleasingly schizoid…the actors from the Haas production (many of whom, though, were playing different parts now) kept trying to root their comedy in some psychological truth; while the actors new to the production, taking their cue from the director, were going for what I viewed as hideous exaggeration.

And my performance was probably odd. I had played Alyosha in the very first production, which was much more innocent than the Haas one; so my kind of rosy male ingenue presence fit that production, but when I tried to do the same thing in this production—which already had two styles going on, the remnants of the Haas, and the beginnings of the Peters—I think I didn't entirely fit in. I felt nervous and confused, and indeed I got a rash on my stomach that lasted for the entirety of the run—a rash I never got again. (But perhaps you're not interested in my dermatological history.)

As we got closer to first preview, it felt like we were in a big bomb. My friend Kate and I couldn't figure out how to play our scenes together, and ended up blocking ourselves; I don't know what Peters was doing. (Though I remember once Kate and I heard Peters telling the designer to cut a particular chair, and we cried out, "No! We use it at the end of the act." It felt as if he wasn't watching our scenes, and didn't know what furniture we used.)

Act I ends with a loony seduction, where Anais gets Alyosha to lie on top of her, and then has the dead body of her father put on top of him, and announces "We make sandwich, Alyosha."

In the Haas production, there were enough odd psychological undercurrents, that this scene worked. In the first preview, which went kind of horribly, Kate and I could sense that the whole audience was going "huh?" I remember the sense of shared, giddy disaster as the lights dimmed, with me on top of Kate and with John Rothman (as the dead father) on top of me; Kate and my bodies both started to shake, and we realized we were laughing at shared theatrical catastrophe.

The next day Brustein made some suggestions for some quick "fixes" that did, surprisingly, help. One of them was to move Alyosha's big number, "Everything's Permitted" to the top of Act II, rather than the end of the act. This did not make much sense thematically—because it marks the end of Alyosha's journey, not its mid-point—but in this production, where things like "journey" were not registering anyway, it made good audience sense because the number was funny and worked, and put the audience in a good mood.

And somehow the production kind of succeeded on its own terms, less special than the Haas one, but offering the audience laughs and strangeness. We all got better as the run went on; and people who saw it mostly seemed to like it.

We did not get good local reviews; but we got one really complimentary review from Mel Gussow in the *New York Times*. It was an early lesson in the power of the *Times*, because that good review wiped away all the negative ones in people's perceptions and memories. And when Albert and I subsequently went to New York, and were reviewed separately for our solo writing, for the longest time the reviewers often would identify us approvingly as the authors of this play.

And so, after this somewhat lengthy introduction, here is *The Idiots Karamazov*. (The script is mostly the one used in the Haas version; though Constance's final speech, geared to capitalize on Meryl's star performance, is from the Yale Rep version.)

ORIGINAL PRODUCTION

The Idiots Karamazov was first presented professionally by the Yale Repertory Theatre in New Haven, Conn. on Oct. 31, 1974. The production was directed by William Peters; setting by Michael H. Yeargan; lighting by Lloyd S. Riford III; costumes by William Ivey Long; music composed by Jack Feldman; lyrics by Durang. The cast was as follows:

CONSTANCE GARNETT	Meryl Streep
ERNEST, her butler	Ralph Redpath
IVAN KARAMAZOV	Charles Levin
DMITRI KARAMAZOV	Robert Nersesian
SMERDYAKOV KARAMAZOV	Stephen Rowe
ALYOSHA KARAMAZOV	Christopher Durang
GRUSHENKA	Franchelle Stewart Dorn
FYODOR KARAMAZOV	John Rothman
FATHER ZOSSIMA	Jeremy Geidt
ALTAR BOYS	Danny Brustein, Evan Drutman
MARY TYRONE KARAMAZOV	Linda Atkinson
DJUNA BARNES	Lizbeth MacKay, Christine Estabrook
ANAIS PNIN	Kate McGregor-Stewart
LEATHER GIRLS	Margot Lovecraft, Dawn Forrest
JOACQUIN PNIN	Peter Blanc

In spring of 1974 there was a student production of the play at the Yale School of Drama, directed by Tom Haas, with music by Walton Jones. The cast was the same as above except for the following: Ivan was Stephen Rowe; Dmitri was Kenneth Ryan; Smerdyakov was Doug Harley; Alyosha was Steven Nowicki; Grushenka II was Nancy Piccione; Fyodor was Barry Marshall; Fr. Zossima was Dan Desmond; Djuna was Alma Cuervo; Anais was Lizbeth MacKay; Leather Girls were Patricia Quinn, and Valerie J. Neale.

The very first production was in 1973 at Silliman College of Yale University and was billed as *The Brothers Karamazov,* starring Dame Edith Evans. That production, directed by Albert Innaurato and with music by Jack Feldman, featured Innaurato as Constance (subbing for the ailing Dame Edith), Durang as Alyosha, Ted Tally as Ivan, Ruth Nerken as Anais, Catherine Schreiber as Mary Tyrone, Patrick Dillon as Fr. Zossima, Roberta Caruso as Grushenka, Patricia Christo as Elena Blumenthal (later Djuna Barnes).

CAST OF CHARACTERS

CONSTANCE GARNETT, translator
ERNEST, her butler
ALYOSHA KARAMAZOV, the monk
IVAN KARAMAZOV, the intellectual
DMITRI KARAMAZOV, the sensualist
SMERDYAKOV KARAMAZOV, the epileptic
FYODOR KARAMAZOV, the father
MARY TYRONE KARAMAZOV, the mother
FATHER ZOSSIMA, the mystic
HIS ALTAR BOYS
ANAIS PNIN, a woman of letters
DJUNA BARNES, her secretary
MISS PNIN'S LEATHER GIRLS
GRUSHENKA, a Russian prostitute
GRUSHENKA II, her bottom half

The Idiots Karamazov

ACT I
Scene 1

Alyosha Karamazov a young innocent-looking monk in black robes, sings the haunting opening strains of Rachmaninov's "Vocalise" in a boy-soprano falsetto. After a moment his father Fyodor Karamazov, a rough man, enters and belts Alyosha one on the head.

FYODOR: Why can't you sing like a man, God damn it? *(Strides off.)*

ALYOSHA: *(Plaintively.)* Poppa! Poppa!

   (Blackout.)

ACT I
Scene 2

A basically empty stage with perhaps some Victorian furniture. Lights up on Constance Garnett, a very old, crone-like woman of letters. She is seated in her wheelchair, a lace doily covers her head. Her butler Ernest stands by her side. Silence for a bit.

CONSTANCE: Ernest.

   (Ernest takes the doily from her face. Constance looks about to get her bearings; addresses the audience.)

CONSTANCE: *The Brothers Karamazov.* I remember when I translated *The Brothers Karamazov.* How do you do? I am Constance Garnett, Bart., eminent translatrix from the savage tongues—the Russian, the Lithuanian, the Polish, the Serbo-Croatian—into the hallowed language we are now speaking. French. Ernest, my monocle, please!

   (Ernest places it before her.)

CONSTANCE: I am not trying to impress you with my credentials, but I have translated all the important Russian works since 1862 to the present, including Chekhov's *The Cherry Orchard,* Tolstoi's *War and Women, The Life of Sessue Hayakawa,* Chekhov's *The Three Siblings, Uncle Sea Gull,* and many others. I've also translated English language novels *back* into their original tongues: *Nightwood* by Djuna Barnes, *Jacob's Womb* by Virginia Woolf, and all the novels of my sister Peter Tchaikovsky, with especial emphasis on *The Nutcracker.* And I was damned by her most gracious majesty when I was thirteen. Never has a comely English girl greeted puberty in such a burst of courtly splendor. I don't think. *The Brothers Karamazov.* I remember when I translated that book I had great difficulty with the Russian word for pestle. The Russian word for pestle is *Anton Diakov.* Pestles are very important in the works of Dostoevesky, vide the use of the word *pestle* in the title of *The Possessed.* The Russian word for vegetable is *lubleevsky. The Brothers Karamazov.* I had kittens today. As a demonstration to my sister of the ways of God, I drowned them in a tub and then I bathed my feet in it. It was quite warm. What sort of God, if there is a God, would bring these diverse characters together? What sort of demon could condemn these unfortunates to so gloomy a fate? Was their fate preordained? Why is this interesting? Is it interesting? Who am I? Where am I? *The Brothers Karamazov.* Part I.

(Constance takes out her books and papers to translate. As she speaks the next section, three of the Karamazov brothers will enter the room and go about their business. Translating.)

CONSTANCE: The intellectual son was Ivan Karamazov, whose favorite song was the "Song of the Olga Boat Men."

(Enter Ivan.)

CONSTANCE: And Olga taught school with five escaped nuns from the convent of Ludun, where her sister Masha married a school teacher named Olga.

(Enter Dmitri.)

CONSTANCE: And the youngest was the bastard son, Irena, whose birthday it is today.

(Enter Smerdyakov. During the above Ivan, Dmitri, and Smerdyakov have been reading, looking at lockets, arranging flowers, other Chekhov-like things. They are dressed in masculine, Russian garb but some of their gesturing and movement has been more delicate than their costumes would suggest. However, they should not appear effeminate. The three brothers now sing "O We Gotta Get to Moscow." Constance should join in obligato in the background.)

IVAN, DMITRI, SMERDYAKOV: *(Singing.)*

> O we gotta get to Moscow,
> O we gotta get to Rome,
> O we gotta get to somewhere,
> Anywhere that isn't home.

> O we gotta get to Moscow,
> Make a check-off list and pack,
> And we'll leave this town behind us,
> And we're never coming back.

> For we find our lives are dull and boring,
> Nous sommes ennui,
> And we find we wake up yawning, snoring—
> Bored three sisters we.

> O let's go off to Alaska,
> O let's go away to Gnome,
> And we'd even go to Texas,
> But we'd skip the Astro Dome,

> The Italian word for window, ceiling,
> Slips through our grasp,
> And we feel like Cleopatra reeling,
> Searching for her asp.

> O we gotta get to Cleveland,
> San Francisco or L.A.,
> And we'll sell the cherry orchard,
> And we'll give the pits away,
> We'll Moscow go,
> We won't take no,
> We'll Chattanooga choo choo off to Buffalo,
> Good-bye now,
> Uncle Vanya, don't you cry now,
> Gotta get to Moscow,
> Moscow right now!
> *(Blackout except for Constance.)*

ACT I

Scene 3

The three brothers exit above. Constance begins her translation again.

CONSTANCE: *The Brothers Karamazov.* By Fyodor Karamazov. Translated by Constance Garnett, Bart. Part I. Chapter I. Alyosha Karamazov was the third son of Fyodor Karamazov, a landowner well known in our district in his own day, and still remembered entre nous parce que son morbidetza et tragica moribunda. Dans le jardin Karamazovi steht der junge Alyosha and his brother Ivan. *(Constance takes off her monocle and smashes it.)* Ernest. Ernest, I've broken my monocle. Send for the optometrist.
(During the above speech of Constance, Ivan Karamazov has been seating himself in the Karamazov home, near the samovar. He is the intellectual and is dressed more elegantly than the other Karamazovs. As he begins to speak Constance remains onstage busy translating and watching her characters.)

IVAN: *(Speaking to "Nurse" who is not there.)* No, thank you, Nurse, nothing from the samovar. It's too hot. Oh, how hot it is here. By the way, how long have we known each other, Nurse? *(Listens.)* That's a long time. Have I changed so much since then? *(Listens.)* Neither have you. Only with you, it's good not to have changed. What? *(Shouts.)* I said, YOU HAVEN'T CHANGED EITHER. How I hate deaf people.
(Enter Alyosha Karamazov, the young monk, carrying a birdcage and an overnight bag.)

ALYOSHA: Ivan! *(Runs to embrace him.)*

IVAN: Alyosha, you've left the monastery. So you've finally realized there is no God.

ALYOSHA: I haven't left the monastery, Ivan. I've come home to help with the family trouble.

CONSTANCE: Dostoevesky here makes a play on the Russian word for trouble, "Nevsky-pudovhkin," which sounds like the Russian word "Nevsky-pudovhkin," which means drainage blockage in the sink. Constance Garnett.

IVAN: I didn't know they taught you plumbing in the monastery, Alyosha.

ALYOSHA: No, Ivan, I didn't say "drainage blockage in the sink," I said "trouble."

IVAN: Alyosha, sit down. No, thank you, Nurse, nothing from the samovar. *(To Alyosha.)* This morning I watched one of my patients die before my eyes.

ALYOSHA: But you're not a doctor, Ivan.

IVAN: Then I am all the guiltier. Oh, Alyosha, how can you look at this barren untranslatable Russian idiom around us, and still believe in God?

ALYOSHA: God's goodness is everywhere, Ivan.

IVAN: There is no God, Alyosha

ALYOSHA: Yes, there is, Ivan.

IVAN: No, there isn't.

ALYOSHA: Yes there is.

IVAN: No there isn't.

ALYOSHA: Yes, there is.

IVAN: No there isn't.

ALYOSHA: Yes there is.

IVAN: No there isn't.

ALYOSHA: Yes there is.

IVAN: Where did you get that bird? *(Points to birdcage.)*

ALYOSHA: Fr. Zossima, who is the saintly mystic who is my teacher and mentor at the monastery where I live as a novice over the hill and away from the home of my father, gave it to me.

ivan: You're like a bird in a cage yourself, Alyosha, locked up in the monastery.

ALYOSHA: Fr. Zossima says that my soul is free like my caged bird.

ivan: A caged bird is not free.

ALYOSHA: A *Christian* caged bird is free.

(*Enter Grushenka, who runs through giggling. She is the lovely town bad-woman. Dmitri, the sensualist Karamazov brother, runs after her and catches her.*)

ALYOSHA: Dmitri!

(*Dmitri pours wine in Grushenka's mouth, kisses her. They both exit.*)

IVAN: All the Karamazovs are sensualists, Alyosha.

ALYOSHA: Was that Grushenka with whom Dmitri and my father are both in love?

IVAN: In a sense.

ALYOSHA: And in another sense?

IVAN: In that sense also.

ALYOSHA: What about Smerdyakov?

IVAN: He is an epileptic.

ALYOSHA: I know. I mean, is there anything new with Smerdyakov?

IVAN: You use words I don't understand. No, thank you, Nurse.

CONSTANCE: Ernest, is my optometrist here yet?

(*Grushenka runs in screaming, perhaps without her dress. She is followed by*

Dmitri. They are both fired at by Fyodor Karamazov, who is carrying a pistol. He is the sensual Karamazov father.)

DMITRI: GRUSHENKA'S MINE!

FYODOR: She's mine! I want her and she's mine! *(Fyodor fires gun at Dmitri, misses.)*

ALYOSHA: Father, don't shoot.

FYODOR: Keep outta this, Alexey. *(Fires at Dmitri, misses.)* Damn, I've missed.

DMITRI: She's mine. You're too old.

FYODOR: I have not lived. I have not lived. *(Shoots, misses.)*

ALYOSHA: Don't shoot Dmitri, father. He's your son.

FYODOR: Shut up, Alexey, or I'll kill you too. *(Grabs Alyosha, puts him in a neck hold, shoots again.)* Oh my life is ruined. I have talent, courage, intelligence. Oh, I'm talking rubbish. *(Fires, misses.)* DAMN. Mother, I'm in despair. *(Just at the end of the above, enter Smerdyakov carrying a black briefcase. He is led in by Ernest, who brings him over to Constance.)*

CONSTANCE: *(In a temper, to Smerdyakov.)* YOU ARE NOT MY REGULAR OPTOMETRIST. My regular optometrist is built differently! I am a busy woman. I can't make out the cyrillic letters without my monocle. Ernest, run to the closet and get my foot. I left it there.

FYODOR: *(Fires.)* Damn, missed again.

ALYOSHA: This is sinful, sinful. I can't breathe.

CONSTANCE: Oh, dear. I forgot the other son. Ernest, what is the English word for epileptic?
(Smerdyakov is seized by a sudden and violent epileptic fit and "leaps into the action.")

ALYOSHA: *(Seeing Smerdyakov on the floor.)* Let me go to my unfortunate half-brother.

FYODOR: The bastard. *(Fyodor lets Alyosha loose.)*
(Alyosha rushes to the writhing Smerdyakov.)

ALYOSHA: Quick, somebody, get a spoon! Did no one hear? Quick, get a spoon.
(Grushenka smiles winningly at Alyosha and produces a spoon.)

GRUSHENKA: Here's a spoon.

ALYOSHA: Thank you. You have a kind heart.

GRUSHENKA: That's just the way I am. I always feel sorry for epileptics.

ALYOSHA: That's the beginning of Christianity. *(Touches her face.)*

FYODOR: Get your mangy hands offa her, you Kraut. *(Grabs Grushenka.)*

GRUSHENKA: Ouch, my arm.

DMITRI: You hurt her arm, I'll kill you.
(Dmitri starts to strangle Fyodor, who fires his gun in the direction of Ivan.)

IVAN: YOU'VE KILLED NURSE! Nurse! *(Ivan picks up the nonexistent body of Nurse.)*

(Alyosha tries to pull Fyodor and Dmitri apart.)

ALYOSHA: Ivan, help me.

IVAN: Nana est morte, Nana est morte.

(Alyosha manages to stop Fyodor and Dmitri for a moment.)

ALYOSHA: Is this how Christ would have acted?

GRUSHENKA: I'm pregnant with both of their children.

DMITRI: Grushenka. I didn't know.

FYODOR: Mein liebe schatzche.

ALYOSHA: You see the outcome of all this sensuality. I came home…

IVAN: Nana est morte, quelle dommage, dommage.

ALYOSHA: Ivan, you're not helping. But I fear you are beyond my meagre help. I beg you all to come to the monastery to let Fr. Zossima settle this problem.

FYODOR: I don't want to see no priest.

GRUSHENKA: I want a settlement. I want a home and a husband and an abortion.

SMERDYAKOV: *(Rising and showing an eye chart to Grushenka.)* What do you see on the top line of the chart?

GRUSHENKA: E.

SMERDYAKOV: And on the second?

GRUSHENKA: G.O.D.O.W.

SMERDYAKOV: And on the third?

GRUSHENKA: A.S.D.F.J.K.L. semicolon.

SMERDYAKOV: I don't think you need glasses at all. *(Has epileptic fit.)*

ALYOSHA: Quick. What did I do with the spoon? *(Alyosha wanders about looking for the spoon.)*

(Fyodor fires at Dmitri, who runs off.)

FYODOR: *(To Alyosha.)* I don't want to see no priest. *(Fires, after Dmitri.)* Damn. *(Exits.)*

ALYOSHA: *(To Ivan.)* Have you see that spoon?

IVAN: What?

(Smerdyakov's fit subsides.)

ALYOSHA: Oh, he's quieter. *(Picks up his overnight bag and birdcage.)*

IVAN: Are you leaving Alyosha?

ALYOSHA: I've said my piece. I believe that I'll see all of you there tomorrow.

IVAN: The faith of an idiot to the end, Alyosha.

ALYOSHA: Good-bye, Miss. *(Alyosha shakes hands with Grushenka, exits.)*

IVAN: *(To Grushenka.)* Do you think that the people who will live a hundred years from now will speak well of us and appreciate our suffering Grushenka?

(Ivan takes out a pistol, aims at the ceiling, fires, a seagull falls from the ceiling.)

(Grushenka looks moved, Ivan takes out a notebook. Writing in his notebook.)

IVAN: Virgin forest. *(Exits.)*

(Grushenka stares at the seagull.)

(Blackout.)

ACT I
Scene 4

Anais Pnin lying face down on a chaise. Djuna Barnes, a depressing-looking, mannish woman in a grey suit, holds her novel Nightwood *in her hands, sets up a music stand, places the book on the stand, and proceeds to read from it, while giving Anais a backrub. We do not see Anais's face.*

DJUNA: *Nightwood*, page 129. "We look to the East for a wisdom that we shall not use—and to the sleeper for the secret that we shall not find. So, I say, what of the night, the terrible night? Wait! I'm coming to the night of nights—the night you want to know about the most of all—for even the greatest generality has a little particular, have you thought of that? We wash away our sense of sin, and what does that bath secure us? Sin, shining bright and hard. In what does a Latin bathe? True dust. We have made the literal error. We have used water, we are thus too sharply reminded."

(Blackout.)

ACT I
Scene 5

The monastery. The sound of Russian chant. The Karamazov family is present, waiting: Fyodor, very grouchy, Dmitri, Ivan, Smerdyakov. Alyosha is apart, praying.

FYODOR: I don't want to see no priest.

DMITRI: You're just afraid the old buzzard'll tell you to keep your hands offa Grushenka. Somebody should kill you with a pestle.

FYODOR: Shut up, you. I wish I'd never given birth to you. Your mother was a Venus-flytrap.

DMITRI: Why do you say that all the time? What do you mean?

ALYOSHA: Father, Dmitri. We're not at home. This is a monastery. You should be preparing your hearts for Fr. Zossima.

FYODOR: I don't want to see no priest.

ALYOSHA: Please, he's almost here. Fr. Zossima is a great saint. He honors us by this audience.

(Russian chant gets louder. Enter two workmen in workclothes, carrying a rolled-up rug. They place the rug on the floor, and Fr. Zossima rolls out of it.)

ZOSSIMA: *(On the floor.)* Come lie with me, Alyosha.

(Alyosha sits with Zossima on rug. A picnic basket has been pre-set nearby, and Zossima prepares to have a picnic on the rug. Two young blond Altar Boys sit with him.)

ZOSSIMA: Everything in the world has a purpose and meaning, Alyosha. This ground we sit on has meaning. This crucifix around my neck has meaning. *(Points to Boy.)* This child on my right has meaning. *(Points to other Altar Boy.)* This child on my left has meaning. *(Picks up a sandwich.)* This has meaning. *(Picks up another sandwich.)* This has meaning. *(Picks up salt shaker.)* This has meaning. *(Carrot.)* This has meaning. *(Celery.)* This has meaning. Everything that God created has a meaning. Even the smallest hair on one's head *(He pulls a hair from his head.)* has a meaning. *(Pulls another.)* And this one. *(Another.)* And this one. *(Another.)* And this one. *(Another.)* And this one. *(Another.)* And this one.

(Alyosha pulls one from his own head.)

ZOSSIMA: And that one.

(Another.)

ZOSSIMA: And this one.

FYODOR: *(Standing.)* I've had enough.

ZOSSIMA: Please. My meaning will become apparent if you will just grant me your patience. *(Smiles.)*

(Fyodor sits.)

ZOSSIMA: I have always felt that if everyone were a little more patient with one another, the world would go around a great deal faster than it does.

DMITRI: But what about Grushenka?

ZOSSIMA: She would move faster too.

DMITRI: No—who should have her?

ZOSSIMA: *(Smiles.)* There is a story in the Bible about a wise ruler named Solomon. *(Closes his eyes for a moment.)* God had granted Solomon great wisdom, and the people came to him to settle their problems.

ALYOSHA: As they do to you, Father.

ZOSSIMA: I do not seek glory, my little son.

FYODOR: *(Standing.)* I've had enough of this.

IVAN: Be quiet. Can't you see the man's a saint.

(Zossima smiles and sends him a sandwich.)

ZOSSIMA: Two women came to Solomon with one baby, and each claimed to be the mother of this child. *(Holds up a hard-boiled egg, smiles significantly at all.)* This is my child, said the one. This is my child, said the other. And Solomon looked from one to the other and said, "Which of you loves the child more?" Who of you knows what the women answered?

ALYOSHA: I do.

ZOSSIMA: Good, Alyosha. *(Pats his head.)* Both women professed to love the child equally.

FYODOR: *(Cranky.)* What about Grushenka?

IVAN: Shut up. The baby's Grushenka.

DMITRI: No. The egg is.

ZOSSIMA: And Solomon saw that both loved the child with an equal heart, and so he said, "The only just way is to cut the child in half." *(Zossima cuts the egg in half.)* One half for you, and one half for you. *(Hands half an egg to Dmitri, and then to Fyodor.)*

DMITRI: You mean...

FYODOR: We should...

ALYOSHA: What is the metaphor, Father?

ZOSSIMA: The metaphor is that the egg represents the baby, and I represent King Solomon.

FYODOR: Which of us gets the bottom half?

DMITRI: I want the bottom half.

FYODOR: Come on, let's just do it.

ALYOSHA: Wait. I don't think you've understood the parable.

FYODOR: I got it okay. So long, Father. Come on, Smerd.

(Fyodor, Dmitri, Smerdyakov exit in a hurry. Ivan follows. Zossima sends the Altar Boys away.)

ALYOSHA: How exactly is Grushenka meant to represent the egg, Father?

ZOSSIMA: A parable cannot be exact, Alyosha, anymore than a poem can be or a human life. Alyosha, do you know what your purpose is at this point in your life?

ALYOSHA: To help my family find the Christ?

ZOSSIMA: No, my child. You must let the world take care of itself. God has seen fit to place you at this juncture of time and history…near me. Do you understand what this means?

ALYOSHA: That I must learn from a saint.

ZOSSIMA: Thank you, Alyosha. *(Smiles.)* Do you really think I'm a saint?

ALYOSHA: You are the most complete Christian I have ever met.

ZOSSIMA: Thank you, Alyosha. Alyosha, for our meditation today, I want us to consider the exhortation of St. Paul in his letter to the Corinthians: "Though I speak with the tongues of men and of angels, and though I have all faith, so that I could move mountains, and have *not* chastity…I am as sounding brass." Do you know what St. Paul means by this, my son?

ALYOSHA: I thought the word was charity, Father, not chastity.

ZOSSIMA: He means to stay away from women. Women are evil, Alyosha. The very etymology of the word *woman* emphasizes her vileness in the eye of the Lord. The Russian word for woman is the same as the Russian word for sickness unto death. The Serbo-Croatian for woman corresponds to the Polish word for anti-Christ. The Lithuanian word woman also means vegetable poison. And the French word La Femme in Classical French means famine, and in colloquial terms is used *as la femme à la tete,* or head cancer.
(During the above Constance has been going through her books, checking Zossima's assertions in a fair frenzy of annoyance.)

ZOSSIMA: Have you understood my meaning, Alyosha?

ALYOSHA: I believe that you wish me to disapprove my father and brother's overlooking of spiritual matters in favor of the earthy Grushenka.

ZOSSIMA: Perhaps. *(Takes a jar from his picnic basket.)* Do you know what these are, Alyosha?

ALYOSHA: I believe they're peanuts, Father.

ZOSSIMA: When Christ washed the feet of his apostles, he did it as an act of humility. Put out your hands.
(Alyosha puts forth his hands, Zossima pours peanuts into them.)

ZOSSIMA: As an act of humility, I will eat from your hand, Alyosha. *(Bends down, eats from his hands, looks up.)* Peeeeeeeeeeeeeeeeeeeeeeeeeennuuuuuuuu-uuuuuuuuuuuuts. Peeeeeeeeeeeeeeeeeeeeeeeeeeennnuuuuuuuuuuuuuuuuuuu-uuuuuts.

Do you understand, Alyosha?

ALYOSHA: I think so, Father.
(Zossima pours more peanuts into Alyosha's hands.)
(Blackout.)

ACT I
Scene 6

Fyodor and Dmitri push Grushenka onstage.

GRUSHENKA: Okay, so who gets me? Did the holy father have a solution?

FYODOR: Yeah, he thought up a way we can both enjoy you without either of us having to give you up.

GRUSHENKA: A menage à trois?

DMITRI: No, sweetheart. He said for both of us to take you into our arms...

FYODOR: Like this...

(They both embrace her.)

GRUSHENKA: And then?

FYODOR: Cut you in half! Smerdyakov, the saw!

SMERDYAKOV: Here, papa.

(Smerdyakov runs on with the saw, has an epileptic attack just as he's about to give the saw to Dmitri. As he falls into the fit, he throws the saw which Dmitri gracefully catches in mid-air.)

DMITRI: Thanks, Smerdy.

GRUSHENKA: *(Struggling.)* You're not going to cut me in half!

FYODOR: *(Still holding on to her.)* You want to bet?

GRUSHENKA: *(Screaming.)* Help! Help!

(They lay her down on the floor. She screams loudly and struggles violently to no avail. Ernest enters with a sheet on his arm. He hears Grushenka screaming and approaches. Ernest puts the sheet on as though it were a cloak and spreads his arms wide, thus creating a curtain. Grushenka continues to scream behind this curtain.)

ERNEST: *(Smiles at the audience.)* Reminds me of the safari. Actually reminds me of Zelda and Scott but that's not polite. A pee-wee woman once gave birth, quite simply in this fashion. African sundown, heat, bug bites, woman's labor pains and me, I was the tent. Dias, my friend, took the meat cleaver and she gave birth to twins, handsome devils both. Maybe I should use this in a short story about bullfighting.

(Grushenka's screaming stops. Ernest wraps the bloody sheet around himself and strides off. Grushenka is now in halves, bottom and top, played by two actresses.)

GRUSHENKA I: You've done it, you've cut me in half!

GRUSHENKA II: I can't speak!

GRUSHENKA I: I can't walk!

GRUSHENKA II: I can't speak, I can't speak, I can't speak!

GRUSHENKA I: *(Walking.)* I can't walk, I can't walk, I can't walk.

DMITRI: *(Embracing bottom.)* Beloved!

FYODOR: *(Embracing top.)* My little Russian octaroon!

GRUSHENKA I: *(In a rage.)* That's enough. Get away from me, you sexist monsters. Have you ever seen anything this disgusting? Have you? That's right, you haven't. Cutting a woman in half. It's sick, it's foul, it's ugly, it's abnormal. And it's all a mockery of women, a damning mockery. Well I for one have had enough. Women are everything that is beautiful and good and kind. They engendered the human race, taught men culture…

GRUSHENKA II: They handed down the rules of democracy.

GRUSHENKA I AND/OR II: That's right. And all they enslaved were men, and they're no better than beasts of burden. And then what happened? Rebellion by the beast, the beast becomes the master, the beauty, the slave. Oh you horrible, vile, disgusting men! Oh for the years of the Amazons when women were warlike, kings, masters; and men were murdered or castrated or both. You don't understand me, read *The First Sex,* read *Matriarchy,* read *They Came from the Sea,* read *Put Your Mouth Where Your Vagina Is.* I cry from my chains: rebellion, slaughter, cessation of injustice!

GRUSHENKA I: Rebellion, slaughter.

FYODOR: That damn priest. I'll kill him.

DMITRI: Damn, damn.

> *(Fyodor, Dmitri, and Smerdyakov exit.)*
> *(Grushenka I and II now sing.)*

GRUSHENKA I AND II: See our arm, see our fist,
And we're feeling good and pissed,
See our legs, stout and strong,
We could even kill King Kong,
We're Omnipotent, We're Woman, Nous Les Femmes!

Watch your step, clear the way,
For we're marching out today,
Duck your head, look out, Mac,
Cause we're ready to attack,
We're Omnipotent, We're Woman, Nous Les Femmes!

Oh yes, we're the Cat's Pajamas,
And men are just underwear,
Oh yes, we're pistol-packin' mamas,
We got balls enough to spare!

Take a stand, follow me,
Hang the vermin from a tree,
Take an axe to their necks,
And eliminate their sex,
We're Omnipotent, We're Woman,
NOUS LES FEMMES!
(Blackout.)

ACT I
Scene 7

Constance in her wheelchair with Russian dictionary before her. Ernest stands nearby, still wrapped in the sheet from the previous scene.

CONSTANCE: Ernest! Ernest! What were you doing in that bloody sheet? I hope you weren't doing research for a new novel, the others were bad enough. All that masculine nonsense. Why must all writers be concerned with matters sexual? What is there in that base itch that propels quill into inkwell and causes it to drip on paper? Ah well, I shall never understand humankind. Now, the Russian verb CHALIAPIN, meaning to be murdered by one's own son with a pestle: CHALIAPINE, CHALIAPINSKI, CHALIAPINSKIYA, CHALIAPINSKOI…CHALIAPINSKINSKI—that's past perfect—having had killing one's own father with a pestle. CHALIA— look at me, do I need sex? No. Writing is all. A writer must save himself. A writer must at all costs save herself from the exhausting impure advances of others. A man came to me once and insisted that I—pure then, a maiden—undress for him. Insisted, I tell you, and told me the law of heaven and earth was on his side. The law indeed! CHALIAPINSKOO. Just because he was my husband he thought that gave him the right to make free with my delicate membrane, the vulgar call the body. Even that odoriferous word makes me shudder. The body…oooooh! *(Shudders in her wheelchair.)* CHALIAPINSKINKI!
(From offstage is heard the scream of Fyodor. Constance, gleefully.)
CONSTANCE: Oh! My sister has just discovered her dead kittens. I've been waiting for this all morning. Ernest, Ernest—go and see…

ACT I
Scene 8

Offstage scream of Fyodor again. Enter Fyodor, holding the back of his head, which has a pestle embedded in it.

FYODOR: CHALIAPIN ! *(Dies.)*
   (Enter Ivan, Smerdyakov, and Dmitri who look down on their dead father.)
IVAN: Father, dead. With a pestle.
DMITRI: Father, murdered.
IVAN: Who does not desire his father's death?
   (Dmitri slaps him.)
IVAN: Why did you do that?
DMITRI: Mosquito. *(Picks bug from Ivan's cheek, eats it, making a "thwap" sound.)*
   Thwap. *(Grabs another bug from air, eats it.)* Thwap.
IVAN: Aujourd'hui mon père est mort. Bon.
DMITRI: Father dead. Thwap. *(Eats fly.)*
SMERDYAKOV: Da da dead. *(Barks, begins to turn into a dog, barks more.)*
IVAN: Oh, curse you, God. God who does not exist. If you do exist, God, strike
   me with a thunder bolt here and now. *(A large bang is heard. Ivan drops to
   the ground.)*
   (Enter Djuna with a large drum, which she is beating, hawking her novel
   Nightwood.*)*
DJUNA: *Nightwood* for sale. *Nightwood.* Won't anybody buy my novel? *(Seeing
   Fyodor.)* But what do these nearsighted-from-writing eyes behold? Why,
   this large, gruff man is dead. Killed with a pestle. *(To Ivan.)* Would you like
   an autographed copy of my novel?
IVAN: Send for my younger brother Alyosha at once.
DJUNA: I must return to my mistress and write up this episode. Night comes on.
   NIGHTWOOD FOR SALE, WON'T ANYONE BUY MY NOVEL?
   NIGHTWOOD. *(Exits.)*
DMITRI: Thwap.
SMERDYAKOV: Arf.
IVAN: *(Lying on the ground, thinking.)* I must stand up, I must stand up, I must
   stand up, I must stand up…
   (Blackout.)

ACT I

Scene 9

Fr. Zossima's cell. Zossima is seen in long johns. His two Altar Boys are dressing him for a party, strapping on pillows to enlarge his bulks; wigs, golden robes, etc. Alyosha appears from outside the cell.

ALYOSHA: Fr. Zossima!

ZOSSIMA: Qui est la?

ALYOSHA: Je m'apelle Alyosha Karamazov. Je suis très desolé!

ZOSSIMA: Answer in English please, I don't know French.

ALYOSHA: It's Alyosha, Reverend Father. I am very desolate.

ZOSSIMA: Attendez-vous une moment, mon cher! *(To Altar Boys.)* Vite, vite mes enfants! *(They tie a pillow around him.)* Excuse-moi, Alyosha, I must prepare to attend one of Anais Pnin's soirees.

ALYOSHA: Who is she, Father?

ZOSSIMA: Un moment, mon cher! *(Altar Boys get robe over Zossima and his pillows.)* Entree! *(Enter Alyosha.)*

ALYOSHA: You look thinner than this morning, Father.

ZOSSIMA: I've changed pillows.

ALYOSHA: What, Father?

ZOSSIMA: Goose feathers instead of eiderdown.

ALYOSHA: *(Kneeling.)* Bless me, Father.

ZOSSIMA: Pas maintenant. I must get ready. One does not wish to be late to Anais Pnin's. Tonight is a party for everyone in volume twenty-three of her famous diary. That puts me in the ranks of Henry Miller, Larry Durrell, Djuna Barnes, and Our Lady of Fatima.

ALYOSHA: Oh most reverend Father, tragedy befalls! My father has been *murdered* with a pestle by one of his own sons.

ZOSSIMA: Ah, Chaliapin!

ALYOSHA: Yes, Father.

ZOSSIMA: Oh, Boris Godounov.

ALYOSHA: What, Father?

ZOSSIMA: That's an archaism for too bad, Alyosha.

ALYOSHA: I pray your permission to return home for his funeral and to comfort my grieving family.

ZOSSIMA: So formal with me, Alyosha. He'd never make an altar boy, would he, mes enfants.

(Boys shake their heads "no.")

ALYOSHA: May I go home, Father?

ZOSSIMA: Do as you like. I can think of nothing but tonight's soiree. *(Puts on wig.)* There are those who think I look like Our Lady of Fatima.

ALYOSHA: Father, I need to make my confession. Might the altar boys leave?

ZOSSIMA: Leave? My little angels? I have no secrets from them. Avancez, mon cher, avancez!

ALYOSHA: Bless me, Father, for I have sinned...

ZOSSIMA: My eyebrows, mes enfants!

ALYOSHA: Father, I had this awful dream about my mother and...

ZOSSIMA: Mes enfants, my blue contact lenses.

ALYOSHA: Father, I had this awful dream about my mother and her...

ZOSSIMA: Not your mother again, Alyosha. My gloves, mes croutons.

ALYOSHA: About my mother and her feet!

ZOSSIMA: *(Looking at his shoeless feet.)* Ah you're right, Alyosha! Mes enfants, mes souliers!

ALYOSHA: No, not *your* feet, Father, my mother's.

ZOSSIMA: Were her feet of clay, my son?

ALYOSHA: No, Father. Strong and muscular. Thick, peasants' feet.

ZOSSIMA: Ah, then they represent holy mother Church!

(Altar Boys applaud.)

ZOSSIMA: Merci, mes enfants. C'est rien!

ALYOSHA: Father, what should my penance be?

(Zossima doesn't answer.)

ALYOSHA: Father Zossima?

ZOSSIMA: I am sorry, Father Zossima is not here. I am his wedding cake. May I take a message?

ALYOSHA: I wanted to know about my penance.

ZOSSIMA: I am sorry. Wedding cakes cannot hear confession.

ALYOSHA: Oh.

ZOSSIMA: However, they can ask their little candles to give the penance. *(To Boys.)* What do you think, my angels?

(Boys whisper to him, shocked.)

ZOSSIMA: Méchant! *(Slaps Boy.)* I'll decide myself. Kneel down, Alyosha. Now pretend to be fourteen and sing in your magic way, sing!

(Alyosha sings in his clear falsetto.)

ZOSSIMA: Ah, the beauty. Now sing, "Bye Bye Blackbird."

(He does.)

ZOSSIMA: I am a wedding cake. I am a wedding cake, Alyosha. Sing, Alyosha.

ALYOSHA: I am, Father. *(Sings again.)*

ZOSSIMA: *(As lights dim.)* Now, mes enfants, the icing, the icing!
(Blackout.)

ACT I
Scene 10
Constance alone.

CONSTANCE: *The Brothers Karamazov.* This is one of the greatest novels ever writ
in any tongue. It deals with the inexorable misery of the condition humain.
Hunger, pregnancy, thirst, love, hunger, pregnancy, bondage, sickness,
health, and the body, let us not forget the body. *(Shudders luxuriously.)*
Now, Alyosha's gruff but beloved father has been murdered by a pestle, just
as my father was blown to bits by a perverted German in the last war.
Alyosha must return to his father's estate. In the novel this beautiful passage reads: Galina Vishnevskeya Irene Archipova loiblu liubasha grigory
warfa evgeny atlantov. Rimsky-Korsakov modeste cui mussprovsky
pushkin, solugub afrodesiac leningrad rasputin. This means: Once again
must I return to thee, land of my fathers, etcetera. Now we are in the next
chapter of *The Brothers Karamazov,* one of the greatest fictions since
Civilization and Its Discontents, which is based on my sister. Alyosha arrives
and finds no one at his progenitor's funeral rites. Where are they? Why do
you ask? The answer is quite clearly in the text. This reads: Dmitri and the
others, cynics all, had repaired to a whorehouse... *(Stops.)* Oh dear. That is
an archaic word which is no longer in use in our tongue. Whorehouse
means..."warehouse." *(Writes in her book.)* Dmitri and the others had
repaired to a warehouse. In the warehouse all the...employees allowed their
bodies, that is, bales of cotton to be tied with wire and brought upstairs to
the...storeroom where they performed sexual...uh, textile activities.

ACT I
Scene 11
*Grushenka's warehouse. Ivan is kissing Grushenka I and Grushenka II.
Dmitri, in a pot, eat flies. Smerdyakov lies asleep as a dog.*

IVAN: Consummatum est. Twice.

GRUSHENKA I: Oh how unhappy it is to be a hostess in a Russian warehouse.

(*Smerdyakov begins to "hump" Grushenka II's legs.*)

GRUSHENKA I: Stop that. Bad, doggie. (*To Ivan.*) I must say your family is all inclusive: a dog, a Venus-flytrap, and a sterile intellectual. Why is your family so degenerate?

IVAN: Alyosha isn't. The monk.

GRUSHENKA: Monk? What order is he?

IVAN: There is no order in the universe.

(*Enter Mary Tyrone Karamazov, the Karamazov family mother. She wears a high-necked, long dress and carries a carpetbag.*)

MRS. KARAMAZOV: Is the Blessed Mother here? (*To Grushenka.*) Are you the Blessed Virgin?

(*Smerdyakov humps her leg.*)

MRS. KARAMAZOV: Not now, dear.

IVAN: Mother, why aren't you at father's funeral?

MRS. KARAMAZOV: No one else was there. I got lonely. Oh, my nose is stopped up. (*Sniffs something.*)

IVAN: (*Bitterly.*) I see you've got your trusy bag, Mother.

MRS. KARAMAZOV: I need it to carry my needles, Ivan.

IVAN: Have you then resumed your…"knitting"?

(*Mrs. Karamazov laughs jovially.*)

MRS. KARAMAZOV: James, it's Edmund you ought to scold for not eating enough. He hardly touched anything except coffee. (*Mrs. Karamazov goes rifling through her carpetbag, finds a hypodermic, and shoots up.*)

IVAN: (*To Grushenka.*) It's Alyosha that did this to mother. She nearly died giving birth to him, and cheap quack doctors got her on the stuff.

GRUSHENKA: The doctors were all men, weren't they?

MRS. KARAMAZOV: (*Getting a faint buzz.*) Thank heaven the fog is gone. I couldn't sleep last night with that awful foghorn. And your father was snoring so hard, I couldn't tell which was the foghorn. That's right. Your father is dead. Who do you suppose it was snoring? (*Passes out.*)

IVAN: Mother, not in front of the children.

GRUSHENKA: You poor woman. How you've suffered.

MRS. KARAMAZOV: Look at all the colors. I'm a color, Cathleen. Guess what color I am.

(*Enter Alyosha, angry.*)

ALYOSHA: Why aren't you all at father's funeral?

MRS. KARAMAZOV: Alyosha! Why aren't you at your father's funeral?

ALYOSHA: Ivan, why have you let this happen to mother again?

IVAN: Am I my brother's keeper?

(Dmitri thwaps, Smerdyakov barks.)

ALYOSHA: Apparently not, looking at Dmitri and Smerdyakov.

MRS. KARAMAZOV: I have a fond memory of Alyosha as a very young baby. *(Screams in agony.)* AAAAAAAAGGGGGHHHH!

ALYOSHA: Mother, why do you do it?

MRS. KARAMAZOV: Do what? I don't know what you're talking about. *(Cries.)* I have to take medicine for the gout in my feet. I don't know why you don't want me to.

ALYOSHA: Don't anybody go away. *(Alyosha exits, returns with the dead body of his father Fyodor, which is contained in a large plastic bag.)* We'll have the funeral right here!

MRS. KARAMAZOV: Don't let James see me this way. Please.

ALYOSHA: Mama, look at me!

MRS. KARAMAZOV: But where are you?

ALYOSHA: Oh, why do you poison yourself? I am angry. Damn. *God* damn. Don't anybody shout at me.

GRUSHENKA: Let's cut the S.O.B. in half.

ALYOSHA: Hush, Magdalena. KNEEL DOWN!

(Everyone kneels, except for Grushenka I, who cannot kneel.)

ALYOSHA: In the name of the Father, of the Son, and of the Holy Ghost. Amen. Our Father, who art in heaven, hallowed… *(Etc.)*

MRS. KARAMAZOV: *(Praying as Alyosha is praying.)* Hail Mary, full of grace; Hail Mary, full of grace…I CAN'T PRAY, SHE DOESN'T BELIEVE ME! *(Weeps. Stands up.)* There's something I must get at the drugstore.

IVAN: Look at you, you pathetic heroin-stuffed old rag. Go ahead. Poison yourself! Forget your sons that need you now more than ever—a dog, a Venus-flytrap, and a sterile intellectual! Damn you!

ALYOSHA: Ivan! *(Slaps him.)*

MRS. KARAMAZOV: *(Weeps, begins to beat Fyodor's corpse with her fist.)* I have to get TOOTH POWDER AND TOILET SOAP AND COLD CREAM…

IVAN: *(Holding his slapped cheek.)* Thanks, kid, I needed that.

ALYOSHA: *(Seeing Mrs. Karamazov beating the corpse.)* Mother, please, don't.

IVAN: Come on, let's go to the funeral parlor. This place has gotten too gloomy. Come on, Poppa.

(Ivan leads off the corpse of Fyodor. Grushenka I and II, Dmitri Smerdyakov all follow off also. Mrs. Karamazov prepares to follow.)

MRS. KARAMAZOV: *(Wandering off.)* When I was at the convent, I used to play the piano with my feet until I got gout. Mother Elizabeth used to say, you don't mean your feet, you mean your hands. I never did though. *(Exits.)*
(All are gone now, except Alyosha, who is downcast.)

CONSTANCE: *The Brothers Karamazov* chapter fifty-three, paragraph six, sentence four, fragment. Alyosha Karamazov leaves the funeral of his dead progenitor in a pique. He decides he must seek counsel from the saintly Fr. Zossima whom he recalls is going to Anais Pnin's soiree… *(Constance busily writes.)*
(Blackout.)

ACT I
Scene 12

The home of Anais Pnin. Djuna Barnes enters with a small pile of wood, which she places on the floor. She exits re-enters with more wood, places it. Exits re-enters with a black cloth which she ceremoniously places over the wood.

DJUNA: *(Proclaiming.)* NIGHTWOOD! Nightwood! Nightwood, nightwood, night wood! Night…wwwwoood! Night…wwwwwoood! N-I-G-H-T-W-O-O-D. Niiiiiiiiiiiiiiightwwwwwwwwwoooooood! Sad indeed is the neglected artist's lot. They told me to become a parfumier. They said, go into odors, Djuna, smells is your life. They said if I did that I'd never experience the dreadful sting of artistic work insensitively ignored. Can any of you understand? Can any of you? Understand? It is very, very sad, if that's how you say it. No one wants my novel. *(Djuna lifts up the black cloth wipes her eyes with it, blows her nose, replaces it over the wood.)* Nightwood in ugly weather!

ZOSSIMA: *(Offstage.)* We're late, we're late! Hurry!
(Zossima and Altar Boys rush in carrying a pole and change of clothes for Zossima.)

ZOSSIMA: *(To Djuna.)* Where's the ladies' room?
(Djuna points off, they exit in that direction.)

DJUNA: *(Announcing.)* Madame Pnin!
(Instead of Madame Pnin entering, the Karamazov family arrives: Mrs. Karamazov, Ivan, Dmitri, Smerdyakov, the dead Fyodor in his plastic bag. They stand in a close group and sway, as one body.)

DJUNA: What do you want?

MRS. KARAMAZOV: As a matter of fact, we have come here in search of an author.

DJUNA: Madame Pnin will be honored. Which novel of hers are you in?

(Enter Alyosha who speaks to Djuna.)

ALYOSHA: I beg your pardon, but is Fr. Zossima…? *(Seeing Ivan.)* Ivan, why have you come?

IVAN: I am often asked that question—and I never see any way out of the existential mess.

ALYOSHA: *(To Ivan.)* Why haven't you buried father?

IVAN: The Grand Duke was shot at Sarajevo. War has been declared.

(All except Alyosha break into a chorus of "Over There." Constance in particular enjoys this, and Ernest wheels her through as she, perhaps, twirls a baton.)

MRS. KARAMAZOV: *(After song is over.)* What an interesting play you've taken me to, Jamie. But I still prefer your father as the Count of Monte Cristo.

DJUNA: Madame Pnin is nigh. She hopes that you will fill out the index cards properly. *(Passes cards out.)* And at the end of this evening's special entertainment, we shall pick a card from a hat, and that person will appear in Madame Pnin's next diary. Madame Pnin!

(Sound of cymbals and trumpets. Enter the Leather Girls, in motorcycle helmets and boots, etc. They carry Anais Pnin, who is wearing flowing robes. She speaks with a quasi Spanish-French accent, whatever that may be, and is very artistic.)

ANAIS: *(Holding up a book with her picture on it.)* This is a picture of me. Here I am in person. Djuna, take a picture.

(Djuna does.)

ANAIS: I have created an irony. A picture of me within a picture of me. I will now walk. But first, a story. My feet were bound at birth in the Oriental tradition. Therefore, my steps are tiny.

(Anais smiles, is let down by the Leather Girls. She begins walking, taking tiny, tiny steps, she barely makes any progress. After a while those present applaud her progress. She rewards them with a smile.)

ANAIS: Thank you for your kind appreciation. It reminds me of my years as a Spanish dancer. I was the most beautiful young girl ever seen. My father always said this to me, between practicing the piano and seducing older women, who were my rivals. A wonderful man, my father, he had eczema.

IVAN: *(Looking in punch bowl.)* There's something in the punch bowl.

ANAIS: My father's hands were so delicate…

IVAN: And it's got big eyes.

ANAIS: …that I feared they would break as he played the piano…

IVAN: And it's staring at me.

ANAIS: Djuna, I am getting interference.

IVAN: It's your doom I see in the punch bowl, Alyosha.

ANAIS: Even if there is something in the punch bowl, it is impolite to say so. Did he fill out an index card, Djuna?

DJUNA: No, Madam Pnin.

ANAIS: Rip it up!

IVAN: I've seen your doom in the punch bowl, Alyosha. For you are to learn what I've already learned: that there is no God, there is no hope, there is no faith, there is no love, there is no light, there is no dark...

ANAIS: Djuna!

IVAN: ...There is no dawn, there is no dusk, the corn has no husk, only voices have husk, there is no point, there is no warmth, there is no cold, there is no...

ANAIS: This is not the special entertainment. This spontaneous.

IVAN: ...cuddling in blankets, there are no episcopal priests...

ANAIS: Subdue this man!

(Two Leather Girls give Ivan a chop on the neck. Anais pointing to whole family.)

ANAIS: Take their measurements and throw them out into the alley.

(The Leather Girls get Karamazov family out of house, except for Alyosha. Fyodor's dead body remains behind.)

ANAIS: Djuna, go taste the punch and see if it's poison.

(Djuna does.)

ANAIS: That young man remind me of Antonia Artaud. Weird. Are you still there, Djuna?

DJUNA: Yes, Madam Pnin.

ANAIS: Make a note. I shall now sit. *(She sits.)*

(Guests applaud.)

ANAIS: I sense an artistic presence.

DJUNA: Is it I, Anais?

ANAIS: No. It is him. *(Points to Alyosha.)* Come to me.

(Alyosha is very embarrassed, and has to be coaxed over.)

ANAIS: Yes, come on, come on. Oh, he's charming, Djuna.

(Alyosha comes to her.)

ANAIS: Oh, what do I smell? Ah, I smell a death stench.

ALYOSHA: I beg your pardon, Madam Pnin. It's my father. He just died.

ANAIS: Oh, and you brought him to me? Thank you! I collect death stenches.

ALYOSHA: He was murdered.

ANAIS: Then I shall cherish him all the more. I have a special room, you know. I keep my dead father in there. I will keep your father in there too—and then, well, we will have something in common, eh? Tell me, what do you do that you have such an artistic presence?

ALYOSHA: I...

ANAIS: Sing, do you? Sing for me!

ALYOSHA: I preach!

ANAIS: You do? Oh, that's for later! *(Blows him a kiss.)*

ALYOSHA: I prepared a homily every Saturday.

ANAIS: *(Confused.)* What?

ALYOSHA: A homily.

ANAIS: What means this? Is this another euphemism? We use quote unquote preach here, don't we Djuna?

DJUNA: Often.

ANAIS: No more words, Djuna. My head is spinning. Sing to me, tiny one. Be David to my Saul. *(Closes her eyes.)*
(Alyosha sings in his falsetto. Gravely.)

ANAIS: Lower.

ALYOSHA: I'm sorry. I was pretending to be fourteen.

ANAIS: That too young for me. Lower.
(Alyosha sings in a lower key, but still falsetto.)

ANAIS: What is that, sixteen? I think you been in a monastery too long. LOWER!!
(Alyosha sings in regular voice.)

ANAIS: Louder.
(He does.)

ANAIS: Very good, very nice! How sweet he is. I put you in my diary. Djuna, make a note. *(To Alyosha.)* Now read to me, you with the big eyes and the tiny waist. My diary, volume forty-two, chapter nine...soothe me...artist... artist... *(Leans back. Closes her eyes.)*
(Djuna gives Alyosha one of Anais's diaries.)

ALYOSHA: *(Reads.)* My father's hands were the most beautiful hands I have ever seen, and they were at their most beautiful when he played the piano. He had eczema. His fingers...

ANAIS: *(Reciting from memory.)* His fingers: how I wish that I, a young, sensitive girl, so sensitive, so beautiful, so fragile, like a white lily plucked by the Blessed Virgin, shuddering, shivering, displaying an artistic sensibility far beyond my years, with a feeling for people so deep, a feeling for secret thoughts, for the innermost sensations of the cook, the maid, the piano, the kitchen mouse, the cockroach, and for all that was somehow—how may I say it?—hushed, delicate, sensitive, beautiful, fragile, poetic in the world which I saw reflected in my eyes in the big mirror in my father's study. *(Takes diary away from Alyosha.)* Thank you, you read with great feeling. *(Smiles at him.)* How well you put things, and how spiritual you are. You must move in with me as my spiritual advisor. I teach you to play the piano. Make a note, Djuna. Have you eczema?

ALYOSHA: No.

ANAIS: Djuna will get you some.

    (Enter Fr. Zossima, now made up to look like Saint Joan. He is tied to a stake, and his Altar Boys wave Christmas tinsel flames at his heels on cue.)

ZOSSIMA: *(Not seeing Alyosha yet.)* I have prepared a parable about St. Joan.

ANAIS: No. This will be derivative.

ZOSSIMA: I hear voices…and there's no one there.

    (Boys shake flamers.)

ANAIS: I only interested in the new. *(Looks at Alyosha.)*

ZOSSIMA: I smell blossoms and the trees are bare.

    (Flamers.)

ANAIS: Zossima, I thank you for your gift.

ZOSSIMA: You mean my parable?

ANAIS: No, your monk.

ZOSSIMA: *(Sees Alyosha.)* Alyosha, what does she mean?

ALYOSHA: But I never…

ANAIS: He is going to convert me twenty-four hours a day. Make a note, Djuna.

ZOSSIMA: *(Taking off his wig.)* It is time for this outrage to stop. Alyosha cannot leave the monastery without my permission.

ANAIS: You find someone new in an hour.

ZOSSIMA: Alyosha, are you ready to abandon me for this relic?

ALYOSHA: Father, please, we must be charitable…

ZOSSIMA: If you leave me and live with her, what will you have? She'll die in a week, and then where will you be?

ANAIS: In my grave, with me!

ALYOSHA: Please, Father Zossima, Madam Pnin. No more. Madam Pnin, I am deeply honored by your invitation. But Fr. Zossima is my mentor. Just as you feel you need me for spiritual solace, so I need him. So I must refuse your kind offer.

ANAIS: I didn't hear you.

ALYOSHA: I said I must refuse your kind offer.

ANAIS: What?

ALYOSHA: I said I must refuse…

ANAIS: What language is this you speak? It not one I understand. Just say yes to me, and I understand you.

ALYOSHA: I can't.

ANAIS: Djuna, I am being opposed. YES!

ALYOSHA: No!

ANAIS: I grow bored with this discussion. MOVE! Ah, how my head aches. It is all the evil in the world that has chosen to attack me this evening in my very salon. Oh, why am I not ringed around with artists as I desire? But still it is time for the entertainment. Djuna, announce the entertainment.

DJUNA: The entertainment.

ANAIS: Thank you, Djuna. This evening, in honor of my father who meant more to me than…my mother, I invite you all to witness the unbinding of my feet. Djuna!

(Djuna kneels and begins to unwrap Anais's feet.)

ANAIS: Be gentle, Djuna, don't hurt me. *(Anais first giggles then laughs, as her feet become more unwrapped, however, she begins to scream in utter agony.)*

(Lights dim, spotting her wriggling feet and Alyosha's horrified face.)

(Blackout.)

ACT I
Scene 13
The monastery. Fr. Zossima is eating peanuts from Alyosha's hand.

ALYOSHA: *(After a bit.)* I had never before noticed how foolishly feet are formed.

ZOSSIMA: I have very nice feet.

ALYOSHA: I guess I just shouldn't think about it.

ZOSSIMA: *(Stopping eating peanuts.)* I think it's time I improve my humility in a new way. Remove your shoes and socks, my son.

ALYOSHA: *(Alarmed a little.)* You ask me to do this to prove that nothing human is disgusting because God has created it?

ZOSSIMA: Do not speak, Alyosha. Obey.

(They both remove shoes and socks.)

ZOSSIMA: When you speak of this, and you will, be kind. I will now place peanuts between our soles, Alyosha.

(Zossima places peanuts between their feet, they rub the soles of their feet together.)

ZOSSIMA: *(Excited.)* Feel the peanuts between our soles, Alyosha. Father and teachers, I ponder, what is hell?

ALYOSHA: *(Putting his feet away.)* Stop it, I can't stand it, feet disgust me, your feet in particular disgust me. All this talk about humility, I don't believe you anymore. I think you're peculiar.

ZOSSIMA: What do you mean, my feet in particular? My feet are beautiful, you only say that because your feet are ugly...

ALYOSHA: I don't care about my feet, I hate all feet...

ZOSSIMA: I don't like this side of you, Alyosha.

ALYOSHA: I think you're crazy!

ZOSSIMA: Then you can pack up and leave the monastery. Disparaging my feet. I order you: You're to leave the monastery and go—to that woman! As your superior, I command you.

ALYOSHA: All right, I'll go. Never again will I diddle peanuts with you. You're not a saint, you're insane. *(Picks up shoes.)*

ZOSSIMA: SAINTS ARE INSANE!

ALYOSHA: I don't believe you! *(Exits.)*

ZOSSIMA: And take your socks!

(Blackout.)

ACT I
Scene 14

Home of Anais Pnin. Djuna Barnes, reading from Nightwood, *is giving Anais a sponge bath [by lifting up folds in Anais diaphanous dress]. Leather Girls are in the background.*

ANAIS: *(To Djuna.)* I have always needed a man to make me an artist. A woman is like a vessel, she does her best fermenting when she is stopped up. Otherwise air get in and make her head light. Djuna, take my plug out.
(Djuna does.)

ANAIS: I feel so lightheaded. *(Anais sings "In Love with the Cloth.")*
It's happened again,
I see a monk—and I'm sunk,
I give my heart automatically,
When I see a monk or priest,
And I find to my concern,

That as to monks, and priests, and monsignors, and bishops, and arch
    bishops, and cardinals, and popes,
I never learn.

I've fallen again for the cloth,
It's happened before with the cloth,
If the priest is the flame, I'm the moth,
And the moth loves the cloth, what to do?

I'm spellbound and feel clergy-caught,
I know it's against what's been taught,
For a girl shouldn't wreck what God's wrought,
Or at least not a priest, what to do?

Sister Ulrica said,
That God would strike me dead,
Mustn't want a man God wanted too,
But I said to her,
God wanted their souls,
Why take their bodies too?

And now there's a new one, alas,
How long, Lord, oh please, let it pass,
And I'd even attend Daily Mass,
To be free,
Clergy free,
God, I plea,
Or at least make that priest
The one priest for me.

DJUNA: *(Reading.)* We wash away our sense of sin, and what does that bath
secure us? Sin, shining, bright and hard…

ANAIS: You remind me of Antonin Artaud. Weird. How blond he was though.
Especially in the Paris spring. Shimmering in the sun in the spring on the
Seine. I have made a speech exercise. Djuna make a note.

DJUNA: I'm reading from *Nightwood.*

ANAIS: Make a note in the margin. Only put Anais Pnin after it so when you
die your editor not make mistake.

(Enter Alyosha, with his suitcase and his bird.)

ALYOSHA: I have just come from crushing peanuts with Fr. Zossima's bare foot.

ANAIS: Don't mention that…give me a euphemism, Djuna.

DJUNA: Faggot.

ANAIS: Faggot, to me.

ALYOSHA: I fear he is not a saint

ANAIS: Oh, you remind me of Antonin Artaud. Weird. Have you come to stay with me?

ALYOSHA: As your spiritual advisor. I've been commanded by Fr. Zossima.

ANAIS: Don't mention that...give me a euphemism, Djuna.

DJUNA: Wedding cake.

ANAIS: Wedding cake. *(Holds up plug.)* This is my plug. It remind me of Antonin Artaud. You know, I am only woman Antonin Artaud ever wanted. To cast in bronze. I say, how bronze look on my skin? It clog my pores. Djuna, sponge my pores.

(Djuna does.)

ANAIS: I am always fascinated by India and all those poor people. Djuna, go into your lotus position.

(Djuna does.)

ANAIS: *(To Alyosha.)* Here, take my picture. *(Gives him a camera.)*

ALYOSHA: I thought I was here as your spiritual advisor, not as your photographer.

ANAIS: Is there a difference? Pose me.

(He does.)

ANAIS: If your picture turns out, little one, I put it on the back of my next diary. I have one volume for each year of my life, only I am twenty-six, so how is that?

ALYOSHA: I don't believe you're twenty-six.

ANAIS: I lie. Lying is a creative act. *(Lies down.)* Sponge me, Djuna. Advise me spiritually.

ALYOSHA: Very well. Saint Paul says...

ANAIS: Sit at my feet.

ALYOSHA: I don't want to sit at your feet.

ANAIS: Ohhh, sit at my feet. Look how pretty my toes are.

ALYOSHA: I don't want to sit at your feet, I've seen enough of feet for one day, feet disgust me.

ANAIS: Yes, sit at my feet.

ALYOSHA: No, I won't.

ANAIS: Oh yesssss.

ALYOSHA: No.

ANAIS: Yesssssss.

ALYOSHA: No.

(Constance is annoyed.)

CONSTANCE: *The Brothers Karamazov,* page 453. At this point, Alyosha Karamazov sits at Madam Pnin's feet.

ALYOSHA: No.

CONSTANCE: Page 453: At this point Alyosha Karamazov sits at her feet!

(Alyosha does.)

ALYOSHA: Saint Paul says in his letter to the...

ANAIS: How wise he is, how handsome, how tiny. Take his picture, Djuna. *(Anais puts her feet in his hair, plays with his hair that way.)* Continue, Alyosha.

ALYOSHA: Saint Paul says in his letter to the...the...please get your feet out of my hair. I don't do that to you. Oh—how can there be a God if there are feet!

ANAIS: Well, of course. There is no God, and there *are* feet. My feet. *(Puts her feet on his shoulders.)*

ALYOSHA: You're right. I should have known when he first brought out the jar of peanuts that there was no God.

ANAIS: Girls!

(Enter the Leather Girls, carrying two dead bodies in plastic bags: of Fyodor and Anais's father:)

ANAIS: Your father and my father are getting on very well together. Thank you girls.

(Leather Girls exit.)

ALYOSHA: Oh. It's strange having these bodies here. You're surrounded by death.

ANAIS: That's life. Come to me, *mia bambino melancholia.*

ALYOSHA: I feel I have no center.

ANAIS: I have a center for you. You be my artist. God has sent you to me...

ALYOSHA: You said there was no...

ANAIS: You are my gift from God. We are both artists. Artist, artist, artist, artist, artist!

CONSTANCE: Ernest, put a cover on that sofa.

(Ernest puts sheet over Anais and Alyosha. Ernest puts one over Djuna, who is reading from Nightwood.*)*

ANAIS: *(Under sheet.)* We pretend we dead, Alyosha.

(Djuna keeps reading aloud.)

(Blackout.)

END ACT I

ACT II
Scene 1

Alyosha and Anais Pnin on divan together. Anais is rolling over and over in her sleep. Alyosha becomes despondent and moves off divan. Constance, per usual, is present.

CONSTANCE: Good evening, and welcome to Alyosha's dark night of the soul.

ALYOSHA: O, I am in a mist.

CONSTANCE: This phrase occurs often in Dostoevesky's letters to my sister.

ALYOSHA: How can there be a God if there are feet?

CONSTANCE: When translating, I had great difficulty with this passage. So I have had to select and simplify. The Russian original goes on for pages and pages, questioning our Savior's existence in a variety of ways, but it seemed to me that it all boiled down to feet.

ANAIS: *(In her sleep.)* Feather, feather, farther, farther...

ALYOSHA: Oh, no she's waking up. It's stupid for me to stay here. I'll just leave.

CONSTANCE: Alyosha, due to a tragic flaw, cannot leave the spider house.

ANAIS: Farther, farther, father, fatash, pop, pop, population.

ALYOSHA: Yes, I can leave.

CONSTANCE: No you will not.

ANAIS: *(Opens her eyes.)* Populist, Popular, Popsicle. Pop Singer. POP SINGER. ALYOSHA, WE MAKE YOU POP SINGER.

ALYOSHA: No.

ANAIS: Yes.

ALYOSHA: Why should I become a pop singer?

ANAIS: It come to me in a dream. I tired of keeping you in the house all the time.

ALYOSHA: This is my second day.

ANAIS: It seem longer.

ALYOSHA: *(To himself.)* I can't go back to the monastery.

ANAIS: Oh, you like singing. You sing poem I write. Djuna!

ALYOSHA: I've come this far, I guess everyone should know my shame and disgust.

ANAIS: Nothing human disgust an artist, Alyosha, unless it is cruel or thoughtless. Djuna, you NO-TALENT NOBODY, I'm calling you.
(Enter Djuna.)

DJUNA: Sorry, Madam Pnin, I was...

ANAIS: I know, you were tattooing *Nightwood* on the insides of your eyelids. But that can wait. Teach Alyosha to sing scales, he going to be my popsicle.

ALYOSHA: She means pop singer.

ANAIS: Who know what I mean? A poet is not exact. Here prose poem of mine. Make up tune for it. *(Hands him paper.)* I go behind curtain to write. Djuna, is that Daddy back there? I pretend to take a shower. *(Anais goes behind large curtain with her diary.)*

(Djuna makes "sssss-ing" sounds like a shower.)

ALYOSHA: I want to go home!

ANAIS: Be quiet. I'm writing. Hotter, Djuna.

(Djuna makes hotter noises.)

ANAIS: Ah, yes, this is helping my writing. Wetter, Djuna.

(Djuna does. Enter Mrs. Karamazov dragging her wedding dress, and walking Smerdyakov on a leash.)

MRS. KARAMAZOV: The Virgin punished me for leaving the nunnery. She'll do the same to you, Alyosha.

ALYOSHA: Mother, why are you here?

MRS. KARAMAZOV: Now, what was it I was looking for? *(Wanders off.)*

ANAIS: Keep singing, Alyosha. Colder, Djuna.

(Alyosha sings. Enter Ivan with birdcage.)

IVAN: Alyosha, don't leave this in your room. Dmitri keeps thinking it's a fly.

(Enter Mrs. Karamazov again with Smerdyakov.)

ALYOSHA: Ivan. I'm going to be a pop star. Are you disgusted?

MRS. KARAMAZOV: Now where was your father?

IVAN: Sure kid. Everything disgusts me.

MRS. KARAMAZOV: *(To dead Fyodor.)* James, Edmund is not well. I don't think its a summer cold at all. It's snowing outside.

IVAN: Oh, Christ.

ANAIS: Djuna, blow soap bubbles.

(Djuna does. Enter Dmitri with flyswatter. He tries to hit bubbles with it.)

ALYOSHA: Mama, should I leave here?

MRS. KARAMAZOV: *(Looking at Djuna.)* I think Cathleen's been drinking.

(Enter Grushenka I and II.)

GRUSHENKA I: Look at this decadence.

ANAIS: Hotter, Djuna. Imitate faulty plumbing.

(Djuna makes loud, deep honking noises.)

MRS. KARAMAZOV: Oh, God, the foghorn. Blessed Mother, make it stop.

GRUSHENKA: This is where headquarters should be.

GRUSHENKA II: We'll tell the Commissar.

GRUSHENKA I: Right on.

(The two Grushenkas exit.)

IVAN: *(To Dmitri.)* They're bubbles, you nut head, not flies. Bubbles.

DMITRI: Da da dead.

MRS. KARAMAZOV: It was something I had once and now have lost.

CONSTANCE: *(Comes to her and takes wedding dress from her.)* Let me hold onto this. You don't want to get this dirty.

MRS. KARAMAZOV: Thank you. You are very kind.

ALYOSHA: *(Despairing.)* Mama, I'm going to be a pop star

MRS. KARAMAZOV: *(Slaps him.)* Edmund, stop saying that! It's just a summer cold!

ANAIS: Sing, Alyosha. All right, Djuna, I'm ready for the stabbing.

(Djuna, shrieking, goes behind the screen and appears to be stabbing Anais.)

ANAIS: ARTIST, ARTIST, ARTIST, ARTIST!

(Alyosha is shocked. Likewise Ivan. Smerdyakov has a fit.)

IVAN: What happened?

DJUNA: Madam Pnin merely wishes to improve her circulation.

ALYOSHA: Does anyone have a spoon?

IVAN: Oh, let him die.

ANAIS: Djuna, I'm ready.

(Djuna opens the curtains, revealing Anais lying down, writing, with the corpse of her father on top of her.)

ANAIS: I writing in volume 98 of my diary today. I have one volume for each year of my life. My father gives me inspiration. Alyosha, my little one, come closer...

ALYOSHA: I don't want to...

CONSTANCE: *The Brothers Karamazov.* Alyosha draws closer to the woman on the divan.

ALYOSHA: I don't want to... *(Draws closer to Anais.)*

ANAIS: Come, get on top. Djuna, help him up. We make sandwich, Alyosha.

(Djuna helps Alyosha on top of dead father.)

IVAN: This is what I saw in the punch bowl.

ANAIS: The mayonnaise, Djuna.

(Djuna spreads mayonnaise.)

(Blackout.)

ACT II

Scene 2

Constance and Ernest alone.

CONSTANCE: *The Brothers Karamazov.* Page 437. Ernest, what is a six-letter word for a great place of entertainment, as in "you haven't lived until you've played the blank?"

ERNEST: Palace.

CONSTANCE: Thank you, Ernest. *The Brothers Karamazov.* Appendix one. Alyosha appears at the palace.

(Enter Djuna.)

DJUNA: Good evening, and welcome to the palace. I am Djuna Barnes, writer, no strike that, composer of *Nightwood,* and I am here, sent by Anais Pnin, to welcome you all. This evening, Anais Pnin is bringing you the debut of Alyosha Karamazov, that is, his first appearance on any stage anywhere except, of course, on the stage we all call life. Thank you. I have been instructed by Madam Pnin to warm you up. Your cooperation will be appreciated. *(Takes out index cards with jokes on them.)* All right. A. Once there were two prostitutes in Ohio. B. And one of these prostitutes bleached her hair. C. And the other one didn't. D. And the one who didn't asked the one who did, E. Do you ever smoke after sex, F. and she said, "What, all the way to Africa?" No. How about another? A. A British man in Hyde Park meets a black prostitute, C. And she says, "Want to take me home? D. And he says E. What? All the way back to Africa? Seriously folks. G. And the bus driver said H. If your ass burns, stick it out the window. Thank you. And now Madam Pnin.

ANAIS: *(Appearing.)* Thank you, Djuna. Good evening. I am Anais Pnin. In honor of my dear father, whose corpse is even this moment in my dressing room, I am presenting to you a young new pop singer, Alyosha Karamazov. He is a young monk who has lost his faith and thus expresses my artistic sensibility. Whether he can sing on pitch or not is an aspect of probability theory and thus expresses the randomness of art in our time more clearly than anything except my diaries. I shall now read from my dairy, volume ninety-six. *(Reads.)* "Grey skies this morning studded with apple stars. The apple stars have worm in their core. I am reminded the French word for heart is 'coeur.' I have a worm in my coeur; it is the worm of sensuality. I go to the theatre with Gore last evening. We drop my stillborn baby off the second balcony, screaming 'Bourgeois pigs who murder children!' Politics is so fatiguing but it is our duty." *(Anais stops reading.)*

(Mrs. Karamazov wanders on.)

ANAIS: Speaking of mothers, this is Alyosha Karamazov's mother, Mary. Isn't she pretty in her lovely dress? Let's have a big hand for her.

MRS. KARAMAZOV: How heavy the fog is. *(Looks at vein.)* Oh, collapsed again. I had a talk with Mother Elizabeth. She is so good and sweet. I told her I wanted to be a nun. I explained how sure I was of my vocation. I had prayed to the Blessed Virgin to make me sure. And I had a true vision of her when I was praying.

ANAIS: Listen to her voice. He gets it from her.

MRS. KARAMAZOV: Mother Elizabeth told me I must be more sure than that. She said I should put myself to a test and go home after I graduate and live as other girls live.

ANAIS: Isn't she pathetic?

MRS. KARAMAZOV: That was the winter of senior year. Then in the spring something happened to me. Yes, I remember. I fell in love with Fyodor Karamazov and was so happy for a time.

ANAIS: Ladies and Gentlemen I give you ALYOSHA KARAMAZOV!

(Enter Alyosha, a raincoat over his shoulder. He is handed a microphone and sings. Constance perhaps shrieks her approval of him from time to time.)

ALYOSHA: *(Sings, à la Frank Sinatra.)*

We'll meet in a pubic place,
I promise to hide my face,
We'll couple and then erase,
All memories of miseries together.

We'll dance and perfume the sheets,
A metronome marks the beats,
We'll send out for sandwich meats,
And try to spurn what we had spawned, together.

Remember when the bellboy had the clap,
What a mess he made upon your lap,
Then we cried for hours at a time,
That in June you would pass your prime.

Pubic places afford no rest,
It took hours to get undressed,
Unclothed you don't look your best,

So good-bye and farewell,
Hope you die and go to hell,
But, alas, strange to tell:
I'll see you Friday.
(Exits.)

ANAIS: And now the Karamazov Family Singers!

(Enter Mrs. Karamazov, Ivan, Dmitri, Smerdyakov, and the dead Fyodor. They sing the following, ringing bells and doing slapping routines. Smerdyakov gets excited and barks a lot.)

KARAMOZOV FAMILY: *(Singing.)*

I'm Poppa, I'm Momma,
I'm Bertha, I'm Dolf,
I'm Ingmar, I'm Inga,
I'm Gerta, I'm Hrolf,
I'm Ulla, I'm Marta,
I'm Zeinholst, I'm Schrolf,
And once we were sitting in Luxury's Lap,
But now we're the travelling SWISS FAMILY TRAPP! *(Ring bells.)*

We like yogurt and sour cream
And butter and cheese,
And sauerkraut and blintzes,
And udders to squeeze,
We like eggnog and whip cream
And Hodgkin's Disease,
We like ice cream and malted and milk shake and frappe,
And now we're the travelling SWISS FAMILY TRAPP! *(Ring bells.)*

Und when we are cranky, we frown,
Und when we stand up, we sit down,
Und when we are gloomy, we weep,
Und when we are happy, we sleep!

We have frostbite and chilblains,
And sniffles and flu,
We have windburn and fungus,
Psoriasis too,
We have nosebleed and nosedrip,
And errands to do,
Been raised by our Momma with Milk and a Slap,
And now we're the travelling SWISS FAMILY TRAPP! *(Ring bells.)*

Und when we are chilly, we sweat,
Und when we are naughty, we wet,
Und when we are leaving, we stay,
Und when we eat strudle, we say:
If Momma has reason,
If Poppa has vice,
If Bertha is freezin',
Then put her on ice,
If winter's a season,
Then nothing is nice,
Und Gott ist in himmel und taking a Napp,
Und we schtick together—
The Swiss family trapp!
(Ring bells chaotically.)
(Blackout.)

ACT II
Scene 3

Alyosha, right after his successful debut. He looks somewhat dazed. A couple of people are in line for autographs. Third in line is Fr. Zossima, in sack cloth. Alyosha looks surprised, signs his book.

ZOSSIMA: Alyosha, you're a success in the world now. Are you happy?

ALYOSHA: Why do you ask? You sent me from the monastery.

ZOSSIMA: I've sold the monastery, Alyosha. It's now a munitions factory.

ALYOSHA: Is that moral?

ZOSSIMA: I no longer judge anything. I am a pilgrim now. I sleep in the open air. I eat nettles. *(Eats nettles.)*

ALYOSHA: And are you happy?

ZOSSIMA: No, but I'm losing weight. You see, I must do penance, Alyosha. We all must.

(Alyosha notices that Zossima is missing an arm.)

ALYOSHA: Where is your arm?

ZOSSIMA: The munitions factory blew up. But it is a good penance. You too must seek penance, Alyosha.

(Blackout.)

ACT II

Scene 4

Constance and Ernest.

CONSTANCE: The Brothers Karaughughughughughughughughughhugghghghg…

(Constance has a horrendous coughing fit.)

(Ernest brings her tea. She stops coughing.)

CONSTANCE: At this point Alyosha and his brothers have tea. *(Tastes her tea, it's awful, she throws it in a potted palm.)*

(Lights up on Alyosha seated with Mrs. Karamazov, Dmitri, Smerdyakov. All seem most catatonic, except Alyosha. Fr. Zossima is seated on a table as a samovar.)

ALYOSHA: What a nice idea to have tea for my success. Thank you, mother.

(No one reacts. Alyosha tries to talk to Dmitri.)

ALYOSHA: How are you, Dmitri? I expect we'll have a blizzard soon. Do you ever hear from Grushenka? I mean since cutting her in half? Did you kill father?

DMITRI: Da da dead.

(Enter Ivan, suffering from brain fever.)

IVAN: The regiment has left town. Everyone of intelligence has gone. How hot it is, absolutely stifling. I saw my children this morning, standing on the doorstep; and I was filled with a horror at thinking of all the senseless boredom they will face in their coming years. Thank God they were the phantoms of my perfervid brain. Now my phantoms will be bored instead of my children, which seems to me more humane.

ALYOSHA: Hello, Ivan. Where is my bird?

IVAN: Where is my bird? The eternal question.

ALYOSHA: *(Picking up birdcage.)* Ah, kukushka, my one comfort in this desert. Would you have tea from the samovar, brother Ivan? *(Getting tea.)* Tea is the stuff of life as is faith to those who have it, Ivan.

(Gets tea from Fr. Zossima, who is seated on the table, his arm held up as a spout, nothing is made of his being a samovar, except he perhaps makes a face of some sort when tea pours from his hand into the cup.)

IVAN: Let us toast our family, Alyosha.

ALYOSHA: Blessed be the Karamazov family, for they shall inherit the earth.

IVAN: Suffer the little Karamazovs to come to me.

ALYOSHA: Forgive the Karamazovs for they know not what they do.

IVAN: Blessed be the wheat fields and rice fields of our great homeland.

ZOSSIMA: *(On table.)* O MOTHER RUSSIA. *(Gets down, kisses floor, resumes position.)*

IVAN: Alyosha, I am greatly troubled. How can we ever know what we perceive? For instance, that samovar didn't just move, did it?

ALYOSHA: I no longer feel certain of anything.

IVAN: You're wrong, it didn't move. How can you sit there in your monastic smugness, believing in the rightness and order of things? Don't you realize we can never be positive of the metaphysical nature of phenomenon? Take cruelty to children! How can God allow it, Alyosha?

ALYOSHA: Fr. Zossima says God does not allow it.

IVAN: Alyosha, open your eyes. I've seen a mother embroidering take her needle and jab it into the eye of her daughter. I've seen a *father* embroidering take a needle and jab it into the other eye of the same child. I then saw this child bitten viciously on the thorax by a rabid seminarian chopping wood. And then this same child was scalded by a peasant woman flinging Russian borscht from her moving troika.

ZOSSIMA: O MOTHER RUSSIA.

IVAN: See there! It didn't move again. O, Alyosha, how can there be a God with such cruelty? I saw that same child, eyeless, burned, scalded, bitten, and rabid, I saw this child forced to swallow Draino, and shoved into a hot oven as a demonstration of the efficiencies of gas heat. I AM THAT CHILD, ALYOSHA, I AM THAT CHILD! And do God's cruelties stop there? Answer me, Alyosha Do they?

ALYOSHA: No.

IVAN: You're wrong. They don't stop there. Look at these pictures. A little girl burned at the stake by her father. A little boy bound and gagged and shoved into an egg beater. Look at this roast beef sandwich. And this one.

ALYOSHA: No—no more pictures.

(Ivan throws pictures on ground, Zossima picks them up.)

IVAN: No, it didn't move, it didn't. It isn't looking at my pictures. It isn't. Give those back to me. *(Grabs them back.)*

ALYOSHA: Ivan, calm down. Let's have some tea. I find our Russian tea very soothing. Ivan, I'm troubled, and feel I must speak my heart.

IVAN: Speak, little brother, and I will listen. I always listen. Artists always listen. Listening is a gift. I'm listening. Go on.

ALYOSHA: Ivan, I've lost something precious to me. All during our singing tours…

IVAN: Loss! It's all loss. It's all absence, all sans signification. You of great faith think you see only manifestations of God's benevolence…

ALYOSHA: Ivan, how can there be a God if there are feet? If only I could…

IVAN: Shut up, Alyosha, I'm listening. You see plenty where there is but nothing. You see a garden, I see but ashes. You see ball gowns, I see sack cloth. *(Picks up grapes.)* Look at these grapes. *(Crushes them.)* CRUSHED! Look at this plum. *(Squashes it.)* SQUASHED! Look at this bird. *(Reaches in to kukushka.)* DEAD!

ALYOSHA: My bird! Dead!

(Ivan shrieks.)

IVAN: Dead. Deadeadeadeadeadeadeadeadeadead. *(Straightens coat.)* Thank you all very much. *(Sits down, has tea.)*

ALYOSHA: *(Picks up dead bird.)* I feel suddenly dizzy. There's a strange smell.

ZOSSIMA: Death stench.

ALYOSHA: Beg pardon?

ZOSSIMA: Death stench. Your bird is not a saint.

ALYOSHA: God spares us no humiliations, Samovar. And it's such a small bird to smell so bad.

ZOSSIMA: Size isn't important, my son.

(Enter Anais and Djuna.)

ANAIS: Quick, Djuna, quick. I smell a death stench. We must bag it.

ZOSSIMA: Hello, Anais.

ANAIS: I do not speak to samovars. That is Djuna's job. Djuna.

DJUNA: That is not a samovar.

ANAIS: Be quiet, Djuna, I conducting business…

DJUNA: That is Father Zossima.

ANAIS: Can you not smile, Alyosha?

DJUNA: And if I had scalding water I'd prove my point.

ANAIS: You always talking about burning people, Djuna. Why you so destructive. Ah, that death stench, where is it? *(Picks up bird.)* Oh, look, it's a pretty dead bird. Yellow dead, beak dead, peep dead. Peep peep peep dead, peep peep peep dead. Bag it, Djuna.

(Djuna does.)

ANAIS: Whose bird is this?

ALYOSHA: It was mine, Madam Pnin.

ANAIS: I've told you and told you to call me Anais. Like the oriental flower. The Oriental flower that means…Djuna, what is it that it mean?

DJUNA: Extension cord.

ANAIS: Extension cord. That why I make a good connection. I have made a joke. Djuna, make a note. On Feb. 15, 1917, on the anniversary of my father's election to the papal college—he was such an archbishop—Djuna, I have made another joke, make a note. Unbinding my feet has set my creative juices flowing, I tink. Kiss me, Djuna.

(Djuna does.)

ANAIS: On Feb. 15, 1917, I make a joke to young Alyosha Karamazov. Add footnotes to explain why they funny. And now, little one, thank you for your bird, it smell lovely.

ZOSSIMA: *(Standing.)* I shall now prophesy.

ANAIS: Oh, look, samovar is rising.

ZOSSIMA: I was only pretending to be a samovar, as a penance. Alyosha, if you stay with this woman…

ANAIS: Listen to that! Why does he call me a woman? It is typical of men in this oppressive society that just because I have two breasts and a vagina, he calls me a woman. That is not necessarily a woman. Now if I had three breasts and four vaginas, *that* would be a woman. Like Djuna. Djuna, write that down. *(Sings softly.)* Djuna busting out all over…

ZOSSIMA: I am trying to speak. Alyosha, if you stay with this woman…

ANAIS: There he go again!

(Alyosha shushes her.)

ZOSSIMA: *(Shouting.)* …and do not return to the monastery at once your father will be murdered with a pestle.

ANAIS: Chaliapin, how base.

ALYOSHA: My father has already been murdered by a pestle.

ZOSSIMA: Then the prophecy is fulfilled.

(Enter Grushenka I and II, dressed in combat boots and Army fatigues. With them enter the Leather Girls who have been transformed into an Army of Legs. The top part of their bodies do not accompany them.)

GRUSHENKA: *(Waving rifle.)* UP AGAINST THE WALL, EVERYBODY, UP AGAINST THE WALL.

(Everybody is forced by the Legs army to stand in a line. This wakes up Mrs. Karamazov, Dmitri, and Smerdyakov considerably.)

GRUSHENKA: Welcome to the Russian Revolution. *(Blows whistle.)*

(Legs search everyone.)

GRUSHENKA: All you sisters, get up and pull yourselves together. The Commissar is coming! You're gonna get it now, pigs, because the big cheese is coming. Whooppee.

ANAIS: This woman have strange vocabulary, maybe I use it in a novel.

GRUSHENKA: The Commissar is coming closer, better dig a mass grave, some-body. Whoopp-ppeee.

(Enter Constance pushed by Ernest, directly into the action for the first time.)

CONSTANCE: Havoc and chaos, have we wreaked havoc and chaos yet, Comrade Grushenka?

GRUSHENKA: I was just about to, Commissar.

CONSTANCE: No time like the present. Kill my sister. Havoc. Chaos. Carry on, Comrade Grushenka.

GRUSHENKA: We burn the diaries. *(To Anais.)* Where are they?

ANAIS: Where are what? I don't know where they are. Only Djuna knows, and she is sworn to secrecy.

GRUSHENKA: *(To Ernest.)* Torture her. *(Points to Djuna.)*

(Ernest moves threateningly toward Djuna.)

DJUNA: Here's the key. They're in the back room.

(Ernest exits with key.)

ANAIS: Djuna, you not an artist.

(Enter Ernest with all the diaries which are kept in a shopping cart.)

GRUSHENKA: *(Emotionally.)* We'll have a fire tonight, we'll be warm for the first time in weeks.

CONSTANCE: Ernest, strike the match.

(Ernest does.)

CONSTANCE: Burn them, Ernest.

ANAIS: Wait. *(Blows out match.)* You mean, you really going to burn them? My diaries, my children? Please, please. Take a village of African children and slaughter them—but spare my words. Or take Djuna, break her limbs, rape her—or kill Alyosha...but don't take my diaries. How can you destroy an art that says "Oct. 26, 1894. Today I had a glass eye made in case I lose my real eye. I play marbles with my glass eye, it reminds me of clairvoyant who play at games with his second sight. Now I put glass eye in my navel and pretend I Indian deity, Siva." And you want to burn this ???? Oh please please please please please please please...

CONSTANCE: Oh, for heaven's sake, let her take them. No one will read them. I haven't translated them. Just get her out of here. Get them all out. Throw them into the snow, the snow, the snow!

(Anais and the rest are pushed out by the two Grushenkas and the Legs.)

ANAIS: Good-bye, house, good-bye, home, good-bye...

(Everyone is gone except Constance, Ernest, Grushenka I and II, Legs.)

CONSTANCE: I want that woman killed, Grushenka. I want them all killed except Alyosha. Ernest, did you kill my sister yet? *(No answer.)* He's so moody. Find out where their camp is, and kill Madame Pnin.

GRUSHENKA: For the Revolution.

(Grushenka I and II, Legs exit.)

CONSTANCE: Have you seen how a white lily grows, Ernest? I only say that because it's an Elizabethan song by John Ferrabosco the Younger, save for the Ernest part, which is mine. Sometime I feel like Sarah Orne Jewett; serve her for dinner next week, Ernest. *The Brothers Karamazov* page 754. This part of the novel is rife with complication; the translatrix's first duty is clarity, clarity like the London fog—dense but simple. The Russian word for mulatto is Pushkin. The Russian word for overcoat is Gogol. The Russian word for epileptic is Dostoevsky. The Russian word for accident at the train station is Anna Karenina. The Russian word for bumble bee is Rimsky-Korsakov. The Russian word for an hysterical homosexual is Tchaikovsky! *The Brothers Karamazov!* At this point...Ernest, do you like me a little? Could you find it in your heart to vouchsafe me a kiss? No? Back to work, solace always in work. *The Brothers Karamazov* page 755. Alyosha Karamazov at this point... *(Takes off her spectacles smashes them.)* Ernest, I've smashed my spectacles, send for my optometrist, the proper one this time. *(Takes her watch smashes it.)* Ernest, my jeweler! *(Rips up book.)* My bookbinder, Ernest. *(Rips her bodice.)* Send for the seamstress, Ernest! That nice one with the heavy beard. DON'T JUST STAND THERE, GET THESE PEOPLE, I HAVE TO GET ON WITH THIS.

(Ernest exits with no expression.)

CONSTANCE: Oh, Ernest, I didn't mean it, oh Ernest... *(Wheels off after him.)*

ACT II

Scene 5

The Russian blizzard. Snow falls. Anais's sleigh is pushed in. In the sleigh are Anais, the dead Fyodor, the dead Joacquin Pnin (father of Anais), Mrs. Karamazov, Alyosha. Pushing the sleigh are Ivan, Zossima, Dmitri, Smerdyakov. The diaries are pulled along by Djuna.

ANAIS: We are dispossessed, we are dispossessed.

(Anais's hands are cold, Djuna blows on them.)

ZOSSIMA: *(To those around him.)* It's cold, mes enfants. I cough. *(Coughs.)* This cough has meaning. *(Coughs.)* And this cough. *(Coughs.)* And this cough. It means I am coming down with pneumonia.

ANAIS: *(Stopping Djuna's blowing on her hands.)* That's enough. We must eat, we must plan. Djuna, come here.

(Anais and Djuna whisper for a moment, then call to Smerdyakov.)

ANAIS: Here, puppy. Here, doggie.

(Smerdyakov follows Anais and Djuna off.)

IVAN: What are you doing with Smerdyakov? *(Exits.)*

MRS. KARAMAZOV: *(To Alyosha.)* Edmund, hurry. I want you to return to the monastery at once.

ALYOSHA: I can't. It's been blown up.

MRS. KARAMAZOV: Please, don't talk about things you don't understand. *(Holds up pestle.)* Look, Edmund. This is the pestle your father was killed with. I'm going to talk to your father. Where is your father?

ALYOSHA: Mama, he's dead.

MRS. KARAMAZOV: You believe that excuse of his? The day he died I confronted him with his guilt. Where is he? Let me confront him again.

ALYOSHA: Mama, Poppa's dead.

MRS. KARAMAZOV: Have you no respect, Edmund? Do you see this pestle? It was a sin I didn't go back to the convent. I'll give up my habit if you go back to the monastery.

ALYOSHA: Would you give it up, Mama?

MRS. KARAMAZOV: Give up what, Edmund? Why are you looking at me that way? Is there something wrong with my hair?

ALYOSHA: If only I could believe you.

MRS. KARAMAZOV: But I've said so many contradictory things, which one did you want to believe? Do you want to believe the Blessed Virgin appeared to me? She did, Edmund. Twice. Do you see this pestle, Edmund? It's too large. I can't get it into my veins. *(Mrs. Karamazov tries to plunge pestle into her veins, cries.)*

ALYOSHA: Mama, don't...

(Enter Anais, Djuna, Ivan. Djuna carries large pot.)

ANAIS: FOOD EVERYBODY. Djuna make casserole.

ZOSSIMA: What is that lovely aroma?

(All begin to eat.)

MRS. KARAMAZOV: Where is Smerdyakov? He should have some.

ANAIS: He's not hungry.

ALYOSHA: Where is Smerdyakov?

(Mrs. Karamazov looks in casserole, takes out dog collar previously worn by Smerdyakov.)

MRS. KARAMAZOV: This was the collar I gave him when he was just a baby. What has happened to him?

ALYOSHA: *(To Anais.)* What did you do?

ANAIS: I can be many things. A writer of diaries, a beautiful woman, an artist, a poet, a novelist. I cannot be hungry.

MRS. KARAMAZOV: Oh, shoot me up, someone, shoot me up.

ZOSSIMA: I used to warn the monks about these literal interpretations of the Eucharist. I leave you with the cannibals, Alyosha. *(Exits.)*

ANAIS: All this fuss over nothing. We have to move on.

ALYOSHA: Give me that pestle, mother. *(Takes it from Mrs. Karamazov.)*

MRS. KARAMAZOV: Don't get hooked, Edmund. Take aspirin.

ALYOSHA: *(Raising the pestle against Anais.)* This is the end, Anais.

ANAIS: This not the special entertainment. This spontaneous.

(Enter Grushenka I and II with guns.)

GRUSHENKA: Die, you revisionist pig!

(Djuna jumps in front of Anais.)

DJUNA: Don't shoot Madame Pnin!

(Grushenka shoots, hitting Djuna, the two Grushenkas exit.)

ANAIS: Djuna!

DJUNA: *(Dying.)* Night…wood.

ANAIS: Her dying words were *Nightwood*. Oh, I am touched. My collection becomes enormous. Who will cook. Oh, I am weeping. Look, this is a tear. Djuna, make a note. I have shed a tear. I must blow my nose. *(Blows her nose into pages she rips from* Nightwood.*)* Poor Djuna, poor *Nightwood*. *(Rips up several pages, crying into them.)* Well, enough of this. Bag her, Ivan. *(Ivan puts Djuna in a plastic bag, similar to the ones containing Fyodor, Joacquin Pnin, and the dead bird.)*

ANAIS: Mush, mush, my hardies, ever onward, the artist never rests.

(Alyosha raises the pestle to kill Anais again. Ivan takes the pestle from him.)

IVAN: *(To Alyosha.)* I love your guts, kid, but I gotta warn you. I hate your guts, you goddam bastard. *(Hits Alyosha over the head with the pestle.)* Gee, kid, I'm sorry, I love your guts. Here, Mama. *(Ivan gives Mrs. Karamazov back the pestle.)*

MRS. KARAMAZOV: This isn't what I was looking for. I was looking…

ANAIS: I said, mush. Come, come.

ALYOSHA: I refuse to go on with you. *(To Mrs. Karamazov.)* Mother, I want you to stay with me.

ANAIS: No, I want her. I make her my new secretary.

ALYOSHA: Mother, we'll find a doctor together.

MRS. KARAMAZOV: Will we, Edmund? Can I get stuff from him?

ANAIS: Come on now, Mary, we stop at drugstore on way. Mush, mush. Get everyone in the sleigh.

(All but Alyosha start to exit in the sleigh.)

ALYOSHA: Mother, why are you leaving?

MRS. KARAMAZOV: I'll be back, Edmund. I'm just going to buy tooth powder.

ALYOSHA: I WANT MY MOTHER!

ANAIS: Take your father instead. *(Pushes Fyodor's dead body at him.)* My father sick of your father. Onward!

(All exit in sleigh except Alyosha and the dead Fyodor.)

MRS. KARAMAZOV: *(Going out.)* I need tooth powder, and toilet soap, and hand cream…

(Alyosha is left alone with the dead body of his father. After a moment the dead Fyodor comes back to life and begins to speak.)

FYODOR: *(Coming to life.)* Ideal weather for my lumbago. Something dripping in my head, ever since the fontanelles. Perhaps it's a little vein. What have you learned, Alyosha?

ALYOSHA: Well…I've learned that it wasn't enough just to want to see Uncle Henry and Auntie Em. And that if ever I go searching for my heart's desire again, I won't look any further than my own backyard. Because if it isn't there, I never really lost it to begin with. Is that right?

FYODOR: That's close.

(Everyone who has just exited, comes back, as in a happy dream, to embrace Alyosha and share in his sudden happiness. Anais, Mrs. Karamazov, Ivan, Dmitri Smerdyakov, Djuna [now alive again]. They sing.)

ALYOSHA: *(Singing.)*
Totem and Taboo, and Toto too,
We've finally forgot what we've been through,
And we'll smile all around us,
The whole day through,
In Toto we'll be happy,
That goes for Toto too.

GRUSHENKA: Totem and taboo, and Toto too,
Man is but a beast in a strange zoo,

With knowledge we are armed now.
We know who's who,
We'll tote our vast new learning,
That goes for Toto too.

ANAIS: Life is a ballet,
Our thoughts are just like toe shoes,
There's no more I can say:
Wear toe shoes, tutus, Toto.
One more thing I'll say,
The concept of a totem,
A totem is a sign,
It represents the scrotum.
(Spoken.) Djuna, I have made a faux pas. Praise me.

ALL: Totem and taboo, the thought ain't new,
We're waiting for Godot, and Toto too,
A happy day upon us,
Our past we rue,
And God created Adam,
That goes for Toto, too.

ANAIS: Taboo may be defined,
No-no words like tinkle,
We must be more refined,
Don't say "tinkle," "ti-ti," Toto.
One more thing I'll say,
Archetypes are through,
If I'm to have my way,
Dump totem and screw taboo.
(Spoken.) Djuna, I have created a slogan.

ALL: Totem and taboo, and Toto too,
We've totally forgot what we've been through,
And we'll smile all around us,
The whole day through,
In toto we'll be
Totally, terribly; thoughtfully, bearably;
Hopefully, warily; truthfully, verily
Happy,
That goes for Toto too.
(At the end of the song, Fyodor and Djuna drop down dead again, and all the

others exit as the lights drop down about them, as if they are pulled out into the
wings. As Alyosha is left alone with the dead bodies onstage, Constance appears.
Constance is dressed in an enormous white wedding gown with a huge veil, the
material seems very, very old. She looks, as the script makes explicit shortly, very
much like Miss Havisham from Great Expectations. *Constance wheels herself*
in slowly and in a pink spot begins to sing.)

CONSTANCE: *(Sings, very showy.)* You may ask,

> Who is she?
> Little one on the sideline,
> Little one with the byline,
> In other people's books.
> You may ask,
> Does she cry,
> Unassuming translatrix,
> Could it be she's the matrix,
> The star of the show,
> If so, you know
> She'll never let it go…

(Lights come up. Constance rolls herself over to Alyosha with great purpose.)

CONSTANCE: Boy. Boy, come here. Come here.

(Alyosha comes over to Constance.)

CONSTANCE: Do you know what I touch here? *(She touches her heart.)*

ALYOSHA: Your heart.

CONSTANCE: Broken! *(Pause.)* What do I touch?

ALYOSHA: Your heart.

CONSTANCE: Broken! And again.

ALYOSHA: Your heart.

CONSTANCE: Broken! *(Constance points to Mrs. Karamazov who did not exit with*
the others after "Totem and Taboo.") What do you think of Estella?

ALYOSHA: That's not Estella, that's my mother.

CONSTANCE: You think she is very pretty. And you, Estella? What do you think
of him?

(Constance whispers to Mrs. Karamazov, who becomes very haughty and cold.)

MRS. KARAMAZOV: I think he is very common. And his hands are coarse.

CONSTANCE: Very good. And you, Pip, do you think Estella can break your
heart?

ALYOSHA: I want to go back to the monastery.

CONSTANCE: Ah, you're as stubborn as my sister.

(Enter Fr. Zossima, coughing and dying.)

ZOSSIMA: *(Coughing.)* Armand, Armand. I didn't want to leave you. Your father forced me to. *(Sings.)* Addio del passato.

(Enter Anais, Ivan, and Dmitri with the plastic bag ready for his death. Constance looks annoyed.)

ANAIS: Get the bag ready, Ivan.

ZOSSIMA: Oh, I am granted a vision of the Blessed Mother. *(To Anais.)* Tell them I'm a saint, tell them. *(Dies.)*

ANAIS: He was a saint. Hurry, Ivan. *(To Alyosha.)* Alyosha, you naughty boy, I wilt your brother. Spray him, Djuna.

IVAN: Djuna dead.

ANAIS: Spray him, Djuna.

IVAN: Djuna dead, therefore everything permitted.

(Ivan sprays Dmitri with insecticide. Dmitri dies.)

ALYOSHA: Wilted.

CONSTANCE: Dead.

(Anais and Ivan hurry off.)

CONSTANCE: Pip, come here. I am tired. I want diversion, and I have done with men and women. Play.

ALYOSHA: Mother, what does she mean?

CONSTANCE: Yust mustn't call Estella mother, or she will laugh at you. Won't you, my beauty?

MRS. KARAMAZOV: Yes.

CONSTANCE: I want you to play for me. Play.

ALYOSHA: I *want* to play. I can play hopscotch. *(Does some.)* Or play tag with myself. *(Runs around, tags himself.)* I'm it! Or hide and seek. Come out, come out, wherever I am. And baseball. Djuna can be first base, and my father second, and Smerdyakov can be third base…

CONSTANCE: PIP! *(Points to Mrs. Karamazov.)* Is she beautiful, graceful, well grown? Do you admire her?

ALYOSHA: *(Calling to Mrs. Karamazov.)* Mother?

MRS. KARAMAZOV: Edmund…

CONSTANCE: No…

MRS. KARAMAZOV: Alyosha…

CONSTANCE: No, no.

MRS. KARAMAZOV: Pip.

(Constance smiles, coaches her.)

MRS. KARAMAZOV: I think you're a common laboring boy. Oh, I didn't take enough. *(Rummages through her bag.)*

CONSTANCE: Now, play. Play for Estella and me.

(With great noise. The Russian Revolution comes back in. Grushenka I and II push before them Anais, Ivan; Anais grabs Alyosha to her.)

GRUSHENKA: WHERE IS THE ROYAL FAMILY? OPPRESSION MUST END.

CONSTANCE: This is not the time for this.

GRUSHENKA: *(To Anais, Ivan, Alyosha.)* Prepare to bid this world good-bye.

ANAIS: Children, stay close together.

CONSTANCE: I'm not ready for this now. Ernest!

GRUSHENKA: Which of you is Nicholas?

ANAIS: I am Nicholas.

GRUSHENKA: Which of you is Alexandra?

ANAIS: I am Alexandra. I both of them. I practice parthenogenesis. I give birth to a homophiliac son, I that kind of mother. *(Gives birth.)* What is it, Ivan?

IVAN: *(Taking a book from under her skirts.)* Volume 99 of your diary.

ANAIS: Good. That save me writer's cramp.

GRUSHENKA: You're Nicholas? *(Slaps Anais.)* You're Alexandra? *(Slaps Anais.)*

CONSTANCE: Kill her and get it over with. Ernest!

GRUSHENKA: *(To Alyosha.)* And you must be the homophiliac son. *(Pinches his cheek.)* How are you, sonny? Want a bruise?

ANAIS: Don't do that, you kill him.

ALYOSHA: Go ahead, kill me.

ANAIS: *(To herself.)* Oh, Nicholas, look how depressed he get. I see that, Alexandra, and I blame it on you. Nicholas! How dare...

GRUSHENKA: Kill them! *(Aims gun.)*

CONSTANCE: No, don't kill Alyosha...

GRUSHENKA: Everybody get killed!

CONSTANCE: NO.

GRUSHENKA: YES. KIIIIIIIIIILLLLL.

(Grushenka I and II fire their guns. Anais, Ivan, Alyosha fall to the ground.)

CONSTANCE: NOT ALYOSHA.

(Constance shoots Grushenka with a blow gun. She dies. Then Constance does the same to Grushenka II.)

CONSTANCE: Pip, where are you? *(Constance finds Alyosha from under all the bodies.)* Play, Pip. I want you to.

(Alyosha prepares to play. Constance, Mrs. Karamazov, and Ernest prepare to be his back-up group.)

ALYOSHA: I want to sing this song for my brother Smerdyakov, who I've eaten; for my brother Dmitri, who was wilted; for my father, murdered; for my mother, a hophead; and for all the other dead people I have known. (Sings.) (Constance, Mrs. Karamazov, Ernest sing background.)

ALYOSHA: Everything's permitted,
Everything's allowed,
And God we have outwitted,
We're moving with the crowd,
We see the soul as zero,
See the soul has fled,
And no one is our hero,
And piety is dead.
Everything's permitted,
All is à la carte,
And nothing has been fitted,
All things fall apart,
Inquisitors are grand,
Christ gets nailed up twice,
A plague is on the land,
The world is far from nice.

CONSTANCE, MRS. KARAMAZOV, ERNEST: We're wearing these boots,
Galoshes through and through,
Like flies to wanton boys,
We'll walk all over you-oo-oo-oo.

ALYOSHA: Everything's permitted,
Full steam race ahead,
Last night I baby-sitted,
The children now are dead,
The seams are splittin' open,
We've headaches all, of course,
We'll try to keep on copin',
Though existentially we're aware that we've foolishly
Placed the philosophic cart,
    Before the nihilistic—horse!
My kingdom for a horse,
My sister's shooting horse,
My voice is getting hoarse.
Ooooo-oooo-ooooooo-ooooooooo.

(Constance finishes this 50s rock song with great satisfaction and opens up her book to translate.)

CONSTANCE: *The Brothers Karamazov.* Page 1803. Ernest ties Alyosha to a chair. *(Ernest does tie Alyosha to a chair.)*

CONSTANCE: Estella, to plant the seeds of her fatal enchantment, grants Alyosha a kiss.

MRS. KARAMAZOV: *(Realizing she's expected to do something.)* Oh, yes, Miss Havis... He's a common laboring boy. Oh I haven't taken enough. *(Takes out her needle, shoots up.)* Oh, Edmund. How heavy the fog is. *(Goes toward him, dies.)*

CONSTANCE: You may say, Don't die, mother.

ALYOSHA: Don't die, mother.

CONSTANCE: Too late! Her heart is broken of an overdose.

ALYOSHA: Let me go back to the monastery.

CONSTANCE: This is your monastery now. Ernest, nail the windows shut. *(Ernest, out of Constance's eyeshot, is aiming a rifle into his mouth.)*

CONSTANCE: Get the gun out of your mouth, Ernest. First things first. *(Ernest exits. Sound of hammering.)*

CONSTANCE: Now, let me just get comfortable. *(Takes out large book, begins to translate.)*

(Alyosha is tied in a chair near her, and watches her throughout.)

CONSTANCE: *The Brothers Karamazov.* Chapter 314. Alyosha Karamazov was the third son of Fyodor Karamazov, a landowner well known in our district... *(Shot offstage.)*

CONSTANCE: Oh, Ernest...well known in our district in his own day, and still remembered among us due to... *(Squints.)* due to...I can't read this. *(Trying again.)* Alyosha Karamazov was the third son of...No. NO. *(Constance rips up the book in a temper, throws all her books off her wheelchair.)* We must begin anew. THE BROTHERS KARAMAZOV. BY FYODOR DOSTO-EVESKY. TRANSLATED FROM THE RUSSIAN BY CONSTANCE GARNETT, BART. PART ONE. CHAPTER ONE. In the beginning was the Word. And there were fishes, and there were winged fowl, and there were Karamazovs. It was the best of times, it was the worst of times. And He looked at the worst times, and He said they were good. Call me Ishmael. I am a sick woman. I am a spiteful woman. I am an unattractive woman. I believe my liver is diseased. Once upon a time and a very good time it was, there was a moocow coming down along the road and this moocow that was coming down the road met a nicens little boy named baby tuckoo Karamazov. There is but one truly serious philosophical question, and that is Baby Tuckoo Karamazov was brought up by hand by his elder sister, Mrs. Joe Gargery. "God bless us every one," said Baby Tuckoo. It *was* a turkey! He could never have stood upon his legs, that bird! They often went shooting quail in the country, oh what a rouge and pheasant slave am I. We shall now listen to the "Dichterliebe" sung by Dietrich Fischer-Dieskau. Papa, potatoes, poultry, prunes and prism are all very good words for the lips; especially prunes, and prism. The following words will be helpful in carrying the thought smoothly from one idea to the next in an argumentative paragraph: moreover, first, second, third, finally, furthermore, in addition, then too, equally important, on the contrary, at the same time, hence, therefore, accordingly, thus, in fact. Thus in fact, I took the babe from my breast and dashed it. All happy families are alike but an unhappy family is unhappy after its own fashion. "Please, sir, I want some more," said Baby Tuckoo. Moreover, they were all at Charing Cross to see Lilia off—Philip, Harriet, Irma, Mrs. Heriton herself. Even Mrs. Theobald, squired by Mr. Kingcroft, had braved the journey from Yorkshire. *The Brothers Karamazov,* page 2, translated from the Russian by the eminent ejaculatrix of the savage tongue. Keep that in mind, Ernest. Oh, he's dead. The orphanage was not kind to Alyosha. Stately, plump Buck Mulligan came from the stairhead, bearing a bowl of lather. In the little world in which children have their existence, there is nothing so finely perceived and so finely felt as injustice. This royal throne of kings, this sceptred isle, this blessed plot, this earth, this realm, this Karamazov. I shall now conjugate the verb Karamazov. Karamazov. Karamazas. Karamazat. Karamazamus. Karamazatis. Karamazant. Past Perfect. Karamazibus. Karamazibutis. Karamazatishibilititis. Karamazalitis serunt…

(Lights dim on Constance and Alyosha.)

END OF PLAY

The Vietnamization
Of New Jersey

INTRODUCTION

After my four months of employment as an actor at Yale Repertory Theatre in *Karamazov* and *The Possessed,* I was faced with what to do next. My co-author, Albert Innaurato, braved moving to New York. I felt I "should" move to New York—historically that's where playwrights seemed to have their careers—but I also was a bit phobic about the city.

Though as a child in New Jersey I often accompanied my parents to Broadway musicals, I usually got a headache from the city itself, which was just too intense and loud for me. And I couldn't figure out what the "first" step would be in New York, or how I'd pay my bills. And I already had a comfortable apartment in New Haven, so I decided to stay on there for a period. And I had two close friends there, Stephen Davis, a Yale undergraduate with whom I had been a singing waiter on Cape Cod, and my fellow Yale playwright, Wendy Wasserstein. (Wendy was two years behind me, and so was still enrolled in the M.F.A. program.)

So I stayed put. But I needed money, so I found three part-time jobs. An acting teaching job opened up last minute at nearby Southern Connecticut Teachers College, and I was recommended and accepted as the part-time replacement. An actress sweetly loaned me her car to commute there; my first day I discovered it was a stick shift, which I didn't drive, but I had to get there. So I learned on the way, sweat pouring out of me every time I approached a stop sign and had to deal with the damn clutch.

I initially felt a terrible fake "teaching" acting. Although I had just worked professionally as an actor, I had never actually taken an acting class. So I wasn't really the most first-rate choice. However, the class was meant for would-be teachers who were taking it for fun, not for future professional actors, so I did actually know more than they did; and a friend helpfully got me to read Viola Spolin's book of theatre games, and that helped me to know what exercises and games to do. And eventually I wrote small acting scenes that the actors worked on. So that job actually worked out fine.

Then I was asked through a friend of Wendy's to help a psychiatrist in the Yale Medical School index his book on schizophrenia. I could do this at home, on an hourly basis, so that was a good thing; and my apartment became littered with file cards saying "reality testing" or "psychosis" or "dementia praecox" (such a pretty name, as Violet Venable says).

But it still wasn't enough money. So Wendy and I went to the Katy Cook Employment Agency in New Haven. The woman running it took an immediate liking to me and Wendy, and tried to place us that very weekend as a butler and maid. Wendy is not incredibly organized and would not be a good maid; I'd be a slightly better butler, but only slightly. So, regretfully, we told Ms. Cook no.

I asked couldn't I get some typing jobs. And she said yes, there was a part-time one at the Yale Medical School for a few months. The task was to go through the files of all the people who had promised to donate their bodies to science upon death, and to write them saying that Yale now had a glut of bodies, and would they make alternative arrangements. So I typed out the endless envelopes and sent this missive out. Perhaps you got a letter from me?

So during this period, I could barely write at all…working, as all of you know, uses up energy, and I'd feel too beat at night to write. I was doing work sporadically on the second or third draft of this play, *A History of the American Film;* Brustein expressed some interest in it for the Rep, but he felt I needed to rewrite it a lot. And for fun and distraction, I co-wrote with Wendy and performed in a show at the Yale Cabaret, *When Dinah Shore Ruled the Earth.*

I rewrote *Film,* improving it, but Brustein didn't choose to do it. But instead he awarded me a CBS Playwriting grant (which CBS-TV funded for a few years); as part of the grant, I was asked to teach once a week at the Drama School (feeling uncomfortably close in age to my "students"; but it went okay), and I was also asked to write a new play for possible production at Yale Rep.

I received the grant in early summer 1975, I think; and I used the grant money to brave moving to New York City. Wendy, as a native New Yorker, helped me shop for an apartment. After being scared off an inexpensive hovel on the supposedly safer East Side that seemed to have a dead pig down the air shaft (it turned out to be a toy pig, Wendy and I realized after our initial shared gasps), I found a sublet through the *Village Voice,* sharing with two divorced men what turned out to be the apartment of Mrs. Burl Ives.

My bedroom was very pretty, with bookshelves filled with Burl Ives records about Christmas and reindeer; and it had a big wooden table, on which I wrote *The Vietnamization of New Jersey,* my commission play for Yale Rep.

This play started as a parody sketch of David Rabe's *Sticks and Bones,* which had won many critical accolades and was about American guilt over Vietnam. I actually think Rabe is very, very talented; but I guess as a young whipper snapper playwright, I found the tone of *Sticks and Bones* to be rather portentious and message-laden; and Rabe's calling his main characters Ozzie and Harriet with their sons David and Ricky (based on the famous 50s sitcom, *Ozzie and Harriet*) seemed kind of heavy-handed.

So the first two and a half scenes of this play were initially a self-contained sketch. Brustein loved the sketch, and was supportive of my turning it into a play.

I wrote all of Act I easily and in a good, giddy mood. Although the "message" parts of the play were take-offs on Rabe, my family—insanely called Ozzie Ann, Harry, Et—quickly became their own entities, and my recurring themes of strong-willed women, overwhelmed men, and the struggles between them came to the fore.

Act I ends rather sweepingly, and it was hard to know what to do with Act II. I initially wrote a version where the family, bereft of all possessions, hitchhikes through the Lincoln Tunnel, and ends up living homeless at Port Authority Bus Terminal, eventually getting into pornographic films. The play ended darkly with a nightmarish academy awards for porno films (written before I knew porno films indeed have award ceremonies; or maybe they didn't back then).

Brustein loved Act I, but thought that Act II, though interesting, felt wrong. He said having the characters leave their house seemed to take us somewhere incorrect. So I threw out my original Act II in its entirety, and rewrote the family so they now lived in a tent where their house used to be. And I added the pivotal character of Larry, who was inspired by the horrific drill sergeant in Rabe's excellent *The Basic Training of Pavel Hummel.*

I think this rewritten act is indeed much better; and Brustein scheduled the play for January, 1977.

It was a very smooth, enjoyable rehearsal process. Walt Jones was the good, friendly director; and the cast was wonderful, and found the play really fun to work on. Of particular note was my friend Kate McGregor-Stewart, an actress graduate from my class, who had just the best, funniest instincts for my plays; and the actor Ben Halley, Jr., who was truly hilarious (and even had some moral stature) as the smart, sassy, angry maid Hazel.

The reviews were the opposite of those for *Karamazov:* The local ones were all good, the one bad one came from Mel Gussow in the *New York Times,* who, though he liked *Karamazov* and liked my one act *Titanic* in New York and was soon to like *A History of the American Film,* just didn't like this one. He saw it the same day he saw Michael Cristofer's serious play about death, *The Shadow Box,* in its excellent original production at Long Wharf Theatre. I think it would be very hard to enter the world of *Shadow Box* in the afternoon, and then enter the world of my play in the evening . So that's one of my theories why he didn't like this one. But it's just a theory.

I find the play funny. I hope you do.

ORIGINAL PRODUCTION

The Vietnamization Of New Jersey was first presented by the Yale Repertory Theatre, in New Haven, Connecticut, on January 28, 1977. It was directed by Walt Jones; the scenic designer was Christopher Clarens; costumes were by Kathleen Armstrong; and the lighting was by James Gage. The cast, in order of appearance, was as follows:

OZZIE ANN	Kate McGregor-Stewart
HARRY	Charles Levin
ET	Stephen Rowe
HAZEL	Ben Halley, Jr.
DAVID	Richard Bey
LIAT	Anne Louise Hoffmann
LARRY	Charles Levin
FATHER MCGILLICUTTY	Jeremy Geidt

CHARACTERS

OZZIE ANN, the mother

HARRY, the father

ET, the son

HAZEL, the black maid

DAVID, the older son

LIAT, his Vietnamese wife

LARRY, Harry's brother (played by same actor as Harry)

FR. MCGILLICUTTY, a priest

Note: The part of Hazel may be played by a black actor, as was successfully done in the Yale Repertory Theatre production; however, if this is done, it is important that the role not turn into a camp turn for a man in drag: The part must be acted for the humor in Hazel's character, and we should, after a while, be able to forget that the part is being played by a man.

THE SETTING

The setting is the interior of a middle-class home in Piscataway, New Jersey. It should mostly be the living room (couch, television, etc.); either Stage Left or Right of the set should turn into a dining area, perhaps near a pass-thru window from the kitchen. The furnishings and whatnot should be in fairly bad taste; the Yale Repertory set included a large red outdoor barbecue in the living room, and several extra, presumably broken, television sets.

The flats representing the walls must be able to be taken apart "at the seams" and removed from the stage at the end of Act I by the repossession men.

Later in Act II the repossession men bring back the walls and put them together again.

When the walls are gone, the audience should see a backdrop of a suburban neighborhood (another house across the street, a driveway, the sky); and in front of the backdrop of Act II is a camping tent, a television, a telephone and a refrigerator.

On one of the walls there must be a large calendar with nothing but the year printed in large letters on it. Throughout the play, a character will rip off the pages of the calendar, indicating passage of a year (or several years). At the top of the play the calendar should read 1967. At the end of Scene 4 Ozzie Ann should change the calendar to 1971. At the top of Scene 5 Ozzie Ann should change the calendar to 1974. At the end of Act I Hazel changes it to 1976. The calendar remains 1976 throughout Act II until Hazel changes it to read July 4.

The Vietnamization of New Jersey

(A American Tragedy)*

ACT I

Scene 1

An American Home. Piscataway, New Jersey. Breakfast. At table: Ozzie Ann, the mother, Harry, the father, and Et, the juvenile delinquent-like son. Calendar reads 1967.

HARRY: Good morning, Ozzie Ann.

OZZIE: Good morning, Harry.

HARRY: Good morning, Et.

OZZIE: Good morning, Et.

ET: Gmorningmomndad. *(Takes a box of cereal, pours it down the front of his pants. Begins to eat the flakes from inside his trousers.)*

OZZIE: Et, don't do that. Harry, speak to your son.

HARRY: Now, Ozzie Ann, Et is a growing boy.

OZZIE: Harry, there are ways of growing, and there are ways of growing.

(Enter Hazel. She rings the bell triumphantly.)

HAZEL: That's one for mother!

OZZIE: Thank you, Hazel. You may clear the breakfast refuse.

HAZEL: You folks sure make a mess. *(Reaches into Et's pants, begins taking flakes out, putting them back in the box.)* All this cereal, lawdy lawdy, the washing machine's clogged up with it.

OZZIE: Hazel, just clear the dishes please. Leave Et alone.

HAZEL: Don't you talk that way to me. *(Throws a cup on the floor, exits in a huff.)*

HARRY: You got her angry.

(Et eats cereal from pants.)

OZZIE: Hazel's bite is worse than her bark. Et dear, there are few things mother likes you to do less than that. Don't do that, dear.

---

* *The grammatically incorrect article "A" is used purposely, like a little child reciting, and curtseying.*

ET: *(Mouth full.)* Do what?

OZZIE: Harry, you speak to him.

HARRY: He doesn't like me.

OZZIE: Very well. Forget it. *(Crossly throws cup on the floor.)*

ET: *(Mouth full.)* When's Davey coming home?

OZZIE: What?

ET: *(Mouth full.)* When's Davey coming home?

OZZIE: Can you understand him?

HARRY: I'm not a linguist.

OZZIE: Did anyone say you were a linguist?

HARRY: You implied it.

OZZIE: I didn't, I didn't. God knows you're not a linguist. You're a turnip!

HARRY: God damn you! *(Throws cup on floor. Hands her spoon.)* Go ahead, castrate me, go ahead.

OZZIE: I can't castrate you with a spoon, stupid. *(Throws spoon on floor.)*
(Enter Hazel.)

HAZEL: Now you pick that up.

OZZIE: I won't, I won't.

HAZEL: You pick that up.

OZZIE: You work for *me.*

HAZEL: People like you are the trouble with America. You pollute the air, the land, the waters, the public park. Every ice cream wrapper that blows along a highway was left there by you. The fish in the water are dying because of you. The cities are dying. Now, pick up that spoon!

OZZIE: I won't, I won't.

HARRY: Oh, Ozzie Ann, pick it up, it's not worth it. *(Picks up spoon himself, to Hazel.)* Here.

HAZEL: I don't want it now. I spit on your spoon. *(Fake spits on spoon, exits.)*

OZZIE: Give me that. *(Takes spoon, hurls it after Hazel.)* Go stick your head in the toilet!

HARRY: That's childish.
(Re-enter Hazel in a fury. She pulls tablecloth and everything on it off table, exits.)

OZZIE: Oh, it's a mess, it's a mess. I'm the worst housekeeper on the Eastern Seaboard. We'll have to pack our bags and move to Anaheim.

HARRY: Pull yourself together, you're talking nonsense.

OZZIE: You're right, I am talking nonsense. Oh my God, I'm talking nonsense.

ET: *(Pretending his mouth is full.)* When's Davey coming home?

OZZIE: Why are you talking that way? You don't have anything in your mouth.

HARRY: He's trying to irritate us.

OZZIE: Why is he trying to irritate us?

HARRY: He's growing up.

OZZIE: There are ways of growing, and ways of growing.

(Enter Hazel, rings bell.)

HAZEL: That's two for mother! *(To Ozzie.)* Bitch. *(Exits.)*

OZZIE: Go back to Africa!

ET: *(Mumbled.)* When's Davey coming home?

OZZIE: I CAN'T UNDERSTAND YOU!

HARRY: He's saying, *(Imitates mumbles.)* WnDvyscmghm?

OZZIE: I *know* that, but it's illegible.

HARRY: You don't mean illegible.

OZZIE: I do mean illegible.

HARRY: You don't.

OZZIE: I do! You can't read it, can you????

(Enter Hazel, rings bell.)

HAZEL: That's three for mother! *(Exits.)*

HARRY: *(Hands Et pad and pencil.)* Write down what you've been saying.

(Et writes it down. Harry hands pad to Ozzie.)

HARRY: Here.

OZZIE: *(Looks at it.)* I can't read it.

HARRY: That's because it's ILLEGIBLE!

(Enter Hazel, rings bell.)

HAZEL: That's one for Daddy!

OZZIE: Get out of here, I hate you, get out.

HARRY: Illegible. You have about as much education as a brass tit in a witch's bra.

OZZIE: Don't say that word. It makes me nauseous.

HARRY: What? Education?

ET: *(Mumbling.)* When's Davey coming home?

HARRY: This'll never work.

OZZIE: Ettie, what does it sound like? *(She pulls her ear.)* Eh?

(Et holds up ten fingers—indicating by charades that it sounds like the word "ten.")

OZZIE: Fingers? It sounds like fingers?

(Et shakes his hand. Holds out "ten.")

HARRY: No. It sounds like hands.

OZZIE: Hands. Hans Brinker?

HARRY: Hans Conreid?

OZZIE: Hansel and Gretel?

(Et shakes head no. Now starts to count with his fingers, trying to get them to do "one, two...etc.")

OZZIE: Finger. Oh, one! One. *(Counts.)* one, two, three, four, five, six, seven, eight, nine, thumb. Sounds like thumb.

(Et has a fit and screams, won't stop.)

HARRY: Behave yourself, young man.

OZZIE: What rhymes with thumb?

ET: *(Screams.)* WHEN'S DAVEY COMING HOME????

OZZIE: That's much too loud to comprehend. That is much too loud for the human eardrum, which is what I'm equipped with, for me to comprehend your statement.

HARRY: We have to settle this. I have to get to work.

OZZIE: All right. Hazel! Come in here.

(Enter Hazel.)

HAZEL: What?

OZZIE: Tell us what Et is saying.

HAZEL: No.

HARRY: You know, don't you?

HAZEL: Yes, I know, but I'm not saying.

OZZIE: YES!

HAZEL: No.

HARRY: Ozzie Ann, wait. *(Whispers to Ozzie.)*

(They both begin to spitefully sing.)

HARRY AND OZZIE: *(Singing.)*

Double your pleasure, double your fun,

With doublemint, doublemint, doublemint gum.

Double your...

(Etc. They keep singing until Hazel is driven crazy enough to stop them.)

HAZEL: All right! Stop it. He said, "When is Davey coming home?"

OZZIE: Oh, is that all. Well, I heard that.

HARRY: He says that all the time. I was hoping for something more.

OZZIE: Hoping, hoping. If only we knew.

HARRY: Thank you, Hazel.

OZZIE: Thank you, Hazel.

HAZEL: I'll be in the sink if you want me. *(Exits.)*

HARRY: You miss your brother Davey, Et?

OZZIE: I bet he does.

ET: When is he coming home?

OZZIE: I don't know, Et. *(Stands.)* I guess, when the other American boys do.

ET: When will that be?

HARRY: When the war is over.

ET: What war?

OZZIE: The war that's described in Davey's letters. Hazel, bring in Davey's letters.
(Hazel brings in a box of letters, large box.)

HAZEL: Davey's the only decent person in this family. The rest of you are just so much cottage cheese.

OZZIE: Thank you, Hazel. You may go.
(Hazel stays. Takes up handfuls of letters, hands them to Et one by one.)

OZZIE: Sept. 2nd.
(Et puts the letter down his pants.)

OZZIE: Sept. 3. Sept. 4. *(Keeps handing them to Et.)* Sept. 5. Sept. 6. Sept. 7. Sept. 8. Sept. 9. Oh, Harry, this is my favorite one. *(Reads.)* Cher Maman, aujourd'hui ma mère est morte. Ou peut-être hier. Je ne sais pas: J'ai lu tous les livres dans la bibliothèque Vietnamienne. Ils sont très biens. Dans la guerre, j'ai peur, j'ai peur, mais j'ai reconnu George Washington et tous les autres heroes Americans. Avec l'amour pour vous—he's like you, Harry, too polite to call me "toi"—vous, Dada, et mon frère Et. Votre fils, David. *(Puts letter down Et's pants.)* Oh, Davey, Davey. *(Ozzie and Harry embrace.)*

HAZEL: *(Taking the letters out of Et's pants.)* I'm afraid Davey won't be home until the American people realize that only they have the power to stop this atrocity.
(Enter David and a Vietnamese girl. Both wear dark glasses, both are blind.)

DAVID: Mother, father.

OZZIE: *(Looks up.)* Davey?

HARRY: Davey?

DAVID: Mother, father, I'm home. Home from the war.

OZZIE: Davey! Come to me!

DAVID: Where are you?

OZZIE: I'm here.

DAVID: Would you mind stamping your foot a little?

OZZIE: Oh. Harry.

HARRY: Ozzie, darling.

OZZIE: *(Stamps her foot, starts to weep.)* I can't do it, I can't.

HAZEL: Oh, I'll do it! *(Stamps her foot.)*

DAVID: Ah, now I hear it. *(Moves, tiny steps, towards Hazel.)* I'm afraid I'm blind. One of the gooks—*(To Vietnamese girl.)* I'm sorry, darling—one of the Vietnamese people blinded me.

OZZIE: Oh, Harry.

(David reaches Hazel.)

DAVID: *(Kisses Hazel.)* Mother!

HAZEL: No, Hazel.

DAVID: Who's Hazel?

OZZIE: Hazel is the new maid, Davey dear, since Grandmother died.

DAVID: Grandma died?

OZZIE: Well actually we had to have her put to sleep. We didn't want to write you about it over there.

DAVID: Oh, mother, no, not Grams. *(Grabs Harry.)*

HARRY: This is Daddy.

DAVID: Father.

OZZIE: Here I am, dear. David, you haven't introduced us to your Korean friend.

DAVID: Mother, this is Liat. *(Pointing to Harry.)* Liat, this is mother.

OZZIE: Oh, isn't she lovely? Is she an exchange student, David?

DAVID: Mother, Liat is not Korean, and she is not an exchange student. She is my wife.

OZZIE: What?

(Very long pause.)

HAZEL: *(Suddenly.)* Oh, oh, oh, six o'clock and the master not home yet. Pray God nothing serious…

OZZIE: Hazel, shush. Go to the kitchen at once. You were polishing the silver, I believe.

HAZEL: Yes, mother. *(Exits.)*

DAVID: Can you say hello, Liat?

LIAT: Allo Amerrrican mozer and fazer of Davey. I am so preezed to be heah. How I wish that I had eyes to see your smiling, happy facesss.

DAVID: You see, mother, Liat is blind as I am.

OZZIE: Oh my God! David, are you blind? *(Rips off his sunglasses.)* David, look at me!

DAVID: I can't. It's all blackness.

OZZIE: LOOK AT ME. Oh, Harry, make him see me.

HARRY: *(Hits David's head.)* That do anything, son?

DAVID: No, Dad. I am afraid it's just an unpleasant reality of life.

ET: *(Takes off Liat's glasses.)* What about her? She see?

DAVID: Only with the eyes of her soul.

LIAT: Allô. I go to American Aramy School. My teachuhs best fucking stick men in the whole Vietnamese bush.

DAVID: Liat, I've told you to stop saying that.

LIAT: Ok, Joe.

DAVID: And don't call me Joe.

LIAT: Sorry Charlie.

OZZIE: I can't stand this. I can't. Wait. I mustn't fall apart. David, you're blind and you've married this blind...Vietnamese person...

LIAT: Herro, Rady, what's new?

OZZIE: ...but the important thing is your home, and we're all here, and we're never going to leave here ever again. Harry, help Davey to his room.

DAVID: Please, no. I want Liat and me to have the enjoyment of finding it ourselves. *(They exit.)*

OZZIE: It's so nice...can they still hear us?

HARRY: They're still near...

OZZIE: How are you doing, Davey?

DAVID: *(Offstage.)* All right, Mom.

OZZIE: Harry, she's a chink. She's got teensy slanted eyes.

HARRY: She's a whore.

OZZIE: She's the enemy.

HARRY: He's brought the enemy into the house.

OZZIE: She's a gook.

HARRY: A goon.

ET: She walks funny.

OZZIE: Oh, Harry, what shall we do?

HARRY: Shall we call Hazel?

OZZIE: Let's try to work this out ourselves. I'm going to be calm. Harry, you know the way that we don't welcome Liat into our home shows that we are hypocrites, and by extension, so are the American people, because, of course, she is one of the people that we are supposedly fighting for. After all, we can't pretend we thought they were all Irish.

HARRY: I can pretend they're Irish.

OZZIE: Well, that's because you're an intelligent man. Perhaps she is Irish.

ET: You know, Mom, on the same subject: *(Holds up Liat's glasses, puts them on.)* the fact that they're blind literally in a way points to the fact that we and the American people are blind figuratively. We suffer, I think, a moral and

philosophic blindness. It raises the question of which is the greater handi-
cap—physical or moral blindness.

(Ozzie puts on David's glasses.)

HARRY: I feel left out. *(Closes his eyes.)*

ET: Which blindness do you think is greater, Dad?

HARRY: I don't know, son.

OZZIE: They're both very bad. If there's a God, moral blindness is worse.

HARRY: But if there isn't, physical is worse.

ET: Ah, but here's something you haven't thought of: What if there is both a
God, and there isn't a God?

OZZIE: Well, in that case, it would be better to be neither blind physically nor
morally!

(Enter Hazel, rings bell.)

HAZEL: That's four for mother!

OZZIE: I've got four, I've got four! *(Suddenly.)* But mother of God, why do I feel
such guilt? *(She looks terrified.)*

(After a moment Hazel embraces her.)

(Blackout.)

ACT I

Scene 2

*The family together. Ozzie and Harry watch David and Liat. David is kneel-
ing in front of Liat. Liat is eating cereal out of Et's pants. David is singing a
romantic song to Liat, such as "Drink to Me Only With Thine Eyes," "I Dream
of Jeannie with the Light Brown Hair," or "Younger Than Springtime."*

LIAT: I like American cereal, Joe. I wish that I could see it. Maybe if I put it in
my eyes, I see it. *(Puts cereal in her eyes, screams.)* Aaaah. It hurts. Aaaah.
(Keeps putting cereal in her eyes.) Aaaaah.

OZZIE: Isn't she cute? Thank you, David. We love her.

DAVID: I love her too. And I hope that she can forgive me for what my country
has done to her country.

LIAT: Aaaaah.

OZZIE: Don't do that, dear. Who knows where the cereal's been before you
touched it.

LIAT: *(Keeping it up.)* Aaaaah.

OZZIE: Dear, don't do that. That causes cancer.

HARRY: Let's give them their presents.

OZZIE: Yes. Hazel!

(Enter Hazel with two gifts.)

HAZEL: Here they are.

OZZIE: (Handing them out.) A present for David, and a present for Maureen O'Hara.

(David and Liat open their gifts. They are trick glasses: the kind with eyes painted on them, that move when the head moves. Ozzie, wearing dark glasses.)

OZZIE: Now we all have glasses.

(Et is wearing dark glasses. Hazel and Harry are not. Harry closes his eyes again, keeps them closed.)

DAVID: Thank you, Mom and Dad. Now I want Liat to tell you about her homeland. I want you to listen carefully because only Liat can forgive us for what our country has done.

OZZIE: We're listening, David.

(Ozzie and Harry stop up their ears. Hazel exits. Et kisses Liat's neck.)

DAVID: Liat, darling, begin.

LIAT: Ok, Joe. You got some Good and Plenty? (Reaches into Et's pants takes out candy bar.) I was just a rittle girl when the American aramy come to my country. They destroy everything, they pillage the village. They cause much havoc and disappointment. I become a go-go dancer at lowlife nightclub. That where I meet Davey.

DAVID: No we didn't, darling.

LIAT: Well, I meet somebody there. Regular S.O.B.

OZZIE: Isn't this pleasant? I love it. Davey, don't you want to call up your old high school sweetheart, Sally? I know she'd like to hear from you, wouldn't she, Harry?

HARRY: Yes she would.

OZZIE: Talk to your father, Davey. He's making an effort, it isn't easy for him.

DAVID: Dad, I like Sally, but I feel responsible for Liat.

LIAT: His name was Billy. We celebrate Chinese New Year together, and he breaks my fingers.

OZZIE: That's lovely, Liat. Thank you. (Quieter.) Davey, your father is calling up Sally Farmington this minute or else we'll have Peggy O'Shaughnessy over there killed by your father's Mafia connections.

DAVID: That does it. You threaten my wife's life in the living room, and I'm leaving.

OZZIE: Davey, it was a joke, we love her. Say something, Et.

DAVID: No. Hazel, pack our things.

HAZEL: They's all packed, Master Davey.

OZZIE: Davey, we love you and we'll learn to love...Princess Pocahontas.

DAVID: That does it. Come on, Liat.

LIAT: Ok, Joe.

DAVID: Good-bye, mother and father. I had a happy childhood here, but right now I'm ashamed to be American.

OZZIE: Davey, we're not typical. Please! Liat, speak to him.

LIAT: Chuck you, Farley.

DAVID: Good-bye, Hazel. You're the only decent member of this household.
   (Takes bags, leaves with Liat.)

OZZIE: Davey, don't leave. Davey!

HARRY: Son!

OZZIE: I thought you'd never say something. Davey! Please come back. Davey!
   (Getting mad.) I hope you walk into walls. I hope you and Anna May Wong fall into a septic tank. I hope you get run over by a truck. Quick, think of more.

ET: I hope you rupture your appendix.

OZZIE: I hope you rupture your appendix.

HARRY: I hope your teeth rot.

OZZIE: I hope your teeth rot. I hope you get leprosy.

ET: I hope you get clap in your eyes.

OZZIE: Et! *(Slaps him.)*
   (Et slaps her back.)

OZZIE: Go straight to your room.

ET: I won't.

OZZIE: Harry, talk to him.

HARRY: He doesn't like me.

OZZIE: Hazel, spank him. Wash his mouth out with something.

HAZEL: It's too late for that sort of thing now, Missy. It's too late for that, and it's too late for just about everything else too.

OZZIE: Hazel, you sound so ominous, I can't stand it.

HARRY: *(Who's been looking out the window.)* Davey and Liat have fallen into the septic tank.

OZZIE: We got one of the wishes!

HAZEL: Well, Mr. B., I guess I better pull them outta there.

OZZIE: I'll help. I'm the mother. Davey, I'm coming.
   (Hazel and Ozzie exit.)

ET: You know, Dad, the way that Davey and Liat are stuck in the mire of our septic tank is a bit like the way the American people are stuck in the mire of the political and military lies of America's Vietnam policies.

HARRY: *(Uncomfortable.)* Oh yes?

ET: And just as the only way to correct Davey and Liat's predicament is to pull them out, so the only answer to the Vietnamese problem is to pull our troops out.

HARRY: How are you doing in high school, Et?

ET: The teachers don't like me. I beat up Miss Willis last week in Home Room.

HARRY: We're having a nice talk, Et. *(Pause; terribly uncomfortable.)* Ozzie Ann, hurry up, I need you. *(Pause. Harry smiles weakly at Et.)*

ET: Is there anything I can advise you on, Dad?

HARRY: *(Laughs.)* No thanks, son. *(Calls desperately.)* Ozzie Ann!

ET: Anything you wanna know about sex, Dad?

HARRY: No thanks, son. The boys at the office fill me in. Ozzie Ann! Ozzie Ann!

ET: Wanna see some pictures? *(Shows him dirty pictures.)*

HARRY: Oh, they're very nice. Ozzie Ann! Ozzie Ann!

(Blackout.)

ACT I

Scene 3

Liat and Davey are in terry cloth robes while Hazel and Ozzie Ann wash their clothes. Harry is wearing his overcoat and holding his briefcase. Et has put on his leather jacket. Hazel and Ozzie Ann have two basins in front of them.

HAZEL: And now Mrs. B. will soak Davey's sewage-soaked shirt in her detergent, while I'll soak Liat's sewage-soaked dress in my detergent. We'll let them soak for a count of ten. One-two-three...

HARRY: I really can't wait. I'm late for the office already...

HAZEL: Just a minute, Mr. B. Four-five-six-seven-eight-nine-ten. And now let's smell the garments.

OZZIE: *(Smells hers.)* I still smell sewage on mine.

HAZEL: *(Offering Ozzie Liat's dress to smell.)* And on the all-temperature Cheer one?

OZZIE: It's completely free of sewage odor.

HAZEL: My detergent wins. I win, I win!

OZZIE: Stop that. We don't need this today.

HAZEL: I win, I win. Your clothes smell of sewage.

OZZIE: Shut up. You have a strident voice and an insufferable manner. Shut up shut up shut up shut up shut up…

DAVID: *(Standing.)* Liat and I must go now.

OZZIE: Davey, you're not dressed. Harry, stop them.

HARRY: I already have my coat on.

DAVID: Good-bye, mother. *(Puts out his hand.)*

OZZIE: NOOOOOOOOOOOO! *(Cries.)* Davey, please, I know I've been harsh with Maureen O'Hara…

DAVID: Mother, that's not her name.

OZZIE: All right, all right. LIAT! LIAT! LIAT! There, are you satisfied?

DAVID: You haven't been kind to Liat.

OZZIE: Davey, people change. If you don't give people a second chance, how can they ever improve?

DAVID: That's true. All right, I'll give you a second chance.

OZZIE: Oh, Harry, a second chance, thank goodness.

DAVID: But it's not going to be easy, Mom. You're going to have to make it up to Liat for what America has done to her country. All of you—Dad, Et, even Hazel.

OZZIE: Oh, anything, Davey, as long as the family can stay together.

HARRY: I'm really late for work.

DAVID: Sorry, Dad, this is more important. We're going to have to institute a reparations plan for Liat.

OZZIE: Anything, Davey. Say anything, Harry.

HARRY: Anything.

OZZIE: Hazel?

HAZEL: Sounds fair to me.

OZZIE: Et?

ET: Sounds great.

DAVID: Then I hereby announce the beginning of Reparations Day. The Tribunal sits in judgment. Liat, you will be the Tribunal.

LIAT: Ok, Joe.

DAVID: First thing: Liat has a right to free elections.

LIAT: Flee erections, I want flee erections.

OZZIE: I'm beginning to have second thoughts.

DAVID: Mom, Dad, Hazel, Et, in 1954 Vietnam, one country, was divided into two countries, North and South, by the Geneva Conference. That conference guaranteed that there would be free elections to unite the country again. The United States and its puppet representatives, the South

Vietnamese government, blocked those elections because they knew Ho Chi Minh would win. Liat is now going to be allowed to vote for whomever she wants.

OZZIE: All right, Davey, all right. Let her vote, for God's sake.

DAVID: Liat, the candidates are Ngo Dinh Diem and Ho Chi Minh. Hazel, bring her a piece of paper.

OZZIE: Davey, this isn't fair. Don't we get to vote?

DAVID: Mother, you're not Vietnamese.

HARRY: Don't argue, dear. Nothing will happen.

DAVID: *(Giving Liat the paper.)* Now, Liat, you're being given the opportunity to choose your destiny as guaranteed by the Geneva Conference of 1954.

OZZIE: I don't see why the Swiss have to butt into everything.

DAVID: Write down your choice for leader: Diem or Ho Chi Minh.
 (Liat does.)

DAVID: Now because Liat and I are both blind, someone else will have to read her ballot.

OZZIE: I will. *(Takes it.)* She voted for Diem. Diem is the winner!

DAVID: I don't believe you.

OZZIE: I'm sorry, as long as you're blind, you'll have to trust me.

DAVID: Liat, whose name did you write down?

LIAT: I don't know, Joe. I don't know how to write. I write down letters I see.

DAVID: I declare this election invalid.

OZZIE: Oh, David, you have absolutely no sense of humor, does he, Harry?

HARRY: None of us do.

OZZIE: Here, Hazel, you read her stupid ballot. What does it say?

HAZEL: *Coca Cola.*

OZZIE: Let me see that. *(Looks at it.)* Liat, dear, you don't hyphenate Coca Cola.

HARRY: I really am late for work.

ET: Hey, Liat, want some free erections?
 (Liat and Et kiss for a while.)

DAVID: Very well, we'll move on. Liat, where are you?

LIAT: *(Talking while kissing.)* Here I am, Joe.
 (David holds her hand, not knowing that Liat is kissing Et.)

DAVID: Mom, Dad, I want you to know what it is to face destruction and terror.

OZZIE: Oh God.

HARRY: Be patient, Ozzie Ann.

DAVID: Pretend that this room is a rice field.
 (Hazel throws Minute Rice all over the floor.)

DAVID: Thank you, Hazel.

OZZIE: You planned that.

DAVID: Now, Mom, Dad, get down on your hands and knees and be picking rice.

HARRY: *(Doing so.)* I hope no one's looking in the window.

DAVID: Now I want you to imagine what it feels like to suddenly have a faceless terror above you, dropping burning fire on you and destroying everything about you. Liat, I am going to give you this gun to let them know how it feels to suffer random violence.

(Liat takes the gun.)

LIAT: I no see you, but I hear you. *(Fires aimlessly about the room.)*

(Ozzie and Harry have hysterics, hide behind couch and so forth. Hazel becomes frightened too. Et holds on to Liat and is amused. David smiles throughout until he gets shot in the arm.)

DAVID: Aaaaaaah. Liat, stop. You got me.

LIAT: Sorry Charlie.

OZZIE: *(Whispers to Harry.)* There *is* a God. Is it over yet, Davey? We both love Liat. I think of her as a daughter.

DAVID: Not yet, Mom. You know what it feels like to suffer random violence, but not specific violence. And not only that, but specific violence when you're blind as Liat and I are. Hazel, pull down the shades and turn off the lights.

(The stage falls into darkness.)

DAVID: *(In the dark.)* We're going to get you. We're coming. We're coming…

LIAT: Hai-ku! Hai-ku!

(Suddenly the sounds of terrible screams, bangings, breakage, chaos. After a while, the lights come up revealing Et holding his father's head in the fish tank or in Hazel's wash basin and shrieking, Liat riding on Ozzie Ann's back while kicking her in the side like a horse and pulling her hair; Ozzie Ann screams. Hazel stands in a corner, breaking cups. David is holding his arm which is bleeding more.)

OZZIE: *(Still being ridden by Liat, but seeing Hazel breaking cups.)* Hazel, stop it. Those are my wedding cups. Hazel!

DAVID: All right, stop, this part's over. Et, you can stop now. Et.

(Et pulls his father's face out of the tank and slaps him several times.)

DAVID: I feel faint from lack of blood.

LIAT: I want Coca Cola.

DAVID: Hazel, get her one.

(Hazel exits. Ozzie and Harry are on their hands and knees on the floor exhausted.)

OZZIE: Please, Davey, please. Do you forgive us yet?

DAVID: Tell Liat you're sorry.

OZZIE: We're sorry, Liat.

HARRY: I'm late for work.

(Ozzie hits him.)

HARRY: We're sorry, Liat.

DAVID: Kiss her foot.

OZZIE: Oh yes, please.

(They kiss her foot. Enter Hazel, gives Liat a Coke.)

DAVID: Now turn around, for Liat to kick you.

(They turn on their knees.)

LIAT: Someone help aim my foot.

ET: I got it.

(Et helps her find the parents' posteriors. Liat kicks both of them.)

DAVID: I call the Reparations to a close. The house is purified, the guilt expunged. The wrongs have been righted! We can live again. We can be a family again!

OZZIE: Oh thank God, it's over.

DAVID: We're purified, we're purified!

HARRY: I don't think Davey's well.

LIAT: *(Suddenly talking without her Chinese accent.)* Mmmmmm, I love Coke. Ever since I was a little girl in Schenectady.

(Everyone looks at her aghast. Liat realizes she's made a mistake, looks embarrassed. David, of all, is the most flabbergasted.)

DAVID: …Liat???????

LIAT: Whoops.

(Blackout.)

ACT I
Scene 4

The same, several minutes later. Liat, Ozzie Ann, Harry, Et. Davey and Hazel are offstage.

LIAT: *(Having taken off the tape from her eyes which made her look Asian.)* You see in 1956 my parents and I were on our way to a vacation in Thailand. You know, ever since I saw *The King and I* with Deborah Kerr and Yul Brynner, I wanted to go to Thailand. I must've been five at the time. Well our plane was shot down over Vietnam. *(Laughs to herself.)*

(We hear Davey's hysterical screams from offstage.)

DAVID: *(Off.)* NOOOO. NOOOOOO! *(Hazel enters.)*

HAZEL: He's hysterical again, Mrs. B. Anymore phenobarb?

OZZIE: There's some in the glove compartment of the car, Hazel.

(Hazel runs out.)

LIAT: Anyway; these Vietnamese people came and they dragged my parents from the burning plane, and they cut their heads off…

HARRY: Were these South or North Vietnamese?

LIAT: They all look the same to me.

DAVID: NOOOOOOOO!

LIAT: So anyway, they had me start work in a child brothel.

OZZIE: Good heavens. Children go to brothels?

LIAT: No, no, silly. The children were the prostitutes. Anyway, when I was twelve, they said I was too old, and they wanted me to fight in the Army.

(Enter Hazel with bottle of pills.)

HAZEL: Ah's a-coming, Ah's a-comin'. *(Runs Off to David.)*

LIAT: So I worked as a go-go girl in the day, and at nights we went around killing people who supported Diem.

OZZIE: Go-go girls worked in the day!

LIAT: They did then! But, let me tell you, by 1966, I was a nervous wreck. I almost couldn't remember Schenectady or *The King and I* or anything. I just knew one thing. That I was born an American, and I had to get back to a country that was sane, that wasn't bursting into flames every minute. And that was when I met your son.

DAVID: NOOOOOOOOOOOOOOO!

LIAT: He was already blind, and he had this real thing about feeling guilt about Vietnam, so I just knew the only way I could get him to marry me and to get back to Schenectady, was to tell him I was Vietnamese and blind too. And that's the story in a nutshell.

DAVID: AAAAAAAAAAAAAGGGGGGHHHHHH!

OZZIE: Well, it's a fascinating story.

ET: You're much more attractive without the slant eyes.

LIAT: Thank you.

OZZIE: Yes, she is. Don't you agree, Harry?

HARRY: I agree.

OZZIE: And how fortunate for you you're not blind.

LIAT: Yes, I know. I just hate being blind.

OZZIE: And, you know, Harry, there's good news for us too: Davey hasn't married a gook, he's married a nice girl from Schenectady. What's your name, dear?

LIAT: Maureen O'Hara.

OZZIE: Then we got it right once! Harry, you were right. She is Irish!

(Enter David, quieter, in a drugged stupor, being led by Hazel.)

HAZEL: Here he is, a little worse for wear and missing some blood, but ready to face life all over again.

OZZIE: Hello, Davey, dear. We're so happy. We knew you couldn't really have married one of those people.

(David moans low, something inaudible.)

OZZIE: He probably doesn't know your name, does he? Davey? Can you hear me? You're married to Maureen O'Hara.

DAVID: I've been betrayed! I've been betrayed!

OZZIE: Really, he's much stupider since he went to Vietnam. I wonder if he took drugs over there?

HARRY: I really have to go to the office now.

OZZIE: That's right, you do. And Hazel has to do the marketing. And Et has to go to high school. And I have to chat on the phone. Oh, Davey, life can go on again. And we'll never have to talk about Vietnam again. That episode is closed. Hurray! Hurray! Hurray!

ALL: *(Except David.)* Hurray! Hurray! Hurray!

(All hold a triumphant pose. Then in a dimmer light, all the characters begin to straighten the furniture, etc., except for Davey, who stares. While they straighten, each character comes down to the footlights, "Matchmaker" style, and speaks to the audience.)

OZZIE: I believe America is resilient. l know I am, and I'm part of America. If thine eye offend thee, pluck it out. That's my motto. If we didn't win the war, or if we fought on the wrong side, or whatnot—well, I say, that's behind us, let's get on with the business at hand. *(She goes back to the cleaning; holding up some broken piece of something.)* Now where does this go?

LIAT: Of course it's not like Schenectady, but I'm so glad to be back in America. I think Davey's family is real nice. I think I can have a whole new life before me and never think of the awful past again. I know now that *The King and I* has nothing to do with Siam. It's right here in America. You create your own Siam. I'm never going to forget that. *(Goes back to cleaning.)*

(Harry comes forward to say something.)

HARRY: *(Pause, thinks and thinks.)* I don't have anything to say.

OZZIE: Oh, Harry, you're such a sieve. Et, you talk for your father.

ET: *(Pause, then gives the finger.)* I learned how to give the finger in seventh grade. And I learned this. *(Puts finger in rounded hole.)* And me and Eddie Duffy took turns laying Eddie's sister under the pool table in their basement, and me and Eddie and John MacMahon and Frank Izzo and Peter Flaherty had a jerk-off contest and...

OZZIE: Et, we don't want to hear about seventh grade. Stop it.

ET: And...

OZZIE: Stop it.

ET: It was a tie. Me and Peter Flaherty.

OZZIE: *(To audience.)* I apologize for Et. He didn't talk about our hopes for the future at all. I hope he finds a nice girl soon to marry even if he is sixteen. That can be something to focus on in the months of rebirth ahead. *(Smiles; goes back to cleaning.)*

HAZEL: I've been cleaning up someone else's mess. That's my job. But I'll tell you one thing. Just because people clean up a mess once, don't mean they ain't gonna make a mess again. So they clean up Vietnam, what next? Let's be honest. I don't like people. I don't believe 'em and I don't trust 'em any further than I can throw 'em. *(Grabs Et, throws him over, self-defense style.)* And if I couldn't throw 'em, I wouldn't trust 'em even that far.

(Et pulls a switchblade out; Hazel pulls a large kitchen knife on him, from her apron.)

HAZEL: And *that's* folk-wisdom for you.

OZZIE: Et, Hazel, please don't play.

(They put their knives away.)

OZZIE: Hazel, you may talk like a nihilistic misanthrope, but underneath it all I know you're really our warm-hearted, loving Hazel.

(Hazel opens mouth to answer.)

OZZIE: Don't contradict me, Hazel. We're about to start over, and I don't want it to be on a sour note. *(Ozzie pauses, looks around.)*

(All action ceases, the house having been cleaned of the mess, etc. A dining room table has been brought out and set also. Ozzie changes calendar to read 1971.)

OZZIE: The 60s are behind us. There, a brand new clean home and a brand new clean slate. We're in the land of Beginning Again.

(Ozzie Ann and Liat smile. Hazel looks doubtful. Harry looks sleepy and haggard. Et rubs his crotch, bored. Davey looks pained and distant.)

(Blackout.)

ACT I

Scene 5

Cheerful opening music. Lights up. Harry reading paper. Davey sits staring. Enter Ozzie Ann. She changes calendar to 1974.

OZZIE: Happy Thanksgiving, Harry.

HARRY: Happy Thanksgiving, Ozzie Ann.

OZZIE: Doesn't the table look nice? How pleasant life is. Et, Maureen, where are you?

(Et and Liat come up from behind couch in their underwear.)

OZZIE: Et, I've told you not to do that with Maureen, it's not fair to Davey.

ET: I've got to do it with somebody.

OZZIE: Speak to him, Harry.

HARRY: He doesn't like me.

OZZIE: Try, please.

(Enter Hazel with bag of groceries, in a temper.)

OZZIE: Hazel, what's the matter?

HAZEL: The price of food is prohibitive!

OZZIE: I'm sure you exaggerate.

(Et and Maureen return behind sofa.)

HAZEL: Look at this. A carton of milk is $3.50.

OZZIE: I don't see why you're upset. Inflation means all the money is worthless, so that what you call $3.50 is probably only worth forty-three cents. Isn't that right, Harry?

HAZEL: Cranberry sauce, $2.85. Celery sticks, $3.25.

OZZIE: Hazel, please, I don't enjoy you when you're in a temper.

HAZEL: Canned sweet potatoes, $4.98.

OZZIE: All right, we'll grow our own.

HAZEL: Mr. B., I've gotta have a larger food budget or else I'm quitting.

OZZIE: Hazel, please, we don't want to think about unpleasant things on Thanksgiving. We're all trying to feel grateful.

HAZEL: Et's feeling Liat.

OZZIE: Her name is Maureen, Hazel. Et, stop hiding behind the couch, we want to see you.

ET: *(Coming up.)* You wanna see me make out?

OZZIE: We want to see you make out in life. Isn't that so, Harry?

HARRY: I wasn't listening.

HAZEL: That's tellin' her, Mr. B.

OZZIE: Hazel, don't you have to check the turkey or something?

(Et and Liat return to behind the sofa.)

HAZEL: There ain't no turkey.

OZZIE: Well, we can do without turkey. Hopefully you have prepared something for us?

HAZEL: Campbell Chunky Beef Soup, two cans, $6.75 each.

OZZIE: Well, please serve them. I believe we're ready.

(Hazel exits. Harry reads paper.)

OZZIE: Hello, Davey. I didn't see you there. How are you today?

(Pause.)

HARRY: Davey's been quiet these past few years.

OZZIE: Davey doesn't talk much.

HARRY: He takes after his father.

(Sounds of orgasm from behind the couch. Harry and Ozzie look distressed but try to ignore it. The sounds subside.)

OZZIE: Anything in the paper?

HARRY: Julie Nixon had a hysterectomy.

OZZIE: Again? *(Pause.)* Seems like only yesterday President Nixon resigned.

HARRY: *(Kindly, gently.)* It was yesterday.

OZZIE: *(Stares at him.)* Oh. *(Dawning on her.)* Then this isn't really Thanksgiving, is it?

HARRY: No, dear, it's not.

OZZIE: Why have I not been corrected then?

HARRY: *(Tenderly.)* You seemed so happy.

OZZIE: I *was* happy. For a time. *(Pause.)* I wonder if Davey should see a psychiatrist.

HARRY: There are so many cranks.

OZZIE: That's true of everything, isn't it? *(Cries.)*

(Harry holds her. Hazel enters with food.)

HAZEL: CHOW'S ON!

(Ozzie keeps crying; Harry helps her to the table. Hazel brings the catatonic Davey to the table.)

HAZEL: Et, Liat, chow time.

(Et and Liat come to table.)

HAZEL: Shall I say the Thanksgiving grace, Mr. B.?

HARRY: It's all right, Hazel. She knows it's not Thanksgiving now.

LIAT: *(Sympathetic.)* What's the matter with Mother B.?

HARRY: She's just sad today.

OZZIE: I'm sorry. It's just that…*(Uncontrollable spasmodic sobbing.)* We only have chunnnnkkkky soo-oou-oup for diiiiiinnnnnnnerrrrrrr…

HARRY: There, there, it's all right.

LIAT: Don't feel bad, Mother B. I *like* chunky soup.

HAZEL: Lots of people can't even afford that.

LIAT: Don't cry, Mother B. We still have each other. I know things will get better. I know that Davey will talk again, and Et will do better in school, and eventually I'll get into the movies, and, besides, you still have Hazel and Mr. B. still has his job. Lots of people don't even have jobs anymore.

OZZIE: *(Still weepy.)* You're right, Maureen. I really have no right to feel sorry for myself. We're all very lucky.

(Doorbell.)

HAZEL: I'll get it. *(Exits.)*

LIAT: It's always darkest before the dawn.

ET: Or the typhoon.

LIAT: Et, show some sensitivity.

OZZIE: That's all right, Maureen. I don't expect it. *(Drying her eyes, smiling.)* Well, I feel much better about that chunky soup now. What about everyone else? Et, some soup? *(Ozzie puts soup in bowls for everyone.)*

(Enter Hazel.)

HAZEL: Mr. B., there are some men at the door with a van.

HARRY: Already?

OZZIE: What do you mean, already?

(Harry tries to speak, can't, begins to sob uncontrollably.)

ET: Oh, brother.

OZZIE: Harry, what is it? Is it something I said? Did I hurt your feelings?

HARRY: *(Crying.)* I'm so ashamed.

OZZIE: Don't be ashamed, dear. No one blames you for the children. We're both to blame.

HARRY: We don't have any money.

OZZIE: We don't need much, do we, children?

HARRY: They've come to repossess the furniture and the car.

OZZIE: Harry, you're exaggerating.

HAZEL: That's what they said at the door, Mrs. B.

OZZIE: Keep out of this, Hazel.

HARRY: I've lost my job.

OZZIE: Harry, you're not amusing any of us. Stop it.

HARRY: Five months ago. I couldn't tell you.

OZZIE: But you've gone to work every day.

HARRY: I've been hiding in the library.

OZZIE: You've lost your job? AAAAAAAAAAAAGGGHHHH! *(Sudden accep-tance.)* Harry, things aren't that bad. We have stocks. We can mortgage the house.

HARRY: The stocks are gone. And the house has been mortgaged three times. The real estate people are showing the house starting tomorrow.

OZZIE: They are not. This is my house and as long as it's standing, I'm staying inside it.

(Doorbell again twice.)

OZZIE: Hazel, don't answer the door. We're going to have our Thanksgiving dinner. *(All try to eat but can't. Doorbell. Sound of door being smashed open. Ozzie screams, shouting to them.)*

OZZIE: AAAAAgggh. Please, please, we're eating. Take the bedroom furniture first. *(Sound of steps going upstairs; calmly to Harry.)*

OZZIE: I told them to go upstairs first. *(Goes to eat soup, screams.)* AAAAAGH!

HARRY: I'm a failure, I'm a failure! I can't support my family!

OZZIE: I'm not being supported!

HARRY: My oldest son is a zombie! My youngest son is a juvenile delinquent! He gets bad grades. He beats up the teachers. My life is nothing, a zero! *(Sound of furniture being taken out.)*

HAZEL: *(Looking out.)* There go the beds.

HARRY: We'll go on welfare. We'll live in a slum. I'll be bitten by a rat and die. I don't want to wait. I want to die now.

OZZIE: All you think about is self, self, self! What about me? You think I want to be bitten by a rat? You haven't protected me. I'm unprotected. You've ruined my life, my furniture, my house. What do I have? Nothing! I hate you, I hate you, I hate you!

HARRY: *(Takes out gun.)* You're right. I want to die. *(Cocks gun to his own head.)*

OZZIE: No! Don't, don't! *(Nasty, bitter.)* We wouldn't get your insurance if you kill yourself.

HARRY: The policy lapsed six months ago.

OZZIE: Oh.

(All look at Harry. No one tries to stop him. He aims gun in his mouth.)

OZZIE: Harry, please, we're at dinner.

(He aims gun at his heart, fires, falls over dead.)

OZZIE: All right, Harold Bartholomew, you've left me to fend for myself. And I will! It's darkest before the dawn, *not* the cyclone. Et, stop eating. I'm not gonna be licked, I promise you, as God is my witness, I won't be licked. Maureen, do you remember that song in *The Unsinkable Molly Brown*? *(She can't remember the lyrics or melody properly but makes up her own rousing melody perhaps lapsing occasionally into "Battle Hymn of the Republic" sings:)*

I'm gonna learn to read and write,
I'm gonna da da da duh duh duh da,
and if I'm da da da da da da duh da,
and then I'll da da da duh duh duh duh.

HAZEL: They've finished with the bedroom, Mrs. B. They're coming in this direction now.

OZZIE: *(Singing a key higher.)*

I'm going to duh duh da da da dum,
I'm going to dum dum dum dum dum,
I'm going to trample out the vineyards
where the grapes of wrath are stored,
I'm gonna dum dum dum duh duh duh...(Etc.)

HAZEL: They're coming closer. They're almost here.

(Ozzie keeps singing. Et looks bored. Liat is distressed. Davey is still trying to figure out if his father is dead. Men break down the set, take away furniture and walls. Note: If wanted the set and furniture can be taken away earlier during the scene if the director wants. Hazel should change the calendar so that it now reads 1976. She should come forward and have a Bicentennial Minute as the men take away the set.)

HAZEL: In Arlington, Massachusetts, Abigail Fritchard something something John Adams Boston Tea Party musket in her face and crows nest around her eyes, took her butter churn and Washington Irving and turned the British boats *back* in the harbor. And that's the way it was 200 years ago today.

ACT END I

ACT II
Scene 1

> *The spot where the house was. A large camping tent has been put up, a pot has been arranged to hang over a pile of wood. Also, scattered about the stage, are a refrigerator, a television, a telephone, all with extremely long extension cords that trail offstage. There are also two large Hefty garbage bags tied up on stage.*
>
> *Hazel is sweeping, singing "His Eye is on the Sparrow." Liat is practicing go-go dancing. Ozzie Ann is on the telephone. The dead Harry is seated next to her, perhaps a blood splotch about his heart. There may be a couple of folding chairs and/or large cartons for them to sit on. David seems transfixed, and is sitting-kneeling very close to the dead Harry, from time to time feeling his father's face. He doesn't appear to pick up on much of what goes on around him.*

OZZIE: *(Into phone.)* I'm sorry, I can't afford to pay that for a coffin. No, I can't. I am not made of money, you know. *(To Hazel.)* Will you shush, Hazel, I'm on the phone. And for God's sake, don't sweep the grass.
(Hazel stops. Back into phone.)

OZZIE: Well, have you anything cheaper? *(Listens.)* I do not consider $15,000 cheaper. My family could eat for three months on $15,000. Good-bye. *(Hangs up.)* That's the last one, Hazel. I guess we just won't be able to bury him.

HAZEL: There's something wrong with this country. It costs too much to live, and too much to die.

OZZIE: Don't criticize all the time, Hazel. Maureen, dear, it really isn't sensitive of you to dance like that until we decide what to do with Harry here.

LIAT: I'm just getting back into practice. We're all gonna have to work, you know.

OZZIE: Work. Oh God. *(To Harry.)* It's your fault this has happened. A woman shouldn't have to work. I hate you, I hate you.
(Enter Et with ten to eleven women's purses.)

ET: I got some money!

OZZIE: Oh, Et, thank goodness. *(Looks at purses. Looks at wallet in one of them: takes out money. Looks at card in wallet.)* Who is Mrs. Stanley Wasserman?

ET: I don't know. Some lady.

DAVID: *(Not having been listening, to Harry.)* You were right, father. You saw it.

OZZIE: He's speaking. Hazel, he's speaking!

DAVID: Father had more wisdom than I knew.

OZZIE: I always said that, didn't I, Hazel? Oh, Davey, you're going to be well again.

DAVID: Father was right to kill himself.

OZZIE: What?

DAVID: Father saw that only by killing ourselves can we atone for our sins in Vietnam and other developing countries.

OZZIE: Hazel, get him the phenobarb.

DAVID: That's thoughtful of you, mother, but an overdose is too gentle a way for us to die. We need guns and knives.

HAZEL: He's right. I'll go get them.

OZZIE: Hazel! Now Davey, you're overwrought. I want you to think pleasant thoughts.

DAVID: Mother, I've been thinking during these three years I've been silent...

OZZIE: Davey, please don't think...

DAVID: And father has made me see. We must all die.

OZZIE: Very well, whatever you think best, dear. *(Whispers.)* Hazel. We've got to bury Harry immediately. It's Harry's body that's upsetting Davey so much.

HAZEL: It ain't just that, missy. It's American history of the past two-hundred years that's upsetting him. Killing the Indians, Manifest Destiny, the Monroe Doctrine...

OZZIE: Look, Hazel, can it, would you? Just can it. Now let's address the subject at hand. Do you think we could sink Harry in the septic tank?

HAZEL: He might keep risin' to the top, Mrs. B.

DAVID: We must give his body an honorable burial. Otherwise his spirit cannot go to the resting place.

OZZIE: You're talking like a member of a minority group, David. I can't take much more.

DAVID: I will ask Buddha to guide us.

OZZIE: How much marijuana did you take over there, Davey? How much?
(David kneels and prays. Sound of garbage truck.)

LIAT: The garbage men are here.
(Hazel goes to gather the two bags of garbage exits.)

OZZIE: Wait. Quick, get another bag. Reenie, help me.
(Liat and Ozzie put Harry in plastic garbage bag.)

DAVID: *(Listening intently.)* What are you doing?

OZZIE: Et, distract your brother.

ET: Hiya, Davey, how ya doin'? *(Flicks David's ears, snaps fingers in his ears, twists his nose, etc.)*

DAVID: *(Through Et's annoyances.)* What are you doing?

OZZIE: *(Calling off.)* Wait, please, don't go yet.

> *(Liat and Ozzie drag off Harry in his bag. Re-enter Liat and Ozzie, followed by Hazel.)*

OZZIE: Well, that's over.

> *(Sound of truck squashing garbage.)*

OZZIE: Good-bye, Harry. Good-bye.

DAVID: Did you put father in the garbage, mother?

OZZIE: Don't be silly, Davey.

DAVID: Lies. Everyone in this country tells lies.

OZZIE: *(Exhausted emotionally.)* Don't generalize, Davey.

DAVID: You've put father in the garbage. You are a moral idiot.

OZZIE: I am not a moral idiot.

DAVID: You are.

OZZIE: I'm not.

DAVID: You are.

OZZIE: Sticks and stones may break my bones, *(Sadly.)* but names can never hurt me.

DAVID: *(Standing with moral dignity.)* You are *all* moral idiots. Mother, Et, and Maureen O'Hara. All of you! *(Goes to exit, walks into the refrigerator.)*

OZZIE: Ha, ha, you think you're so smart. You just walked into the refrigerator! Ha, ha! Ha, ha!

> *(David exits.)*

HAZEL: That's tellin' him, Mrs. B.

OZZIE: I told him! I told him! But oh, Hazel, why do I feel so alone?

HAZEL: Cause you is alone, Mrs. B., you *is* alone.

> *(Blackout.)*

ACT II

Scene 2

> *The same later. Et and Liat are on the ground, kissing. Hazel sits behind them watching them, disapproving. Ozzie Ann wafts about, feeling sad.*

HAZEL: *(Looking at Et and Liat.)* Tsk, tsk, tsk. Diss-gusting.

OZZIE: And this is where the dining room table used to be. And this is where the couch used to be. And there used to be a wall here. And a wall here. And a wall here. *(Getting her bearings.)* And the things we have left are the refrigerator. And the telephone. *(Picks it up.)* Hello? Hello? Hello? *(Puts it down.)* And the television. *(Ozzie turns on the television, sits before it.)*

HAZEL: Your brain gonna turn to jello, you watch the television, Mrs. B.

OZZIE: I like jello, Hazel.

(We hear the sounds of the TV show, sort of: that is, we hear silence, then canned laughter; then silence, then laughter etc. Ozzie watches it blankly for a while, then decides she likes it and laughs delightedly with the audience on TV.)

OZZIE: *(Merry.)* Don't you like this show, Hazel?

HAZEL: Sure I likes it. I just doesn't laugh much.

OZZIE: We should all laugh more. Hazel, how many phenobarb have we?

HAZEL: Two hundred and six.

OZZIE: Bring them to me.

LIAT: *(Coming out of her kissing.)* Mother B!

OZZIE: I'm sorry, Reenie.

LIAT: Et, Mother B's going to kill herself. Stop her.

HAZEL: *(With pills.)* Here ya go, Mrs. B.

LIAT: Hazel, how can you?

HAZEL: I does what I's told.

LIAT: Davey, Davey, come quick. Your mother's going to kill herself. *(Runs off.)*

OZZIE: *(Takes one pill.)* Good-bye, Hazel. *(Laughs with TV.)* This really is an excellent show. *(Laughs cries, takes a pill.)*

(Re-enter Liat and David. David is now in Buddhist robes.)

LIAT: Quick, Davey.

DAVID: Mother! *(Kneels by her.)* You've seen, you've understood.

OZZIE: There's a good program on, Davey.

DAVID: Yes, yes. Now say after me. This is for all the wrong America has done.

OZZIE: What?

DAVID: This is for Vietnam. *(Gives her pill.)* Swallow. And this is for the Indians. *(Gives pill.)* Swallow. And this is...

OZZIE: STOP IT, STOP IT? Hazel, get him away from me.

DAVID: Mother!

OZZIE: Don't you call me mother! Turn the damn television off, Hazel.

HAZEL: You don't want to watch it?

OZZIE: Turn it off, Hazel. You've ruined the program for me, Davey. You've ruined everything for me.

HAZEL: You don't want any more phenobarb?

OZZIE: No, I don't want any-more-phenobarb. What is the matter with everyone?

I'm in despair and my son feeds me pills. The family unit. What has happened to the family unit?

LIAT: I'm here, Mother B.

OZZIE: Oh God, help me. Help us. Help. Our father who art in heaven... *(She kneels, desperate.)*

DAVID: *(To Hazel's direction.)* What did I do?

OZZIE: ...hallowed be thy name. Pray, everybody, pray! Thy kingdom come, thy will be done...

(Liat joins her, forces Et to; Hazel looks doubtful, knits.)

OZZIE AND LIAT: ...on earth as it is in heaven; give us this day our daily bread, and forgive us our trespasses...

(Thunder, lightning. Deafening sounds of an airplane. Lights dim up and down. From the sky drops a man in a large white, silver-sparkled parachute. He is Larry [played by same actor as played Harry]; he is dressed in a military uniform, spanking clean and neat. He is spotlit and looks dazzling.)

OZZIE: Harry?

LARRY: Ozzie Ann, I came as soon as I could. Everything is going to be all right now.

OZZIE: Harry? Is Harry alive?

LARRY: I'm not Harry, Ozzie Ann. I'm his brother Larry.

OZZIE: Larry?

LARRY: Yes.

OZZIE: Did Harry have a brother Larry?

ET: Sure he did, Mom. Don't you remember? Larry is Dad's brother in the Mafia.

OZZIE: But he looks like a general.

LARRY: I'm in the reserves, Ma'am, and proud of it. *(Salutes.)*

DAVID: *(Worried.)* Do I hear a uniform?

OZZIE: You can't hear a uniform, Davey.

LARRY: *(At David.)* Who've we got here?

OZZIE: This is David, Larry. He's been upset lately.

LARRY: *(Referring to his Buddhist robes.)* He looks like Barbra Streisand. Stand up straight, son. Straight! Shoulders back, stomach in. *(Punches David's stomach.)*

ET: Look at me, Uncle Larry. *My* stomach's in!

LARRY: Good for you, Ettie boy. This family could use some Army discipline, you know that, Ozzie Ann?

DAVID: *(Soft.)* I've been in the Army.

LARRY: What you say?

DAVID: I said I been in the Army.

LARRY: *(Suddenly, violently twisting his arm.)* I don't like your tone, greenhorn. Now say I'm sorry, Sergeant.

DAVID: *(In pain.)* I'm sorry, Sergeant.

LARRY: And why you sorry, Soldier? Huh?

DAVID: I don't know.

LARRY: Because I'm a stupid-ass raw recruit motherfuckin' S.O.B., that's why. Say it.

ET: I can say it, Uncle Larry!

LARRY: I want Davey to say it.

DAVID: Cause I'm a stupid-ass raw recruit motherfuckin' S.O.B.

LARRY: Good! *(Throws him down.)*

ET: Cause I'm a stupid-ass raw recruit motherfuckin' S.O.B.!

LARRY: Good boy, Ettie.

OZZIE: *(With great politeness.)* Larry, I normally ask the children not to use bad language in the house.

LARRY: You gotta have discipline, Ozzie Ann. Otherwise this country's gonna fall apart.

ET: He's right, Mom.

OZZIE: Well, I suppose discipline is more important than polite language.

LARRY: Goddam right.

ET: Goddam right.

LARRY: *(Ruffles Et's hair.)* You're a good kid, Ettie. *(Sees Liat, leers.)* I don't think I been introduced to everybody.

OZZIE: Oh, I'm sorry. Larry, this is David's wife, Maureen O'Hara.

LARRY: Hiya, Marine.

LIAT: It's More-reen.

ET: Uncle Larry, she's been a go-go dancer and a prostitute and a guerilla fighter.

LARRY: Oh yeah? How'd ya like to fight this gorilla, huh, Marine?

ET: Gee, Uncle Larry, you got a great sense of humor.

LARRY: You got to in my business, Ettie. *(To Liat, offers her chocolate bar.)* Haben-ze das chocolate bar, Fraulein? Nein, ja?

LIAT: What?

LARRY: *(Trying to explain.)* Choc-olatz.

OZZIE: Larry, Maureen is American.

LARRY: Oh, yeah, right. Chocolate, Marine?

LIAT: It's More-reen.

LARRY: How about a kiss? *(Kisses her.)*

ET: I've kissed her too, Uncle Larry!

OZZIE: Larry, Maureen is married to Davey.

ET: But I kiss her, Mom.

OZZIE: Well, I know, but…

ET: Mom, Uncle Larry is a guest…

OZZIE: Yes, I suppose he is.

LARRY: Davey, don't mind, do you, Davey?

DAVID: *(Sullen.)* What?

LARRY: You don't mind if I kiss Marine here, do ya?

DAVID: It's More-reen, not Ma-rine.

LARRY: Hey, soldier…STANDUP, STOMACH IN, TEN HUT! I said, Ten-Hut! *(Knocks David around.)*

ET: Look at me, Uncle Larry. I'm at Ten-Hut!

LARRY: Good boy, Ettie. *(To David.)* Hey, ugly, TEN-HUT!

    (David and Et stand at attention.)

LARRY: You too, Marine.

    (Liat stands at attention.)

LARRY: You see that, Ozzie Ann. That's order.

OZZIE: Thank you, Larry. It's lovely.

LARRY: Who's the tar baby over there knitting?

OZZIE: That's Hazel, Larry. We don't normally call her a tar baby.

LARRY: Hey, tar baby, where are the walls?

OZZIE: The repossession men took them, Larry. And please call her Hazel.

LARRY: Well…Hazel…you get them repossession bastards on the phone and you tell 'em Uncle Larry is in town and he wants the house back.

OZZIE: Larry, we have no money.

LARRY: I got money. I ain't in the Mafia for nothing.

OZZIE: You mean—we can have the walls back?

LARRY: Sure.

ET: Gee, Uncle Larry, you're gonna buy the house back for us?

LARRY: That's right, Ettie boy. Okay, Hazel, let's see you get to the friggin' telephone and don't take too long bouncin' your titties about it, you understand?

    (Hazel, aghast, tries to say something back. Gives up, takes phone, exits with it.)

OZZIE: I don't understand it. Hazel's usually so talkative.

LARRY: *(To Liat.)* Haben-ze das nylons, Fraulein?

LIAT: Oh, look. Ones with seams. What year is this?

OZZIE: Oh, and they're hard to come by. I don't like the ones without seams.

(Larry throws her a pair.) Thank you, Larry. Larry, will you be staying with us for long?

LARRY: TEN-HUT!

(Everyone stands at attention.)

LARRY: I think so, Ozzie Ann. I think so.

(All freeze. The Repossession Men come back and set up the house again and all its old furnishings. The calendar reads 1976 still. The characters help with the set-up [not David though], and come forward once again, "Matchmaker-style.")

OZZIE: *(Comes forward; a little doubtful.)* I think everything's going to be all right again. I know Harry's brother Larry uses rough language and he's maybe a little hard on Davey, but don't forget Harry Truman used bad language and, judging by that book by Doris Kearns on Lyndon Johnson, he used bad language too; and this is what I think: The important thing isn't the language you use but the meaning of your language. And Larry's language is America's language: "Stand up straight, stomach in, work hard and you'll survive." I'm afraid I'm awfully woozy from all that phenobarb I took… *(Gets dizzy has to sit down.)*

LARRY: Get off your butt, Ozzie Ann.

OZZIE: Oh. You're right, Larry. *(Gets up to continue work.)*

LARRY: I've worked my butt off all my life, and I'm proud of it. I been through World War II, and I been through Korea. I was a POW in Korea, and I had to sit in a little box in my own shit for eight months.

OZZIE: Don't say shit, Larry. Say feces.

LARRY: Them Commie chinks wanted me to crack but they couldn't make me because *I knew where I was going.* America used to know where it was going too, but we got things too easy and we got soft. America is about personal initiative, about people who get up in the morning and go to work. America has succeeded because it wanted to be the best. But then in the 60s we got all these jerk-off kids who get handed all this money and education and they fart around doin' nothin' and protesting because things got too easy for them! Well maybe this recession is a good thing because I say when it ain't easy for these kids no more, then things'll start bein' right again. *(Hits Davey.)* Move your ass, kid. Everybody's workin'. Let's see you work.

OZZIE: Larry, please, he *is* blind.

LARRY: Move it, buddy. *(Pokes Davey: He has to work.)*

ET: Uncle Larry says I can be anything I want to be, but the important thing is to have ambition. I never used to have ambition, but now I want to be just like Uncle Larry. I guess this has to do with having the proper male model. Before Uncle Larry the strongest identity figure I had was Hazel, and a guy can't grow up to be a maid.

OZZIE: *(Proud of him.)* Et, that's the smartest thing you've ever said. Maureen dear, have you anything to say?

LIAT: I remember the day President Kennedy was killed. I was a go-go dancer in Vietnam at the time and I was killing Diem supporters in the evening. And I was go-going away when I heard the news Kennedy was shot, and I thought, "Oh God, life is awful." I wish life were like *The King and I.* You know President Kennedy's favorite musical was *Camelot* and mine is *The King and I.* Well, I presumed *Camelot* must really be terrific, I mean he was the President and he went to Harvard and everything. But then I saw it. I mean, no wonder we got involved in Vietnam if that was his judgment. *Camelot* isn't very good at all, the book is very weak, and it's about this king whose wife commits adultery with Robert Goulet. I mean, do you think Jacqueline really did things like that? And they say *he* slept with Marilyn Monroe. I mean, no wonder things are a mess. *(Cries.)* I want to be in *The King and I.* I don't like this house any more. Nothing's worked out the way I wanted. *(Cries.)*

LARRY: Cut the crybaby crap, Marine.

DAVID: *(Steps forward.)* I feel that this house is...

LARRY: Shut up, you.

DAVID: I feel...

LARRY: SHUT UP.

OZZIE: Larry, Davey has a right to have his say.

LARRY: I don't want him to.

OZZIE: Larry, please. We've all got to try to get on. Please. Davey. Go ahead, dear.

DAVID: I feel that this house is becoming like Vietnam. I am Vietnamese, and Larry is the military-industrial complex, and ahead of us is nothing but terror and destruction. *(To Hazel.)* Mama San. Mama San, I'm afraid. Hold me, Mama San.

HAZEL: *(Holds David.)* I don't really have sympathy for any of these people.

LARRY: What did you say?

HAZEL: I said, I don't have sympathy for any of you.

(Larry starts to take out his gun to kill her.)

OZZIE: Larry, no! She's only kidding. That's how Hazel talks. Underneath she loves us a lot.

LARRY: I don't like that kind of talk.

OZZIE: Larry, please, the house is ready for us to start over again. Please, it can't be with a shooting.

LARRY: OK. *(To Hazel.)* But look, goon face, one more crack outta you and you're gonna get it. Got me?

HAZEL: Yes, Ma'am.

LARRY: What?

OZZIE: She said, yes, sir. Larry, please, the house wants us to start the morning. *Please* Larry.

(Larry looking ugly at Hazel, relents. Cheerful situation comedy music. Alarm. Hazel stands with spatula. The family goes to the table. David exits upstairs.)

LARRY: Good morning, Ozzie Ann.

OZZIE: Good morning, Larry.

LARRY: Good morning, Et.

OZZIE: Good morning, Et.

ET: Good morning, Mom. Good morning, Uncle Larry.

OZZIE: Good morning, Maureen.

LIAT: Good morning, Mother B.

LARRY: *(Wolf call at Liat.)* Hot pussy. *(Whistles.)* Look at them apples. Sit on my face. Hot pussy.

ET: Hot pussy!

OZZIE: Please, we don't like the word pussy! Hazel, I believe we're ready for our Bicentennial Minute now.

HAZEL: In Morristown, New Jersey, General George Washington on the banks of the Potomac and the subzero weather unable to withstand the deadly lust of the Mohicans woke up with Natty Bumppo on his Chingachgook, threatening to spread to the entire camp until Benjamin Franklin, inventing penicillin five days later, caused the Bumpo to go away and had a restful few days with Martha at Lake Erie. And that's the way it was two hundred years ago today.

OZZIE: I don't see what Lake Erie has to do with anything. Please serve breakfast now.

LARRY: *(To Liat.)* Et tells me you used to be a go-go dancer.

LIAT: Yes.

LARRY: You wanna shake it for me a little?

LIAT: I haven't had breakfast yet.

LARRY: Can't you eat and dance at the same time?

OZZIE: Larry, let her eat her...

LARRY: I want her to dance !

LIAT: All right! I'll dance. *(Stands on her chair, does go-go dance.)*

ET: Gee, this is great, Uncle Larry.

(Et and Larry look up her dress.)

LIAT: *(Praying to herself.)* I'm in *The King and I;* I'm in *The King and I;* I'm in *The King and I....*

OZZIE: *(Depressed.)* Breakfast is delicious, Hazel.

LARRY: Somebody's missing. Where's your gooney son?

OZZIE: I think he meditates in the morning, Larry.

LARRY: Oh he does, does he? *(Storms off.)*

LIAT: *(Still dancing.)* I'm in *The King and I;* I'm in *The King and I....*

OZZIE: You can stop dancing, Maureen.

(David screams offstage. Larry drags him in.)

LARRY: Whatsa matter, smart guy, you too smart to join our company? Huh? Look at this goddam dress. Know what you look like? Barbra Streisand! That's what! You look like Barbra fuckin' Streisand!

OZZIE: Larry, please say copulating or having sexual congress or something.

HAZEL: Breakfast is getting cold.

OZZIE: Davey, dear, won't you sit down and have some breakfast with us?

LARRY: Goddam right he will, and he'll eat every bit. *(Slams David into the chair.)* Okay, Barbra Streisand, I want to see you eat your food like a soldier. Every time I hit the table, you put this fork in your mouth, you got me, friend? Ready, about face, eat! *(Larry shoves a fork into David's hand and makes him eat at a nerve-racking pace, beating the table with his fist in time to how he wants David to eat.)*

(David at first complies, then finally flings forkful of food in Larry's face.)

DAVID: You know what you are! You're the American as imperialist! You think you know what's right about everything, and you go in and you keep little people in little countries from voting for who they want and you try to make them just like America and maybe they don't want to be like America. You're an imperialist! Imperialist pig! Imperialist pig!

(Larry starts to strangle David.)

OZZIE: Larry, please, he's blind.

LARRY: *(Stopping.)* Okay. But he's got two minutes to take it back or, blind or not, I'm gonna kick the shit outta him. *(Sits down.)* You little jerk-off.

OZZIE: Say ejaculating or something, can't you?

LARRY: You wanna swallow your teeth?

OZZIE: No. Let's just have breakfast.

(They eat in silence.)

LARRY: *(To Liat.)* Who told you to stop dancing?

   (Liat dances.)

ET: You got a son, Uncle Larry?

LARRY: Sure do, Ettie boy. I got a son and a daughter and a wife.

OZZIE: They must be missing you.

LARRY: Here's their picture.

ET: Gee, your son's about my age.

LARRY: He was, Ettie. He was.

OZZIE: Did he die?

LARRY: They all died. They wuz murdered two months ago.

OZZIE: Murdered? Why?

LARRY: Mafia infighting, you know. This Mr. Big and I had this disagreement how to sell this German pornography and so he says to me, you wanna find your wife and kids with their heads cut off, and I said, I dare ya; and then he did it. *(Shows another picture.)*

OZZIE: That's awful.

ET: What did you do back, Uncle Larry?

LARRY: I got this horse, ya see, and I cut his head off, and then I put the bloody head in his bed when he was asleep. *(Laughs uproariously.)*

HAZEL: That's derivative.

LARRY: What?

HAZEL: You saw that in the movies.

OZZIE: *(Desperately trying to keep peace.)* You know, movies and television really are to blame for a lot of our troubles. I know that *Bonnie and Clyde* caused at least ten deaths that I know of personally; and Et never had naughty thoughts until he saw *Therese and Isabel.* All those breasts.

DAVID: What did you to before you were in the Mafia?

   (Silence. Everyone is worried that David spoke.)

LARRY: You talkin' to me, Soldier?

DAVID: What did you do before you were in the Mafia?

LARRY: *(Pauses, stares at him.)* I manufactured napalm.

DAVID: *(Becomes hysterical.)* Mother, we can't accept his money. It's contaminated. We've got to send the walls back!

OZZIE: Davey, calm down, there are lots of peaceful uses of napalm too.

DAVID: Like what?

OZZIE: I don't know. Burning crops, heating homes, that sort of thing.

DAVID: This house is evil!

   (Larry gets David in a neckhold.)

LARRY: We got to teach you some manners for your elders, sonny boy. Hazel, keep these hot cakes *hot. (Larry drags David offstage.)*

ET: You know, the way that Uncle Larry and Davey don't get on is rather like the difficulties the generations had getting on in America, particularly in the late 60s, Kent State, etc.

OZZIE: That's true, Et.

(We hear Larry whipping David.)

OZZIE: Larry, Larry, stop it! *(Runs off.)*

ET: *(To Liat who's stopped dancing.)* I'll give you a chocolate bar if you dance again.

LIAT: I don't want to hear chocolate bar mentioned again, is that clear?

(Et either forces Liat under the table, or carries her off to the kitchen, struggling. The sounds of David and Larry continue too.)

HAZEL: *("Matchmaker" style.)* It was the worst of times, it was the worst of times. There were Puerto Rican traveling companies of *Hello, Dolly,* and they would go from town to town, mugging the audience sometime during the "So Long, Dearie" number. There were all-black productions of *Fiddler on the Roof,* and there were all Jewish landlord productions of *To Be Young, Gifted, and Black;* and after these performances the blacks and the landlords would meet in empty parking lots and rumble. The American people, feeling sorry for Nixon, re-elected him. And the National Endowment for the Arts gave grants to the makers of snuff movies. Mere anarchy was loosed upon the world. And the mayor of Newark was a beast like a lion, and the mayor of Trenton was a beast like a calf, and the third beast had a face as a man, and the fourth beast was like a flying eagle, and these beasts were full of eyes before and behind, and...

(Enter Ozzie screaming.)

OZZIE: Run, children, run!

(Liat, Hazel, Et look for shelter. Larry runs in holding his belt; David runs in hysterical, brandishing a gun.)

DAVID: I kill you! Yankee imperialist pig! I kill you!

LARRY: Go ahead! Shoot me! Gook! Dirty friggin' gook!

(David shoots. Liat gets shot in shoulder.)

LIAT: Aaaaaaaggghhh!

OZZIE: Hazel, do something.

HAZEL: Davey, give me the gun.

DAVID: Don't come near me, Mama San. I'm going to kill all of us.

HAZEL: Davey...

DAVID: I mean it, Mama San... *(Fires.)*

(Ozzie dials the phone.)

DAVID: Do I hear a phone?

OZZIE: No, Davey. No phone. *(Into phone, whispers.)* Operator, get me St. Mary's Rectory at once.

(Blackout.)

ACT II

Scene 3

In blackout we hear sounds of guns, explosions, general sounds of warfare. Then the sounds become less frequent. Silence. Lights up on living room, it is night. Liat, with wounded shoulder, is on couch. Ozzie is reading, trying to hold onto normality. After a bit, Et and Larry stalk through with guns and kitchen knives. There is barbed wire in living room.

LARRY: *(Calling softly.)* Davey! Davey! *(Exits.)*

(Doorbell. Et stays on guard by door.)

OZZIE: I'll get it, Hazel. *(Ozzie lets in Fr. McGillicutty, a sweet-natured, rather nervous man.)* Oh, Father, thank God, you've come.

FR. MC GILLICUTTY: Hello, Mrs. Bartholomew, how are you?

OZZIE: Come in please.

(Fr. McGillicutty enters, almost steps in bear trap on floor.)

OZZIE: Look out! *(Pulls him aside.)* It's a bear trap. Larry's set them all through the house.

FR. MC GILLICUTTY: What seems to be the matter?

(Shots offstage.)

LARRY: *(From off.)* I see him! I see him!

OZZIE: My brother-in-law and son are fighting.

FR. MC GILLICUTTY: Have they had a disagreement?

OZZIE: Yes, I fear they have.

(Terrible clamp offstage. David screams in agony.)

LARRY: *(From offstage.)* I caught him! I caught him!

OZZIE: Oh dear, excuse me. *(Ozzie exits.)*

(Fr. McGillicutty smiles awkwardly.)

FR. MC GILLICUTTY: Hello, Et.

ET: Hello. This is Maureen O'Hara. She used to be a go-go dancer.

FR. MC GILLICUTTY: How do you do?

(Re-enter Larry and Ozzie and David. David has huge trap closed on his foot.)

OZZIE: We've got to get this off Davey's foot.

LARRY: No we ain't. *(To David.)* Sit down, you fuckin' bastard.

OZZIE: Please, Larry, Fr. McGillicutty is here.

LARRY: I say we cut the gook's ears off.

OZZIE: Larry! Fr. McGillicutty is here to counsel us. We can't go cutting Davey's ears off.

(All sit.)

OZZIE: Father, this is Laurence Bartholomew, my late husband's brother, and this is my son David, and David's wife Maureen.

FR. MC GILLICUTTY: How do you do?

OZZIE: And I believe you know Et from Sunday School.

FR. MC GILLICUTTY: Yes.

ET: Father's a queer.

OZZIE: Et!

ET: Well, he is. Look how he's sitting.

OZZIE: Please, this isn't the issue now. Father, Davey has been very upset since he came back from Vietnam in 1968.

FR. MC GILLICUTTY: Perhaps his experiences over there bothered him.

OZZIE: Yes, I'm sure they did, but you see I thought he should be over them by now. Perhaps you might speak to him.

FR. MC GILLICUTTY: I can try. Hello, Davey. I'm Fr. McGillicutty.

DAVID: Where's Liat?

OZZIE: Maureen is here, dear. She's still bleeding a little.

DAVID: I don't care about Maureen. I WANT LIAT! I HAD A VIETNAMESE WIFE AND I WANT HER!

LARRY: Shut up, asshole!

OZZIE: *(Mad.)* Rectum, Larry.

LARRY: Rectum.

FR. MC GILLICUTTY: Did Davey have an Asian wife?

OZZIE: Well, in a way.

LIAT: I pretended to be Vietnamese for awhile.

OZZIE: *(Explaining.)* Davey's blind, you remember.

FR. MC GILLICUTTY: Oh he is? Perhaps that's why he's bitter. Is that why you're bitter, Davey?

DAVID: I am not bitter anymore. I merely wish to atone for America's genocide.

FR. MC GILLICUTTY: My son, you must not judge man so harshly. God does not. Don't you know why God allows wars? God looks down from heaven and he sees a poor country with too many people and he says to himself, "Oh dear, think how much poverty and degradation these people are going to face because there are so many of them," and then he whispers into the President's ear at night, and then in the morning there is a war; and when the war is over, there are fewer people, and these fewer people are happier. The same is true of earthquakes, floods, plagues, epidemics. It all has to do with population control. *(To Et.)* And likewise homosexuality, though this isn't widely accepted yet, is also God's way of dealing with the overpopulation problem; but once this is more fully realized, we will no longer fear the homosexual or the war or the flood or the earthquake, and in a while there will be fewer of us, and we will all be happier. We need air to breathe, space to move our arms, to stretch out, to extend our arms to their outermost positions. God knows this, He will help us, there will be fewer of us.

OZZIE: *(A little disturbed.)* Some coffee, Father?

FR. MC GILLICUTTY: No, thank you. Have you ever been on a turnpike or a parkway in a traffic jam with all those people in all those cars? And you don't move, and you can't move, and there's all that gaseous air; and some of the people honk their horns, and some swear, and it's just awful. And sometimes as I sit in my stalled automobile, I think to myself, I CAN'T STAND IT, there are too many people alive, they're all crazy, there's probably a sniper in one of these cars right now, I have this pain in my head, what can I do? But then I get ahold of myself and say, Father, you're a priest, have faith, remember there are wars and floods and pestilences and homosexuals, and then such a flood of peace and understanding surges through my body that my heart cries aloud with hosannas for our Lord, hosanna, hosanna in the highest.

OZZIE: Can you help Davey?

FR. MC GILLICUTTY: I have to go now.

OZZIE: Please don't go.

FR. MC GILLICUTTY: Yes. It's rather close in here, there are so many of you. They're transferring me to Arizona, you know. I really don't think I can stand New Jersey another minute, but then I guess I'll have to til I leave. But then that's what being a priest is really all about it, isn't it? Good-bye and God bless. *(Exits.)*

HAZEL: It's up to you now, Mrs. B. You've got to be the mediator.

OZZIE: All right. *(Paces, psyches herself up, thinks desperately, then she starts.)* Davey, dear, do you remember how when your father was alive, how you made him and me crawl about on the floor with Minute Rice while

Maureen shot at us? Now after we did that, you said the house was purified of guilt for Vietnam. And now here you are going on about it again.
Now even if Uncle Larry did manufacture napalm, if he hadn't, someone
else would have. Just as if we hadn't bombed Cambodia, someone else
would have. Now, Davey, I think you're mixing things up a little bit: your
idea of right and wrong, and your love for your family. Now if it's a question of some Vietnamese person being hit with napalm and with your
mother able to lead a happy life, I think you know what the answer should
be. And so does Uncle Larry, which is why he was so mad about you showing all this preference for Asians. I mean, empathy is a lovely thing, Davey,
and I'm proud you have it; but you must have it in proportion. Isn't it
Buddha who said "Everything is moderation"? Of course, that sounds like
the Methodists too, but whoever said it, can't we have a little moderation
here, I mean, don't I get any happiness ever? Or what? *(She's hysterical.)* You
tell me, David! Now for God's sake, shake hands with Uncle Larry or else
I'm going to cry.

DAVID: I won't.

OZZIE: Davey, we can't take your foot out of the trap if you're going to kill Uncle
Larry.

DAVID: I won't kill him. I know now that Uncle Larry is indestructible. I must
atone for sins on my own. I must join my father beyond the grave.

LARRY: Good.

OZZIE: Larry, Please.

DAVID: I wish to set myself on fire.

OZZIE: Davey, is that a constructive remark?

LARRY: I'd like to see him on fire. Give me a good excuse to piss on him.

OZZIE: What is the matter with you? Piss on him! Can't you say urinate? Piss,
fart, shit, ass. I don't like that kind of language, Larry. I WANT NICE
LANGUAGE!

DAVID: You really are a moral idiot, aren't you? You don't care that he made
napalm, but you're offended by the word piss.

OZZIE: EVERYONE IS OFFENDED BY THE WORD PISS. And I am not a
moral idiot, you keep saying that! *(Stands.)* All right, Davey, two people
can play at this game. I am not going to let you out of the bear trap until
you apologize to me. And I don't care how many months it takes. *(Exits.)*

DAVID: I must set myself on fire.

*(Larry makes a pssss sound and makes motion as if to urinate on David; David
moves his lips, soundlessly saying "I must set myself on fire" over and over.)*

ET: *(Pointing to Liat, in a leering manner.)* Hey, Uncle Larry—wanna play some ball? *(Larry goes over with a grin to Liat. She suddenly begins to speak.)*

LIAT: Excuse me. Now, Your Majesty, when I came to Siam several months ago you promised me a cottage away from the Palace for my little son Louis and myself. Now…Heavens! Are all these children yours, Your Majesty? I had no idea. *(Begins to sing manically, to no recognizable melody.)*

March of the Siamese children-dren-dren,

dum dee dum dum dee dum, we kiss in a shadow quite often;

happy talk talk talk talk…

HAZEL: O, what a noble mind is here o'erthrown.

LIAT: Oh, are you Prince Chinga-acorn? How do you do? *(Sings:)*

Getting to know chop suey, Flower drum drum

drum drum drum drum song, swinging Siamese in the trees…

(Enter Ozzie Ann, distracted.)

OZZIE: SHUT UP SHUT UP SHUT UP! Hazel, do something to the calendar. I've had enough of this, I want to start tomorrow.

HAZEL: Yes, ma'am. *(Pulls calendar leaf off: It's July 4.)* Happy Fourth of July, everyone.

OZZIE: Breakfast. Everybody sit down!

(All but David do. Liat is late.)

OZZIE: *(To Liat.)* Come on, Looney Tunes, move it over here.

LIAT: *(Sing-song.)* Shall I tell you what I think of you? You're spoiled! You work hard and long in the factory, but you're spoiled! *(Sings:)*

Getting to know chop suey…

OZZIE: SHUT UP! Hazel, our Bicentennial Minute please.

HAZEL: When in the course of human events it becomes necessary for one Thomas Jefferson to dissolve the political bands Glenn Miller, Benny Goodman and to assume the powers based on the theory of natural rights, ours not theirs; then it comes to pass that we hold these truths to be self-evident—that all men are created evil, that they are endowed by their Creator with certain unavoidable blights, that among these are the cities, the politicians, the Nixon years, the Johnson years, Mr. Wipple commercials, plague, pestilence, famine…

OZZIE: *(Cutting her off.)* Thank you, Hazel. You may serve breakfast now. Davey, are you ready to apologize yet?

DAVID: I must set myself on fire.

OZZIE: I see. Good morning, Et dear. How are you doing in school now?

ET: Swell, Mom, ever since Uncle Larry started helping me with my homework.

And for Social Studies Uncle Larry helped me write my Bicentennial pageant which is all about what makes our country…

OZZIE: That's nice, dear. Good morning, Maureen. How are you?

LIAT: *(Sing-song.)* Whenever I feel afraid I hold my head erect…

OZZIE: What a good idea, I'm so glad.

LIAT: *(Sings.)*

And then I cheerfully whistle…

(Whistles.)

OZZIE: Hazel, have we already had our Bicentennial Minute?

HAZEL: Yes, sir, Mrs. B.

OZZIE: Fine. Thank you. And what a lovely breakfast. *(Ozzie suddenly grabs the tablecloth and pulls it and all the dishes to the floor. She stands, screaming.)* It's a mess, it's a mess. I'm the worst housekeeper on the Eastern seaboard, we're going to have to sell the house and move back to Anaheim. I want to die, I want to die!

LARRY: *(Shakes her violently.)* Stop it, stop it. This is no way to start the morning.

OZZIE: I don't know what time it is. It's dark out.

LARRY: It doesn't matter that it's dark out. You're American and it's the Fourth of July. Aren't you proud?

OZZIE: I don't know what I'm doing!

ET: Let's set off our fireworks, Uncle Larry. That'll cheer her up.

LARRY: That's a good idea, Et. But she needs more than cheering up. She needs reminding.

OZZIE: *(Terrified.)* Reminding of what?

LARRY: Of why you're an American.

OZZIE: I was born here.

LARRY: It's more than that, Ozzie Ann. Et, give me your homework. *(Takes notebook.)* Ozzie Ann, your son Et wrote this for his 11th grade Social Studies class, but we're going to perform it right here in the living room among the barbed wire and the ruined breakfast, because we've got to learn again why we're proud to be Americans.

ET: Gee, Uncle Larry, are we gonna perform my pageant right here?

LARRY: We sure are, Ettie. Okay, everybody, TEN-HUT!

(Everyone stands at attention but David, Larry moves them toward the couch.)

LARRY: HUT, TWO, THREE, FOU', FIVE, HUT, TWO, THREE, FOU', FIVE. At ease. Now, siddown. Okay, Et, you begin.

ET: *(Stands, reads from his notebook.)* "A American Tragedy," by Et Bartholomew, written on the eve of this country's Two-hundredth Bicentennial celebration for Social Studies B, Miss Willis, teacher, Piscataway Senior High, Piscataway, New Jersey. Scene One. Enter the First President.

LARRY: That's you, Ettie.

ET: Thanks, Uncle Larry. "I am George Washington. I am the first President of the United States and I have wooden teeth."

HAZEL: Does this get any better?

LARRY: Pipe down, Hazel.

ET: "And I threw a silver dollar across the Delaware." *(Takes out dollar bill, throws it, it falls limply.)* "And I cannot tell a lie. I represent the spirit of '76 because I am the First President, and also because I am a young person— that is, I, Et, am—and America's hope is in its youth." Enter a famous colored person.

LARRY: That's Hazel.

(Hazel shows mock surprise and pleasure.)

HAZEL: *(Reads.)* "I am George Washington Carver, and I invented the peanut. I represent the Melting Pot of America because even though I was born in Africa, I have been accepted in America because everyone eats peanuts."

ET: And now for comic relief, enter an intellectual from Princeton, which is in New Jersey.

LARRY: Let's let Angel Boobs do this.

LIAT: *(Is handed script, looks confused, reads.)* "I am Woodrow Wilson, and these are my fourteen points. Point Number One. Point Number Two. Point Number Three. Point Number Four. Point Number Five. Poi..."

LARRY: *(Taking script.)* "And tell me, Mr. Wilson, what do we get if we follow your fourteen points?"

LIAT: *(Reads.)* "One helluva piece!"

ET: Uncle Larry made that line up. You've got a great sense of humor, Uncle Larry.

LARRY: Now enter Teddy Roosevelt. I'll be him. "I am Teddy Roosevelt, the Bully President, and I've got gumption. As a youth, my ill-health necessitated tutors and withheld me from the rough-and-tumble companionship of boys my own age; but deliberately and with great persistence, I built up my frail body til I could give any motherfuckin' sonovabitch who needed it one helluva lickin'. I represent the spirit of '76 cause I got balls!"

OZZIE: Say testicles, Larry. Or gonads even.

LARRY: Enter the First Lady through history. That's you, Ozzie Ann.

OZZIE: *(Sighs, takes notebook, emotionally she's had it.)* "I am the First Lady through history. I am Martha Washington, I had to scrub those wooden teeth. I am Mary Todd Lincoln, my mental health is tenuous. I am Dolly

Madison, I invented ice cream. I am Eleanor Roosevelt, I have Red sympathies. I am Jacqueline Kennedy Onassis, I survived a tragedy and married a wealthy Greek for extravagant financial security. I am Ladybird Johnson, I beautified America. I am Pat Nixon, I drink secretly. I am the woman behind the man; I am the spirit behind the brawn; I am the Statue of Liberty. Bring me your tired and your poor, and I will give them self-respect, freedom, and a clerk-typist position for the women and a laborer position for the men. I will not give the tired and poor welfare, though, because a country on welfare isn't *well* and a country on welfare isn't *fair* to those who work. And now let us sing our National Anthem.

LARRY: Give her a note, Hazel.

(*Hazel gives an incredibly high note.*)

OZZIE: (*Starts on that very high note.*)

O say can you see,
By the dawn's early light, What so proudly we hail,
At the twilight's last gleaming; And the Rocket's red glare…
…It's too high, I can't finish it. It's exhausting.

LARRY: Finish it!

OZZIE: (*Breaks into uncontrollable hysterics.*) It's too high, I can't sing it, I can't sing it. It's too high, I can't… (*Weeps.*)

(*Hazel holds her.*)

LARRY: Finish it.

OZZIE: I can't, I can't.

ET: Uncle Larry, can I set up the fireworks outside now?

LARRY: Okay, go ahead.

(*Et runs out.*)

LARRY: Ya shoulda finished it. Finish it!

OZZIE: Hazel, hold me, hold me…

DAVID: Mama San, free my foot. I must set myself on fire.

LARRY: Okay, buddy, I got it. (*Larry opens up bear trap.*)

(*Everyone watches David. David limps to cabinet, gets can of gasoline, pours it on himself. There's a lot of gas in the container, it takes a long time to pour out. He finishes.*)

DAVID: Does anyone have a match?

(*Enter Et.*)

ET: I lit off the fuse. They should go off in about a minute.

DAVID: Et, could I have your matches?

ET: Sure, Davey. (*Gives them to him.*)

(David is about to strike the match when:)

OZZIE: NO! *(Pleading, sad.)* No. Not on the rug, Davey. I'm going to have to clean up the breakfast mess as it is.

DAVID: Very well.

(Exits.)

OZZIE: I remember when they used to do this on the news all the time, but I never imagined my own Davey would…

(Sound of fireworks, bangs, lights, etc.)

ET: Look, the fireworks have started!

(Et and Larry look out window.)

ET: Gee, they're so beautiful. Red and blue and purple.

(A flash of orange.)

ET: Oh, and look, there's Davey, all orange. Gee, Uncle Larry, it looks terrific. Red and blue and orange and purple. And red and blue and orange and purple…

HAZEL: *(Rocking Ozzie.)* Oh, oh, oh, six o'clock and the master not home yet. Pray God…

OZZIE: No more, Hazel. No more. *(Goes to kitchen table, sits down; begins to pour corn flakes slowly all over table.)*

ET: Red and blue and orange and purple…red and blue…

OZZIE: It's a mess, it's a mess. It's a mess, it's a mess. *(Plays with the corn flakes.)*

END OF PLAY

A History of the American Film

A MUSICAL

Book & Lyrics by Christopher Durang
Music by Mel Marvin

INTRODUCTION

I was inspired to write this play after seeing the 1933 Frank Borzage film *A Man's Castle*, a beautiful, one-of-a-kind depression romance starring Spencer Tracy and Loretta Young.

The film is set mostly in a hobo's shantytown, where Tracy lives; and pre-Production Code—before there were rules that proscribed how morality was presented in movies, and insisted that all "evil" was punished, and all adulterers committed suicide or were run over by cars—Spencer's character lived "in sin" with the beautiful, penniless Loretta Young.

I like actors who do the play to try to see this movie (it's obscure, but it shows up on cable; I originally saw it at the Yale Film Society) because it helps communicate the kind of innocence I want the character of Loretta to have in my play.

Loretta Young gives a truly luminous performance in the film, as a woman totally in love with this man who doesn't want to be tied down. But it's a truly modern, realistic performance—it has no silent screen posing, or archaic film acting. Young's character seems totally open, good, vulnerable; and that's the kind of "good girl" I ended up wanting to refer to in my character called Loretta.

(When people don't see the film, they sometimes play Loretta as a self-consciously mock innocent Mary Pickford—okay, but I like something warmer, and simpler, as in the real Loretta Young performance.)

Spencer's character is a charming tough guy, innately worldly, who knows how to get in and out of scrapes.

I realized watching the film that these two 1933 characters seemed to represent a very positive view Americans had about themselves as both innately good and innately resilient in the face of adversity.

Spence is stuck in the Depression with few options, but he seems to have total confidence that he'll find ways to survive by being smart and cagey and making do; but he's also gallant about taking the more helpless Loretta under his wing. And Loretta seemed good and loyal and willing to expect little from life; when Spence somehow manages to buy her a stove for their shantytown shack, she breaks down and weeps.

I was very charmed by the film, and by the intensity of the romance between the two characters.

And looking at the film made me have thoughts about how America's sense of itself, as reflected in the movies, seemed to have changed a lot since the 30s and 40s.

I lived my college years during the torturous Vietnam era; I went to movies obsessively, both old and new; and the frequent belief in American goodness and optimism that was rather casually in films of the 30s and 40s seemed to change radically in the movies of the 60s.

Using the movies as a prism of national consciousness, Americans seemed to be entertaining the idea that maybe we weren't always on the right side or making the right decision. We were clearly on the right side (and fought gallantly) in World War II; but we also dropped the bomb; maybe we had become insane, like the characters in 1963's *Dr. Strangelove.*

Or if we weren't insane, maybe we just didn't know what we were doing, we were innately innocent and meant well (we said we were helping people in Vietnam) but were extremely disconnected from the results of our actions. Even though 1967s *Bonnie and Clyde* wasn't about Vietnam, its main characters seemed innocent (they didn't mean any harm), and yet they caused death and destruction for themselves and others.

Or then, more on the nose, there was 1967's megahit *The Graduate,* very funny, but reflecting our sense of a loss of purpose or belief in where we were going. In the 50s, we had all that stultifying "keep up with the Joneses" mentality; in *The Graduate* that seemed to break down, as reflected in the memorable moment when recent grad Dustin Hoffman, lolling about in the pool with no career plans or aspirations, is asked by his father what the purpose of his going to college had been. "Ya got me," Hoffman says, and the college movie audiences in the 60s would cheer at that moment.

Well, I guess I didn't have quite such organized thoughts when I saw *A Man's Castle,* but I did feel that the 1933 film seemed to reflect a belief in American goodness and future that we were no longer feeling. And that's why I was drawn to writing the play.

(The other reason for writing the play, though, was a simpler one: I loved movies, and knew a lot about them; and parodying them seemed a fun way of celebrating and remembering them.)

The first draft of my play started out set in the mythical Shanty Town I had seen in *A Man's Castle;* this draft was, though, stylistically more surreal, in the style of my early one acts, than the play eventually was to be.

I thought it would all take place in Shanty Town, but early in my writing, I stumbled on the idea that Loretta, separated from Spence, wandered about and ended up in Hollywood, making a Busby Berkeley musical. (Berkeley's loony "We're in the Money" number from *Gold Diggers of* 1933, with women dressed as coins and with Ginger Rogers singing the lyrics in pig Latin, was as much an innocent pop culture image of the Depression as *A Man's Castle* was).

Once I thought of Loretta moving from a "depression romance" to a "Busby Berkeley" musical, the idea for my play crystallized—I realized I wanted the characters to stay the same (as archetypes), but to move through different movie genres—from Shantytown romance to gangster film to screwball comedy to World War II drama, etc.—while American history sort of wafted by in the background.

And I knew that the result of moving through movie history this way would ultimately give us a feeling of loss—of lost innocence, of lost optimism, of lost sense of purpose.

I called the characters Loretta and Spence, but early in my first draft, Spence got mad at Loretta and pushed a grapefruit in her face—an indelible moment from the 1931 *Public Enemy* with Jimmy Cagney.

And I realized that, as much as I loved Spencer Tracy's performance in the Borzage film, in terms of film history, and public perception, it was Jimmy Cagney who represented the tough guy, the bad boy, the gangster...Tracy's acting persona evolved rather quickly into the good priest (which he played several times, notably in *Boys Town* and the earthquake extravaganza, *San Francisco*), then later into the stolid "tamer" of Katherine Hepburn, then finally into the wise, good father. So the "gestalt" of his career didn't conjure up the tough guy image that I wanted; so I renamed the character Jimmy.

For the tough girl, it was easy to choose Bette, thinking of all those tough girls that Bette Davis played in the 30s (as well as those played by Barbara Stanwyck and Joan Crawford: tough, wised-up broads, very unlike the sweet-souled Loretta figure). And for the sweet, good guy, it was easy to think of Henry (Hank) Fonda, his face permeated with decency and goodness as he stares into the distance talking about "Preacher Casey" in *The Grapes of Wrath*.

When I showed an early draft to Robert Brustein to consider for Yale Rep, his main note was that I should "play the movie game" more exactly, keeping things in the right period; and also, he thought, I should choose to refer to more famous movies.

So I rewrote the play several times, taking his note about keeping film references more accurate. (For instance, in an early draft Loretta went to prison in the 30s, but the aura of the scenes was 1950s women's prison sadism, very over the top; funny, but not really belonging in the 30s; so I threw those scenes out.) And I brought in really famous films, like *Citizen Kane* and *Casablanca*, that I did not originally include.

I wrote the play in 1974–75, but wasn't getting any productions for it. (People kept saying, how can you produce it, it's too big, though I never thought it was a problem.)

In 1976 I submitted a fourth or fifth draft to the Eugene O'Neill National Playwrights Conference, and was accepted.

The O'Neill is a wonderful place, and each summer it accepts about twelve playwrights; and over a four week period, each play receives a rehearsed, staged reading with first rate actors. It was (and is) a very prestigious place. I had tried to get accepted four times previously (with other plays) before finally getting in with this play.

This summer event was fantastic for me; and once again, in terms of best case scenario, I kind of "won the lottery" with it.

Regional theatres had started attending the O'Neill, looking for new plays to do; you weren't supposed to focus on that aspect of it, you were to do your work and your rewrites; but nonetheless for a starting writer, it was hard not to hope you would get a theatre to be interested in a production of your play.

My play was the final play of the conference, and went really well. And I got three offers from three major regional theatres to do the play.

At first, I was asked to choose only one of the three because each wanted the "premiere." My new agent, Helen Merrill, went to bat for me and convinced the three theatres to have a "triple premiere," pointing out that they could reap publicity from this; and also pitching that I needed the money.

And indeed I did. I went to the O'Neill with about $100 in the bank and that was it. But suddenly I had these three pending productions; and Lloyd Richards, who ran (and runs) the O'Neill, very kindly nominated me for a Rockefeller grant, which I won. So I was very lucky in my early playwriting years.

In 1977 I had back-to-back productions of the play at the Hartford Stage Company in Hartford, Conn., the Mark Taper Forum in Los Angeles, and the Arena Stage in Washington, D.C.

I got a lot of publicity as an "up and coming writer"; *People* Magazine printed a photo of me looking like a wary sixteen year old, and quoted me as saying I didn't believe there were any solutions to the problems of our lives. (At the time I guess I didn't; but in a short article, the comment really stood out.)

I'm not going to tell the production history of the play in a long form, but here are some miscellaneous memories of the productions:

At the O'Neill, the cast was magical—Jerry Zaks, Cynthia Herman, Gale Garnett and Richard Backus were wonderful as the leads; Cara Duff

McCormick and Gary Bayer were funny and poignant as Clara and Mickey; Bryan Clarke stopped the show with his Victor Henreid routine; the fabulous Dianne Wiest, whom I had only seen play poetic drama, showed her amazing comic ability as wisecracking Eve; the late Jo Henderson was so good as the screwball mother and then as the lovely, lovely Blessed Mother; the late Robert Christian (now lost to AIDS) so, so funny as Viola.

The Hartford production partially disappointed me—I was in disagreement with the director, who insisted on going to blackout between the play's many, many scenes. (He was afraid if you saw an actor moving a chair, you wouldn't know if it was the actor or the character. This kind of thing just doesn't worry me…while letting the audience sit in the dark between scenes in a play with fifty scenes does.)

However, the good part was that Jerry Zaks and Cynthia Herman repeated their wonderful Jimmy and Loretta; Jerry had not started directing yet, and was an excellent actor, his small wiry body and urban rhythm a perfect match for Jimmy; and Cynthia was a different image of Loretta—she was like a tomboyish Doris Day, all crinkly smile and sincerity—but she was truly funny, and a good physical comedienne as well. The other actors were also good, especially Jeff Brooks as Mickey, fresh from my play *Titanic*.

The Mark Taper Forum production, directed by the late Peter Mark Schifter (also lost to AIDS), was probably the funniest production, and also the best sung. The talented leads were Udana Power, Robert Walden, June Gable, Rick Lenz; also terrific were Lu Leonard, Barry Dennen, Frank O'Brien, Gordon Connell, James Gleason, and Roger Robinson as Piano Man; but the supporting players also included three fabulous performers with impressive Broadway musical credits—Alice Playten *(Henry, Sweet, Henry; Gypsy)*, Teri Ralson *(Company; A Little Night Music)*, Jane Connell (the original Agnes Gooch in *Mame*); and so when the company would sing any of the songs, the audience (and I) went to musical comedy heaven.

The Arena Stage production, directed by David Chambers, was the most over-all successful (I thought), and was certainly a big hit for the theatre. It was the first production that took some of the characters' "pain" for real; as played by April Shawhan and Gary Bayer, there was such ache and longing when Loretta and Jimmy met at the Club Intimate, and when Loretta said she wanted to go back to Shanty Town.

I had been feeling that my work was in danger of being considered only camp; and I liked the serious colors that Chambers brought to the production. And Arena had a wonderful acting company, and they had just done a good, but very serious production of *The Lower Depths;* so part of the fun for the Arena audience was to see the company members (Richard Bauer, Leslie Cass, Stanley Anderson, Halo Wines, Howard Witt) doing really, really silly things.

The reviews for the three regional productions were all good; and Arena's reviews were probably the best (including a rave from Mel Gussow in the *Times*).

It seemed ear-marked to be a Broadway success. And I also felt that it was the first play I had written that was likely to be accepted by a broad audience; so many of my other plays alienated and frightened some of the audience. (*Titanic,* for instance, got a nice notice from Gussow, but got hideous reviews from the other critics. Indeed the *Daily News* review began "Horrors!"; and the *New York Post,* in the mean persona of Martin Gottfried, wondered how I was ever awarded an M.F.A.)

But *Film* felt friendly and sweet (even though it turns darker as it goes on). And I was now approached by two Broadway producers. One wanted to mount a totally new production, with new director, a name composer, some name stars. And the other producer (well, a team, Judy Gordon and Richard Bright) wanted, more or less, to bring in the Arena production.

I had enjoyed working on the three productions (four, if you count the O'Neill); but I felt a little worn out by the idea of doing yet another one from scratch. And I left out that each of the three theatres had insisted I use a different composer—so there were three different scores, which was very schizoid for me, and made for some bad feeling among the composers.

So I decided to go with bringing in the Arena production. I thought it was really good, and I didn't see the point of throwing it out and starting over from scratch.

But here the "winning the lottery" luck kind of broke down, alas.

The Broadway version was good, I still run into people who remember it fondly; but nonetheless it wasn't as good as it was at Arena.

Transferring a production that worked in one theatre (Arena's 500 seat Kreeger Theatre) to another, bigger theatre (the Broadway ANTA Theatre, about 1300 seats; it's now called the Virginia)—well, this was something that the director and I had little experience with.

So among the mistakes we made were: The theatre was too big for the play (and the production's somewhat subtle comic style); the set, not rebuilt but brought in from Arena in order to save money, looked different on the bigger stage. A big mistake: Due to union rules requiring we pay many musicians, we moved from having a simple piano at Arena to having about twenty-five pit musicians—and this disastrously changed audience responses. Indeed, in all three regional productions, whenever Jimmy first started to sing "Shanty Town Romance," there was always a gentle laugh at the cliché of it all; on Broadway there was no laugh—the orchestra sound made it seem like it was just the first song in a conventional musical. So a wrong tone was set.

We were an almost-success; the reviews weren't horrible, they were just a bit tepid; and we were also overwhelmed by opening near to Bob Fosse's *Dancin',* which became the hot ticket. And the title of my play, of course, sounded like a dissertation…well, anyway, we had about two weeks of previews and two weeks of run; and then we closed.

I had made some money from the regional productions; but I hadn't yet realized that because royalties do not have taxes taken out of them, you have to plan ahead to pay your taxes. I didn't plan ahead, so all of a sudden that safety net I thought I had was gone to pay taxes, and I had very, very little money left…enough for a few months rent, just about.

Well, so that's how that ended up.

But you're about to read the play, and it's fun, I think; and so were the actors in the Broadway cast, whom I wish to remember fondly—repeating their roles from Arena were April Shawhan, Gary Bayer, Joan Pape, David Garrison, Eric Weitz, and the marvelous Swoosie Kurtz as Bette; repeating from Hartford was Jeff Brooks as Mickey; repeating from the O'Neill was Bryan Clark as Victor; and new to the play were Brent Spiner, Maureen Anderman, Walter Bobbie, David Cromwell, Mary Catherine Wright, and my two *Vietnamization* buddies, Kate McGregor-Stewart and Ben Halley, Jr.

By the way, this printing of the play is the first one that is "updated" to the present. The original play ended with film references up to the mid 70s about.

I kept wondering how to update it, and then decided it could be quite simple. At the end of the play, the characters start to change identities quickly…I just added several more recent "identities," and I'm pretty sure the effect is that we've traversed twenty years, even though it's only been a couple of pages. (The rewrite affects only the last several pages.)

I wrote this update for a production that the Juilliard School Drama Division did in the fall of 1995, directed by Michael Mayer.

I thought it was an excellent production; and I think the acting class that did it are going to go on to have notable careers, so I'd like to give their names too: Claire Lautier was Loretta, Sean Arbuckle was Jimmy, Kate Jennings Grant was Bette, Bill Gross was Hank, Maya Thomas was Eve; the other parts were played by Opal Alladin, Ryan Artzberger, Christian Camargo, Matthew Daniels, Danyon Davis, Julia Ditelberg, Juan Hernandez, T.J. Kenneally, Kristen Thomas, and Michael Tisdale.

So I like this play. I hope it comes back sometime.

CHARACTERS

The Stars:

LORETTA

JIMMY

BETTE

HANK

EVE

The Contract Players:

(a group of eight to ten actors who play the following roles with much doubling:)

THE MOTHER	INDIAN
POLICEMAN	MICKEY
GOD	FRITZ VON LEFFING
JESUS	SALAD GIRLS
BLESSED MOTHER	SALAD CHEF
ORPHANAGE LADY	SALAD BOYS
MINSTREL SINGER	DOLORES DEL REEGO
TICKET MAN	HARKNESS
NEWSBOY	PIANO MAN
MA O'REILLY	ITO
MICHAEL O'REILLY	OPERA PEASANTS
BARTENDER	UNCLE SAM
SPEAKEASY PIANO PLAYER	SOLDIERS
FERRUCHI	WWII WOMEN
FERRUCHI'S HENCHMEN	SAILOR IN CANTEEN
JUDGE	TELEGRAM BOY
REPORTER NO. 1	WOMAN MOVIE PATRON
REPORTER NO. 2	VICTOR HENREID
NURSE	ANDREW SISTER
VIOLA	SOLDIERS COMING HOME
CLARA MORTIMER	ROBOT
EDWARD MORTIMER	ALCOHOLIC NO. 1
ALLISON MORTIMER	ALCOHOLIC NO. 2

ABDHUL	ALCOHOLIC NO. 3
MA JOAD	OSCAR VOICE
PA JOAD	OSCAR USHERS
GRANDMA JOAD	PRISON MATRON
PRISON WARDEN	VOICE OF GOD
CAROLERS	STUART
SANTA CLAUS	THEATRE MANAGER

The use of "contract players" who double is meant to reflect the recurrence of certain character actor types in movie after movie (Spring Byington was everyone's mother, Edna May Oliver was everyone's aunt, Hattie MacDaniels was everyone's maid). On Broadway there were ten actors playing all these roles; in the regional theatres there were eight. Note: I intend one black actor to play *all* the minority roles: Viola, Indian, Piano man, Ito, Robot, and Stuart.

ORIGINAL PRODUCTION

A History of the American Film was given its first New York production, under the direction of David Chambers, at the ANTA Theatre, New York City, March 30, 1978. It was produced by Richard S. Bright and Judith Gordon. Scenery was by Tony Straiges, Lighting by William Mintzer, Costumes by Marjorie Slaiman and Musical Staging by Graciela Daniele.

LORETTA . . . . April Shawhan
JIMMY . . . . Gary Bayer
BETTE . . . . Swoosie Kurtz
HANK . . . . Brent Spiner
EVE . . . . Joan Pape

The Contract Players:
BLESSED MOTHER, MA JOAD, etc.. . . . . Maureen Anderman
MICHAEL O'REILLY, SALAD CHEF, etc. . . . . Walter Bobbie
MICKEY, NEWSBOY, etc. . . . . Jeff Brooks
VICTOR HENREID, EDWARD, etc.. . . . . Bryan Clark
ABDHUL, PA JOAD, etc. David Cromwell
MINSTREL, SAILOR, etc.. David Garrison
VIOLA, PIANO MAN, ITO, etc.. . . . . Ben Halley, Jr.
ALLISON, MA O'REILLY, etc. . . . . Kate McGregor-Stewart
GOD, TELEGRAM BOY, etc.. Eric Weitz
CLARA, MOTHER, etc. . . . . Mary Catherine Wright

Prior to the New York production, the play was first performed at the Eugene O'Neill National Playwrights Conference in Waterford, Connecticut; and then, as a joint premiere, in three separate productions at the Hartford Stage Co., the Mark Taper Forum in Los Angeles, and the Arena Stage in Washington, D.C.

MUSICAL NUMBERS
ACT I
Pre-Show

"The Silent Years"	Piano
"Minstrel Song"	Minstrel
"Shanty Town Romance"	Jimmy, Loretta
"They Can't Prohibit Love"	Bette
"O Come, All Ye Faithful"	Prison Warden, Santa Claus, Carolers
"We're In A Salad"	Hank, Loretta, Eve, Salad Girls, Chef, Salad Boys
"Euphemism For Sale"	Loretta
"Ostende Nobis," Tosca	Hank, Bette, Opera Peasants
"Off-To-War"	Eve, Company

ACT II

"Pin-up"	Eve, Loretta, Bette, Clara
"Apple Blossom Victory"	Bette, Eve, Andrew Sister
"Search For Wisdom"	Jimmy, Loretta, Company

This acting version of *A History of the American Film* is based on the Broadway production, which in turn was based on the Arena Stage production. These two productions chose to produce the play elaborately; and, particularly in the Arena Stage's five-hundred-seat Kreeger Theatre, this giddy attempt at opulence was, in an unspoken way, evocative and satiric of America's grandiose self-image, as reflected in American movies.

This version reflects those production choices, in terms of noting flypieces for certain scenes, rolling platforms for others, electric flags, etc. But I do want to stress to anyone considering putting on this play that it is possible to simplify greatly many of the production ideas noted in the script; and that to choose to do the play simply can be another, equally valid artistic choice. For instance, although I have greatly enjoyed the various excesses of the "We're in a

Salad" number (which I've seen in three different productions), the crazily simple device of having girls merely wave pieces of celery in rhythm (at a staged reading at the Eugene O'Neill National Playwrights Conference) seems as viable, and as funny, a way to approach the play as any.

THE SETTING

In the productions designed by Tony Straiges (Arena Stage and Broadway), the play is set in a large, nonrealistic movie palace. This movie palace has an upstage balcony, behind which is a movie projection booth (which later explodes); it has two small side balconies, right and left, which represent at various times an opera box, Hoboken, and heaven. On the stage floor are ten to fifteen movie theatre seats (on rollers, for fast movement on or off) which, spaced irregularly and with members of the cast seated in them, suggest a movie audience. For the non-movie house sections of the play, these seats are removed, or else stand in for regular furniture (chairs in the gangster or screwball comedy sections, for instance).

In the scenes which take place specifically in the movie house, the actors stare out ahead of them, as if the film they are watching is just over the live audience's heads.

Act I is performed in black and white—that is, the costumes and props are black, grey, and white only. (Face, hair, lip color should be left normal.) The movie palace set should be painted grey and silver so as not to contradict this.

The play turns to color at the end of Act I, as specified in the script.

THE PRE-SHOW

At Arena Stage and on Broadway, the director David Chambers came up with the idea of the "pre-show" sing-along. As the audience entered the theatre, members of the cast entered the movie theatre on the stage, sitting in their movie seats, fidgeting, looking around them, etc., waiting for the "film" to begin. While waiting, the two audiences (real and onstage) had a pre-show, follow-the-bouncing-ball sing-along. A screen (upstage, behind the actors' heads; the actors pretended to see it in front of them) was lowered, and popular songs of the 20s were projected onto it. The songs chosen (from the public domain) were "My Darling Clementine," "Beautiful Dreamer," and "On the Sidewalks of New York." Many other choices, of course, are possible. Between the songs, the pianist played "specialty numbers," such as "Humoresque"; an original piano specialty number, "Jumpin' Jehosophat," is included in the score.

It's important that the pre-show begin almost as soon as the house is opened, so that the entering audience doesn't think that the play has begun early and that it must be hushed and attentive. If the audience doesn't catch on that it can talk and read the programs and generally move about, then the pre-show will backfire.

This pre-show, very successful at Arena in particular, should be considered optional. At the end of the pre-show, the play proper begins.

A History of the American Film

ACT I

Scene 1

A beam of light shines from the projection booth, and we hear the sound of a projector. Silent movie piano music begins ("The Silent Years").

Spot on the Mother, D.R., rocking a large cradle. She is dressed in old-fashioned, Lillian Gish-like clothes. A screen is lowered U. C., onto which the silent movie titles are projected. (Characters freeze during titles.)

Title: *Out of the cradle, endlessly rocking...*

(The mother continues rocking the cradle. After a moment, she frowns, takes the baby from the cradle, walks to L. and places it on a "doorstep." [Doorstep is another area of the stage which lights up as she gets there.] The mother hesitates, then resolutely leaves the baby there, returning to her chair by the cradle.)

Title: *The Selfish Mother gets into the cradle herself.*

(The Mother does this. Lights dim on her rocking.)

(A Policeman, who perhaps has a Charlie Chaplin-like gait, comes by the "doorstep" L. and sees the baby. He does a large take and speaks soundlessly.)

Title: *"A foundling!"*

(He picks up the baby, exits. Lights fade on whole stage.)

(Complete dark.)

Title: *Time passes.*

(Lights up on The Mother still in the cradle. She coughs silently, very ill. She prays.)

Title: *Near death, the mother prays to God to forgive her for deserting her child.*

(Lights up in heaven [L. balcony]. God [with white beard], Jesus and the Blessed Mother talk silently together. The Blessed Mother points down toward The Mother. God says something, we don't know what, and they all look down at The Mother.)

Title: *God refuses to forgive her.*

(The Mother is crushed by their refusal, weeps.)

Title: *The Mother dies.*

    (The Mother dies. Lights fade on her area.)

    (Up in heaven. The Blessed Mother talks with God and Jesus, makes motions of rocking baby in her arms.)

Title: *"But what has happened to the baby? Can we help it?"*

    (God looks stern and speaks to the Blessed Mother.)

Title: *"It is not up to Us to help those on earth. We can only watch."*

    (All three look down to earth to watch.)

    (The music turns sweet and romantic. Enter Loretta, young and innocent, very lovely in a white dress. She gives the audience the look of a startled fawn, D.C.)

Title: *The Baby grows up to be a lovely girl in the orphanage.*

    (Enter the Orphanage Lady, who hands Loretta a small suitcase, speaks soundlessly, and points away.)

Title: *Loretta is told she is too tall to remain in the Home but must make her own way now.*

    (Loretta hesitates, worries, takes the suitcase. The Orphanage Lady hands her a coin, speaks soundlessly.)

Title: *"Here is a nickel. Spend it wisely."*

    (Loretta smiles, takes it. The Orphanage Lady waves and exits U.C. [Walking backwards.] Loretta wanders L., unsure where to go next.)

    (Honky-tonk music begins. A Minstrel Singer in blackface is lit, D.R., singing silently. Loretta looks interested. A Ticket Man appears and bars her from coming too close, putting his hand out for money. She gives him her nickel.)

Title: *Loretta reluctantly pays the nickel to see the talking picture.*

    (Loretta sits in a movie seat to watch the Minstrel Singer. He finishes what he's been singing and is ready to sing a new one. A musical introduction to the Minstrel Singer's song is heard over the sound system. The Minstrel Singer's voice is on the "sound track" and the actor playing the Minstrel Singer mimes the song, noticeably out of synch. Toward the end of the song, the actor's real voice can be heard as the sound track voice fades out. Thus the recorded voice fades into the live voice.)

MINSTREL: *(Miming sound track.)*

The sun shines south,

The sun shines north,

And Laz'rus, he's a-comin' forth

But I'm alone,

With my song,

And I guess I better move along…

(Actor starts to sing with live voice as sound track fades out. Now in synch.)

Well, well,—I'm goin' back to my dear old Alabammy,

And sleep in the bosom of my mammy,

Mammy, cradle me and hold me,

Mammy, the massuh's gone and sold me,

Mammy, I'm sick a pickin' cotton,

Mammy, I know you ain't forgotten,

So I'm comin' back,

To that old shack,

To see my ma-a-amy!

(Loretta cries.)

Title: *Loretta's heart is wrenched apart by the word "Mammy."*

(Lights fade to an "iris" spot on Loretta.)

ACT I

Scene 2

Loretta in a tight spotlight, walking about. Sounds of a city (car horns, etc.) are played on the sound system, perhaps on a very scratchy tape. (During Loretta's spotlit movement a major scene change occurs: The movie audience exits with their movie seats; and actors or stage hands set up a park bench stage L., a table and two chairs stage R.)

Lights come up C. and L. Loretta bumps into a Policeman (the same one as in the silent section.)

POLICEMAN: Whaddya doin' there, young lady?

LORETTA: Nothing, officer.

POLICEMAN: Well, a nice girl oughtn't to be about on the streets at this hour. Shanty Town's not a safe place for a nice girl.

LORETTA: Yes, officer.

POLICEMAN: *(Kindly.)* Run along home now, Missy.

(She nods. He exits L.)

LORETTA: Yes, officer. Oh, look, a kitty. Hello, kitty, hello. Oh, it's someone's hair. Oh. *(A bit alarmed.)* Officer! Oh dear, oh dear. Nowhere to go, just like that little kitty. That's right, it wasn't a kitty. *(Shudders.)* Maybe if I sleep, things will be better. *(Sits on park bench, L., to sleep.)*

(Enter a Newsboy with a cap on his head, holding newspapers, from R.)

NEWSBOY: Extra, extra, read all about it. Unemployment Reaches New Low

Point. Hoover Appoints Commission to Study. Extra, extra, read all about it. St. Valentine's Massacre Marks Peak of Gangster Wars. Extra, extra, Garbo talks in Metro Movie. Says "Gif Me A Whiskey, Ginger Ale on the Side, and Don't Be Stingy, Baby." Extra, extra, Actor John Gilbert Unable to Make Transition to Talkies. Hoover Appoints Commission to Study. *(To Loretta.)* Paper, Miss?

LORETTA: Oh...I don't have any money.

NEWSBOY: Here ya go, Miss. *(Gives her one.)*

LORETTA: Oh, thank you.

NEWSBOY: *(Going off L.)* Extra, extra, read all about it. Unemployment Reaches New Low Point. Hoover Appoints Commission to Study...

LORETTA: *(Reading to herself at same time Newsboy says it.)* Unemployment Reaches New Low Point. Hoover Appoints Commission to Study. *(Yawns.)*

NEWSBOY: *(From Offstage, his voice gets sleepy, as if heard through Loretta's sleepiness.)* Extra, extra, read all about it....

(Loretta falls asleep. Lights get dimmer.)

(As Loretta sleeps, Jimmy, a young and energetic tough, sits next to her on the bench, pulls his cap over his face, and goes to sleep. After a beat, we hear the sound of birds chirping. Lights up brighter again, it's morning. Jimmy mumbles in his sleep a bit, then suddenly jerks awake and fires his gun. Loretta screams awake.)

JIMMY: Take that, you dirty copper! *(Looks about, sees he's been dreaming.)*

(Loretta looks at him aghast.)

JIMMY: Whatsa matter, I wake you? *(Pause.)* Say, you're a pretty scrawny looking lamb chop, ain't ya?

LORETTA: *(Feeling very faint from hunger and fear.)* I feel...

JIMMY: I bet you could *use* a lamb chop, couldn't ya? Ya hungry?

LORETTA: *(Mumbles.)* I...need...

JIMMY: Hey, Sadie, speak up.

(He pokes her; she whimpers; he listens closely to her.)

LORETTA: *(Softly.)* Get me...

JIMMY: Yeah, get me. Get me what?

LORETTA: ...Get me...to...

JIMMY: Get me two. Two what? Two lamb chops?

LORETTA: ...get me...to...the hospital...

JIMMY: Hospital? Whatsa matter?

LORETTA: Can you help me?

JIMMY: I'm American, ain't I? *(Jimmy helps Loretta off the bench.)*

ACT I

Scene 3

(Lights fade on this area, fade up on another area, R., representing Jimmy's shack in Shanty Town. Music plays on the sound track while he moves her. They arrive at the shack, represented by a table and two chairs. On Broadway a flat was flown in, U.R., representing a drab wall of Jimmy's shack, with a window and a nearly bare shelf.)

JIMMY: Well, here we are. It ain't much, but I call it home. *(Sits her down.)* Hey, sourpuss, how d'ya like it?

LORETTA: It's very nice.

JIMMY: Call me Jimmy, why don'tcha?

LORETTA: OK, Jimmy.

JIMMY: That's the ticket.

(Mock punches her jaw; she starts to faint.)

JIMMY: We gotta get you well.

LORETTA: Thank you.

JIMMY: Where ya from, sourpuss?

LORETTA: I'm from an orphanage.

JIMMY: Oh yeah?

LORETTA: Are you an orphan too?

JIMMY: Nah, I got a Ma, but I spent most of my time in a reform school.

LORETTA: You did?

JIMMY: What's wrong wid that?

LORETTA: *(Scared.)* Nothing. Why were you put in reform school?

JIMMY: For robbin' the poor box at St. Raphael's and settin' Fadder MacNeil on fire.

LORETTA: Jimmy, you didn't.

JIMMY: Sure I did. I sang in the choir, too. Fadder MacNeil was a real dodo anyways. I liked seein' him on fire.

LORETTA: Did he die?

JIMMY: Nah. It's hard to kill priests.

LORETTA: But did reform school change you?

JIMMY: Yeah, I'd never try to burn somebody anymore. I'd shoot 'im.

(There is a sudden clap of thunder and flash of lightning. Loretta screams and inadvertently embraces Jimmy.)

LORETTA: What was that?

JIMMY: Whaddya tink it was?

LORETTA: It sounds like a storm. *(She moves away from him a bit.)*

JIMMY: Whatsa matter? You scared of me?

LORETTA: A little.

JIMMY: Ah, relax, sourpuss. I ain't gonna bite ya.

> *(Sound of the rain coming down, steadily, on the roof. Music introduction of a romantic song begins. Jimmy starts to sing in a soft Bing Crosby style.)*

JIMMY: *(Sings.)*

> Hear the pitter patter on the roof,
> The raindrops sing a pleasant song,
> Pennies fall from heaven up above,
> Inside we're cozy and in love,
> The roof may leak but we don't care,
> We have a future life to share,
> Anyone could tell it at a glance,
> We share a Shanty Town romance.
> It's not the Ritz,
> It's not the Riviera,
> Who wants a villa in Rome,
> When you've got a Shanty Town home…

LORETTA AND JIMMY: *(Together.)*

> Hear the pitter patter on the roof,
> The raindrops say that nothing's wrong,
> Pennies fall from heaven up above,
> Inside, we're sleepy and in love,
> Anyone could tell it at a glance,
> We share a Shanty Town, a Shanty Town,
> A Shanty Town romance.

LORETTA: Oh, Jimmy. When you sing to me like that, I don't mind being poor at all. And I know whatever happens, everythings going to be alright.

> *(Loretta rests in Jimmy's arms; the lights iris in on the two of them, and then out.)*

ACT I

Scene 4

> *Lights on a large, daily calendar. Leaves fall off the calendar, signifying time passing. (On Broadway, God turned the leaves on an oversize calendar in the L. balcony.) Lights off the calendar.*

Lights up on Loretta in the shack, some time later. She is alone, ironing a shirt on the kitchen table and humming to herself.

LORETTA: *(Singing without accompaniment.)*
It's not the Ritz,
It's not the Riviera,
Who wants a...
(Enter Bette, a tough-looking woman in a print dress.)

BETTE: Hey, Jimmy, I'm back... *(Sees Loretta, stares.)*

LORETTA: Oh, hello. I'm ironing.

BETTE: Oh?

LORETTA: Are you a friend of Jimmy's?

BETTE: Yeah. Who are you?

LORETTA: I'm Loretta. Jimmy's letting me stay here until I'm well.

BETTE: Oh yeah? How ya feelin'?

LORETTA: Well, I still feel a little weak.

BETTE: You look weak. Look, sister, I'll give you five minutes to pack your things and get yourself outta here.

LORETTA: But...I'm ironing.

BETTE: I'm very good at ironing. *(Picks up iron.)* How d'ya like your face done, honey—starch or no starch?
(Loretta screams. Enter Jimmy.)

JIMMY: Hey. What's this?

BETTE: Just givin' a couple of pointers on how to do your shirts, Jimmy.

JIMMY: Look, baby, let's get one thing straight—you ain't never done my shirts.

BETTE: But...

JIMMY: We're through, Bette.

BETTE: But...But...

JIMMY: Cut the small talk. *(To Bette.)* Whatcha hear when you wuz in Chicago?

BETTE: Louie the Hook says you don't guarantee his beer in town and he's gonna put on the squeeze.

LORETTA: But beer is prohibited.
(Jimmy and Bette stare at her.)

JIMMY: *(To Bette.)* And Ferruchi's boys?

BETTE: They're standing by Louie. You don't take his beer, your speakeasy don't stay open.

LORETTA: Speakeasy!

BETTE: You should get her a monkey and put her on the stage.

JIMMY: Lay off her, Bette. She don't mean nothin'.

LORETTA: I mean something.

JIMMY: Keep outta this, sourpuss.

BETTE: Sourpuss. That's cute.

JIMMY: Beat it, Bette. I wanna talk to Loretta.

BETTE: *(Hurt.)* Okay, Jimmy. *(To Loretta.)* So long, sourpuss. Hope to see you again real soon—preferably on the obituary page. *(Exits.)*

LORETTA: She took the iron.

JIMMY: Look, bright eyes, I don't want you givin' me no advice about how to run my business, you got me?

LORETTA: But if something isn't legal…

JIMMY: I got big plans. You think I wanna live in this dump forever?

LORETTA: But I love it here.

JIMMY: Boy, you're a real fruitcake, you know that?

(Sound of rain falling. Loretta looks up happily.)

LORETTA: Jimmy, what does happiness feel like?

JIMMY: Whatcha wanna know for?

LORETTA: Because I think I'm happy.

(Sound of rain, louder. Music of "Shanty Town Romance" also. Lights dim.)

ACT I
Scene 5

The same, some time later, breakfast. Loretta and Jimmy eating grapefruit.

LORETTA: Jimmy, can we get married?

JIMMY: Ah, just eat your grapefruit.

LORETTA: Jimmy, I'm going to have a baby, and I want him to have a name.

JIMMY: Why don't you call him nitwit? Jeez, you dames is all alike.

LORETTA: Jimmy, every baby should have a mother *and* fa…

JIMMY: Yeah ? You wanna know what I think of that? *(Jimmy violently pushes his grapefruit in her face.)*

(Lights off them.)

ACT I

Scene 6

Ma O'Reilly, Jimmy's mother, sits on a chair L. Near her is a bucket. Ma is paging through a large photograph album. Loretta crosses to her and kneels by her side.

MA O'REILLY: And here's a picture of Jimmy when he was two and a half. And here's a picture of Jimmy when he was three. And here's Jimmy when he was four.

LORETTA: Oh, Mrs. O'Reilly, I'm so ashamed. I've come to see you because I haven't seen Jimmy in six months and I'm going to have his baby.

MA O'REILLY: And here's Jimmy when he was five.

LORETTA: Mrs. O'Reilly, didn't you hear me?

MA O'REILLY: Yes, I heard you, but I was thinking. Maybe you should talk to my other son. Michael!

(Enter Michael, Jimmy's policeman brother, upstanding and serious-looking.)

MICHAEL: Yes, Ma.

MA O'REILLY: Oh, Michael... *(She cries.)*

(So does Loretta.)

MICHAEL: It's Jimmy again, isn't it? Why do you cry, Ma? You know he's no good.

MA O'REILLY: Michael was always the good boy, and he became a policeman, but Jimmy had a harder time of it. He was too short for the police force.

MICHAEL: He's a rat, Ma.

MA O'REILLY: It's the environment that made him be bad. If a boy grows up on a city street and he's poor, why then he's bound to get confused.

MICHAEL: I didn't get confused.

MA O'REILLY: I know, but you fought in the World War and that made you think straight, but Jimmy didn't have that advantage. *(To Loretta.)* Were you brought up on the street?

LORETTA: No. I was brought up in an orphanage. I have no excuse.

MA O'REILLY: That's an excuse. A lot of orphans become criminals because they have no love.

LORETTA: I wish I had a mother.

MA O'REILLY: I have a daughter, but I always liked Jimmy the best, didn't I, Michael?

MICHAEL: He's a crook and a killer, Ma.

MA O'REILLY: It's not his fault, Michael. It's the society.

MICHAEL: *(To Loretta.)* Come on, Miss, we'll find that rat if we have to look in every crummy gin joint and speakeasy in the whole state.

MA O'REILLY: Tell him I'm making corned beef for supper, Michael.

(Michael takes Loretta out, U.C. Ma gets on her hands and knees and scrubs the floor with a hard hand brush.)

MA O'REILLY: He always liked that. Poor Jimmy. *(Scrubs.)*

(Lights off Ma.)

ACT I
Scene 7

Spot on Bette, extreme R., in a glittering gown, singing a song in Jimmy's speakeasy. Once her song is established, Jimmy and a few gangster-ish men and B-girls fill in the R. and C. areas. Jimmy sits at a table, R. (Note: The Broadway production opted for a very filled-in stage picture—three tables [Jimmy's and two others]; a piano U.R., played by a black piano player; a bar and bartender U.C.)

BETTE: They can take away my whiskey,
And my vodka and champagne,
They can take my rubbing alcohol,
And pour it down the drain,
They can take my sloe gin fizz away,
But, baby, then here's what I say,
They can't prohibit love
—We'd make it in the bathtub!
They can't prohibit love, they can't prohibit love!
(Applause. Bette bows, comes over to Jimmy, looks concerned.)

BETTE: Jimmy, you promised you wuz gonna lay low.

JIMMY: I ain't layin' low for Ferruchi or anybody else.

BETTE: Ferruchi and his boys are gunnin' for ya, ya big lug.

JIMMY: Don't ride me, Bette.

BETTE: Oh, go ahead, get killed, see if I care. *(Cries, takes handkerchief from her purse.)*

JIMMY: You're really stuck on me, ain't ya?

BETTE: Oh, go drink your beer.

JIMMY: *(Sees a gun in her purse, holds it up.)* Since when you start carryin' hardware?

BETTE: *(Recklessly unhappy.)* It ain't nothin'. It's a cigarette lighter. *(Puts cigarette in her mouth, aims gun at it, shoots it in half.)*
(Sudden dead silence in the speakeasy.)

JIMMY: What are you, crazy?
(Speakeasy noise starts up again.)

BETTE: I love ya, Jimmy.

JIMMY: You coulda shot your nose off.

BETTE: What do I need my nose for? You don't love me.

JIMMY: *(Puts the gun back in her purse.)* You dames is drivin' me crazy.
(Enter Michael in his police uniform and Loretta, L. All noise stops.)

SOMEONE: It's the cops!

JIMMY: It's OK. It's my brudder.
(Michael and Loretta come to him.)

JIMMY: Hiya, Mike. How's Ma?

MICHAEL: She prays for ya, Jimmy.

JIMMY: That's nice.

MICHAEL: She doesn't want you to be a gangster, Jimmy.

JIMMY: And I don't want her to be a gangster.

LORETTA: Michael, leave me with Jimmy please.
(Michael exits.)

JIMMY: Hiya, sourpuss. Whatcha drinkin'?

LORETTA: I don't drink, Jimmy.

BETTE: You wanna know why nobody likes you? Cause you're so good you're dull.

JIMMY: And what makes you think a B-girl's so interesting? Beat it, Bette.
(Bette, extremely stung, gasps, moves away.)

JIMMY: Whaddya want, Loretta?

LORETTA: I want a proper life. I want every transgression to be punished. I want no conversation to have salacious content. I want never to discuss themes of incest or white slavery. I want to be a married wife and have children and have a bedroom with two beds in it and when you're on the bed you always have to keep one foot on the floor. That's what I want.

JIMMY: Loretta, you're a good kid. But I ain't the marryin' kind. I'm a rat, Loretta. You don't wanna marry a rat.

LORETTA: Yes I do. *(Cries.)*

JIMMY: Here, honk on this. *(Offers her his handkerchief.)*

LORETTA: Thank you, I have my own *(She opens Bette's purse, thinking it's her own; takes out Bette's gun.)* Oh. This isn't mine. I…

(Several raincoated Gangsters—Ferruchi and his Henchmen—burst into the room, L. balcony.)

BETTE: Ferruchi! No!

(The Gangsters machine-gun Jimmy to death. Then they rush out.)

LORETTA: *(Still holding Bette's gun.)* JIMMY!

BETTE: JIMMY!

(Enter Ma O'Reilly, hysterical.)

MA O'REILLY: JIIIIIIIMMMMMMMMMMMMMYYYYYYYYYYY!

(Enter Michael, stands by the dying Jimmy and Ma.)

MICHAEL: *(Looking at Jimmy.)* They all end this way, every one of them.

JIMMY: *(Dying.)* Mother of God, is this the end of Jimmy O'Reilly? *(Dies.)*

(A large The End sign, in cut-out letters, is lowered in front of this tableau. Sound: Gangster music soars, crescendos, finishes as at end of movie. Everyone holds this. Music stops. The End sign goes up again. The Characters—as opposed to the Actors—seem a trifle surprised that they have to go on with their lives, as if they had expected to stay frozen behind The End sign forever. After a bit of silence, Bette breaks the impasse by breaking into hysterics.)

BETTE: *(Pointing to Loretta, who still holds the gun.)* She did it! I saw her! She killed Jimmy!

LORETTA: That's a lie.

MA O'REILLY: My son, my son!

BETTE: Murderess! Murderess!

MA O'REILLY: I made you corned beef for supper, Jimmy.

BETTE: She did it! She killed Jimmy!

LORETTA: That's a lie.

(Michael tries to comfort Ma O'Reilly.)

MA O'REILLY: *(To Michael.)* Take your hands off me! My only son is dead!

(During the above, the speakeasy has been changing into a courtroom. The bar and bartender become Judge's desk and Judge.)

ACT I
Scene 8

Judge bangs his gravel, C. Loretta is put in the witness box; Bette, Ma O'Reilly and Michael are L. Also present, R., are three reporters: Eve (in a woman's business suit and hat) and two male reporters. All three hold telephones.

JUDGE: Order in the court, order in the court. If there is another such outburst I shall have to clear the courtroom.

MICHAEL: *(To Loretta; in a state because of Ma O'Reilly.)* Alright, Miss—did you on the night of November 23 kill James T. O'Reilly?

LORETTA: Please, Michael, I'm going to have a baby.

JUDGE: What did she say?

MICHAEL: She said she's going to have a baby.

JUDGE: Now?

(Loretta starts to have birth pangs.)

JUDGE: Get a nurse in here.

(A nurse enters, helps Loretta off. The reporters spring into action, each holding his own telephone.)

EVE:	REPORTER NO. 1:	REPORTER NO. 2:
Jack, it's Eve	OK, Louie, tell	Hello, Harry?
down at the	'em to hold the	It's Ernie.
courtroom, get	front page and get	No. Nothing
this down: A	your pencil.	much new. The
hushed courtroom	It's pandemonium	dame's gonna have
viewed the fourth	down here as	a baby.
day of the murder	Loretta Moran is	How are you
trial of Loretta	in the back room	doin'? Win
Moran, a beautiful	giving birth to	anything at
orphan girl from	a baby. The	the horses?…
the wrong side	crowd's goin' wild…	
of the tracks…		

(The Reporters' voices trail off, and courtroom noise stops, when all see that the Nurse has grimly re-entered the room.)

NURSE: The baby is dead.

(Pandemonium breaks out. Ma O'Reilly faints. Michael and Bette help her off, with great difficulty. Judge bangs his gavel. Most of the audience focus should go to the three reporters who are shouting back into their phones.)

(Eve, Reporter No. 1, Reporter No. 2, simultaneously.)

EVE: Jack, listen fast: Death in The courtroom. Loretta Moran has a dead lover and now she has a dead baby too. Minutes after court was called to order...

REPORTER NO. 1: Hey, Louie, you hear that? Dead as a doornail and closed as a clam shell. Boy, this Moran kid's really got the breaks...

REPORTER NO. 2: Hey, Harry? The dame's kid's kicked off. Yeah. Too bad. How's your kid? What? Say, who is this? I wanted Tarrytown 9-8760.

(The Reporters' voices trail off again as Loretta walks slowly back into the courtroom. Lights should dim now, leaving a spot on Loretta, a spot on the Judge, and an area on the reporters, especially Eve.)

JUDGE: Loretta Moran, you have been found guilty of murder in the first degree, and it is the duty of this court to sentence you. In view of your unfortunate state in life, but mindful of the seriousness of your crime, I sentence you to twenty-five years hard labor on a chain gang. *(Bangs gavel.)* *(Loretta gasps. Lights focus on Loretta.)*

JUDGE'S VOICE: ...twenty-five years hard labor on a chain gang...twenty-five years hard labor on a chain gang...

(Lights spot Loretta alone. We no longer see the Judge. Eve is on the phone again. The two male reporters play cards or shoot dice.)

EVE: Jack? It's Eve again. Get your pencil ready. Orphan Girl Sentenced to Chain Gang. Loretta Moran. No mother. No father. Nobody to love but a gangster husband and, for a few minutes, a baby. But somehow love wasn't enough. If you want it too bad, love's never enough. But it wasn't just love that finished off Loretta Moran. It was the gangs; it was the system; and it was the world. *(Pause.)* Well, that closes the last chapter on the Loretta Moran case. What? Yeah, I want a chicken on rye with lots of mayo and eighty-six the pickle. *(Hangs up, exits.)*

(The spot intensifies on Loretta. Sound: The prison movie music crescendos. The End sign lowers itself in front of Loretta's despairing face. The music finishes. Complete blackout.)

ACT I

Scene 9

In the dark we hear cheerful silly-comedy music, leading us into a screwball comedy. An elegant white couch is R. A large picture window with reams of ruffled curtains is flown in, U.R. In front of the window is a small table and chair. A large white door (on rollers) is U.L. Another small table, with a telephone on it, and a chair are L. (This may be simplified.)

The lighting up to now has been Warner Bros. ominous—harsh and with lots of shadows. Now it becomes Paramount romantic—very bright, soft.

Lights up as the phone rings. Enter Viola, a heavy colored maid in a frilly uniform, from L.

VIOLA: *(Answering phone, very slurred accent.)* Hlo, Misser-en-Misszzes Morimer's reszdence. No, I'm sorry, Misszzes Morimer isn't heah. She's out on a scabinger hunt. Scabinger. S-K-E...*(Thinks.)*...I-B-Z-R-Y, Scabinger. Ahright, thank *you*.

(Enter a young heiress, Clara Mortimer, dressed in a shiny negligee, from R.)

CLARA: Was that for me, Viola?

VIOLA: No, Miz Clara, dat done be for Misszzes Morimer.

CLARA: *(Sinking onto the sofa with world-weariness.)* Oh, why are there never any calls for me, Viola?

VIOLA: I jus' don' know, Miz Clara. *(Plops down on sofa next to her, opens up a box of chocolates, eats them voraciously.)*

CLARA: I'm pretty, I'm reasonably intelligent, I'm rich, so why am I condemned à la maison de mes parents?

(Enter Edward Mortimer, the father, age fifty, in a smoking jacket, from R.)

EDWARD: Good morning, dear. *(Kisses Clara.)* Where is your mother?

VIOLA: She on a scabinger hunt. S-K-E-I-Z-B-R-T.

EDWARD: What?

CLARA: Viola says mother went on a scavenger hunt last night, and I guess she's still there.

EDWARD: Is the Turkey with her?

CLARA: He's a Turk. And mother doesn't like you to call him a turkey. His name is Abdhul, and he's a wonderful, handsome poet. And he unfortunately doesn't know I'm alive.

EDWARD: He's too busy living off of me.

CLARA: He's an artist!

EDWARD: That doesn't appear to have affected his eating habits any. Viola—what are you doing?

VIOLA: Ah'm eatin' chocklits.

EDWARD: Well stop it. And serve breakfast.

VIOLA: Yassuh. *(Exits with box of chocolates, still eating, off L.)*

EDWARD: There's no discipline in this house anymore. *(He sits to read his paper at the table U.R.)*

(Enter Allison Mortimer and Abdhul, through the door U.L. She is a forty-ish scatterbrained rich lady in evening clothes; he is her protégé and wears evening clothes and a turban.)

ALLISON: Hello, children, we're home! And you'll never guess what—Abdhul and I won the scavenger hunt! You should have seen Dolly Adams, she was simply livid! We got absolutely everything. We got a goldfish bowl, and a goat—

EDWARD: And you already had a turkey.

ALLISON: I don't think that's funny, Edward. And then we found a ship's anchor, and a rosebush—oh, and then, Edward, guess what? Abdhul and I were the only ones to find an escaped prisoner from a chain gang—we found two!

CLARA: Mother!

ALLISON: Abdhul saw them really. Tell them how, Abdhul!

ABDHUL: I see stripes.

ALLISON: That's right, he did. Dolly Adams was just green with envy.

CLARA: But what happened to the prisoners?

ALLISON: Oh, I forgot. I've asked them to breakfast. Abdhul, be an angel, and go bring them in.

(Abdhul exits through the door.)

EDWARD: Allison, are you mad? Bringing two murderers into this house?

(Viola sluffs in with plate.)

ALLISON: We don't know that they're murderers, Edward. Maybe they're arsonists.

VIOLA: *(Putting plate in front of Edward.)* Heah are your eggs. *(Sluffs out.)*

EDWARD: Allison, I will not have you turn this house into a penitentiary.

ALLISON: Oh, Edward, eat your eggs.

CLARA: I think it's wonderful. I've never been in love with a criminal before.

ALLISON: Now, Clara, behave.

(Abdhul brings in the two escaped criminals—Loretta and Hank, through door U.L. They are both dressed in the striped convict outfits. Loretta looks extremely upset and disoriented. Hank wears a cap, seems uncomfortable in the rich home, but attempts to carry it off with a down-home politeness.)

ALLISON: *(Being very cheerful.)* Well here they are!

(Edward looks away, reads his paper.)

ALLISON: Now. Let me present my family. This is my husband, Edward Mortimer.

(Edward doesn't look up.)

ALLISON: And this is my daughter, the madcap heiress, Clara.

CLARA: Oh, mother.

HANK: *(To Clara.)* How do you do, Ma'am.

CLARA: I'm very pleased to meet you. Are you lovers who committed a crime of passion together?

ALLISON: Clara, don't be rude. They may not wish to discuss it.

(Enter Viola carrying a plate.)

ALLISON: Oh; and this is Viola. I don't know her last name.

VIOLA: *(To Edward.)* Heah's your English muffins. *(Sluffs out.)*

ALLISON: *(To Hank and Loretta.)* Now what are *your* names?

HANK: My name's Hank, Ma'am.

ALLISON: Hello, Hank. *(To Loretta.)* And you, dear?

LORETTA: My name's Loretta. *(Weeps.)*

ALLISON: Oh, forgive me, you must be famished. *(Takes plate of eggs from Edward.)* Give them your eggs, Edward. Viola will bring you more. *(Allison gives eggs to Loretta.)*

CLARA: *(Fascinated, to Hank.)* What do you think of when you kill people?

ALLISON: Clara! *(To Hank.)* You must excuse my daughter. She has a glandular condition.

HANK: That's alright, Ma'am, but I've never killed anyone.

ALLISON: Good for you, Hank.

CLARA: *(Disappointed.)* Well, why were you put on a chain gang then?

HANK: I was falsely accused of robbing a grocery store in Tulsa, but I didn't do it.

CLARA: I've never been to a grocery store. What are they like?

HANK: I don't know. They're sort of small, they have food in them...

CLARA: *(Enthusiastically.)* But don't you just want to *kill* whoever sent you to prison unjustly?

HANK: No, Ma'am. Even though American justice didn't work in my particular case, I still believe in it.

(Enter Viola.)

ALLISON: The exception proves the rule, isn't that so, Edward?

VIOLA: *(To Edward.)* Heah's your orange joose. *(Sluffs off.)*

EDWARD: Is there never to be a morning in which I can have all my breakfast at once?

ALLISON: Edward, please, your manners. *(Gives orange juice to Hank.)*

CLARA: *(To Hank.)* Would you like to see my playroom? I grew up there. We could swing on the monkey bars and do headstands and…

ALLISON: Clara, time for your pill, dear. Abdhul, won't you favor our guests with one of your poems?

EDWARD: That does it! *(Throws down paper, starts to exit.)*

(Enter Viola with plate of pancakes.)

VIOLA: Heah's your wheat cakes.

EDWARD: *(Takes plate.)* You may send the syrup to my office! *(Edward stalks out.)*

(Viola exits.)

ALLISON: You must excuse Edward. He doesn't understand the artistic temperament. Abdhul, your poem.

ABDHUL: Ah! *(Rises, recites.)*

Ganna tooey,

Appasooft,

Digannasuey, la spleece,

Swalla wimba

Sreni vassa

La breena zunu treest.

(During above enter Viola in hat and coat, carrying a bottle of syrup. She exits out front door with it.)

ALLISON: Viola!

(Clara laughs; then so do Allison and Abdhul. Hank and Loretta look bewildered and out of place. Sound of happy Scene's-over music. Music finishes. Allison keeps laughing the longest.)

ALLISON: *(To herself mostly.)* Now, have I finished laughing? Yes. What should we do next? Polo? Charades?

(Doorbell rings.)

ALLISON: Oh, good, the door. Now who could it be? Well, it could be Dolly Adams. *(To Loretta.)* Or it could be the police for you, or it could be the wealthy industrialist and his wife I met at the scavenger hunt and who I invited to breakfast.

(Doorbell again.)

ALLISON: Oh, the doorbell. Viola! *(Realizing Viola is not there.)* Oh, could it be Viola? *(Grandly.)* Loretta, dear, could you get that for me?

(Loretta goes to the door. Hank follows behind her, to get away from Clara. Loretta opens the door, revealing Jimmy and Bette dressed as Wallace Berry-

Jean Harlow social climbers now, instead of gangsters. Seeing the still alive Jimmy, Loretta faints .)

LORETTA: Jimmy! *(Faints.)*

(Jimmy bends down to rouse her.)

ALLISON: Oh, dear. I'm so sorry. Do come in.

LORETTA: *(Coming to.)* Jimmy! You're supposed to be dead.

JIMMY: Nah, they just nicked me a little. I been stayin' outta circulation til the heat was off, and then after Bette and me got hitched, I kinda drifted into big business.

LORETTA: *(Horrified.)* Got hitched?

BETTE: Yeah. That's American slang for got married.

LORETTA: But I've been on a chain gang for killing you.

JIMMY: Gee, if I'd-a known, I coulda sprung ya.

BETTE: *(Pokes him.)* Siddown.

(Bette and Jimmy cross into the room and sit on the sofa, Bette trying to fit into "society," Jimmy merely uncomfortable. Clara goes and hangs on Hank, Upstage. Loretta sits next to Jimmy on the sofa also, to Bette's annoyance.)

ALLISON: *(Trying to make conversation.)* Well…Abdhul, why don't you go whip up your thrilling souffle?

(Abdhul nods and rushes out L. to the kitchen, laughing.)

ALLISON: *(To Bette.)* It's a Turkish delicacy.

BETTE: Oh, I love exotic food. My husband and I are goin' to the Alps for the Bavarian Cream Pie.

(Enter Viola through the door.)

VIOLA: I gave him the syrup. *(Exits L.)*

ALLISON: *(Explaining to her guests.)* That's Viola.

CLARA: I take ballet lessons. Watch me dance, Hank.

(She starts to dance about the room, to Hank's embarrassment.)

ALLISON: Oh yes, and that's Clara.

(Enter Viola, upset.)

VIOLA: Mrs. Morrimer, you bettah come out heah. Abdhul, he in there, and he throwin' this, and he throwin' that. He gwine make a mess in my kitchen.

ALLISON: There is no such word as gwine, Viola.

(Enter Edward, upset, though the door.)

EDWARD: I can't go to the office in my bathrobe.

ALLISON: Oh, dear, I think I'm going to laugh again. *(Sits and laughs and laughs.)*

(Abdhul enters with flour bowl and laughs too; Clara and Edward laugh also. Viola grabs back her bowl and probably doesn't laugh. Throughout all the

above, Loretta and Jimmy have been stealing unhappy, uncomfortable looks at each other. Loretta now stands.)

LORETTA: I want this over.

ALLISON: *(Startled.)* What?

LORETTA: I want it over. I HATE SCREWBALL COMEDIES!

ALLISON: *(Deeply offended.)* Are you attempting to criticize our way of life?

LORETTA: You don't follow. I want the music to soar and the sign to come down and it can be *over.*

ALLISON: Edward, I think she's gone mad.

LORETTA: Please, you can do it. I'll show you. Look—Hank and Clara have fallen in love because they're screwballs and social class doesn't matter. *(Loretta pushes Hank and Clara together.)*

HANK: I'm not a screwball.

LORETTA: And Jimmy marries…well, he can't marry me, so Abdhul marries me, and I'm miserable for the rest of my life…but Mr. Mortimer, on the other hand, is so happy that Abdhul is leaving his house that he takes Mrs. Mortimer over his knee and he spanks her and then The End sign comes down and we don't feel anything anymore.

(There is a long pause while everybody looks at Loretta as if she's crazy. Loretta seems relieved that she's discovered a way to end things. Suddenly the expressions on Edward's, Allison's, Clara's, Viola's and Abdhul's faces change, and they begin to act out what Loretta has just described as if it were the most natural thing in the world and as if anything should be tried once. Throughout the following, Hank, Bette, and Jimmy look extremely bewildered and occasionally aghast. Jimmy, though, also seems to feel bad for Loretta. Edward now grabs Allison, puts her over his knee and spanks her.)

ALLISON: Edward, stop this! Stop it!!

EDWARD: *(With Allison still over his knee.)* I'm not taking any more of your foolish behavior, Allison Mortimer. You bring home one more Turkey, or rahjah, or any other foreigner in a turban, and you'll get a paddling from me you'll never forget.

VIOLA: Thash tellin' huh, Mr. Morrimer.

ALLISON: *(Thrilled.)* Oh, Edward, I've never seen you like this!

CLARA: Oh, mother, at last I'm in love too. *(To Hank.)* And I hope when I'm bad, you'll spank *me.*

ALLISON: All my children are leaving the nest. *(Cries.)* I'm so happy.

VIOLA: *(To Allison.)* Why, if Miz Clara is gettin' married, can Ah be a flower girl?

ALLISON: But, Viola, would you know how?

VIOLA: Sure. Ah knows all about flour! *(Viola throws flour in Allison's face.)*
(Pause. Everyone laughs: Viola, Clara, Edward, Abdhul, Allison. Loretta looks possessed. Hank, Bette, Jimmy look very baffled and a bit alarmed. There is extremely cheerful music, and The End sign descends in front of the tableau. The music crescendos, finishes. Everyone holds the scene; the laughter continues. After a moment, the laughter stops, the music has ended, and The End sign goes back up. There is a long uncomfortable silence.)

BETTE: Perhaps we better go now.

ALLISON: *(Stiffly.)* No need to go yet. *(Suddenly irate.)* I will not allow the servants to behave this way. VIOLA! Go pack your things at once. We're putting you on the first bus back to Georgia!
(Viola exits, crying.)

CLARA: Can we still get married?

ALLISON: CLARA—stop that. *(To Bette and Jimmy, crossly.)* Sit down!
(They reluctantly do. Doorbell.)

ALLISON: *(In a foul temper.)* I suppose someone *else* has come to breakfast now. Loretta, do you think you could answer the door—*without* fainting this time?
(Loretta goes to the door, opens it. Enter Michael the policeman.)

MICHAEL: I'm looking for two convicts who've escaped from a chain gang.
(Loretta screams. She and Hank run R. Michael chases them, is tripped by Jimmy. Lights dim, frantic escape music starts, and a spotlight moves frenetically about the stage as we go to the next scene.)

ACT I

Scene 10

The escape. Sirens and the sound of dogs barking are added to the escape music. A large map of the United States is lowered (or projected onto the screen) U.C. A pinspot focuses on Connecticut and moves with determination westward. It finally settles somewhere around Oklahoma; and the map goes out.

The escape music and dogs barking fade to the sound of wind and a melancholy harmonica.

Lights up on Ma and Pa Joad. Ma is C., staring out stoically, Pa is U.L. of her, playing his harmonica. Grandma Joad lies dead in an old tire D.L.

PA JOAD: Ma, we got to bury Grandma.

MA JOAD: I wish Hank were here, Pa. Maybe he'll escape.

PA JOAD: Ya can't escape a chain gang, Ma.

MA JOAD: A Joad can, Pa. Cause We're the People, and you can't keep us down.

PA JOAD: Ya can't escape a chain gang, Ma.

MA JOAD: Look, here he comes now, Pa.

(*Enter Loretta and Hank, out of breath and exhausted from* R.)

MA JOAD: Hank boy!

HANK: Ma!

PA JOAD: How'd ya escape, son?

HANK: Don't have time to talk. The bloodhounds'll be after us in a minute. Ma, this is Loretta.

MA JOAD: Welcome, Loretta.

HANK: Ma, where's the farm?

MA JOAD: There ain't no farm, Hank. They run us off and they razed it down.

PA JOAD: Dang bulldozers. Dang tractors.

MA JOAD: It's alright, Pa.

(*Sound of the bloodhounds.*)

LORETTA: They're coming!

MA JOAD: Don't be afraid, honey. We're the People.

HANK: Ma, I'm gonna head me out for California. They say they got jobs in the movies for folks, Ma.

LORETTA: Please, we have to go.

MA JOAD: Hank, I don't wancha bein' in no movies, son. There's no life out there. You're too far from the soil.

HANK: I gotta try, Ma.

(*Sound of bloodhounds somewhat closer.*)

MA JOAD: How am I gonna know about you, son, out there in the movies?

LORETTA: Please!

HANK: Well, maybe it's like Preacher Casey says, a fellow ain't got a soul of his own, just a little piece of a big soul. Then…

MA JOAD: Then what, Hank?

HANK: Then it don't matter. I'll be wherever ya look. Wherever there's a fight so hungry people can eat, I'll be there. Wherever there's a cop beating up a guy, I'll be there.

LORETTA: Please! Talk faster!

HANK: (*Talking faster.*) I'll be in the way guys yell when they're mad, I'll be in the way kids laugh when they're hungry and they know supper's ready, and when people are makin' movies about the West and how this country got started, I'll be there too.

LORETTA: *Please!*

MA JOAD: *(Gives Loretta a hard look.)* I don't understand it, Hank.

HANK: Gimme your hand, Ma. Good-bye.

MA JOAD: Good-bye, Hank.

(Loretta and Hank start to exit.)

MA JOAD: Wait, Hank, we ain't the kissin' kind but…

HANK: I'm gonna have to do a lot of it in the movies.

(They laugh sadly at his joke, kiss. The sound of the bloodhounds abruptly stops.)

LORETTA: *(Alarmed.)* The barking's stopped!

MA JOAD: I don't hear nuthin'.

MICHAEL'S VOICE: *(Offstage R.)* Put your hands up or we'll shoot.

HANK: Loretta! Run! *(Hank runs.)*

(Much gunfire. Hank dies violently.)

LORETTA: Hank!

(Enter Michael. He takes Loretta into custody.)

MICHAEL: Loretta Moran, you're under arrest. *(He takes her out U.L.)*

MA JOAD: *(Looks at Hank and dead Grandma; teary at first.)* Well, Pa. I guess he ain't gonna make no movies now. They're tryin' to break my will, but they ain't gonna do it. Cause We're the People. They can't wipe us out, they can't lick us. We'll go on forever, Pa, cause We're the People.

(Pa starts to play his harmonica.)

MA JOAD: Put that dang thing away, wouldja, Pa?

(Pa and Ma look sadly at one another. Lights dim.)

ACT I

Scene 11

Ominous return-to-prison music. Sound of heavy prison door closing. Michael delivers Loretta to her cell in a small pool of light U.C. He exits.

LORETTA: Oh please, God, please. Don't leave me here in prison for twenty-four years. Our Father, which art in heaven, hallowed be thy name, thy kingdom come… *(etc.)*

(During Loretta's above praying, music begins. The Prison Warden [a woman] enters in the L. balcony. As she reads from a sheet of paper, Offstage singing of "O Come, All Ye Faithful" begins.)

PRISON WARDEN: I have good news for some of you girls. In honor of Christmas,

I have Governor's pardons for the following prisoners: Alice Adams, Susan Alexander, Crystal Allen, Esther Blodgett, Nora Charles, Stella Dallas, Norma Desmond, Rebecca DeWinter, Dorothy Gale from Kansas, Regina Giddens, Tracy Lord, Rosa Moline, Loretta Moran, Mildred Pierce, Terri Randall, Addie Ross, Sylvia Scarlett, Tootie Smith, Judith Traherne, and Florence Ziegfeld. I wish all of you girls the best of luck, and Merry Christmas. *(During the above, when the Prison Warden says Loretta's name, the Blessed Mother wafts in U.L. and stands, smiling, near Loretta; Loretta cannot see her though. At the finish of the Warden's speech, the music swells, and many Carolers enter, in overcoats and mufflers, holding candles, still singing. The Warden joins the singing, moving to U.C. balcony; she is joined by a black-and-white Santa Claus, who rings a bell. Snow falls. During the singing, the Blessed Mother graciously waves her hand, like the Ghost of Christmas Past, showing Loretta the warmth and loveliness of the world. Loretta smiles and is happy. Toward the end of the singing, she looks up, expecting The End sign to come down, although it does not. As the singing finishes, the Carolers exit off back to their worlds; Loretta is the last to exit, finally giving up on waiting for the sign.)*

ACT I
Scene 12

Hollywood, the set of a western. An obviously painted western drop is lowered. Hank, D.R., is dressed as a Gary Cooper-like cowboy; Eve, D.L., is dressed in a frontier woman's dress; and the black actor plays an Indian, seated on the floor, D.C., motionless, wrapped in a blanket with a couple of feathers in his head. Mickey, the Newsboy of earlier in the play, is running around with a clap board.

DIRECTOR: *(Over loudspeaker.)* Everyone on the set for "Dobson's Pass." Places, Mr. Joad, Miss Sheridan. Lights, camera. Sticks, Mickey.
    (Mickey steps forward with a clapboard.)
MICKEY: Shoot-out at Dobson's Pass, Scene forty-three, Take eighty-eight.
DIRECTOR: Action.
EVE: *(To Hank.)* You can't go up there!
HANK: I gotta.
EVE: You can't. They'll kill you if you go up there.
HANK: I gotta.

EVE: What do you care if they kill Dakota Pete? What did Dakota Pete ever do for you?

HANK: Somethin'.

EVE: Well what?

HANK: Somethin'.

EVE: Alright, go ahead, get killed, what do I care? You're insufferably monosyllabic, and I hate you. Good-bye.

HANK: G'bye. *(Walks out of the action; stands by the side.)*

EVE: Oh, I hate you, I hate you!

INDIAN: Why white squaw squawk?

EVE: *(Crying.)* I can't help it, I love him so much…

INDIAN: Why White Squaw not soft like woman? Woman should be soft like fur of raccoon, woman should have babies. Why White Squaw not have babies?

EVE: *(Thinks, can't resist wisecracking.)* Well, I've been to the Stork Club several times, but nothing seemed to work out.

DIRECTOR: Cut!

MICKEY: Cut!

DIRECTOR: You speak to her, Mickey. I give up.

MICKEY: Miss Sheridan, that's not your line. Your line is "I want to have babies more than anything else, Chief Big Feather."

EVE: I know, but it's such a stupid line.

DIRECTOR: Miss Sheridan, if you ruin one more take with another one of these wisecracks, you will find yourself back in the newspaper business faster than you can whistle "Dixie."

(Eve whistles "Dixie" quickly.)

MICKEY: *(Covering for her, before Director can respond.)* Shoot-out at Dobson's Pass, Scene forty-three, Take eighty-nine.

DIRECTOR: Action.

EVE: *(Almost starts to laugh, collects herself.)* You can't go up there!

HANK: I gotta!

(Enter Loretta, dazed.)

LORETTA: Help!

DIRECTOR: Cut! No visitors on the set, please.

(Indian exits in irritation.)

HANK: Loretta!

EVE: Loretta Moran!

LORETTA: Hank!

HANK: I've been trying to contact you.

LORETTA: What happened?

HANK: Well, I was in the hospital for a while, but now I'm fine. I've been looking all over Hollywood for you.

LORETTA: You should have tried the prisons.

HANK: I didn't think of that.

DIRECTOR: I said no visitors.

HANK: *(Out to Director.)* Oh, please, Mr. von Leffing, won't you give her a job? She's a swell kid, and I know she has lots of talent and she's had it so rough. Oh please.

DIRECTOR: Very well, Mr. Joad. Put her in the next number.

HANK: Loretta, you're in. And if you work hard, I just know you're gonna succeed. Things are lookin' up for us, kid. *(Hank kisses Loretta.)*
(Eve notices this wistfully; Mickey notices Eve's look.)

MICKEY: *(Points thumb to Hank and Loretta.)* Tough luck, kid. Looks like she's going to be Hank's girl now.

EVE: Oh, I'm used to it. I've been turned down so many times I feel like a bedspread.

HANK: Hey, Eve, take Loretta back to the dressing room and help her learn the lyrics fast.

LORETTA: *(To Eve.)* Which door do I use?

EVE: Well, there's the trap door, the humidor, and the cuspidor. Which door did you want?

LORETTA: Oh, God.

(Eve and Loretta exit, R. Hank removes his cowboy costume to reveal a tuxedo.)

DIRECTOR: Lights. Camera. Action.

(Western drop goes out, revealing a shimmer curtain.)

MICKEY: "Clamdiggers of 1937," scene one-hundred-seven, take two.

HANK: *(Sings.)*

My favorite part of dinner,
Is not the rich dessert,
Desserts don't keep you thinner,
Or bright-eyed and alert.
You may think that I'm crazy,
You may think my choice is pallid,
But once you see them all dressed up, you'll know:
Why my favorite is the *salad.*

(As Hank begins to sing the chorus, All the girls [including Eve and Loretta] come out dressed as vegetables: lettuce, carrots, celery, etc. On Broadway there

was also a Chef and two Salad Boys [in tuxedos] who pushed the girls forward on a three-tiered platform.)

HANK: *(Sings.)*

    I love *the salad,* I love *the salad,*

    I love to toss it up and pour the roquefort on,

    I love to eat the celery and the lettuce and the bean,

    Cucumbers are the jokers, and a red tomato is the queen,

    I love *the salad,* I love *the salad,*

    I love to eat it up as you can plainly see,

    I love *the salad,* I love *the salad,*

    Won't you come dancing in the *salad bowl* with me?

    (All the girls come forward, Ziegfeld Follies style.)

GIRLS: *(Sing, in nasal showgirl style.)*

    We're in a *salad,* we're in a *salad,*

    We've got a lot of what it takes to fill a bowl,

    Bring vinegar and oil, French and Russian, Roquefort too,

    As ladies of the *salad,* we have vegetation just for you,

    We're in a *salad,* we're in a *salad,*

    So whip out your salad fork and knofe,

    We're in a *salad,* we're in a *salad,*

    Won't you come dancing in the *salad bowl of life?*

EVE: *(Sings conversationally to another piece of the salad.)*

    I want a honeymelon honeymoon,

    A ripe banana crooning me a tune,

    My daddy says, "Absolutely nope,"

    Cause a grapefruit would be fine—but you cantaloupe.

LORETTA: *(Comes forward; she has to sing the pig Latin verse and seems dazed a bit.)*

    Ereway-in-ay alad-say, ere-way in-ay alad-say,

    Eve-way ot-gay ot-lay at-whay akes-tay oo-tay ill-fay owl-bay.

EVE: *(Whispers to Loretta.)* Good for you, honey.

    (Girl comes forward as a sexy tomato.)

GIRL: *(Bette.)*

    I'm a tomato, tomato, tomato,

    I'm a tomato, I'm red and I'm ripe,

    The farmers who grew me, they all took right to me,

    I'm a tomato, I take dictation, and I type.

HANK: You're hired! Take a letter.

    (The Tomato takes shorthand.)

HANK: *(Sings.)*
    Dear Department of Agriculture,
    No more cakes,
    No more soup,
    No more ice cream,
    Not one scoop,
    Just one thing can make us sing:
ALL: Salad, salad, salad, salad!
    (The girls each speak solo lines in tempo.)
GIRL 1: I love radish,
    Red and snappy.
GIRL 2: Only lettuce,
    Makes me happy,
GIRL 3: I love dressing,
    Tart and sassy,
EVE: I love God,
    And I love Lassie,
LORETTA: I love blue cheese,
GIRL 1: I love oil,
TOMATO: Thousand Islands
    Rich and royal,
GIRL 2: More than Garbo,
GIRL 3: More than Gable,
EVE: I love salad
    On the table,
ALL: Salad, salad, salad, salad, Salad, salad, salad, salad, Salad, salad, salad,
    salad, Salad, salad, *salad!*

HANK, CHEF AND BOYS:

HANK, CHEF AND BOYS:	GIRLS:
We love…the salad	La la la la la…
We love the salad,	La la la la la la la,
We love to toss it up	Toss it,
and pour roquefort on,	Pour it on!
We love to eat the celery, and the	Ah ha!
Lettuce and the bean,	Lettuce and the bean!
Cucumbers are the jokers,	Ah————
and a red tomato is the queen,	Ah————ah!

ALL: *We're in a salad, we're in a salad,*
    So whip out your salad fork and knife,
    We're in a salad, we're in a salad,
    Won't you come dancing?
    Won't you come dancing?
    Won't you come dancing in the…

HANK: *(Out to Director.)* Do you like Loretta, Mr. von Leffing?

DIRECTOR: Finish the number, Mr. Joad.

HANK: But do you like her?

DIRECTOR: Very much. I think she's going to be a great star.
    (Everyone beams good-naturedly at Loretta.)

ALL: *(Finishing.)* …salad bowl of life!
    (The End sign majestically descends. Everyone holds pose. Loretta notices the sign a bit uncomfortably.)

DIRECTOR: Cut. OK, print it.
    (The End returns up again.)

DIRECTOR: Good work, kids. Places for the "Wrath of God" number. Mickey, get Dolores on the set.
    (Much moving about and exiting of Chorus.)

MICKEY: Miss del Reego, Miss del Reego, on the set for "Wrath of God" number.
    (Loretta and Hank exit; Eve stays on. Enter Dolores, U.C., an enormous fruit hat on her head; Mickey follows behind her.)

DOLORES: Here I am, Fritz. *(Slips, falls to ground.)* Aggggh, who left this piece of lettuce here? Oh. Oh. MY LEG, MY LEG, MY LEG!

DIRECTOR: OK, one of the kids in the chorus will have to take over the part.

EVE: Me, Mr. von Leffing?

DIRECTOR: You make too many wisecracks to be a star.

DOLORES: I can do the number, Fritz. It's just my leg.

EVE: You can't do the number with a broken leg.

DOLORES: Jes, I can.

EVE: You can't!

DOLORES: I can!

DIRECTOR: Ladies, ladies, schweigen sie doch! I want the new girl to do it, Loretta…

DOLORES: But, Fritz…

EVE: Fritz…

DIRECTOR: Mickey, take the hat off Dolores.
    (Mickey does, then exits R.)

DOLORES: Fritz! *(To Eve.)* How would you like a piece of my mind?

EVE: Oh, I couldn't take the last piece.

(Dolores limps off in anger, L. Mickey runs in quickly from R.)

MICKEY: Here she is, Mr. von Leffing.

(Loretta hurries in behind Mickey, followed by Hank.)

EVE: *(Good-naturedly.)* Oh, break a leg, honey.

(Loretta falls, breaks her leg, cries out.)

EVE: Oh, I'm sorry, I'm sorry!

DIRECTOR: Gott in Himmel!

HANK: Loretta, are you alright?

(Hank helps Loretta hobble toward R.)

MICKEY: I don't think she can walk, Mr. von Leffing.

DIRECTOR: Alright, we give the part to Elissa.

MICKEY: She has scarlet fever, Mr. von Leffing.

DIRECTOR: Then get me the Swedish girl with all the hair.

MICKEY: She's been deported, Mr. von Leffing.

DIRECTOR: Alright, we make it a dog picture. Get me Rin Tin Tin.

MICKEY: *(As he exits L.)* Mr. Tin, Mr. Tin!

(Eve brings Loretta crutches, which she's gotten from off R.)

HANK: Don't be sad, Loretta. You can be in other movies.

LORETTA: Nothing ever works out, Hank.

HANK: Ma always says it does.

LORETTA: I don't know, Hank. I get put in prison, I break my leg. After a while it becomes discouraging. I think I better leave Hollywood.

HANK: Don't go, Loretta. I want to marry you.

LORETTA: I'm sorry, Hank, but I still love Jimmy. And that won't work out either, so I'm just going to go away somewhere and try to forget everything for a while.

HANK: Please marry me.

LORETTA: I can't, Hank.

HANK: Loretta, I can't let you go like this.

EVE: I'll marry you, Hank.

(Loretta cries.)

HANK: Why are you crying, Loretta? Does your leg hurt?

LORETTA: No, it's not that. It's just that sometimes I think that the thirties aren't ever going to be over. *(Loretta hobbles off L.)*

(Hank and Eve go off R., sadly.)

ACT I

Scene 13

Xanadu. Citizen Kane-like music—brooding and ominous—is heard. Bette, well-dressed, enters with an oversized jigsaw puzzle; she sits on the floor D.R. and tries to fit various pieces together, without success. Jimmy sits far U.L., stern, brooding.

BETTE: There are too many pieces to this puzzle. And it's all sky anyway. Six million pieces of blue cardboard. I'm gonna go crazy. *(Pause.)* Ain't you talkin' anymore?

JIMMY: I was thinking of someone.

BETTE: Who?

JIMMY: Finish your puzzle, Elizabeth.

BETTE: *Her* again?

JIMMY: Shut up. You got what you wanted, you're a big shot in society so shut up.

BETTE: OK, I wanted to be successful, ain't I allowed? But you—you overdo everything. You run five newspapers, two auto factories, a glue works, two Senators, all those so-called nightclubs; you started the Spanish-American War, for God's sake. All you do is achieve, achieve, achieve. IT'S NEUROTIC!

JIMMY: Practice your singing, Elizabeth.

BETTE: And that's another thing. I DON'T WANNA BE NO OPERA SINGER!

(Jimmy starts to choke her, won't stop. Enter Harkness, their butler from R.)

HARKNESS: Sir. Sir.

(Jimmy stops his choking.)

HARKNESS: Sir, I have the information you wanted on the whereabouts of that certain person.

JIMMY: Where is she, Harkness?

HARKNESS: Miss Moran left Hollywood several months ago, sir. The agency has traced her to—I'm sorry to say—the Club Intimate.

JIMMY: I see. That will be all, Harkness.

HARKNESS: Yes, sir. *(Exits.)*

JIMMY: I've got to see her.

BETTE: Please, not now, Jimmy. I need help with the Italian pronunciation.

JIMMY: Ito can help you with *Tosca.*

BETTE: Ito is Japanese.

JIMMY: Practice your singing, Bette. *Sing. (Chokes her again.)*

(She has to sing a scale with his hands around her throat. Lights dim on them.)

ACT I

Scene 14

> *Club Intimate. We hear the sound of a piano tinkling. Lights up on Piano Man, an amiable Black Man playing the piano,* L. *Jimmy moves to a small side table,* D.R.

PIANO MAN: *(To the room at large, show about to start.)* Hi, everybody, this is Piano Man, welcoming you back to the Club Intimate and reminding you all to be real nice to our pretty hostesses. And now the Club Intimate is happy to present, back from a month of drying out in White Plains, Lady Loretta from Room 779. Let's have a big hand for the little Lady, and don't nobody buy her a drink.

> *(Enter Loretta in slinky, nightclub garb,* U.C. *She is startled by a spotlight.)*

LORETTA: Oh my God. Is this the hospital?

PIANO MAN: Just sing, honey. Piano Man'll tell you where you are later.

LORETTA: Okay.

> *(Piano Man plays introduction; she doesn't come in.)*

LORETTA: Excuse me. I have something in my ear. *(Knocks side of her head.)*
> *(Introduction again.)*

LORETTA: I'm sorry, I can't quite hear the piano. Would someone buy me a drink?

> *(Piano Man looks sternly at the audience. No one offers. Loretta starts to cry.)*

LORETTA: Oh…I…

JIMMY: *(Outside of spotlight.)* I'll buy the lady a drink.

LORETTA: *(Can't see straight.)* Thank you, whoever you are.

> *(Piano Man reluctantly pours her drink at the piano. She gulps it right down.)*

LORETTA: Mmmmmm, that was delicious. I think I'll try again, Piano Man.

> *(Piano Man plays introduction. She has trouble climbing on the piano but finally, if awkwardly, does so.)*

LORETTA: *Euphemism for sale,*
> What am I bid for my whatchamacallit?
> *Euphemism for sale,*
> What does it matter what people call it?
> I'm just a ship in a storm,
> I need a captain, to keep me warm,
> Drop your anchor—if you're male,
> I've got a *euphemism for sale.*
> I'm traveling down a certain road,

That's forbidden by the production code.
My name's Taxi, stay a while,
I don't charge—for the first mile...
Euphemism for sale,
What am I bid for my whosamadoosey,
I get sent through the mail,
Special rate for a fourth class floozie,
(Longingly.)
I like to play by the sea,
Hey little boy there, please play with me,
(Raucously.)
You've got a shovel, I've got the pail,
I've got a *euphemism for sale,*
What am I bid for?—
My euphemism for sale?

JIMMY: Loretta.

LORETTA: Have I stopped singing?

JIMMY: Hey, sourpuss. Don't you know me?

LORETTA: Your voice is familiar. Are you a disc jockey?

JIMMY: Loretta, it's Jimmy.

LORETTA: *(Not comprehending.)* Jimmy, Bobby, Harry, the Mayor. Buy me another drink, huh, baby?

JIMMY: You shouldn't drink, kitten.

LORETTA: *(Crosses to his table.)* But I have to do such awful things, and I mustn't remember them, and...there's someone I have to forget. His name was Jimmy. *(Realizing it's Jimmy in front of her.)* Oh, Jimmy. *(Cries.)* Our vines have such tender grapes. *(Pause.)* Can I have some wine?

JIMMY: No more, kid. We gotta get you well. Hey, Piano Man, play "Shanty Town Romance."
(Piano Man does.)

LORETTA: *(Hearing song.)* Oh, Jimmy—let's go back to Shanty Town.

JIMMY: We don't need Shanty Town, sourpuss. I got ambition. I'm runnin' for Governor, I'll be elected tomorrow. And then after that I'll be President, and after that...

LORETTA: I want Shanty Town. I want it to be raining and for you to sing that song, and then for The End sign to come down and then we can stay frozen behind it forever.

JIMMY: Ya can't have that, kid.

LORETTA: Can I drink?

JIMMY: No more.

LORETTA: Can we go to the movies then?

JIMMY: Not now. How'd ya like to see a really bad opera?

(They look at one another. We hear Bette's singing of scales. Lights dim on their looking at one another.)

ACT I

Scene 15

Backstage at the Opera House, L. Bette, dressed as Brunnehilde, is singing scales, with an hysterical edge in her voice. With her is her houseboy Ito (played by the black actor).

Enter Mickey, L.

MICKEY: Fifteen minutes, Mrs. O'Reilly. *(Exits.)*

BETTE: Oh my God, I still don't know the Italian. Say something Italian, Ito.

ITO: Nooky nooky.

BETTE: Don't say that, Ito. It's annoying.

(Enter Mickey.)

MICKEY: Here's a note from your husband, Mrs. O'Reilly. And ten minutes. *(Exits.)*

BETTE: You read it, Ito.

ITO: Good ruck on your opening. So solly you cannot sing. Am divorcing you to mally Lolletta, she plegnant with my baby. Hope you choke on own spit. Jimmy.

(Enter Mickey.)

MICKEY: Two minutes, Mrs. O'Reilly.

BETTE: You just said ten minutes.

MICKEY: Time flies when you're having fun. *(Exits.)*

ITO: Why you dressed this way? That not right for Tosca.

BETTE: I don't know what I'm doing!

(Enter Mickey.)

MICKEY: Places! *(Exits.)*

BETTE: What is the matter with him? Ito, before I go on, find Loretta in the audience. And tell Harkness I want a gun.

(They exit L. with purpose.)

ACT I

Scene 16

Sound of orchestra tuning up.

> *Lights up in "opera box." (Balcony* R.*) Seated are Allison and Clara. Jimmy enters looking about for Loretta.*

JIMMY: *(To Allison.)* Hey, you seen Loretta?

ALLISON: Oh, Mr. O'Reilly. You remember my daughter, the madcap heiress, Clara.

CLARA: *(On edge.)* Mother! You have got to stop saying that.

JIMMY: *(Calling.)* Loretta!

ALLISON: Ssssh.

> *(The opera begins. Enter a Gypsy Peasant, played by Hank.)*

HANK: *(Sings.)*

> Ostende nobis, Tosca,
>
> Ostende nobis, Tosca,
>
> Hip, Hip, Oremus!

> *(Enter Bette* U.C. *as Brunnehilde, dragging Loretta who's bound and gagged. Bette is brandishing a gun madly.)*

BETTE: *(Sings.)*

> Hoy-a-ta-ho! Hoy-a-ta-ho!
>
> Hoy-a-ta-ho! Hoy-a-ta-ho! Ah—

> *(Bette shoots the gun in Jimmy's direction. He and Clara duck.)*

ALLISON: I love Verdi. He *begins* with climaxes.

BETTE: *(Occasionally singing, but more often addressing the audience)*

> Hoy-a-ta-ho! Hoy-a-ta-ho! Ah!

> *(Shouting.)* You must not vote for my husband for governor!

JIMMY: This isn't *Tosca*, Bette.

> *(Enter two Opera Peasants.)*

OPERA PEASANTS: *(Singing.)*

> Hic, haec, hoc,
>
> Huius, huius, huius,
>
> Hic, haec, hoc,
>
> Huius, huius, huius…

> *(They repeat this twice more under Bette's next speech.)*

BETTE: *(Shoots randomly at the Peasants.)* You must not vote for him. He shares a love nest with an alcoholic floozie.

OPERA PEASANTS: *(Singing.)*

    Alla gallia est divisa in partes tres!

JIMMY: Sing, Bette.

BETTE: *(Sings)*

    I love you, I love you!

    Je t'aime, Jimmy!

    (Shoots at him; Allison dies.)

CLARA: Mother!

BETTE: I'm going to kill Loretta, Jimmy.

    (Aims gun at Loretta.)

    (Enter Harkness.)

HARKNESS: Excuse me for interrupting the performance, Madam. I must speak with you.

BETTE: *(Very annoyed.)* What is it, Harkness?

HARKNESS: Madam. They've bombed Pearl Harbor.

BETTE: Who has?

HARKNESS: The Japanese, Madam.

BETTE: Why?

HARKNESS: I don't know, Madam.

BETTE: Oh.

HARKNESS: This will mean war, Madam.

    (Hank and Peasants run off; Jimmy comes down to Loretta.)

BETTE: Well, I presume so.

HARKNESS: I've taken the liberty of firing Ito, Madam. We've placed him in a camp.

BETTE: Very good. Thank you, Harkness.

    (Harkness exits.)

BETTE: *(To audience.)* Well, you have all heard Harkness. The United States is at war. *(Exits U.C.)*

LORETTA: *(Being untied by Jimmy.)* Jimmy, what's going to happen?

JIMMY: I can think of one thing.

LORETTA: What?

JIMMY: I'm going to enlist.

    (Jimmy and Loretta run off U.R. Clara runs in, frantic, D.R., as Mickey runs in from D.L.)

CLARA: *(Calls to him.)* Hey! Please, don't leave me. My mother's dead and I need you.

MICKEY: But I don't even know you.

CLARA: Funny things happen during wartime. I love you.

MICKEY: You're a funny kid.

(They kiss.)

CLARA: Oh, Mickey, I don't understand what the war's for.

MICKEY: I do. It's so that a little kid in Kansas can grow up on a farm and be President or Senator or dogcatcher or whatever he wants to be. It's for that lady with the light, it's for the Fourth of July and the Declaration of Independence. It's so that a young girl like you can be free to buy herself an ice cream soda in a soda shop in Vermont.

CLARA: I'm hungry.

(They kiss, then run off U.L. A drum roll. Eve enters, U.C. dressed as the Statue of Liberty.)

EVE: *(Sings.)*

You've got to take a stand,

You've got to lend a hand,

So pack your gear, as thousands cheer,

Go march off to that band.

(Behind Eve an enormous American flag, studded with lightbulbs, is lowered. The flag appears to be black and white—unlit, the red and blue bulbs tend to read gray and black. At a point in the music, the flag switches on and becomes bright red, white, and blue. The play has switched to color. The Blessed Mother appears in color in the L. balcony, marching in time; Uncle Sam appears in the R. balcony.)

EVE, BLESSED MOTHER, UNCLE SAM: Take a stand, lend a hand,

Take a stand, lend a hand…

(They keep repeating this.)

(From R. enter Hank and the Gypsy Peasants, now dressed as the Spirit of '76; from L. enter Jimmy, Mickey, and the rest of the men dressed in uniform— Army, Navy, etc. All women, dressed in color now too, stand on the side to wave them on.)

HANK AND CHORUS 1:

Columbia, the gem of the ocean,

The home of the brave and the free,

The shrine of each patriot's devotion,

Is borne by the red, white, and blue…

JIMMY AND CHORUS 2:

Anchors aweigh, my boy,

Anchors over hill, over dale,

We have hit the dusty trail,

From the halls of Montezuma

to the shores of Tripoli…

(Loretta runs over to Jimmy.)

LORETTA: Be careful, Jimmy.

JIMMY: Don't worry, sourpuss.

LORETTA: What should I do about the baby?

JIMMY: Name him Jimmy.

LORETTA: Alright, Jimmy.

(Enter Bette, her Brunnehilde costume now in color too.)

BETTE: I'm pregnant also. What would you like me to call *my* baby? Have you any suggestions, Loretta?

LORETTA: No.

JIMMY: Well I have. I want you both to put aside your differences until this war is over. Because we all have to act as one nation now because whatever these babies are called it's for them we're gonna be fighting. We're all Americans.

LORETTA: *(Waves.)* Good-bye, Jimmy.

(Simultaneously.)

MEN: *(Sing, marching in place.)*

We've got to...	
Nip the nips in the bud,	WOMEN:
Zap the Jap and spill his blood,	Oooooooh—
Rout the Krout, wipe him out,	Oooooooh—
Chop Hitler into sauerkraut,	Rout the Krout, wipe him out—
If we are really men,	
It's war again, world war again,	America, America,
I't a great world war again.	Ahhhhhhh—

WOMEN: So raise your voice, increase your stride,

ALL: We all have Roosevelt and God on our side
America is number one,
We are never number two,
And over there we're gonna win,
For the red, the white, and the blue!

(Blackout.)

END ACT I

ACT II

Scene 1

Lights flash, Sound of explosions. Jimmy, in his Army uniform and helmet, is writing a letter, in R. balcony. Near him is Mickey, also in uniform and helmet. Mickey, terrified of the bombs, shivers and whimpers throughout scene.

JIMMY: Dear Sourpuss. Tomorrow I am going on a dangerous mission behind enemy lines. I don't know if I'll get back alive. But if I die I will die for a good cause. I realize now that when I killed people in the early 1930s, it was wrong because it was done for selfish reasons, for personal gain. However, I find that my years as a gangster were an excellent training for dealing with these stinkin' Nazis. Shootin' Joe Ferruchi and seein' his head roll about in a plate of spaghetti has prepared me for the worst these Nazis can dish out. Even the memory of settin' Fadder MacNeil…
(Annoyed at Mickey's whimpering, Jimmy suddenly shoots his gun at Mickey, who screams.)
JIMMY: Look, kid, you don't quit the crybaby stuff, I'm gonna aim better next time, got me?
(Mickey nods.)
JIMMY: What's your name, kid?
MICKEY: Mickey.
JIMMY: Well, keep it down, Mickey. *(To himself.)* Kids. War ain't for kids.
MICKEY: *(Softly.)* No…
(Lights dim on them.)

ACT II

Scene 2

Lights up on Eve, D.R., dressed as a Wac. With her is Loretta.

LORETTA: Eve, what can I do to help the war effort?
EVE: *(Lifts up Loretta's skirt, points to Loretta's leg.)* See that? Hitler's afraid of that.
LORETTA: Oh, Eve, you're joking.
EVE: *(Grimly.)* I never joke anymore. You wanna help our boys? Then come to the canteen tonight. And bring those gams with you.
LORETTA: *(Thinks.)* The canteen…
(They exit R., lights dim on them.)

ACT II

Scene 3

We hear the Sound of 40s big band dance music. A Sailor sits at a USO table, D.L. *Clara enters, nervous and hyped-up, dressed in a fluffy school-dance kind of dress. She goes over to the Sailor.*

CLARA: You wanna dance, soldier?

SAILOR: No thanks.

CLARA: My boyfriend's overseas. His name's Mickey.

SAILOR: Uh huh.

CLARA: Actually, he's my husband. We only had one night together. My mother got shot at the opera.

SAILOR: Oh yeah?

CLARA: *(Kisses him passionately.)* That's for Mickey, wherever he is! *(Kisses him again, long.)* I'm an emotional wreck.

(They kiss passionately. Enter Eve in her Wac uniform. She salutes.)

EVE: Good evening, soldiers of the United States Military forces, and welcome to the Stage Door Hollywood Canteen, Lt. Eve Sheridan reporting. *(Sees Clara kissing.)* You've met our hostesses, and now meet our entertainment! *(Enter Loretta and Bette wearing only lingerie. Cat calls.)*

EVE: You said it!

LORETTA AND BETTE: *(Singing.)*
  Keep you chin up,
  With a *pretty pin-up,*
  We will keep out chest up,

LORETTA BETTE AND EVE: You can keep the rest up,
  Keep your chin up,
  With a *pretty pin-up,*
  While you're in the action,
  We'll give you satisfaction,

LORETTA: Just think of Grable and her legs,
  And you can scramble Hitler's eggs,

BETTE: If Rita Hayworth makes you hot,
  That's one more Nazi who gets shot!...
  (All "purr," imitating machine gunfire.)

LORETTA BETTE AND EVE: Keep your chin up with a *pretty pin-up,*
  Keep your chin up, GI Joe.

(Clara, who has been watching from the side with the Sailor, suddenly stands up with an unstable look in her eye.)

CLARA: *(Takes off her dress.)* THIS IS FOR MICKEY!

(She starts to pose and to shimmy; Eve in particular notices her with some alarm.)

LORETTA: Betty has her legs,

EVE: And Lana has her sweater,

BETTE: Rita Hayworth's mouth

Is like a mouth but wetter,

LORETTA, BETTE, EVE AND CLARA: Our patriotic duty lies,

In keeping up our legs and thighs…

Keep your chin up

With a *pretty pin-up,*

You make Hitler's knees shake,

We will give you cheesecake,

We won't make you have to beg,

Show some bust and then some leg,

Keep your chin up…

CLARA: *(Maniacally.)* I LOVE YOU, MICKEY!

ALL FOUR: Keep your chin up…

LORETTA AND BETTE: *(Spontaneous, and identical, outburst.)* I LOVE YOU, JIMMY!

(Glare at each other.)

ALL FOUR: Keep your chin up, GI Joe!

CLARA: *(Suddenly exhausted.)* I'm a wreck.

(Lights dim on them.)

ACT II

Scene 4

Sound of explosions. Back to Jimmy writing his letter, in R. balcony. Mickey is still with him.

JIMMY: …and Loretta, if I should be killed tomorrow on this dangerous mission that I mentioned earlier in the letter, I want you to know how proud I am that you've become a pin-up girl. And I know the little guy inside of you will be too when he arrives on the scene. I've got to stop writing now,

Loretta. The dawn is beginning to creep up over the hillside, like old Landlord Death come to collect his final rent...

(Lights dim on him and Mickey; they exit from balcony in dark.)

ACT II

Scene 5

Loretta, at USO table L., reading Jimmy's letter to Eve.

LORETTA: ...I've got to stop writing now, Loretta. The dawn is beginning to creep up over the hillside, like old Landlord Death come to collect his final rent...

(Enter Telegram Boy.)

BOY: Telegram for Miss Moran.

LORETTA: *(Looks at it, faints.)* Oh...

EVE: *(Reads it.)* James T. O'Reilly. Missing in action.

BOY: Gee.

EVE: And her about to have a baby. It's not fair.

(Blackout.)

ACT II

Scene 6

Sound of a hospital; "Calling Dr. Martin, Calling Dr. Martin." Then the sound of a slap and then a baby crying.

In dark, Loretta is seated L., a blanket over legs. Bette is seated R., a blanket over her legs.

Lights up L. on Loretta. With her are Eve and Hank, now a priest.

EVE: *(Holding baby.)* It's a fine healthy-looking boy, Loretta. What are you going to call him?

LORETTA: *(Pause.)* Missing in action. *(Cries.)*

(Everyone looks disturbed. Lights dim.)

ACT II

Scene 7

Sound of a baby crying at birth, again; a slap.

Lights up on Bette, propped up with pillows in a chair, recuperating. Viola, the colored maid of the Mortimers, has become a Nurse and is holding a baby.

VIOLA: You gave birth to your baby jus' fine, Miz O'Reilly.

BETTE: Let me see it. *(Looks at it; grimly.)* Did you do something to this baby?

VIOLA: No, Miz O'Reilly. Ah didn't do nothin'.

BETTE: This baby is Japanese.

VIOLA: Yassum.

BETTE: *(Thinks.)* That damn Ito! *(Pause.)* What about Loretta's baby? Is it Japanese?

VIOLA: No, Ma'am. Miz Loretta's baby looks jus' like Mr. O'Reilly.

BETTE: I am sick of always coming second to Loretta. Sick, do you hear me?

VIOLA: Yes, Ma'am. Ah hears you.

BETTE: Gimme a piece of paper.

VIOLA: Yassum. *(Viola does.)*

(Bette turns baby over, uses it to write on.)

BETTE: Dear Miss Loretta Moran, the United States Army regrets to inform you that Mr. James T. O'Reilly, previously reported as missing, has been found dead. Our regrets, signed General... *(Thinks.)* Douglas MacArthur. *(Folds the paper.)* I'm going to find my husband and win him back if I have to join the military to do it. Viola, send this telegram to Loretta and send this baby to a camp.

VIOLA: Yassum. *(Exits R. with baby and telegram.)*

(Lights dim.)

ACT II

Scene 8

Lights up on Loretta's hospital room again. Loretta is depressed and staring off, the baby in her lap. Eve, Hank still present.

HANK: Eve, I've never seen her this depressed.

EVE: Hank, I'm going to talk to her. *(Goes closer to Loretta.)* Loretta, listen to me. I've watched you for the last ten minutes. Do you know what you are? You're a quitter! That's right, a quitter. You're full of self-pity—self, self, self. Well I don't feel sorry for you. You know why? Because you have a baby, and you have a career as a pin-up girl, and if Jimmy is alive, you'll have a husband, and even if he's dead at least you will have been loved! Who do you think you are to feel sorry for yourself? Jane Froman doesn't have the use of her legs, but do you see her carrying on this way? No! She's out entertaining the troops on crutches. Where are you? Where would the Allies be if they acted the way you do? *(Tears in her voice.)* Well I don't feel sorry for you because you're nothing but a quitter! *(Cries, hides her face in Hank's shoulder.)*

LORETTA: Thank you, Eve. I feel strong again. And Hank, how nice you've become a priest.

HANK: Well, when I couldn't get into the Army to fight this war, I thought I should fight another kind of war. His war.

EVE: Oh, brother.

(Enter Telegram Boy.)

BOY: Telegram for Miss Moran. From General MacArthur.

(Loretta looks worried, reads telegram. Pause. She screams, faints, dropping the baby along the way.)

EVE: *(Takes telegram.)* The United States Army regrets to inform you… *(Looks at Hank.)* He's dead, Hank. *(Looks at Loretta.)* Poor kid. *(Sees baby.)* Pick up the baby, Hank.

HANK: *(Picks it up.)* The baby's dead.

EVE: Well, there's the trap door, the humidor, and the cuspidor.

HANK: Cut it out, Eve.

EVE: You're right, Father.

(Lights off them; they exit in dark.)

ACT II

Scene 9

At the movies. A few chairs, facing out to the "Screen." In the U.C. balcony, seated, are a woman patron and Victor Henreid, a suave European in his 40s. We hear the sound track of the picture. After a bit, Loretta enters and watches the picture, upset and crying.

WOMAN: *(On sound track.)* Oh, John, I love you more than I love skating!

MAN: *(On sound track.)* But, darling—why not love me *and* skating?

WOMAN: *(On soundt rack.)* You mean—you don't mind? Oh, John, let's skate forever!

(On the sound track the music soars cheerfully, and there is the sound of skating

on ice. These skating sounds should continue until indicated. Loretta has been crying throughout above.)

PATRON: Ssssssssh. Why are you crying? This picture is a comedy.

LORETTA: I hate skating.

PATRON: Then you shouldn't have come to this picture.

LORETTA: I hate skating. And the Nazis made me drop my baby, and I hate the Nazis. I HATE THE NAZIS. I HATE THE NAZIS.

PATRON: Sonja Henie is not a Nazi.

LORETTA: She sounds like she is. And she's not doing anything to stop them. What do the Nazis care whether she skates or not? I HATE THE NAZIS. *(The sound track crescendos, the skating stops, the picture's over.)*

PATRON: I am going to report you to the manager. *(Exits.)*

VICTOR: *(To Loretta.)* I could not help overhearing you. My name is Victor Henreid.

LORETTA: You don't sound American.

VICTOR: I am Austrian. I hate what the Nazis have done to my country. I am a member of the Austrian underground. I am on my way to Tunis. Would you like to help us?

LORETTA: My life is worth nothing to me. If it can be worth something to the underground...why not?

VICTOR: *(Lights two cigarettes in his mouth, offers her one.)* Cigarette?

LORETTA: I'm sorry, I don't smoke.

VICTOR: You will have to learn. May I be your teacher?

(Sound track starts again; sound of music and skating.)

VICTOR: On our way to Tunis we must stop at Casablanca to get letters of transit. Shall we go?

LORETTA: Wait. I missed the beginning. *(Loretta sits down, watches the movie.)* *(Victor does likewise, smokes his two cigarettes. Lights dim on them.)*

ACT II

Scene 10

Lights up on a cafe in Casablanca. Piano Man, the black man from the Club Intimate, is seated at the piano, R., playing a Hoagy Carmichael-like song.

With him is Jimmy, dressed in a white dinner jacket, seated at a table D. L. of the piano. He is smoking and staring off.

PIANO MAN: How's your amnesia today, Mister Rick?

JIMMY: Fine, Piano Man. I ain't remembered nuthin' since I came to Casablanca eight days ago.

PIANO MAN: You come here six months ago, Boss. Why you come to Casablanca, Boss?

JIMMY: I came to Casablanca for the waters.

PIANO MAN: But there ain't no waters here, Boss.

JIMMY: Stick to your piano playin', why don'tcha?

(Piano Man starts to play "Shanty Town Romance.")

JIMMY: Don't play that one.

PIANO MAN: Why not, Boss?

JIMMY: I dunno. Just don't play it.

(Enter Bette and Michael from U.L. in their military uniforms.)

MICHAEL: *(To Bette.)* Major O'Reilly, this is futile. We can't keep looking for Jimmy all over Europe. It's doomed.

BETTE: Americans don't give up, Major O'Reilly. *(Sees Jimmy.)* James!

JIMMY: You lookin for somebody?

BETTE: James, it's me! Your wife!

JIMMY: *(Truly not recognizing her.)* You tell her, Piano Man.

PIANO MAN: Mister Rick here has amnesia, Ma'am. He don't remember nuthin'.

BETTE: *(Looks at them both as if they're crazy.)* But you've got to remember. I'm your wife. *(Points to Michael.)* This is your brother. You tried to make me an opera singer. Don't you remember? *(Sings.)* Hoy-a-ta-ho!

MICHAEL: Major O'Reilly, keep a hold of yourself.

BETTE: Perhaps it's my uniform. I wasn't always a Wac, James. I used to do big puzzles. You used to hit me.

JIMMY: Look, I got a lousy memory about dames. Beat it.

BETTE: JAMES, I'M YOUR WIFE!

JIMMY: Have a grapefruit! *(Jimmy pushes a grapefruit in her face.)*

(Bette has hysterics.)

MICHAEL: *(To Jimmy.)* That was a rotten thing to do. *(To Bette.)* Are you alright?

BETTE: I have a seed in my eye.

(Michael checks her eye. Enter Loretta, r., looking lovely. No one sees her right away except for Piano Man. Piano Man plays "Shanty Town Romance.")

JIMMY: *(Violent.)* I thought I told you never to play that!

LORETTA: Jimmy!

(He looks at her.)

LORETTA: You're alive...

JIMMY: (*Looks at her; his amnesia leaves.*) Your name is Sourpuss. My name is Jimmy. It's 1943.

PIANO MAN: That's right, Boss!

JIMMY: I remember everything.

BETTE: (*Sees Loretta.*) Oh no.

LORETTA: Jimmy, I didn't know you were alive.

JIMMY: I'm American, ain't I?

(*Enter Victor, R. He goes up to Loretta, kisses her.*)

VICTOR: I'm sorry to take so long, darling. I was afraid the hatcheck girl was a Nazi.

JIMMY: Who's this Bozo?

LORETTA: Jimmy, this is my husband, Victor Henreid.

(*Bette looks up hopefully.*)

VICTOR: How do you do? (*Puts out his hand.*)

JIMMY: Your what? (*Pause.*) I'll kill him! (*Goes to hit Victor.*)

LORETTA: Jimmy, don't hit him! He's a member of the underground.

(*Victor glares at her, she realizes her gaffe. Jimmy pauses, starts to punch Piano Man.*)

JIMMY: I thought I told you to stop playin' that lousy song. Ya dumb head!

(*Jimmy continues to beat up Piano Man.*)

(*All else looks embarrassed.*)

BETTE: I love you, James. Hit *me*. Hit *me*.

JIMMY: (*Finished with Piano Man.*) I'm takin' this here bottle and I'm gonna drink it until I get amnesia all over again. (*Jimmy exits with the bottle, U.C.*)

(*Bette, crying, is taken off by Michael, L.*)

LORETTA: I'm sorry he hit you like that, Piano Man.

PIANO MAN: That's alright, Miss Loretta. He hurtin' inside.

LORETTA: We all are, Piano Man.

PIANO MAN: You white folks like me to play somethin' to cheer you up?

VICTOR: Do you know the "Marseillaise"?

LORETTA: Oh not now, Victor. I have the most awful headache.

VICTOR: Very well. We only have a few minutes before the plane leaves. (*Gets an odd look in his eye.*) Excuse me, I must check something. (*Exits R.*)

LORETTA: Play it, Piano Man.

PIANO MAN: I'm a bit rusty, Miss Loretta.

LORETTA: (*Smiles sadly.*) Play it.

(*Piano Man starts to play "Shanty Town Romance."*)

LORETTA: (*Singing.*)

Di di di di di di di di di di...

(*Shots Offstage R. Enter Victor from R.*)

VICTOR: The hat checkgirl *was* a Nazi. I had to kill her.

LORETTA: Yes, Victor.

VICTOR: Killing is wrong, Loretta. I want you to understand that. Do you remember when I read Victor Hugo's *Les Miserables* to you aloud, and how I said it was wrong for a man to steal bread, but a necessary wrong, so he could feed his family?

LORETTA: Yes, Victor. I remember. The book was a trifle long, I thought.

VICTOR: Killing Nazis is like stealing bread, Loretta. It is wrong, but it must be done until the world is a just one.

LORETTA: You better dispose of the bread, Victor.

VICTOR: Yes, you're right. *(Pause.)* That man with amnesia. He meant something to you once, didn't he?

LORETTA: Who? Mr. O'Reilly? *(Laughs hilariously.)* Really, Victor, you are too much. Go bury the Nazi and I'll practice smoking.

(Victor exits. Loretta practices. Re-enter Jimmy from U.C. He crosses down to Loretta.)

JIMMY: I've come to say good-bye to you and your dull husband before your plane leaves.

LORETTA: Victor is a wonderful man. He's good and noble, he's everything you're not, but it's true—I am bored to death with him! Oh, Jimmy, I don't want to get on the plane to Tunis with him. I don't want to read any more Victor Hugo. Jimmy, let's run away together.

(They kiss. Piano Man starts to play "Shanty Town Romance.")

LORETTA: You'll have to think for both of us, for all of us.

JIMMY: Alright, I will.

(Sound of the plane.)

LORETTA: The plane. Oh, Jimmy, I'll never leave you again.

JIMMY: You have to, sourpuss. If that plane leaves the ground and you're not on it with him, you'll regret it. Maybe not today, maybe not tomorrow, but soon and for the rest of your life.

(Piano Man begins to play the theme very dramatically and loudly.)

LORETTA: What about us?

JIMMY: We'll always have Shanty Town. But I've got a job to do, too. And where I'm going, you can't follow, what I've got to do you can't be any part of.

LORETTA: Don't play it now, Piano Man. I can't concentrate.

JIMMY: Loretta, I'm no good at being noble, but it doesn't take much to see that the problems of three little people don't amount to a hill of beans in this crazy world. Someday you'll understand that.

LORETTA: What about beans? *(Very upset.)* I don't want you to play now!

JIMMY: Here's looking at you, sourpuss.

(Enter Victor.)

LORETTA: Here's looking at me? What does that mean? Are you confusing me with someone else?

VICTOR: Loretta, dear, the plane for Tunis is waiting.

LORETTA: What about Tunis? I haven't heard a word anyone has said.

(Victor and Loretta exit R. Piano Man stops playing.)

JIMMY: That didn't go the way I wanted.

(Sound of plane take-off. Enter Bette and Michael from L.)

BETTE: Did you tell her good-bye?

JIMMY: Yeah.

BETTE: Good. Now you have two alternatives. You can tell me you love me and I can tear up these orders—or you can reject me and be sent on an extremely dangerous mission and probably be killed. Which is it to be?

JIMMY: Gimme the orders.

BETTE: Very well. No hard feelings. I hope you die in that mission. I hope your eyes shrivel up and fall out of your head. I want you to know that I love your brother. I'm divorcing you and marrying your brother right after we invade Normandy. Forget I said anything about Normandy. Kiss me, Michael.

MICHAEL: Darling, I'm so happy.

BETTE: *(Pushing him away.)* Me too, me too... *(Exits L., distraught.)*

MICHAEL: She's very high strung, but militarily quite brilliant.

JIMMY: *(Looking at his orders.)* Now what about this bomb I'm supposed to drop?

MICHAEL: Well, it's very powerful, and if all goes well we have hopes of its bringing this war to a close. Now your first target is Hiroshima. Now what you need to know is that the atom is the smallest particle of matter which has the characteristic chemical properties of an element. There are three fundamental subatomic particles:

JIMMY: Michael, I have a feeling this is the beginning of a beautiful friendship...

MICHAEL: ...the proton having unit positive charge and mass number one; neutron, having neutral charge and mass number one; electron...

(Lights fade as Jimmy and Michael walk off, U.C. The End sign is lowered. Sound of an enormous, long explosion. The End sign shakes considerably, goes up again.)

(Blackout.)

ACT II
Scene 11

In blackout we hear the music start of the following song. Lights up on Three 40s Singers singing in front of a radio microphone like the Andrews Sisters, D.C. (They are normally Eve, Bette, and a third actress.)

THREE SINGERS: Well we got ourselves an *apple blossom victory,*
  And they're ready with confetti Maine to Tennessee,
  Gonna learn to live with the atomic bomb,
  Cause it's back to God and apple pie, and back to Mom,
  Come home, boys, come home to your wives,
  These are the best years of our lives...
  Welcome ba-ack,
  Welcome ba-ack,
  You were there at Iwo Jima,
  You flew over Hiroshima,
  You're a hero in Khaki,
  You destroyed Nagasaki,
  Well we'll never drop another,
  But if we should drop another:
EVE: Don't sit under the atom bomb with anyone else but me...
THREE SINGERS: Welcome back,
  It's an apple blossom victory!
  Zya-ba-doo-ba-dee-ba-doo ba-bop! Yeah!
  (The Three Singers exit.)
  (Enter Loretta and Victor, in R. balcony.)
LORETTA: The war is over, Victor.
VICTOR: Yes, Loretta.
  (Soldiers come home, embracing girls.)
LORETTA: The soldiers are coming home now, Victor.
VICTOR: Yes, Loretta. We are entering a new decade. It will be called the post-war decade. It will be a period of building up, of restoring. There will be a baby boom, and much will be accomplished in the coming years.
  (Loretta and Victor exit. Enter Mickey and Clara from opposite sides; they call across to each other.)
CLARA: Mickey!
MICKEY: Clara!
CLARA: I've been promiscuous!

MICKEY: I have no hands! *(Holds up his handless arms.)*

(Mickey and Clara run together and embrace. Enter Eve and Father Hank from U.C.)

EVE: The war is over, Hank.

HANK: Yes, Eve.

(Enter Michael, R. From other side enter Bette.)

MICHAEL: Bette!

BETTE: Michael!

(They embrace, kiss.)

EVE: Everyone's kissing, Hank.

HANK: Yes, Eve.

EVE: Do you ever give up celibacy, like for Lent?

HANK: Celibacy is a serious thing, Eve.

EVE: I love you, Hank. *(Kisses him.)*

HANK: You shouldn't have done that, Eve. *(Exits L.)*

EVE: *(Calling after him.)* Don't worry. You can always get a tetanus shot. *(Exits after him.)*

MICHAEL: Bette. It's good to see you.

BETTE: It's good to see you. Who are you?

MICHAEL: I'm your husband, Michael.

BETTE: Jimmy is my husband.

MICHAEL: Jimmy is your ex-husband. I'm his brother.

BETTE: I married his brother? Why did I do that?

(Enter Jimmy, R., back from the war.)

BETTE: Jimmy!

MICHAEL: *(Holding her back.)* I'm your husband now, Bette.

(Michael pulls Bette Offstage. Enter Loretta and Victor, U.C. Loretta sees Jimmy.)

LORETTA: *(Clutched throat.)* Jimmy!

JIMMY: Loretta!

(They face each other, do not embrace.)

LORETTA: You remember my husband Victor?

JIMMY: How ya doin'?

VICTOR: Well thank you. And yourself?

JIMMY: Okay.

LORETTA: How is your wife Bette?

JIMMY: She married my brother Michael. I'm free now, Loretta.

LORETTA: Oh. You remember my husband Victor?

VICTOR: I understand that you were the pilot who dropped the atom bomb.

LORETTA: Oh, did you do that, Jimmy?

VICTOR: I have great hopes that atomic energy will be used for the general betterment of mankind in the coming post-war years.

LORETTA: Victor's full of hopes. It makes him fun to be with. *(Cries.)*

VICTOR: Loretta, Liebchen, did I say something wrong?

LORETTA: No, Victor. Something's flown in my eye.

JIMMY: Lemme see if I can get it out. *(Jimmy takes Loretta a few steps away from Victor.)* Meet me at the Club Intimate in an hour, and we'll talk about killin' this dodo for his insurance.

LORETTA: Jimmy, we couldn't.

JIMMY: I dropped the bomb, didn't I?

LORETTA: I know, but that was mass slaughter, this would only be killing one man.

JIMMY: You love me, don'tcha? Meet me in an hour.

VICTOR: Liebchen, we'll be late for the concert.

LORETTA: Yes, Victor. *(To Jimmy.)* We're very fond of Schubert.

(Loretta and Victor exit, R. Re-enter Bette; Michael follows after her.)

BETTE: Yoo-hoo, Jimmy, I'm here! *(Smiles.)*

JIMMY: Oh yeah? Drop dead.

MICHAEL: *(Grabs ahold of Bette.)* You'll learn to love me, Bette.

BETTE: Yes, I'm sure I will. *(Bette gets an uncontrollable facial tic; then turns on Michael and beats on his chest hysterically.)*

MICHAEL: Bette! Do you think you should see a psychiatrist?

BETTE: Yes, maybe I should. *(Facial tic returns.)* What's a psychiatrist?

(Bette is dragged off struggling by Michael. Clara and Mickey break free from their embrace.)

MICKEY: How promiscuous were you?

CLARA: Well, how much of your hands are you missing?

TWO SINGERS: *(Now minus Bette; singing in L. balcony.)*
Welcome back, welcome back…
(Fading out.)
Zya-ba-doo-ba-dee-ba-doo ba-bop…
Zya-ba-doo-ba-dee-ba-doo ba-bop…
(Their singing is interrupted by the intrusion of eerie science fiction music. Clara, Mickey, Jimmy look about in panic. Enter a Robot, all silver, in U.C. balcony. His voice comes from over the speaker system, not from himself.)

ROBOT: People of the planet earth. I have come with a warning to you from the planet Zabar. Beware atomic power, people of earth. Within it you hold the possibility of destroying the entire universe, including Zabar. People who have been near the deadly radiation emanating from the atomic bomb may have mutant children or, among the male species, find themselves sexually impotent. If you have been near atomic radiation, go to a doctor at once. You must join the United Nations. My name is Edward. *(Exits.)*

CLARA: *(Screams hysterically.)* AAAAAAAAAAAAAAAAAGGGGGGGGGGGHH-HHHHHHHH…Mickey, what did he mean?

MICKEY: I don't know.

CLARA: You've never been near the atom bomb, have you?

MICKEY: No, never.

CLARA: Thank goodness.

(Jimmy has overheard them, looks worried.)

CLARA: It's so terrifying. AAAAAAAAAAAAAAAAAGGGGGGGGGGGGHHH-HHHHHHHH!

(Mickey and Clara run off R. Jimmy stays on, worried.)

ACT II
Scene 12

The Club Intimate. Piano Man, L., playing "Shanty Town Romance." Jimmy crosses to him.

JIMMY: Piano Man, if you had a friend who loved a woman but he couldn't marry her because he had been near some nuclear power or something, and he'd been to a doctor and the doctor said he couldn't, well, this person couldn't be a man anymore, well, if you were this friend, what would you do?

PIANO MAN: I'd kill myself.

JIMMY: But if you didn't do that, what would you do?

PIANO MAN: I'd send myself back to Africa.

JIMMY: Look, you keep playin' that song, I'm gonna break your hands.

(Piano Man stops.)

JIMMY: Play somethin' else.

PIANO MAN: OK, Boss. *(Plays, "As Time Goes By.")*

JIMMY: *(Scribbles on a piece of paper.)* Piano Man, when Loretta comes, give her this note. And now…good-bye. *(Exits, L.)*

(Enter Loretta, R.)

LORETTA: Piano Man.

PIANO MAN: Good to see you, Miss Loretta,

LORETTA: Is Jimmy here yet?

PIANO MAN: He done left you a note. *(Gives her the note.)*

LORETTA: *(Reads it.)* But all it says is "Good-bye."

PIANO MAN: I guess it ain't meant to be, Miss Loretta.

LORETTA: But it's so...terse. *(Cries.)* Gimme a drink, Piano Man.

> *(He goes to pour her one; she grabs the bottle from him, gulps it. He looks worried. Lights dim as we hear 50s sleazy sax music, which continues until the next scene.)*

ACT II
Scene 13

> *Hank, a drunk Loretta, Eve, Clara, and three other people at an Alcoholics Anonymous meeting. They stand in line. Eve, Hank, and Loretta are five, six, and seven, respectively.*

PERSON 1: My name is Wally Marvin, and I am an alcoholic.

EVE: Good for you, Wally, that's an important step.

LORETTA: *(Drunk.)* Where are we, Gustaf?

HANK: Don't be afraid, Loretta.

PERSON 2: My name is Elizabeth Purtridge, and I am an alcoholic.

LORETTA: I gotta get outta here. These people are drunks.

HANK: You can't keep running away, Loretta.

PERSON 3: My name is Daniel Goldman, and I am an alcoholic.

HANK: God'll help you, Loretta.

LORETTA: No, He won't. He doesn't like me.

CLARA: My name is Clara Myrna Mortimer, and I am an alcoholic.

LORETTA: They're getting closer.

EVE: My name is Eve Sheridan, and I am an alcoholic.

HANK: I pass. Your turn, Loretta.

LORETTA: I pass.

HANK: You can't keep running away, Loretta.

LORETTA: I can, I can!

HANK: Say your name.

LORETTA: I don't remember it.

HANK: Say it after me, my name is Loretta...

LORETTA: My name is...

HANK: Loretta...

LORETTA: My name is nobody and I'm not anything! *(Runs out.)*

EVE: Well, you tried, Father. I guess she wasn't ready.

PERSON 1: I bet she goes out and has a drink.

PERSON 2: What does she drink mostly, Father?

HANK: I don't know really.

PERSON 2: I wonder if she likes scotch.

PERSON 1: I never liked scotch. I liked bourbon a lot though.

   (They all look thirsty and unhappy; exit L.)

ACT II

Scene 14

   Sleazy sax music again. Loretta enters R., in her slip and drinking from a bottle. Unsteady, she ends up on the floor.

LORETTA: This is the bottom. Hello, bottom, hello. *(Cries.)* It's the war really. When the war was on, none of us had time to be neurotic. But now that it's over, there's just all this time… *(Cries.)*

   (Supernatural music. The Blessed Mother appears, dressed in blue, in the L. balcony.)

BLESSED MOTHER: Loretta.

LORETTA: Oh God, the D.T.'s.

BLESSED MOTHER: Loretta, don't turn away from God. I'll intercede for you.

LORETTA: I'm afraid.

BLESSED MOTHER: Don't be afraid. Did you see *The Song of Bernadette* with Jennifer Jones?

LORETTA: Yes, Your Grace.

BLESSED MOTHER: She wasn't afraid. And what happened to her?

LORETTA: *(Confused and crying.)* She won an Oscar.

BLESSED MOTHER: That was during the war. To win an Oscar now you must overcome great personal difficulties. Do you think you can do this?

LORETTA: *(Standing.)* I want The End sign to come down and I want to stay frozen behind it.

BLESSED MOTHER: Loretta, do you have faith enough in God and in yourself to overcome polio?

LORETTA: But I don't have polio.

   (The Blessed Mother gracefully waves her hand, as if bestowing a great gift. Loretta falls down, stricken with polio.)

BLESSED MOTHER: Find the strength within yourself, Loretta. It's within your-self... *(Disappears.)*

LORETTA: No, don't leave me, no...no...

(Music. A platform is pushed on by two ushers in tuxedos. Enter Mickey, dressed up for an awards ceremony and holding an Oscar under his arm.)

VOICE: And now the next major award of the evening.

MICKEY: The nominations for Best Actress are: Bette O'Reilly as an unhappily married woman still in love with her former husband Jimmy but fast for-getting him due to several rounds of shock treatments in *Love Me or Leave Me in the Snake Pit.*

(Applause. Enter Bette in an evening gown. She has a completely blank stare and has to be helped to her place. She doesn't seem to know where she is.)

MICKEY: Eve Sheridan as an alcoholic spinster shamefully in love with a Catholic Priest and fast finding her wisecracks unable to protect her from an empty bed in *Losing Her Sense Of Humor.*

(Applause. Enter Eve in an evening gown. She is led to her place by an usher, and seems glum indeed.)

MICKEY: Clara Mortimer as a dimwitted socialite who can't cope with her hus-band's losing his hands in the war in *We the Victors.*

(Mickey looks self-conscious on We the Victors. *Applause. Enter Clara in an evening gown. An usher leads her to her place; she holds his hand too long, and he has to pull it away.)*

MICKEY: Loretta Moran as an alcoholic ex-ingenue who must overcome polio in *I'll Cry With a Song in My Heart Tomorrow.*

(Applause. Loretta waves.)

MICKEY: And the Blessed Virgin Mary in *Sunset Boulevard.*

(Applause. Enter the Blessed Mother.)

MICKEY: And the winner is... *(Tries to open the envelope, can't.)* ...Clara, would you help me with this?

(Clara does.)

MICKEY: ...LORETTA MORAN!

(Applause. Clara gracefully applauds; the Blessed Mother is perhaps bitter, up to the actress; Eve is glad for Loretta; Bette tries to applaud but has trouble get-ting her hands to hit one another. Loretta drags herself with great difficulty over to Mickey and the Oscar. Eve eggs her on with encouraging "You can do it, come on," etc., type statements. As courageous background music soars Loretta manages to get to her feet and to stand and walk once again. Tears stream down her face. The applause is immense.)

LORETTA: *(Weeping, holding the award.)* I am…so deeply grateful. I haven't really even made a movie, and yet you have given this to me. If only we can find our way again—maybe we can—through the courageous stories of recovery of people like myself or Lillian Roth or Marjorie Lawrence or…
(Jimmy, in a leather outfit like Brando's in Wild One, *stumbles in, drunk from U.L.)*

LORETTA: …oh.

JIMMY: Congratulations…

(Everyone Onstage is embarrassed for Loretta.)

LORETTA: Hello, Jimmy. You're wearing leather.

JIMMY: I'm a Rebel. *(Hardly audible.)* Ya know what I'm sayin'?

LORETTA: What are you rebelling against?

JIMMY: I dunno. *(Thinks.)* What've ya got? *(Laughs; moves drunkenly; accidentally knocks the Oscar from her hand; the Oscar breaks.)* I'm sorry, I'm always hurting people. I just killed this old woman with my motorcycle out front…

LORETTA: Don't cry, Jimmy…

JIMMY: I don't mean to be bad.

LORETTA: None of us do.

JIMMY: I dropped the bomb, but now there's no place for me to fit in.

LORETTA: Maybe we'll have to drop the bomb again…

VOICE: The next award please.

MICKEY: I'm sorry, we have to give the next award now.

JIMMY: *(Really violent.)* Don't hassle me. *(Shakes him.)* You understand me. Don't hassle me!

CLARA: Please, don't hurt him, he hasn't any hands!

MICKEY: *(Suddenly hysterical.)* Will you shut up, will you just shut up!

LORETTA: Oh, this is all so public, I can't stand it.

JIMMY: Loretta, I'm impotent. Will you marry me?

VOICE: The next award please.

LORETTA: Please, we can't talk here. Everyone's listening. Come on, Jimmy…
(Starts to lead him off, U.L.*)*

CLARA: *(Crying with Mickey.)* Don't forget your Oscar…

LORETTA: *(Taking it.)* Thank you. I'm sorry you didn't win.

CLARA: Please, just go away.
(Loretta and Jimmy exit U.L.*)*

VOICE: And now, Clara Mortimer and her husband, Mickey, will sing the next nominated song from the film *Seven Brides for Twelve Angry Men.*

(Musical introduction. Mickey and Clara look out horrified. They try to sing but are overcome with grief again, and have to exit, U.R., crying. The ushers help the others off too, especially Bette who hasn't quite followed anything that's gone on but has felt instinctively that what ever it was was upsetting. Lights dim on the whole area.)

ACT II
Scene 15

The sound of foghorns and seagulls. A rooftop. Enter Jimmy, still in leather, with Loretta, still in her slip, in the L. balcony.

LORETTA: Why are we on this rooftop, Jimmy?

JIMMY: Well…Hoboken ain't much but…I call it home.

LORETTA: It's so ugly.

(Jimmy cries.)

LORETTA: Don't cry, Jimmy.

JIMMY: You don't unnerstan'. I coulda been a contender, I coulda been somebody.

LORETTA: We'll move away from here. We don't have to stay in Hoboken. We'll go back to Shanty Town.

JIMMY: What are you talking about? This is Shanty Town.

LORETTA: What do you mean?

JIMMY: This is where it was. Right here in Hoboken.

LORETTA: I don't believe you. This isn't Shanty Town. It isn't. You're lying to me.

JIMMY: I swear to God, sourpuss. It's the truth.

LORETTA: *(Looks out.)* I remember it differently.

(Jimmy puts his arm around her, and they stare out, sadly. Lights dim on them.)

ACT II
Scene 16

Abrupt sound of gavel on a desk. The House Un-American Activities Committee. Michael stands, U.C., behind a lectern on which are papers and the just-heard gavel. A Prison Matron places a chair D.L. of the lectern. From L. a very elderly Ma Joad is helped in by Fr. Hank, followed by Eve.

HANK: Be strong, Ma.

MA JOAD: I ain't afraid, son. We're the people.

MICHAEL: Name.

MA JOAD: Ma Joad.

MICHAEL: Age.

MA JOAD: I'll be one-hundred-two this Febr…

MICHAEL: Now, Mrs. Joad, are you now or have you ever been a member of the Communist Party?

EVE: You don't have to answer these questions, Mrs. Joad.

MA JOAD: I'm a Democrat.

MICHAEL: Mrs. Joad, you were heard to say by a witness friendly to this committee—your son—the phrase, "We're the people."

HANK: I'm sorry, Ma. I felt I had to.

(Eve and Ma look at Hank in shocked surprise.)

MICHAEL: What did you mean by that phrase?

MA JOAD: It don't mean nothin'. It's just a little somethin' I say to raise my spirits a little.

MICHAEL: Did it ever cross your mind that it might raise the spirits of the *Russian* people a little?

MA JOAD: I didn't say it in Russian.

MICHAEL: Mrs. Joad, I have here a needlepoint pillow bearing the aforementioned phrase, "We're the people." *(Holds up red pillow.)* Do you deny having made it?

MA JOAD: *(Cheerfully.)* No. I love it.

MICHAEL: Do you deny it's *red*?

MA JOAD: *(Agreeably.)* No, it's red.

EVE: Don't answer any more of these questions, Mrs. Joad. They're idiotic.

HANK: Eve, this isn't your place.

MICHAEL: There aren't going to be any more questions. Mrs. Joad, if we don't execute you, the next thing we know you'll be needlepointing *state secrets* to the Communists.

EVE: Execute!

MA JOAD: But I don't know no state secrets.

MICHAEL: We only have your word for that, don't we? Guilty as charged. *(Bangs gavel, exits U.L., pushing his lectern [on rollers] before him.)*

MA JOAD: Why'd you do it, Hank?

HANK: Ma, we have to stop Communism somewhere.

(Enter Prison Matron.)

MATRON: It's time now, Mrs. Joad.

MA JOAD: No, I don't want to die. I want to live.

HANK: Come, Ma, let's pray.

MA JOAD: I ain't gonna pray. I'm gonna scream. *(Screams horribly.)*

(Matron drags off Ma, R., who continues to scream and scream.)

HANK: I mean, she did say it. We're the people. She said it all the time.

EVE: I've wasted a lot of time being in love with you, Hank.

HANK: Eve, don't go now.

EVE: So long, Hank. *(Exits, L.)*

(Sound of an electrocution and a flashing light come from Offstage, R. A spot hits Hank's face.)

HANK: Ma! Ma! *(Rips off his priest's collar.)* Ma's dead! Ma's dead!

(Blackout.)

ACT II

Scene 17

On the sound track we hear crashing cymbals and then the music to what sounds like a Biblical epic. This music should continue on until almost the end of the scene, though at a low and hopefully unobtrusive level.

We are at the movies again. The following characters push in their movie seats and then stare ahead at the movie: Bette and Michael, D.R.; Clara and Mickey behind them; Eve by herself, just R. of Center. Center is an imaginary aisle. D.L. is Hank in pants and T-shirt, an empty seat next to him. Behind him is Stuart, a well-dressed black man; there are two empty seats, one on each side of him. And several feet U. of his seat there is another empty seat; toward the end of the scene, the Blessed Mother comes into the theatre and watches the movie from this seat.

Michael is in his military uniform. Bette looks odd. She has on a blond wig, lots of red lipstick, and a tight dress which has been awkwardly padded to suggest an extremely ample figure. She should look something like Marilyn Monroe, but it should not be too exact. It should look like the attempt of a crazy person to look like Monroe. She should purse her lips a lot, like Monroe.

VOICE OF GOD: These are the Ten Commandments. Honor the Lord thy God. Thou shalt have no molten images.

BETTE: *(Southern accent, like Monroe's in* Bus Stop.*)* What's a molten image?

MICHAEL: Bette, why are you talking in that accent?

BETTE: I'm talkin' about what's a molten image.

MICHAEL: Be quiet, Bette.

VOICE OF GOD: *(On sound track.)* Thou shalt not take the name of the Lord thy God in vain.

BETTE: Is that Esther Williams?

MICHAEL: No. That's Charlton Heston.

BETTE: You told me Esther Williams was going to be in this.

MICHAEL: I didn't, Bette.

BETTE: You did.

EVE: *(Annoyed.)* Ssssssssssh.

BETTE: *(Hurt.)* Sssssssss y'self.

VOICE OF GOD: Honor thy Father and thy Mother. Thou shalt not kill.

BETTE: I'm tryin' to sound like Kim Novak in *Picnic.* Actually she didn't talk that way. It's more like Marilyn Monroe in *Bus Stop.* Do you think I look like her? Maybe I'm Carroll Baker in *Baby Doll.*

EVE: Will you be quiet?

BETTE: I'm tryin' to be quiet, if you'd all just quit hushin' me.

(Enter Loretta U.C. by herself; sits next to Stuart; her clothes are middle-aged slutty.)

BETTE: *(Sings.)*

It's that ol' black magic, that ya hear so well…

MICHAEL: *(Furious.)* Will you pull yourself together? Bette, I am going home now. I hope you pass through this period of your life. I find it very depressing. *(Exits U.C.)*

EVE: *(To both of them.)* Shut up!

BETTE: *(Calling sadly.)* Hey! Oh well.

LORETTA: Is that Bette?

BETTE: Who's that?

LORETTA: *(Moving over to her.)* It's Loretta.

BETTE: Oh, hi honey! You come to the movies?

EVE: I am going to get the manager! *(Exits in huff U.C.)*

LORETTA: I'm married to Jimmy now.

BETTE: That's nice.

LORETTA: You look different.

BETTE: Do I? Well I bleached my hair. Or maybe it's a wig. *(Takes off her wig; looks at it.)* No. I bleached it. You look different too.

LORETTA: I know. I feel different. I feel like I'm in a Lana Turner movie about adultery.

BETTE: Oh, I love those. I don't know what movie I'm in. *(Cries.)*

LORETTA: I want to commit adultery.

BETTE: *(As if she heard a question.)* Oh, I'm fine. I'm a member of the Joint Chiefs of Staff now. Ever since we had Hank Joad's momma executed.

LORETTA: Hank. He always found me attractive, I think. Do you know where he's living now?

BETTE: Over there.

(Points to Hank in theatre. Loretta moves over next to Hank.)

LORETTA: Hello, Hank. It's Loretta.

HANK: Ssssssh, I'm watching the movie.

LORETTA: You're not a priest anymore, I see.

HANK: No, uh, I left.

LORETTA: I have an unhappy marriage, Hank. I want to commit adultery.

HANK: Uh…Well… *(Smiles, nervous.)*

LORETTA: I always liked you, Hank, ever since we first met on that chain gang. Why are you fidgeting so much?

HANK: Uh, I dunno. Uh, Ma was just sayin' the other day that I'm too shy with girls.

LORETTA: *(Taken aback.)* Hank. Ma is dead.

HANK: What?

LORETTA: Hank, Ma is dead.

HANK: No she ain't. Ma ain't dead. Are you, Ma? *(Speaks in a falsetto voice for "Ma.")* No, son, I'm fine. We're the people. *(Normal voice.)* You see.

LORETTA: Hank!

HANK: What, Ma? *(Falsetto.)* Loretta looks dirty, son. Tell her to take a shower. *(Normal.)* You need a shower, Loretta.

LORETTA: Hank, you need help. Psychiatric help.

HANK: Ma, you want to say hello to Loretta? *(Falsetto.)* Let me just put on my lip rouge, son. Hello, Loretta. Nice to see you.

(Loretta screams, runs to another seat L. of Stuart. Hank has raised his knife to kill Loretta but she hasn't seen him. Enter Eve and the Theatre Manager, U.C. Hank puts his knife away. Bette screams, echoing Loretta's scream.)

EVE: *(Pointing at Bette.)* There she is.

MANAGER: *(To Bette.)* I'm sorry, Miss. We'll have to ask you to leave now.

BETTE: What? Is the picture over?

MANAGER: Yes, it's over.

BETTE: *(Looking at screen.)* What are all those people doing up there?

MANAGER: They're worshipping molten images. Come on. *(He starts to pull her up the Center aisle.)*

BETTE: *(Licks her lips lasciviously.)* Do you think I'm Elizabeth Taylor in *Raintree*

County? I could be Joanne Woodward in *Three Faces of Eve.* Hello. I'm Eve White. Hi there, I'm Eve Black. Hi…*(Exits with Manager.)*

HANK: Loretta, Ma wants you to come back and sit with us. *(Falsetto.)* Come on back, Loretta honey. I won't bite you.

LORETTA: Oh God.

HANK: *(Falsetto.)* Don't be sad, son. You'll see Loretta again. *(Normal.)* I know, Ma.

EVE: Sssssssssshhh.

HANK. *(Falsetto.)* Hello, Eve. Nice to see you today.

EVE: Nice to see you, Mrs. Joad. Now if you and your son will both do me the favor of being quiet, I will consider my life fulfilled. Alright?

HANK: *(Falsetto.)* Alright. *(Regular.)* Alright.

CLARA: *(Depressed.)* Why do they call it the *Red* Sea? It's blue.

MICKEY: Clara, our marriage just hasn't worked out.

CLARA: It's just post-war adjustment problems.

MICKEY: Clara, we can't keep saying everything is post-war adjustment problems. It's been twenty years.

CLARA: Well then it's tension about the bomb. Or Krushchev not liking *Can Can.* It's more than I can stand.

EVE: Sssssssssh.

MICKEY: Clara, you're just not a good wife. You commit adultery, you're an alcoholic, you neglect the children…

CLARA: I'm sorry, I just don't like the children.

MICKEY: Maybe if I'd had hands it would have been different. Good-bye, Clara. *(Exits; Clara cries.)*

EVE: *(Mad.)* Why are you crying? The movie is not sad. *(Clara runs out.)*

HANK: *(Muttering in falsetto.)* We're the people. Ya can't keep us down, ya can't lick us…

EVE: BE QUIET!

HANK: *(Looks at her with hatred; falsetto.)* Go get her, son. *(Hank takes out knife, stabs her repeatedly. Stuart sees the stabbing, looks away, keeps his eyes riveted on the screen. Loretta, who is seated on one side of Stuart, stares ahead, seemingly not noticing the killing. Jimmy enters U.C. in a temper, looking for Loretta. On his entrance, Hank stops stabbing and sits the dead Eve up in her seat. The Blessed Mother enters here too, watching the movie and eating popcorn.)*

JIMMY: Loretta. I want you to come home.

LORETTA: I'm watching the movie, Jimmy.

JIMMY: The children miss you, Loretta. They miss their mother.

LORETTA: Screw the children.

JIMMY: Watch your mouth, Loretta.

LORETTA: Screw you! *(Jimmy sits on other side of Stuart. Stuart is seated between Loretta and Jimmy.)*

JIMMY: You're gonna get it when we get home.

LORETTA: Screw you, cluck!

(Enter Bette from U.C. in a motorized wheelchair. She is dressed as before, but has on wire-rimmed sun glasses and one black leather glove. The Theatre Manager follows her, upset.)

MANAGER: Miss, Miss.

(Bette fires a gun, killing him. Loretta and Jimmy don't notice, Stuart thinks he's in a nuthouse. Bette settles herself comfortably in her wheelchair in the front, D.R.)

BETTE: What a dump! *(Bette does the Bette Davis circular hand gesture, maniacally, and it turns into the Dr. Strangelove-strangling-himself gesture. She wears a black leather glove on her strangling hand. When she stops strangling herself, she should push a button on a small device on her wheelchair.)*

LORETTA: Hey, what's that from?

JIMMY: What's what from?

LORETTA: She just did it for you. What a dump!

JIMMY: I don't know what it's from.

LORETTA: It's from some goddamn Bette Davis movie. *(To Stuart.)* Hey, you, what's it from?

STUART: Excuse me?

LORETTA: Yeah, you. What's it from? What a dump!

STUART: *(Uncomfortably.)* I don't know. is it from *Lilies of the Field?*

LORETTA: No, cluck, it's not from *Lilies of the Field.*

STUART: *(Standing, to leave.)* Excuse me.

JIMMY: Sit down.

STUART: *Excuse* me.

JIMMY: Stop him, Bette.

(Bette shoots gun in his direction, doesn't hit him. Stuart sits down, further alarmed.)

LORETTA: *(To Stuart.)* We have the most lovely daughter.

JIMMY: Yeah, a real knockout.

LORETTA: Would you like to come to dinner and marry her? We don't care you're Negro, do we, Jimmy?

JIMMY: Hell, no, we're very liberal.

LORETTA: Goddamn right.

HANK: *(In falsetto.)* Hello, Loretta.

LORETTA: Not now, Hank. Or if not our daughter Deidre, how about our son Bob?

JIMMY: Sure, come to dinner and marry Bob.

LORETTA: If Bob would want it, we would want it.

STUART: What's the matter with you two?

LORETTA: Do you have children?

STUART: No.

LORETTA: We have twelve children. There's Robert and Deidre and Ernestine and Joel and Barbera and Maxine and William and Michael and David and Lily and Martha and Susie.

JIMMY: You know what they say…

JIMMY and LORETTA: IT'S CHEAPER BY THE DOZEN! *(Laugh hilariously.)*

BETTE: You have children? Take that and that and that…*(Pushes button.)*

JIMMY: *(Crosses to Bette.)* Whatcha got there, Bette?

BETTE: This is the button. I got access to the button. I'm a member of the Joint Chiefs of Staff now. We bomb things.

LORETTA: Hello, Bette. Have you met our son-in-law?

BETTE: Where your parents from, black boy?

STUART: Chicago.

BETTE: *(Pushes button.)* Not any more.

HANK: There's a fly on my nose, Ma. *(Falsetto.)* Just leave it be, son, it'll go away.

JIMMY: *(Crosses back to Stuart.)* You know some people may not want you to marry our daughter, black boy, but you know what I say to those people?

LORETTA: You tell 'im, Jimmy.

JIMMY: They can eat shit!

LORETTA: That's tellin' 'em, baby!

JIMMY: Eat shit, eat shit, eat shit.

STUART: Please! I don't come to the movies for this kind of thing!

JIMMY: No? Well what do you come for then, huh? You come for a skin flick? Well we can fix that. Why don't you hump my wife? Hey, Loretta, he wants you to spread for him.

LORETTA: Oh, Jimmy, you're sick, you're really sick.

JIMMY: Isn't that the game we should play first?

LORETTA: Well, you sure as hell can't play it. *(To Stuart.)* You wanna know why?

JIMMY: Don't tell him, Loretta.

HANK: The fly's still there, Ma.

LORETTA: You wanna know why?

JIMMY: Cut it, Loretta.

LORETTA: Because I am more of a man than my husband is. Tell them about your souvenir from the war, Jimmy.

JIMMY: You went too far, Loretta.

LORETTA: Tell them about your dead badge of courage. Tell them our marriage is nothing but a limp noodle.

JIMMY: I'm going to kill the children, Loretta.

HANK: Got it. *(Kills fly on nose, eats it.)*

JIMMY: I'm going to kill them.

LORETTA: I don't care, go ahead.

JIMMY: Alright, I've just killed Robert.

LORETTA: Go ahead! I've killed Ernestine.

JIMMY: I've killed Joel and Maxine!

LORETTA: I've killed William!

JIMMY: I've killed David!

BETTE: *(Pushing button.)* I got Thailand!

LORETTA: Barbara's dead!

JIMMY: Michael's dead!

LORETTA: Susie's dead!

BETTE: I got Norway!

JIMMY: Deidre's dead! *(To Stuart.)* Deidre's dead, get outta here, boy.

STUART: *(Stands; proud, firm.)* They call me *Mister* Tibbs.

BETTE: *(In a low voice; like in* The Exorcist.*)* I'm the devil, fuck me, fuck me! *(Sticks her tongue out, tries to make her head rotate.)*

JIMMY: Get outta here, boy.

STUART: They call me Shaft.

JIMMY: Get outta here, Shaft.

STUART: They call me Super-fly.

BETTE: *(Slapping herself.)* My sister, my daughter! My sister, my daughter! *(Jimmy aims a gun at Stuart.)*

STUART: You gonna shoot me, Dirty Harry? *(Jimmy points gun up against Stuart's head.)*

JIMMY: Make my day.

BETTE: *(Happy.)* Violence, violence! *(Sound of* Jaws *theme.)*

BETTE: Oh, good, a shark! *(Someone in a back row screams and is eaten by a shark.)*

SOMEONE: Help, help!

BETTE: Oh, I must've eaten something. *(Squirms in agony.)*

STUART: *(While Bette squirms.)* What choo fussin' about, Miz Daisy?

BETTE: Oh my God, I have an alien in my chest. *(Screams.)*

(An alien comes out of her chest.)

STUART: Miz Daisy got an alien in her chest.

BETTE: *(Happy, Diane Keaton in* Annie Hall.*)* La dee dah, la dee dah.

JIMMY: Look! *(Looking out at screen.)* A towering inferno. A tidal wave. An earthquake!

(An earthquake takes over. The characters sit in their chairs and watch the screen for a moment. The sound of an earthquake starts, first on the screen, and then it spreads to the movie theatre itself.

The characters start to shake, first just a little, then wildly. As the noise grows, various pieces of the set fall off. Pieces of The End sign fall to the ground. There are explosions; and at the final peak, the projection booth explodes, spewing out reels and reels of film on the people below.

The shaking and the noise stop. Everyone lies still, perhaps dead.

During the above, the Blessed Mother has sat in her seat, not shaking and not affected by the earthquake. She now, having enjoyed the chaos, applauds; and then gets up and exits.

Everyone else seems to be dead. Though after a moment, four people stir: Jimmy, Loretta, Bette, and Hank.

They stumble to their feet, look around, dazed, disoriented.)

JIMMY: Gosh. I feel thirty years older after that.

LORETTA: I think you are thirty years older. We're having very, very long lives.

HANK: *(In a happy idiot sort of tone.)* Stupid is as stupid does.

JIMMY: That's right, Hank. You know, I feel better after the earthquake. Sometimes you have to knock everything down in order to get a perspective on things.

LORETTA: What's this on the ground? *(Picking something up.)* Did The End sign fall to pieces?

JIMMY: Yeah, I guess so.

BETTE: *(With authority.)* Christina! No wire hangers! *(Disoriented.)* Who's Christina?

JIMMY: Pipe down, Bette, would ya? So, we'll have to start all over again…building towns, railroads, inventing the telephone.

LORETTA: Jimmy, I really don't want to start over again. I want The End sign to come down, and then I can stay frozen behind it forever, and then nothing else can happen to me.

JIMMY: Ya can't have that, kid. *(Back to his plans.)* So, we'll invent the telephone.

And we'll procreate. I can't, of course, as Loretta was saying before the earthquake. But Hank here is a man, and we have two women. And what a race we can engender.

BETTE: *(Wandering about happy, like Jodie Foster's* Nell.*)* Chick-a-pee, chick-a-pee.

HANK: Ma always says life is like a box of chocolates. *(Falsetto.)* Life is like a box of chocolates.

JIMMY: Uh huh. Now we have to move forward.

LORETTA: I don't want to go forward. I want to go backward. I don't like it here. I want to go back to the way it was.

BETTE: *The Way We Were,* with Barbra Streisand.

LORETTA: No, before that. *Way* before that.

JIMMY: Well, we have to go forward, but we could sort of be looking backward at the same time.

BETTE: *(With accent.)* I hat a farrum in Afreeka.

JIMMY: What, Bette?

BETTE: I'm not quite sure who I am. I'm working on it.

LORETTA: No, I don't want you to be someone recent. I want you to be someone from the past.

BETTE: But who?

LORETTA: Sylvia Sidney's nice.

BETTE: Who?

LORETTA: Or Loretta Young. Jeanette MacDonald.

BETTE: I could be Jeanette MacDonald at the end of *San Francisco,* right after the earthquake. And we've just had an earthquake. See, I'm making connections. I'm alright.

JIMMY: Okay, Bette will be noble like Jeanette MacDonald after the earthquake.

BETTE: *(Sings, in fruity, high soprano.)*
San Francisco,
Open your golden gates…

JIMMY: And we'll start over. But we'll be better this time.

LORETTA: Oh, starting over, it sounds so hard.

JIMMY: Come on, sourpuss, where's that good old American spirit? Okay. And Bette's gonna be noble.

BETTE: I'm noble, I'm noble.

JIMMY: And Hank is good-hearted, and full of folk wisdom.

HANK: Life is like a box of Kleenex.

JIMMY: And I'll be the smart one. I'll be crafty and resilient. And Loretta will be…well she's depressed now, but she'll get better. Won't you, Loretta?

LORETTA: Yeah, yeah, yeah.

JIMMY: *(Upset, sincere.)* Loretta, don't you love me anymore?

LORETTA: I guess I do, Jimmy. I'm just so tired.

BETTE: *(Garbo accent.)* Ah haf nevah been so tired in all my life. *(No accent.)* That was Greta Garbo. In 1932. She was tired back then.

JIMMY: Yeah, but she wasn't American, most Americans weren't tired. We gotta build on what's positive. Isn't that right, Loretta?

LORETTA: Okay, Jimmy. I'll go forward with you. But this time we have to recapture from the past only what was good. And build on it.

JIMMY: Now you're talkin', Loretta. And what a race the four of us can engender. We'll have leaders like Henry Fonda in *Young Mr. Lincoln*. Of course, we'll have to earn money.

HANK: I could start a shrimp business. *(Falsetto.)* That's true, Forest. Or you could hold an auction. *(Regular.)* I could hold an auction.

JIMMY: You do that, Hank. And we'll share our money with other people, like Gary Cooper in *Mr. Deeds Goes to Town*.

HANK: *(Holds up iron.)* This is the iron Loretta used in *A Man's Castle*.

LORETTA: I remember that iron. In Shanty Town.

HANK: Do I hear three hundred dollars?

VOICES: *(Starting to sing off-tage; or on the floor; in stately, somewhat somber tones.)* San Francisco…

JIMMY: *(Hearing the singing.)* Listen…

HANK: *(Paying no attention.)* Fifty dollars?

(Bette hears the voices singing "San Francisco." She's delighted and joins them, happy to have her "role" clear; she initially sings in her chirpy-happy soprano way; but soon she picks up the other voices' serious, otherworldly tone as well.)

VOICES: San Francisco…

BETTE: San Francisco…

San Francisco…

JIMMY: Listen!

HANK: Fifty cents? *(Falsetto.)* Fifty cents! *(Regular.)* Sold to Ma Joad for fifty cents!

VOICES: SAN FRANCISCO…

(Jimmy, buoyed up by the sound and promise of the voices, begins to set forth his vision of the future.

As he starts this, many of the characters from earlier in the play begin to crawl in, out of the earthquake rubble: Mickey, Clara, Viola in her maid's uniform, Allison, Michael, the Policeman from the silent section; Eve comes back to life, brushes herself off. The characters' clothes are ripped and distressed from the earthquake.

The Blessed Mother and Jesus appear in the balcony, survey the doings below; and then eventually come down and join the other characters.

During the song, Loretta stands by and behind Jimmy, agreeing with his vision of the future, rooted in the past. She sings along with the chorus when it seems appropriate. She is very happy with the idea that they are going to change how life has been since…well, since Shanty Town.)

JIMMY: Our race will have spiritual values…

CHORUS: Spiritual values…

JIMMY: …like Spencer Tracy in *Boys Town.*
We'll be idealistic…

Idealistic…

JIMMY: …like James Stewart in *Mr. Smith Goes to Washington.*
We'll be for racial tolerance…

Racial Tolerance…

JIMMY: …like Gregory Peck in *To Kill a Mockingbird.*
We'll suffer with patience…

Suffer with Patience…

JIMMY: …like Luise Rainer in *The Good Earth*…
(Explaining.)…the locusts…

[Note: in the above section, the chorus sings after Jimmy says the phrase. In what follows, the chorus and the song's examples begin to move on their own steam, ahead of Jimmy's examples; and indeed Jimmy starts to have trouble thinking or remembering the examples.]

JIMMY: We'll search for wisdom, like Tyrone Power in *The Razor's Edge.*
We'll take disappointment with dignity like Mickey Rooney in *Love Finds Andy Hardy.*
We'll discover radium like Greer Garson in… uh, *Madame Curie.*
We'll…we'll invent penicillin like…

CHORUS:
We'll search for wisdom like Tyrone Power,
Take disappointment Like Mickey Rooney,

Discover Radium Like Greer Garson

We'll invent penicillin

...like Paul Muni in,
in...*(At a loss.)* The
Life of Emile Zola...

(Hearing Ronald Coleman.)
...in *Lost Horizon!*

(Hearing John Wayne.)
...in *Stagecoach!*

HANK: *(Ripping off Clara's dress.)*
This is Clara's dress.
Do I hear sixty cents?
(Falsetto.)
Sixty cents!

Like Paul Muni,

We'll search for wisdom
Like Ronald Coleman,

Have pioneer spirit
Like John Wayne

We'll be tough-minded,
Like Lucille Watson
We'll live by
Moral Values
Like Priscilla Lane

(Suddenly the Chorus, which has been moving chaotically up to now, finds itself more or less in a straight line. And as the melody of the song peaks, all the characters, including Jimmy, Loretta, Bette and Hank, now step forward, down to the audience and sing with strong focus and energy.)

JIMMY, LORETTA, BETTE, HANK CHORUS: *(Singing.)*

We'll start again,
We'll start anew,
We'll search for wisdom,
For what is true,
We'll relive our past
And keep the best,
And edit out the rest!

JIMMY: Sssssh!!!!

(Chorus sings softly while Jimmy speaks.)

JIMMY: Our children will be
like Jackie Cooper...
in *Skippy*; Patty
McCormick in *The Bad
Seed*...uh, no, no,
that's a bad one...uh,
Dicky Moore! Little
Dicky Moore in *Blonde
Venus*...

CHORUS:
Glory, glory, glory,
Lionel Barrymore,
Glory, glory, glory,
Dorothy Lamour
Glory, glory,
Glory,
Little Dicky Moore,

And we shall rise
once more...

(The Blessed Mother comes forward, and offers a heartfelt, gracious prayer.)

BLESSED MOTHER: Our Father,

Who art in heaven,

Give us this Doris Day

Your Grace and Nancy Kelly,

And Robert Donat

into temptation,

But deliver us Gene Tierney

HANK: *(Having taken off his pants.)* These are my pants! Who'll give me thirty cents? *(Falsetto.)* Thirty cents!

BLESSED MOTHER: As it was in the beginning,

Is now, and ever shall be,

Zasu Pitts, Amen.

LORETTA: *(Spoken; happy, determined.)* And this time we're going to do it right, right, Jimmy?

JIMMY: You got it, sourpuss.

(All the characters bond together to sing the final verse of their plans.)

ALL: We'll search for wisdom

Like Leslie Howard,

Take disappointment

Like James Dean,

We'll be tough-minded

Like Wallace Beery,

We'll live by moral values,

Like Butterfly McQueen,   VIOLA: *(Singing.)*

We'll search for wisdom   Fall on your knees!

Like Marjorie Main,

Take disappointment

Like Joan Fontaine

What time's put asunder

We shall mend,

Triumphant to

The end!

(The song ends triumphantly, but immediately Loretta breaks and with great purpose, she motions them to follow her and Jimmy as they leave to start this new life of re-building.

Everyone starts to follow Loretta and Jimmy when suddenly a projector light comes on and shines out into the house. Everyone, including Jimmy, looks out for a moment, mesmerized by whatever they see on the screen. Then they rush and get seats, or as many seats as they can. They sit and stare out at whatever this next movie is.

Loretta looks upset. She keeps gesturing for them to get up and follow her out, to start the re-building. Loretta goes up to Jimmy, and pulls on him, trying to get him to move. But he waves her away, in an offhand manner, looking with interest at the screen. Loretta realizes after a bit she can't get them to budge. She looks out at the screen. She looks distressed, trapped. Nothing is going to change. The sound of the projector whirring is the last sound we hear. Loretta's face, looking out, is the last image we see.)

END OF PLAY

NOTE ABOUT THIS ENDING OF *A HISTORY OF THE AMERICAN FILM*:

A History of the American Film was written in 1976 and 1977, and performed on Broadway in 1978. And so its references to movies stopped with the films of the late 70s.

In the fall of 1995, the Juilliard School Drama Division, where I have been co-chairing (with Marsha Norman) a playwriting program since 1994, decided to present the play. I chose this production opportunity to update the ending of the play.

The updating is fairly simple. In the original play, shortly before the earthquake section, the characters start to change identities in a lightning quick fashion, taking us quickly through many film references of the 70s. For the rewrite, I just added some other film references from the 80s and 90s *(Chinatown, Alien, Mommie Dearest, Forrest Gump);* and the feeling is, I hope, that we have raced through those two decades as well.

The other change I made was with the last song.

As it was written for Broadway, Loretta resisted Jimmy's vision for the future and wanted to be "rescued" by The End sign. In this older version, the Blessed Mother, sort of like the Wizard of Oz, waved her hand and a "magic" The End sign descended and Loretta got on it, and started to ascend to some sort of heaven, when suddenly the projector turned on and everyone sat down to watch the next movie again. And so Loretta ended up, stuck, unable to escape.

For this rewrite, I chose to write out the magic The End sign: It's too expensive for almost any theatre to rig properly. Plus, the The End motif didn't quite register as strongly as I thought it would, when we did it on Broadway. Plus, in the original version, the song didn't finish...the projector came back on before the final notes of "The End" were sung. I think the "Search for Wisdom" song that Mel Marvin and I wrote is a very effective and stirring song; and years later, I decided it was pointlessly frustrating to the audience not to finish it.

So at Juilliard we finished the song (though the musical director chose to modulate the final chord so it sounded a tiny bit less final, and so there wouldn't be applause; I think you could also let the song end, and have the silent action that follows it happen during applause, as a second choice).

In this rewrite, Loretta is in synch with Jimmy about planning to re-start the human race, just as long as everyone agrees to only take the best from the past. Her frustration and upset does not happen until the end, when everyone refuses to face the future with her, because they want to see the screen.

If you try to do this new ending, I should point out that in the Samuel French version of the score, Loretta sings counterpoint to the Blessed Mother's prayer, with lyrics about how she wants to leave the earth on The End song. These lyrics and musical phrases should simply be cut; let the Blessed Mother's prayer happen, uninterrupted.

And, during the final chorus, Loretta has an obligato that occurs. In the original version, she sang this obligato as she ascended into "heaven" on the sign. In this new version, she can still sing the obligato, but now its meaning should simply be that she is happy that everyone is joining together, planning to build a better future.

As I write these notes, Samuel French does not yet have a printed copy of this new ending; only this book has the new ending. In the future, I hope Samuel French will be convinced to add this new ending to its scripts.

Well, that's all on the new ending, except to say I thought it worked well at Juilliard; and that the cast and director (Michael Mayer) did a superb job, in my opinion.

Beyond Therapy

INTRODUCTION

After the closing of *A History of the American Film,* I went into a bit of a writer's block. And then my mother's cancer worsened, and for the next year I was involved with the painful ups and downs of her health. (My mother had breast cancer in 1972, was okay for a while seemingly, but then got bone cancer in her hip in 1976.)

I was very close to my mother, at the same time I was trying to become an adult and separate from her. There were many unspoken feelings from her and her family that due to her illness, I should move home to New Jersey and live with her full-time. Three of her siblings all lived with their mother; there was a lot of anger coming toward me (I believe) of how dare I not follow the family rule. Plus, my mother now moved next door to her siblings, for comfort; but part of the "comfort" seemed to be to bicker and fight incessantly, as that was what was familiar; and this constant embroilment among the siblings was one of the main reasons I needed to live away from home.

As it was, I was out in New Jersey three days out of seven; then back in New York, I would be emotionally spent and go to bed for two days.

Anyway, it was an awful time. I don't mean to make my upset more important than my mother's illness; she was going through the most painful events. But I need to acknowledge that I was both numb and paralyzed (though I did very well dealing with the doctors and medical treatments and updates and theories, etc.).

My mother died on March 10, 1979. Her bone cancer had become extremely painful, she would break bones merely moving in bed; and so, truthfully, I was extremely relieved. I am grateful I had her as a mother for as long as I did; but I am sad some of her life wasn't more consistently happy. (She would have made a wonderful comic actress, but never went that route.)

I needed to heal and re-group. I was blessed with winning another fellowship, a Guggenheim; this good news I learned about a week after my mother died. The grant meant I could refocus on writing, and not have to get a "survival" job.

I went to visit my friend Stephen Davis in Washington, D.C., to do nothing for a couple of months but rest and maybe write. Steve now worked for the Library of Congress and lived literally next door to Arena Stage, where I had a lot of friends and could hang out. So that stay was wonderfully healing.

My writer's block did lift. I had started *Sister Mary Ignatius Explains It All For You* during my mother's illness, but then got stuck and put it aside. I picked it up again (on the train down to Washington, I recall) and had the idea of

Sister's ex-students coming in to confront her; this idea allowed me to finish the play. And when the character of Diane began to tell Sister the story of her mother's death from cancer, I was unprepared for my writing turning so direct and so serious, but I went with it.

I also started to work on *The Marriage of Bette and Boo* (more on that later). And after I finished *Sister Mary*, I started to write *Beyond Therapy*. (*Sister Mary*, by the way, is a long one act, and thus not in this volume. But it is in Smith & Kraus' *27 Short Plays* and in Grove Weidenfeld's *Christopher Durang Explains It All For You*.)

Beyond Therapy is, so far, the friendliest, sunniest play I've written. And it seems to be my most produced play as well, even now.

All my friends in college and after tended to be in therapy; and daily phone calls with these friends (including Wendy W.) would invariably be to recount what we had been told by our therapists, and what they thought we should be doing, and so on and so forth.

Years earlier, I wrote a play called *Therapy* in which the entire world was in therapy with this one person; the play's not too good, and I put it in a drawer, but it included an early sketch for Mrs. Wallace, the woman therapist in *Beyond Therapy*.

The off-Broadway Phoenix Theatre had offered me a playwriting commission sometime after *Film* closed; the money and the vote of confidence were very helpful, and I started to write *Beyond Therapy* for them.

Usually I didn't write on a schedule—I preferred to wait for inspiration to strike—but since I now was worried about whether I'd return to writer's block, I forced myself to write every afternoon on the play, no matter how I felt. And if the material seemed terrible, I would look again the next day, and either find it better than I thought; or I would now be clearer how to fix it.

Writing the play I heard the vocal inflections of Kate McGregor-Stewart in my head for Charlotte Wallace; and for the part of Prudence, the sensible woman trying to find a relationship, I heard the voice of my friend Sigourney Weaver.

Sigourney and I became friends in 1971, when we met as fellow students at Yale School of Drama. Due to her height and beauty, she was an immediate stand-out in her class; and over lunch one day in the Graduate Hall dining room, we discovered we had similar senses of humor.

She then acted in my first cabaret show at Yale—which I wanted to call *Better Dead Than Sorry*, but was encouraged to change to the friendlier *Darryl and Carol and Kenny and Jenny*. Sigourney played sensitive Jenny, who received shock treatments while singing the song "Better Dead Than Sorry." An actor dropped out, and I replaced him as Darryl; and thus I got to play worried, caring brother Darryl to Sigourney's Jenny. And this cabaret ended up being her and my first "success" in the Drama School. (Although, more accurately, half the school loved it, and half the school hated it. But among those who loved it were Brustein, head of the school, and Howard Stein, head of the playwriting program. So it was fortunate for us.)

Anyway, we got to be very good friends; acted in several other plays together (not just by me). And when some of the acting teachers turned cool on Sigourney and she felt great discouragement (with the vocal teacher one day saying to her, in her cadenced, British accent, "You know, Sigourney, there are other acting schools..."), our friendship was cemented since she could tell how much I believed in her talent.

In my early plays—she also played Soot in the student one-act version of *The Marriage of Bette and Boo* at Yale, and she played the put-upon housewife Eleanor in *The Nature and Purpose of the Universe* in a New York workshop—Sigourney played the sensitive roles, the sensible person looking askance at the craziness around her. (Intriguingly, most all her movie roles have cast her as strong and invincible, but this is not how she was cast in my plays.)

And in 1976 she played the triple-personalitied daughter, Lidia, in *Titanic*. She and I also co-wrote and performed our crackpot Brecht-Weill parody cabaret, *Das Lusitania Songspiel,* first as a curtain-raiser to *Titanic;* and then again in 1980 as a late-night show at the Westside Arts, where it received great reviews and became a cult event. (And we did a segment of that show on *Saturday Night Live* in 1986, when Sigourney was guest host.)

I had written Loretta in *American Film* with Sigourney in mind, but I was never able to convince the various directors to cast her in the part; since this was early in her career, this disappointed her a lot.

So I was extremely happy that the Phoenix Theatre was happy to cast Sigourney as Prudence and Kate as Charlotte without any resistance. (Of course, Sigourney's leading part in the hit movie *Alien* gave her that celebrity clout now.)

To direct the play we got Jerry Zaks, who had just directed my *Sister Mary Ignatius*...to rave reviews in its initial, three-week run at Ensemble Studio Theatre.

The Phoenix production was mostly terrific, and Sigourney and Stephen Collins were charming, funny, and sweet in the leads.

The schedule, though, was odd—there were only two previews, which was not good. The newspaper critics came on the second preview, and all the actors were still finding themselves, and the comic rhythms weren't confident yet. The magazine critics came to the third performance—the opening actually—and at this performance the play clicked together and was very good, very funny.

And the newspaper reviews (based on the second preview) were all bad; and the magazine reviews (based on the third performance-opening) were almost all good.

However, magazine reviews come out slowly, a week to two weeks to three weeks later; so the actors and I had to deal with some prove-it-to-me audiences who had read that it wasn't good. And Jerry Zaks had to leave immediately after the opening, to rehearse full-time as an actor in the musical *Tintypes* (in which he was terrific); but it then fell to me to give acting notes, since with only two previews the actors hadn't had enough guidance in dealing with the audience yet.

Ultimately, the run went very well. But I was thrown by the newspaper critics not liking it, even granting the slight bumpiness of the performance they saw. In the past I made sense of some of my bad reviews—I like *Titanic,* but it's really weird, I can see it's not to everyone's taste; I know we made mistakes in our Broadway production of *A History of American Film,* so the slightly so-so response, unfortunately, made sense to me. But *Beyond Therapy* was funny; I didn't understand the critics who said it wasn't.

I got a Broadway producer, however, Claire Nichtern, who loved the play but wanted me to rewrite the ending. I was in total agreement with her; and rewrote the last two scenes (collapsing them into one) and removing the extraneous character of Paul, an ex-boy friend, who showed up in the Phoenix production.

By the time I did the rewrite, and money was raised, and a theatre was found (again, we couldn't get the one we wanted—the 500 seat Little Theatre, now called the Helen Hayes—but settled on the bigger, though nice, Brooks Atkinson Theatre), Sigourney was no longer available, but was off in Australia, making one of her best movies, Peter Weir's *Year of Living Dangerously.*

Claire would have been happy to cast Sigourney, but we didn't want to wait until the following season (it was already a year after the Phoenix production), so we went looking for a mostly new cast.

And a new director. Jerry Zaks has become such a whoppingly successful director (deservedly so) that it must seem insane to imagine that he was turned down for a job. But at this point, he had only directed a few times, never on Broadway; and it was true that the transitions between scenes were not well done at the Phoenix. (Both Jerry and I learned a lot about how to prepare for scene changes in the future; the beautiful-to-look-at set at the Phoenix was designed to change and move around, but it had to be done by stagehands, and it took a really, really long time and looked clunky.)

I pitched to Claire that Jerry could do it; that it was the limitations of the Phoenix Theatre space that made the scene changes not work. But she held firm to her belief that she needed someone with Broadway experience.

Jerry was very disappointed, but I was so grateful to him that he understood the position I was put in, and didn't turn against me because I didn't make his being hired an "either-or" demand to Claire. (I don't believe it works to force someone to work with someone.) So because of Jerry's modest understanding, he and I worked together several other times after this.

Claire and I then chose John Madden to direct. Madden had directed Arthur Kopit's *Wings* on Broadway, and was about to do Jules Feiffer's *Grown Ups*. He was (and is) very talented, and I thought he did a great production.

To step in for Sigourney, John and I thought of Dianne Wiest. She was not yet famous from her Woody Allen film work, but John and I had both seen her numerous times be fabulous. Dianne, though, had just received very bad notices as Desdemona in a production of *Othello,* and Claire didn't seem very interested in her. Then Dianne came in to audition, and Claire turned around and suddenly couldn't imagine anyone but Dianne in the part. Which was fine with me.

The previews went great, the audience seemed to laugh nonstop, the actors all were doing well. And then the reviews came out: we got some raves, some okay mixed, and one pan from the damn *New York Times* again.

You know, it isn't reading negative things that upsets me; it's my sense of reality. If I stand in the back of the theatre and hear an audience laugh over and over, what am I to make of a review that says no, it's not funny. Am I to think that the audience is in reverie, laughing at something they saw last week? Or that I'm insane, and the laughter is in my head? Or that the audience is stupid, and only the critic is smart, and he knows not to laugh?

Yes, I know people's taste varies; and I do sometimes sit in an audience that laughs its head off, and I sit there, silent.

But that's what's so hard—if there is disagreement, why are we dealing with a system in which the individual at the *New York Times* is carrying weight, while the critic at, say, just anywhere else isn't.

Listen to the contrasting opening lines in Frank Rich's review in the *Times* and in Brendan Gill's review in the *New Yorker*:

Rich: "Some day, I swear, the explosive comic brilliance of Christopher Durang will erupt on Broadway. The only question is when. It didn't happen in 1978, when the playwright's *A History of the American Film* capsized in a spectacularly ill-conceived production. And it didn't happen last night, when Mr. Durang's latest play, *Beyond Therapy,* pretty much wilted of its own volition at the Brooks Atkinson."

Gill: "It has been the ambitious dream of many an author throughout history to begin a piece of writing with a sentence—"Call me, Ishmael," "For a long time I used to go to bed early"—so irresistible that his readers couldn't fail to proceed to the next sentence and then to the next and the next, pitching headlong as far into the piece as the author's literary ingenuity was able to entice them. This dream came true last week for Christopher Durang, at the opening of his delightful little farce, *Beyond Therapy,* at the Brooks Atkinson: the audience laughed at the very first line of the play, then at the second, and then at the third; I can bear witness to the fact that I wasn't alone in continuing to laugh with something like the regularity of a metronome through most of the rest of the play."

So on the one hand, one man's opinion that the play "wilted." Another man's opinion: An author's dream is fulfilled, and the audience laughs at almost every line.

Now it's fine with me that people have different opinions. It isn't fine with me that the opinion I don't agree with is the one carrying the weight; and two weeks later the play is closed (with a final kick from *Times Sunday* writer Walter Kerr).

So I don't like this aspect of this business.

And I also regret that more people didn't see the production, in which Dianne Wiest and Kate McGregor-Stewart were sublimely funny; and in which John Lithgow, Jack Gilpin, Peter Michael Goetz and David (Hyde) Pierce (in his first Equity performance, years before his *Frazier* success) were also wonderful.

By the way, I realize Rich says many nice things about me in his review; and at the time I even took the review in stride—you lose some, you win some. But a few more shows under Rich's eye—and under his agenda, perhaps unconscious, of how he wanted theatre to be, and how he "graded" you if you were living up to his beliefs of what you should be doing—I really found writing in New York theatre to be a big whopping problem.

A nice coda, for my play at least. After the closing on Broadway, regional theatres started to do the play, cautiously at first; but each production had great successes with audiences, usually got good reviews, and usually got extended. And so *Beyond Therapy*, in terms of stock and amateur rights, has been my most performed and most financially successful play.

(By the way, one more bit of negativity. The film version Robert Altman made of the film is horrific…unfunny, pushed, the script rewritten by him so that all psychology is thrown out the window, and the characters dash around acting "crazy" but with literally no behavioral logic underneath. I should have taken my name off the film, but for complicated, wrong reasons I didn't. I meet some people who only know my work through renting that film; and it isn't my work. I like many of Altman's films; but he makes stinkers too, and this was one of them. He also does not have a sense of humor compatible to my play; and he has great arrogance, fancying himself a writer. A nightmare experience for me.)

Well, goodness, have I put you in a bad mood? Maybe you should go take a bath before you read the play. And I'll go soak my head, and rinse my brain out.

Well, I was in a good mood when I wrote the play. Let's forget everything I've just said. Everything is fine. Life is amusing. Bruce and Prudence are about to meet. Life is droll, life is droll, breathe, breathe, smile, breathe.

ORIGINAL PRODUCTION

Beyond Therapy had its Broadway premiere on May 26, 1982, at the Brooks Atkinson Theatre. It was directed by John Madden. It was produced by Warner Theatre Productions (Claire Nichtern) and FDM Productions (Francois de Menil and Harris Maslasnky). Settings were by Andrew Jackness, costumes by Jennifer Von Mayrhauser, lighting by Paul Gallo. Production Stage Manager was Craig Jacobs. Music coordinator was Jack Feldman.

(In order of appearance:)

BRUCE:.	John Lithgow
PRUDENCE:.	Dianne Wiest
STUART:	Peter Michael Goetz
CHARLOTTE	Kate McGregor-Stewart
BOB	Jack Gilpin
ANDREW	David Pierce

Beyond Therapy was previously presented by the Phoenix Theatre in New York City on January 1, 1981. The production was directed by Jerry Zaks; scenery by Karen Schultz; costumes by Jennifer von Mayrhauser; lighting by Richard Nelson; sound by David Rapkin. The cast was as follow:

BRUCE . . . . Stephen Collins
PRUDENCE . . . . Sigourney Weaver
DR. STUART FRAMINGHAM . . . . Jim Borelli
MRS. CHARLOTTE WALLACE . . . . Kate McGregor-Stewart
BOB . . . . Jack Gilpin
ANDREW . . . . Conan McCarty
PAUL* . . . . Nick Stannard

*The character of Paul, a former suitor of Prudence's, appeared in the final scene of the play at the Phoenix. This scene was changed for the Broadway version, and the character was written out.

SYNOPSIS OF SCENES
ACT I
Scene 1: A Restaurant
Scene 2: Dr. Stuart Framingham's Office
Scene 3: The Office of Charlotte Wallace
Scene 4: The Restaurant Again
Scene 5: Dr. Framingham's Office
Scene 6: Bruce's Apartment

Intermission

ACT II
Scene 1: Mrs. Wallace's Office
Scene 2: The Restaurant Again
Scene 3: The Restaurant Still

Beyond Therapy

ACT I

Scene 1

A restaurant. Bruce is seated, looking at his watch. He is 30–34, fairly pleasant looking, probably wearing a blazer with an open shirt. Enter Prudence, 29–32, attractive, semi-dressed up in a dress or nice skirt and blouse. After hesitating a moment, she crosses to Bruce.

PRUDENCE: Hello.

BRUCE: Hello.

PRUDENCE: *(Perhaps referring to a newspaper in her hand—*The New York Review of Books?*)* Are you the white male, thirty to thirty-five, 6'2", blue eyes, who's into rock music, movies, jogging, and quiet evenings at home?

BRUCE: Yes, I am. *(Stands.)*

PRUDENCE: Hi, I'm Prudence.

BRUCE: I'm Bruce.

PRUDENCE: Nice to meet you.

BRUCE: Won't you sit down?

PRUDENCE: Thank you. *(Sits.)* As I said in my letter, I've never answered one of these ads before.

BRUCE: Me neither. I mean, I haven't put one in before.

PRUDENCE: But this time I figured, why not?

BRUCE: Right. Me too. *(Pause.)* I hope I'm not too macho for you.

PRUDENCE: No. So far you seem wonderful.

BRUCE: You have lovely breasts. That's the first thing I notice in a woman.

PRUDENCE: Thank you.

BRUCE: You have beautiful contact lenses.

PRUDENCE: Thank you. I like the timbre of your voice. Soft but firm.

BRUCE: Thanks. I like *your* voice.

PRUDENCE: Thank you. I love the smell of Brut you're wearing.

BRUCE: Thank you. My male lover Bob gave it to me.

PRUDENCE: What?

BRUCE: You remind me of him in a certain light.

PRUDENCE: What?

BRUCE: I swing both ways actually. Do you?

PRUDENCE: *(Rattled, serious.)* I don't know. I always insist on the lights being out. *(Pause.)*

BRUCE: I'm afraid I've upset you now.

PRUDENCE: No, it's nothing really. It's just that I hate gay people.

BRUCE: I'm not gay. I'm bisexual. There's a difference.

PRUDENCE: I don't really know any bisexuals.

BRUCE: Children are all innately bisexual, you know. If you took a child to Plato's Retreat, he'd be attracted to both sexes.

PRUDENCE: I should imagine he'd be terrified.

BRUCE: Well, he might be, of course. I've never taken a child to Plato's Retreat.

PRUDENCE: I don't think they let you.

BRUCE: I don't really know any children. *(Pause.)* You have wonderful eyes. They're so deep.

PRUDENCE: Thank you.

BRUCE: I feel like I want to take care of you.

PRUDENCE: *(Liking this tack better.)* I would like that. My favorite song is "Someone to Watch over Me."

BRUCE: *(Sings softly.)* "There a somebody I'm longing duh duh…"

PRUDENCE: Yes. Thank you.

BRUCE: In some ways you're like a little girl. And in some ways you're like a woman.

PRUDENCE: How am I like a woman?

BRUCE: *(Searching, romantically.)* You…dress like a woman. You wear eye shadow like a woman.

PRUDENCE: You're like a man. You're tall, you have to shave. I feel you could protect me.

BRUCE: I'm deeply emotional, I like to cry.

PRUDENCE: Oh I wouldn't like that.

BRUCE: But I like to cry.

PRUDENCE: I don't think men should cry unless something falls on them.

BRUCE: That's a kind of sexism. Men have been programmed not to show feeling.

PRUDENCE: Don't talk to me about sexism. You're the one who talked about my breasts the minute I sat down.

BRUCE: I feel like I'm going to cry now.

PRUDENCE: Why do you want to cry?

BRUCE: I feel you don't like me enough. I think you're making eyes at the waiter.

PRUDENCE: I haven't even seen the waiter.

(Bruce cries.)

PRUDENCE: Please, don't cry, please.

BRUCE: *(Stops crying after a bit.)* I feel better after that. You have a lovely mouth.

PRUDENCE: Thank you.

BRUCE: I can tell you're very sensitive. I want you to have my children.

PRUDENCE: Thank you.

BRUCE: Do you feel ready to make a commitment?

PRUDENCE: I feel I need to get to know you better.

BRUCE: I feel we agree on all the issues. I feel that you like rock music, movies, jogging, and quiet evenings at home. I think you hate shallowness. I bet you never read *People* magazine.

PRUDENCE: I do read it. I write for it.

BRUCE: I write for it too. Freelance actually. I send in letters. They printed one of them.

PRUDENCE: Oh, what was it about?

BRUCE: I wanted to see Gary Gilmore executed on television.

PRUDENCE: Oh, yes, I remember that one.

BRUCE: Did you identify with Jill Clayburgh in *An Unmarried Woman?*

PRUDENCE: Uh, yes, I did.

BRUCE: Me too! We agree on everything. I want to cry again.

PRUDENCE: I don't like men to cry. I want them to be strong.

BRUCE: You'd quite like Bob then.

PRUDENCE: Who?

BRUCE: You know.

PRUDENCE: Oh.

BRUCE: I feel I'm irritating you.

PRUDENCE: No. It's just that it's hard to get to know someone. And the waiter never comes, and I'd like to order.

BRUCE: Let's start all over again. Hello. My name is Bruce.

PRUDENCE: Hello.

BRUCE: Prudence. That's a lovely name.

PRUDENCE: Thank you.

BRUCE: That's a lovely dress.

PRUDENCE: Thank you. I like your necklace. It goes nicely with your chest hair.

BRUCE: Thank you. I like your nail polish.

PRUDENCE: I have it on my toes too.

BRUCE: Let me see.

(She takes shoe off, puts foot on the table.)

BRUCE: I think it's wonderful you feel free enough with me to put your feet on the table.

PRUDENCE: I didn't put my feet on the table. I put one foot. I was hoping it might get the waiter's attention.

BRUCE: We agree on everything. It's amazing. I'm going to cry again. *(Weeps.)*

PRUDENCE: *Please,* you're annoying me.

(He continues to cry.)

PRUDENCE: What is the matter?

BRUCE: I feel you're too dependent. I feel you want me to put up the storm windows. I feel you should do that.

PRUDENCE: I didn't say anything about storm windows.

BRUCE: You're right. I'm wrong. We agree.

PRUDENCE: What kind of childhood did you have?

BRUCE: Nuns. I was taught by nuns. They really ruined me. I don't believe in God anymore. I believe in bran cereal. It helps prevent rectal cancer.

PRUDENCE: Yes, I like bran cereal.

BRUCE: I want to marry you. I feel ready in my life to make a long-term commitment. We'll live in Connecticut. We'll have two cars. Bob will live over the garage. Everything will be wonderful.

PRUDENCE: I don't feel ready to make a long-term commitment to you. I think you're insane. I'm going to go now. *(Stands.)*

BRUCE: Please don't go.

PRUDENCE: I don't think I should stay.

BRUCE: Don't go. They have a salad bar here.

PRUDENCE: Well, maybe for a little longer. *(She sits down again.)*

BRUCE: You're afraid of life, aren't you ?

PRUDENCE: Well...

BRUCE: Your instinct is to run away. You're afraid of feeling, of emotion. That's wrong, Prudence, because then you have no passion. Did you see *Equus?* That doctor felt it was better to blind eight horses in a stable with a metal spike than to have no passion. *(Holds his fork.)* In my life I'm not going to be afraid to blind the horses, Prudence.

PRUDENCE: You ought to become a veterinarian.

BRUCE: *(Very offended.)* You've missed the metaphor.

PRUDENCE: I haven't missed the metaphor. I made a joke.

BRUCE: You just totally missed the metaphor. I could never love someone who missed the metaphor.

PRUDENCE: Someone should have you committed.

BRUCE: I'm not the one afraid of commitment. You are.

PRUDENCE: Oh, dry up.

BRUCE: I was going to give you a fine dinner and then take you to see *The Tree of Wooden Clogs* and then home to my place for sexual intercourse, but now I think you should leave.

PRUDENCE: You're not rejecting me, buddy. I'm rejecting you. You're a real first-class idiot.

BRUCE: And you're a castrating, frigid-bitch!

(She throws a glass of water in his face; he throws water back in her face. They sit there for a moment, spent of anger, wet.)

PRUDENCE: Absolutely nothing seems to get that waiter's attention, does it?

(Bruce shakes his head "no". They sit there, sadly.)

(Lights fade.)

ACT I

Scene 2

Psychologist's office. Dr. Stuart Framingham. Very masculine, a bit of a bully, wears boots, jeans, a tweed sports jacket, open sports shirt. Maybe has a beard.

STUART: *(Speaking into intercom.)* You can send the next patient in now, Betty.

(Enter Prudence. She sits.)

STUART: *(After a moment.)* So, what's on your mind this week?

PRUDENCE: Oh I don't know. I had that Catherine the Great dream again.

STUART: Yeah?

PRUDENCE: Oh I don't know. Maybe it isn't Catherine the Great. It's really more like *National Velvet.*

STUART: What do you associate to *National Velvet?*

PRUDENCE: Oh I don't know. Childhood.

STUART: Yes?

PRUDENCE: I guess I miss childhood where one could look to a horse for emotional satisfaction rather than a person. I mean, a horse never disappointed me.

STUART: You feel disappointed in people?

PRUDENCE: Well, every man I try to have a relationship with turns out to be crazy. And the ones that aren't crazy are dull. But maybe it's me. Maybe I'm really looking for faults just so I won't ever have a successful relationship.

Like Michael last year. Maybe he was just fine, and I made up faults that he didn't have. Maybe I do it to myself. What do you think?

STUART: What I think doesn't matter. What do you think?

PRUDENCE: But what do *you* think?

STUART: It's not my place to say.

PRUDENCE: *(Irritated.)* Oh never mind. I don't want to talk about it.

STUART: I see. *(Makes a note.)*

PRUDENCE: *(Noticing he's making notes; to make up:)* I did answer one of those ads.

STUART: Oh?

PRUDENCE: Yes.

STUART: How did it work out?

PRUDENCE: Very badly. The guy was a jerk. He talked about my breasts, he has a male lover, and he wept at the table. It was really ridiculous. I should have known better.

STUART: Well, you can always come back to me, babe. I'll light your fire for you anytime.

PRUDENCE: Stuart, I've told you you can't talk to me that way if I'm to stay in therapy with you.

STUART: You're mighty attractive when you're angry.

PRUDENCE: Stuart…Dr. Framingham, many women who have been seduced by their psychiatrists take them to court…

STUART: Yeah, but you wanted it, baby…

PRUDENCE: How could I have "wanted" it? One of our topics has been that I don't know what I want.

STUART: Yeah, but you wanted that, baby.

PRUDENCE: Stop calling me baby. Really, I must be out of my mind to keep seeing you. *(Pause.)* Obviously you can't be my therapist after we've had an affair.

STUART: Two lousy nights aren't an affair.

PRUDENCE: You never said they were lousy.

STUART: They were great. You were great. I was great. Wasn't I, baby? It was the fact that it was only two nights that was lousy.

PRUDENCE: Dr. Framingham, it's the common belief that it is wrong for therapists and their patients to have sex together.

STUART: Not in California.

PRUDENCE: We are not in California.

STUART: We could move there. Buy a house, get a jacuzzi.

PRUDENCE: Stuart…Dr. Framingham, we're not right for one another. I feel you have masculinity problems. I hate your belt buckle. I didn't really even like you in bed.

STUART: I'm great in bed.

PRUDENCE: *(With some hesitation.)* You have problems with premature ejaculation.

STUART: Listen, honey, there's nothing premature about it. Our society is paced quickly, we all have a lot of things to do. I ejaculate quickly on purpose.

PRUDENCE: I don't believe you.

STUART: Fuck you, cunt.

PRUDENCE: *(Stands.)* Obviously I need to find a new therapist.

STUART: Okay, okay. I lost my temper. I'm sorry. But I'm human. Prudence, that's what you have to learn. People are human. You keep looking for perfection, you need to learn to accept imperfection. I can help you with that.

PRUDENCE: Maybe I really should sue you. I mean, I don't think you should have a license.

STUART: Prudence, you're avoiding the issue. The issue is you, not me. You're unhappy, you can't find a relationship you like, you don't like your job, you don't like the world. You need my help. I mean, don't get hung up on who should have a license. The issue is I can help you fit into the world. *(Very sincerely, sensitively.)* Really I can. Don't run away.

PRUDENCE: *(Sits.)* I don't think I believe you.

STUART: That's okay. We can work on that.

PRUDENCE: I don't know. I really don't think you're a good therapist. But the others are probably worse, I'm afraid.

STUART: They are. They're much worse. Really I'm very nice. I like women. Most men don't.

PRUDENCE: I'm getting one of my headaches again. *(Holds her forehead.)*

STUART: Do you want me to massage your neck?

PRUDENCE: Please don't touch me.

STUART: Okay, okay. *(Pause.)* Any other dreams?

PRUDENCE: No.

STUART: Perhaps we should analyze why you didn't like the man you met through the personal ad.

PRUDENCE: I…I…don't want to talk anymore today. I want to go home.

STUART: You can never go home again.

PRUDENCE: Perhaps not. But I can return to my apartment. You're making my headache worse.

STUART: I think we should finish the session. I think it's important.

PRUDENCE: I just can't talk anymore.

STUART: We don't have to talk. But we have to stay in the room.

PRUDENCE: How much longer?

STUART: *(Looks at watch.)* Thirty minutes.

PRUDENCE: Alright. But I'm not going to talk any more.

STUART: Okay.

    (Pause; They stare at one another.)

STUART: You're very beautiful when you're upset.

PRUDENCE: Please don't you talk either.

    (They stare at each other; lights dim.)

ACT I

Scene 3

    The office of Charlotte Wallace. Probably reddish hair, bright clothing; a Snoopy dog on her desk. If there are walls in the set around her, they have drawings done by children.

CHARLOTTE: *(Into intercom).* You may send the next patient in, Marcia. *(She arranges herself at her desk, smiles in anticipation.)*

    (Enter Bruce. He sits.)

CHARLOTTE: Hello.

BRUCE: Hello. *(Pause.)* Should I just begin?

CHARLOTTE: Would you like to begin?

BRUCE: I threw a glass of water at someone in a restaurant.

CHARLOTTE: Did you?

BRUCE: Yes.

CHARLOTTE: Did they get all wet?

BRUCE: Yes.

    (Silence.)

CHARLOTTE: *(Points to child's drawing.)* Did I show you this drawing?

BRUCE: I don't remember. They all look alike.

CHARLOTTE: It was drawn by an emotionally disturbed three year old. His parents beat him every morning after breakfast. Orange juice, toast, Special K.

BRUCE: Uh huh.

CHARLOTTE: Do you see the point I'm making?

BRUCE: Yes, I do, sort of. *(Pause.)* What point are you making?

CHARLOTTE: Well, the point is that when a porpoise first comes to me, it is often immediately clear…Did I say porpoise? What word do I want?

Porpoise. Pompous. Pom Pom. Paparazzi. Polyester. Pollywog. Olley olley oxen free. Patient. I'm sorry, I mean patient. Now what was I saying?

BRUCE: Something about when a patient comes to you.

CHARLOTTE: *(Slightly irritated.)* Well, give me more of a clue.

BRUCE: Something about the child's drawing and when a patient comes to you?

CHARLOTTE: Yes. No. I need more. Give me more of a hint.

BRUCE: I don't know.

CHARLOTTE: Oh I hate this, when I forget what I'm saying. Oh, damn. Oh, damn damn damn. Well, we'll just have to forge on. You say something for a while, and I'll keep trying to remember what I was saying. *(She moves her lips.)*

BRUCE: *(After a bit.)* Do you want me to talk?

CHARLOTTE: Would you like to talk?

BRUCE: I had an answer to the ad I put in.

CHARLOTTE: Ad?

BRUCE: Personal ad.

CHARLOTTE: *(Remembering, happy.)* Oh, yes. Personal ad. I told you that was how the first Mr. Wallace and I met. Oh yes. I love personal ads. They're so basic. Did it work out for you?

BRUCE: Well, I like her, and I tried to be emotionally open with her. I even let myself cry.

CHARLOTTE: Good for you!

BRUCE: But she didn't like me. And then she threw water in my face.

CHARLOTTE: Oh, dear. Oh, I'm sorry. One has to be so brave to be emotionally open and vulnerable. Oh, you poor thing. I'm going to give you a hug. *(She hugs him and kisses him with her Snoopy doll.)* What did you do when she threw water in your face?

BRUCE: I threw it back in her face.

CHARLOTTE: Oh good for you! Bravo! *(She barks for Snoopy and bounces him up and down.)* Ruff ruff ruff! Oh, I feel you getting so much more emotionally expressive since you've been in therapy. I'm proud of you.

BRUCE: Maybe it was my fault. I probably came on too strong.

CHARLOTTE: Uh, life is so difficult. I know when I met the second Mr. Wallace…you know, it's so strange, all my husbands have had the same surname of Wallace, this has been a theme in my own analysis…Well, when I met the second Mr. Wallace, I got a filing cabinet caught in my throat…I don't mean a filing cabinet. What do I mean? Filing cabinet, frying pan, frog's eggs, faculty wives, frankincense, fornication, Follies Bergère, falling falling fork, fish fork, fish bone. I got a fish bone caught in my throat. *(Smiles.)*

BRUCE: And did you get it out?

CHARLOTTE: Oh yes. Then we got married, and we had quite a wonderful relationship for a while, but then he started to see this fishwife and we broke up. I don't mean fishwife, I mean waitress. Is that a word, waitress?

BRUCE: Yes. Woman who works in a restaurant.

CHARLOTTE: No, she didn't work in a restaurant, she worked in a department store. Sales…lady. That's what she was.

BRUCE: That's too bad.

CHARLOTTE: He was buying a gift for me, and then he ran off with the saleslady. He never even gave me the gift, he just left me a note. And then I was so very alone for a while. *(Cries.)*

(After a bit, he gives her a hug and few kisses from the Snoopy doll. She is suitably grateful.)

CHARLOTTE: I'm afraid I'm taking up too much of your session. I'll knock a few dollars off the bill. You talk for a while, I'm getting tired anyway.

BRUCE: Well, so I'm sort of afraid to put another ad in the paper since seeing how this one worked out.

CHARLOTTE: Oh, don't be afraid! Never be afraid to risk, *to risk!* I've told you about *Equus,* haven't I? That doctor, Doctor Dysart, with whom I greatly identify, saw that it was better to risk madness and to blind horses with a metal spike, than to be safe and conventional and dull. Ecc, ecc, equus! Naaaaaaaay! *(For Snoopy.)* Ruff ruff ruff!

BRUCE: So you think I should put in another ad?

CHARLOTTE: Yes I do. But this time, we need an ad that will get someone more exceptional, someone who can appreciate your uniqueness.

BRUCE: In what ways am I unique? *(Sort of pleased.)*

CHARLOTTE: Oh I don't know, the usual ways. Now let's see. *(Writing on pad.)* White male, thirty to thirty-five, 6'2" no—6'5", green eyes, Pulitzer Prize–winning author, into Kierkegaard, Mahler, Joan Didion and sex, seeks similar-minded attractive female for unique encounters. Sense of humor a must. Write box whatever whatever. There, that should catch you someone excellent. Why don't you take this out to the office, and my dirigible will type it up for you. I don't mean dirigible, I mean Saskatchewan.

BRUCE: Secretary.

CHARLOTTE: Yes, that's what I mean.

BRUCE: You know we haven't mentioned how my putting these ads in the paper for women is making Bob feel. He's real hostile about it.

CHARLOTTE: Who's Bob?

BRUCE: He's the guy I've been living with for a year.

CHARLOTTE: Bob. Oh dear. I'm sorry. I thought you were someone else for this whole session. You're not Thomas Norton?

BRUCE: No, I'm Bruce Lathrop.

CHARLOTTE: Oh yes. Bruce and Bob. It all comes back now. Well I'm very sorry. But this is a good ad anyway, I think, so just bring it out to my dirigible, and then come on back in and we'll talk about something else for a while. I know, I mean secretary. Sometimes I think I should get my blood sugar checked.

BRUCE: Alright, think you, Mrs. Wallace.

CHARLOTTE: See you next week.

BRUCE: I thought you wanted me to come right back to finish the session.

CHARLOTTE: Oh yes, see you in a few minutes.

　　(He exits.)

CHARLOTTE: *(Into intercom.)* Marcia, dear, send in the next porpoise please. Wait, I don't mean porpoise, I mean…pony, pekinese, parka, penis, no not that. I'm sorry, Marcia, I'll buzz back when I think of it. *(She moves her lips, trying to remember.)*

　　(Lights dim.)

ACT I
Scene 4

　　A restaurant again. Bruce waiting, looking at his watch. After a bit enter Prudence.

PRUDENCE: *(Sees Bruce.)* Oh.

BRUCE: Hello again.

PRUDENCE: Hello.

BRUCE: Odd coincidence.

PRUDENCE: Yes.

BRUCE: *(Stands.)* Are you answering an ad again?

PRUDENCE: Well, yes, I am.

BRUCE: Me too. I mean I put one in again.

PRUDENCE: Yes, well…I think I'll wait over here. Excuse me. *(Prudence sits at another table.)*

　　(After a bit he comes over.)

PRUDENCE: Yes?

BRUCE: I'm afraid it's crossed my mind that you answered my ad again.

PRUDENCE: I would not be so stupid as to answer the same ad twice.

BRUCE: I changed my ad.

(She stares at him.)

BRUCE: I was hoping to get a different sort of person.

PRUDENCE: Are you then the Pulitzer Prize-winning author, 6'5", who likes Kierkegaard, Mahler, and Joan Didion?

BRUCE: Yes I am. Sorry.

PRUDENCE: I see. Well that was a ludicrous list of people to like anyway, it serves me right. I feel very embarrassed.

BRUCE: Don't be embarrassed. We're all human.

PRUDENCE: I see no reason not to be embarrassed at being human.

BRUCE: You should be in therapy.

PRUDENCE: I am in therapy.

BRUCE: It hasn't worked.

PRUDENCE: Thank you very much. Do you think we're the only two people who answer these ads?

BRUCE: I doubt it. Maybe we're fated.

PRUDENCE: Jinxed seems more like it.

BRUCE: You think you're unlucky, don't you? In general, I mean. *(He sits down.)*

PRUDENCE: You're going to sit down, are you?

BRUCE: Well, what else should I do? Go home to Bob?

PRUDENCE: Oh yes. How is Bob?

BRUCE: He's kind of grumpy these days.

PRUDENCE: Perhaps he's getting his period.

BRUCE: I don't know much about menstruation. Tell me about it.

PRUDENCE: *(Stares at him.)* Yes, I do think I'm unlucky.

BRUCE: What?

PRUDENCE: In answer to your question. I mean, I am attractive, aren't I? I mean, without being conceited, I know I'm *fairly* attractive. I mean, I'm not within the world's two percent mutants…

BRUCE: I don't think you're a mutant at all. I mean, I think you're very attractive.

PRUDENCE: Yes, well, I don't know if I can really credit your opinion. You're sort of a crackpot, aren't you?

BRUCE: You really don't like me, do you?

PRUDENCE: I don't know you really. Well, no, I probably don't like you.

BRUCE: Well I don't like you either.

PRUDENCE: Well, fine. it was delightful to see you again. Good-bye. *(Starts to leave.)*

(He starts to cry, but tries to muffle it more than usual.)

PRUDENCE: I really hate it when you cry. You're much too *large* to cry.

BRUCE: I'm sorry, it's not you. Something was just coming up for me. Some childhood something.

PRUDENCE: Yes, I miss childhood.

BRUCE: I thought you were leaving.

PRUDENCE: *(Sits.)* Alright, I want to ask you something. Why did you put that ad in the paper? I mean, if you're living with this person named Bob, why are you trying to meet a woman?

BRUCE: I want to be open to all experiences.

PRUDENCE: Well that sounds all very well, but surely you can't just turn on and off sexual preference.

BRUCE: I don't have to turn it on or off. I prefer both sexes.

PRUDENCE: I don't know, I just find that so difficult to believe.

BRUCE: But why would I be here with you if I weren't interested in you?

PRUDENCE: You might be trying to murder me. Or punish your mother.

BRUCE: Or I might just be trying to reach out and touch someone.

PRUDENCE: That's the slogan of Coke or Dr. Pepper, I think.

BRUCE: The telephone company actually. But it's a good slogan. I mean, isn't that what we're all trying to do, reach out to another person? I mean, I put an ad in a newspaper, after all, and you answered it.

PRUDENCE: I know. It's very hard to meet people. I mean I do meet people at the magazine. I met Shaun Cassidy last week. Of course, he's too young for me.

BRUCE: Bob really likes Shaun Cassidy.

PRUDENCE: Oh, I'll have to try to set them up.

BRUCE: I don't think your therapist is helping you at all.

PRUDENCE: Well I think yours must be a maniac.

BRUCE: My therapist says you have to be willing to go out on a limb, to risk, to risk!

PRUDENCE: My therapist says... *(At a loss.)* I have to settle for imperfection.

BRUCE: I know it's unconventional to be bisexual. My wife Sally didn't deal with it at all well.

PRUDENCE: You were married?

BRUCE: For six years. I married this girl Sally I knew all through grammar school and everything. She was runner-up for the homecoming queen.

PRUDENCE: I didn't go to the prom. I read *Notes From The Underground* instead.

BRUCE: You should have gone to the prom.

PRUDENCE: I don't like proms. Why did you and Sally break up?

BRUCE: Well, I didn't understand about bisexuality then. I thought the fact that I wanted to sleep with the man who came to read the gas meter meant I was queer.

PRUDENCE: I'm never home when they come to read the gas meter.

BRUCE: And so then Sally found out I was sleeping with the gas man, and she got real angry and we got a divorce.

PRUDENCE: Well I guess if you're homecoming queen runner-up you don't expect those sorts of problems.

BRUCE: You haven't been married, have you?

PRUDENCE: (Uncomfortable.) No.

BRUCE: Has there been anyone serious?

PRUDENCE: I have two cats. Serious, let's see. Well, about a year and a half ago I lived for six months with this aging preppie named Michael.

BRUCE: (Pleased—a connection.) I'm an aging preppie.

PRUDENCE: Yes I know. Michael was a lawyer, and…

BRUCE: I'm a lawyer.

PRUDENCE: (Registers this fact, then goes on.) And he was very smart, and very nice; and I should've been happy with him, and I don't know why I wasn't. And he was slightly allergic to my cats, so I broke it off.

BRUCE: And you haven't gone out with anyone since?

PRUDENCE: Well I do go out with people, but it never seems to work out.

BRUCE: Maybe you're too hard on them.

PRUDENCE: Well should I pretend someone is wonderful if I think they're stupid or crazy?

BRUCE: Well no, but maybe you judge everybody too quickly.

PRUDENCE: Well perhaps. But how many nights would you give David Berkowitz?

BRUCE: You went out with David Berkowitz?

PRUDENCE: No. It was a rhetorical question.

BRUCE: You must ask yourself what you want. Do you want to be married?

PRUDENCE: I have no idea. It's so confusing. I know when I was a little girl, Million Dollar Movie showed this film called *Every Girl Should Be Married* every night for seven days. It was this dumb comedy about this infantile girl played by Betsy Drake who wants to be married to this pediatrician played by Cary Grant who she sees in a drugstore. She sees him for two minutes, and she wants to move in and have babies with him. And he finds her totally obnoxious, but then at the end of the movie suddenly says,

"You're right, you're adorable," and then they get married. *(Looks baffled by the stupidity of it all.)*

BRUCE: Well it was a comedy.

PRUDENCE: And what confused me further was that the actress Betsy Drake did in fact marry Cary Grant in real life. Of course, it didn't last, and he married several other people, and then later Dyan Cannon said he was insane and took LSD and so maybe one wouldn't want to be married to him at all. But if it's no good being married to Cary Grant, who is it good being married to?

BRUCE: I don't know.

PRUDENCE: Neither do I.

BRUCE: Well you should give things time. First impressions can be wrong. And maybe Dyan Cannon was the problem. Maybe anyone married to her would take LSD. Maybe Cary Grant is still terrific.

PRUDENCE: Well he's too old for me anyway. Shaun Cassidy's too young, and Cary Grant's too old.

BRUCE: I'm the right age.

PRUDENCE: Yes I guess you are.

BRUCE: And you haven't left. You said you were leaving but then you stayed.

PRUDENCE: Well it's not particularly meaningful. I was just curious why you put the ad in the paper.

BRUCE: Why did you answer it?

PRUDENCE: I don't wish to analyze my behavior on the issue.

BRUCE: You're so afraid of things. I feel this overwhelming urge to help you. We can look into the abyss together.

PRUDENCE: Please don't say pretentious things. I get a rash.

BRUCE: *(Depressed.)* You're right. I guess I am pretentious.

PRUDENCE: Well I really am too hard on people.

BRUCE: No you're probably right to dislike me. Sally hates me. I mean, sometimes I hear myself and I understand why no one likes me.

PRUDENCE: Please don't be so hard on yourself on my account. Everyone's stupid, so you're just like everyone else.

(He stares at her.)

PRUDENCE: I'm sorry, that sounded terrible. I'm stupid too. We're all stupid.

BRUCE: It's human to be stupid. *(Sings romantically.)* There's a somebody I'm longing duh duh, Duh duh duh duh, duh duh duh duh...*(Stops singing.)*

PRUDENCE: *(Sings.)* Someone to watch...*(Realizes she's singing alone.)* Oh I didn't realize you were stopping.

BRUCE: Sorry. I didn't realize you were...starting.

PRUDENCE: Yes. Stupid of me to like that song.

BRUCE: It's a pretty song.

PRUDENCE: Well I guess it is.

BRUCE: I want to say something. I like you.

PRUDENCE: (*Surprised anyone could like her.*) You do?

BRUCE: I like women who are independent minded, who don't look to a man to do all their thinking for them. I like women who are persons.

PRUDENCE: Well you sound like you were coached by Betty Friedan, but otherwise that's a nice sentiment. Of course, a woman who was independent minded wouldn't like the song "Someone To Watch Over Me."

BRUCE: We have to allow for contradictions in ourselves. Nobody is just one thing.

PRUDENCE: (*Serious.*) That's very true. That wasn't a crackpot comment at all.

BRUCE: I know it wasn't. And just because I'm a crackpot on some things doesn't mean I'm a total crackpot.

PRUDENCE: Right. You're a partial crackpot.

BRUCE: You could be a crackpot too if you let yourself go.

PRUDENCE: That wasn't what I was attempting to do when I got up this morning.

BRUCE: To risk, to risk! Do you like me?

PRUDENCE: Well, I don't know. I don't really know you yet.

BRUCE: Do you want to get to know me?

PRUDENCE: Well I don't know. Maybe I shouldn't. I mean, we did meet through a personal ad, you don't have a Pulitzer Prize...

BRUCE: I have a membership in the New York Health and Racquet Club.

PRUDENCE: Well similar, but not the same thing.

BRUCE: As a member I can get you a discount.

PRUDENCE: I don't know if I'm ready to exercise yet. I'm thinking about it, but I'm cautious still.

BRUCE: We're getting on, aren't we?

PRUDENCE: Well yes, in a way. (*Smiles warmly; he smiles back; she then looks around.*) Do you think maybe they don't have waiters in this restaurant?

BRUCE: Maybe they're on strike. Why don't we go to another restaurant? I know a good Mexican one.

PRUDENCE: I don't like Mexican food, I'm afraid.

BRUCE: Japanese?

PRUDENCE: Well no.

BRUCE: Chinese?

PRUDENCE: Well more than Japanese, but not really.

BRUCE: Where do you want to go?

PRUDENCE: Well could we go to an American Restaurant? I know I'm very dull, but I didn't even like vanilla ice cream when I was a child. I was afraid of it.

BRUCE: That's a significant statement you've just made.

PRUDENCE: It does sound pathological, doesn't it?

BRUCE: Don't be afraid to sound pathological. That's what I've learned from my therapy so far.

PRUDENCE: I don't think I've learned much from mine yet.

BRUCE: Maybe I can help you. We can look into the abyss together. Oh that's right, you didn't like it when I said that before.

PRUDENCE: That's alright. I'll look into the abyss for one evening.

BRUCE: Oh you're becoming more open. Good for you. Ruff, ruff, ruff!

PRUDENCE: *(Very taken aback.)* I'm sorry?

BRUCE: *(Very embarrassed.)* Oh, my therapist barks. For encouragement.

PRUDENCE: Ah, of course.

BRUCE: *(Back to getting to know her.)* Now tell me about your fear of vanilla ice cream.

PRUDENCE: *(As they walk out.)* Well, I had gotten very used to baby food, and I also liked junket, but there was something about the *texture* of vanilla ice cream…

(They exit.)

ACT I

Scene 5

Dr. Stuart Framingham's office again.

STUART: *(On phone.)* Hiya, babe, it's me. Whatcha doin'? Oh, I'm just waiting for my next patient. Last night was great, wasn't it? It was great. What? So quickly. What is it with you women? You read some goddamned sex manual and then you think sex is supposed to go on for hours or something. I mean, if you're so frigid you can't get excited in a couple of minutes, that's not my problem. No it isn't. Well, fuck you too. *(Hangs up.)* Jesus God. *(Into intercom.)* Betty, you can send in the next patient.

(Enter Prudence.)

STUART: Hello.

PRUDENCE: Hello.

STUART: What's on your mind this week?

PRUDENCE: Nothing.

STUART: *(Furious.)* Goddam it. I don't feel like dragging the words out of you this week. Talk, damn it.

PRUDENCE: What?

STUART: You pay me to listen, so TALK! (Pause.) I'm sorry, I'm on edge today. And all my patients are this way. None of them talk. Well this one guy talks, but he talks in Yiddish a lot, and I don't know what the fuck he's saying.

PRUDENCE: Well you should tell him that you don't understand.

STUART: Don't tell me how to run my business! Besides, we're here to talk about you. How was your week? Another series of lonely, loveless evenings? I'm still here, babe.

PRUDENCE: Don't call me babe. No, I've had some pleasant evenings actually.

STUART: You have?

PRUDENCE: Yes I have.

STUART: You been answering ads in the paper again?

PRUDENCE: Well, yes actually.

STUART: That's a slutty thing to do.

PRUDENCE: As a therapist you are utterly ridiculous.

STUART: I'm just kidding you. You shouldn't lose your sense of humor, babe, especially when you're in a promiscuous stage.

PRUDENCE: I am not promiscuous.

STUART: There's nothing wrong with being promiscuous. We're all human.

PRUDENCE: Yes, we are all human.

STUART: So who is this guy? Have you slept with him?

PRUDENCE: Dr. Framingham....

STUART: Really, I gotta know for therapy.

PRUDENCE: Yes, we have slept together. Once. I wasn't really planning to, but...

STUART: Is he better than me?

PRUDENCE: Stuart...

STUART: No really. You liked him better? Tell me.

PRUDENCE: Yes I did. Much better.

STUART: I suppose he took his time. I suppose it lasted just hours. That's sick! Wanting sex to take a long time is sick!

PRUDENCE: Well he was attentive to how I felt, if that's what you mean.

STUART: So this fellow was a real success, huh?

PRUDENCE: Success and failure are not particularly likable terms to describe sexual outings, but if you must, yes, it was successful. Probably his experiences with men have made him all that better as a lover.

STUART: What?

PRUDENCE: He's bisexual.

STUART: *(Starting to feel on the winning team again.)* Oh yeah?

PRUDENCE: So he tells me. Masters and Johnson say that homosexuals make much more responsive sex partners anyway.

STUART: BULLSHIT! You are talking such bullshit! I understand you now. You're obviously afraid of a real man, and so you want to cuddle with some eunuch who isn't a threat to you. I understand all this now!

PRUDENCE: There's no need to call him a eunuch. A eunuch has no testicles.

STUART: I GOT BALLS, BABY!

PRUDENCE: I am so pleased for you.

STUART: You're afraid of men!

PRUDENCE: I am not afraid of men.

STUART: You're a fag hag. *(To himself.)* I gotta write that down. *(Writes that down, makes further notes.)*

PRUDENCE: Look, I admit I find this man's supposed bisexuality confusing and I don't quite believe it. But what are my options? A two-minute roll in the hay with you, where you make no distinction between sexual intercourse and push-ups; and then a happy evening of admiring your underarm hair and your belt buckles? *(Irritated.)* What are you writing?

STUART: *(Reading from his pad.)* I'd like to give this patient electroshock therapy. I'd like to put this patient in a clothes dryer until her hair falls out. I'd like to tie her to the radiator and… *(Stops, hears himself, looks stricken.)*

PRUDENCE: I think this is obviously my last session.

STUART: No, no, no. You're taking me seriously. I'm testing you. It was a test. I was just putting you on.

PRUDENCE: For what purpose?

STUART: I can't tell you. It would interfere with your therapy.

PRUDENCE: You call this therapy?

STUART: We're reaching the richest part of our therapy and already I see results. But I think you're entering a very uncharted part of your life just now, and so you must stay with your therapy. You're going out with homosexuals, God knows what you're going to do next. Now I'm very serious. I'm holding out the lifeline. Don't turn away.

PRUDENCE: Well I'll think about it, but I don't know.

STUART: You're a very sick woman, and you mustn't be without a therapist even for a day.

PRUDENCE: *(Not taken in by this; wanting to leave without a scene.)* Is the session over yet?

STUART: We have thirty more minutes.

PRUDENCE: Could I go early?

STUART: I think it's important that we finish out the session.

PRUDENCE: I'd like to go.

STUART: Please, please, please, please…

PRUDENCE: Alright, alright. For God's sake.

(They settle down, back in their chairs.)

STUART: When are you seeing this person again? I'm asking as your therapist.

PRUDENCE: Tonight. He's making dinner for us.

STUART: *He's* making dinner?

PRUDENCE: He says he likes to cook.

STUART: I don't think I need say anything more.

PRUDENCE: I don't think you do either.

(They stare at one another; lights dim.)

ACT I

Scene 6

Bruce's apartment. Bruce fiddling with pillows, on couch, looking at watch, etc. Doorbell. Bruce lets in Prudence.

BRUCE: Hi. Come on in.

PRUDENCE: Hello. *(They kiss.)* I brought some wine.

BRUCE: Oh thanks.

PRUDENCE: You have a nice apartment.

BRUCE: Thanks.

PRUDENCE: It looks just like my apartment.

BRUCE: Yeah I guess it does.

PRUDENCE: And like my office at the magazine. And like the lobby at the bank. Everything looks alike.

BRUCE: Yes, I guess it does.

PRUDENCE: I'm sorry, I'm just rattling on.

BRUCE: That's alright. Sit down.

(They sit.)

BRUCE: Can I get you a drink?

PRUDENCE: Ummm, I don't know.

BRUCE: Do you want one?

PRUDENCE: I don't know. Do you want one?

BRUCE: Well I thought I might have some Perrier.

PRUDENCE: Oh that sounds good.

BRUCE: Two Perriers?

PRUDENCE: Well, do you have Poland water?

BRUCE: I think I do. Wait here. I'll be right back. *(Bruce exits.)*

    (After a moment Bob enters. Bob sees Prudence, is rattled, ill at ease.)

BOB: Oh. You're here already. I...didn't hear the bell ring.

PRUDENCE: Oh. Hello. Are you Bob?

BOB: Yes. *(At a loss, making an odd joke.)* And you must be Marie of Roumania.

PRUDENCE: I'm Prudence.

BOB: Yes, I know. *(At a loss how to get out of room.)* Is Bruce in the kitchen?

PRUDENCE: Yes.

BOB: Oh. *(Starts to go there; stops.)* Oh, well, never mind. When he comes out would you tell him I want to see him in the other room?

PRUDENCE: Alright.

BOB: Excuse me. *(Exits back to bedroom presumably.)*

    (Enter Bruce with two glasses of sparkling water.)

BRUCE: Well here we are. One Perrier, and one Poland water.

PRUDENCE: I thought you said Bob was away.

BRUCE: Oh, you met Bob already? Yes, he was going away, but then he changed his mind and I'd already bought the lamb chops.

PRUDENCE: You mean he's going to be here all through dinner?

BRUCE: Oh I don't think so. He said he was going to his mother's for dinner. He has a very funny mother. She's sort of like Auntie Mame.

PRUDENCE: Oh yes?

BRUCE: Now don't let Bob upset you.

PRUDENCE: Well he seemed very uncomfortable. He asked me if I was Marie of Roumania.

BRUCE: Oh, he says that to everyone. Don't take it personally. *(Raising drink.)* Well, cheers.

PRUDENCE: *(Remembering.)* Oh. He said he wanted to see you in the other room.

BRUCE: Oh. Well, alright. I'll just be a minute. Here, why don't you read a magazine?

PRUDENCE: *People,* how nice.

BRUCE: Be right back. *(Exits.)*

(Prudence reads magazine uncomfortably, and tastes his Perrier water to compare it with her Poland water. We and she start to hear the following offstage argument; initially it's just a buzz of voices but it grows into anger and shouting. Prudence looks very uncomfortable.)

BRUCE: *(Offstage.)* This isn't the time to talk about this, Bob.

BOB: *(Offstage.)* Well, when is the time?

BRUCE: *(Offstage.)* We can talk about this later.

BOB: *(Offstage.)* That's obviously very convenient for you.

BRUCE: *(Offstage.)* Bob, this isn't the time to talk about this.

BOB: *(Offstage.)* Well when *is* the time?

BRUCE: *(Offstage.)* Come on, Bob, calm down. *(Softer.)* Now I told you this doesn't have anything to do with us.

BOB: *(Offstage. Very angry.)* Oh God!

BRUCE: *(Offstage.)* I'm sick of this behavior, Bob!

BOB: *(Offstage.)* Well I'm sick of it too!

(There is a crash of something breaking. Pause. Then re-enter Bruce.)

BRUCE: Everything's fine now. *(Pause.)* We broke a vase. Well, Bob broke it.

PRUDENCE: Maybe I should go.

BRUCE: No, everything's fine now. Once Bob vents his anger then everything's fine again.

PRUDENCE: I thought you told me that Bob didn't mind your seeing me, and that the two of you had broken up anyway.

BRUCE: Well, I lied. Sorry. Some members of Bob's group therapy wrote me a note saying they thought if I wanted to see women, I should just go on and see women, and so I just sort of presumed they'd convince Bob eventually, but I guess they haven't yet.

PRUDENCE: They wrote you a letter?

BRUCE: It's a very intense group Bob is in. They're always visiting each other in the hospital and things.

PRUDENCE: But what shall we do about this evening?

BRUCE: I think you and Bob will really like one another once you get past this initial discomfort. And besides, I'm sure he'll be going to his mother's in a little while.

PRUDENCE: Maybe we should go to a restaurant.

BRUCE: No really I bought the lamb chops. It'll be fine. Oh my God, the rice. I have to go see about the rice. It's wild rice; well, Rice-a-roni. I have to go see about browning it. I won't be a minute.

PRUDENCE: No, no, don't leave…

BRUCE: It's alright. *(As he leaves.)* Bob will come talk to you… *(Exits.)*

PRUDENCE: *(As she sees he's gone.)* I know…Oh dear.

(Enter Bob.)

BOB: Hello again.

PRUDENCE: Oh hi.

BOB: I didn't mean to make you uncomfortable about Marie of Roumania. It's just something I say.

PRUDENCE: Oh that's alright.

BOB: *(Offering it as information.)* I just broke a vase.

PRUDENCE: *(Being pleasant.)* Oh yes, I thought I heard something.

BOB: Bruce says that I will like you if I can just get past my initial hostility.

PRUDENCE: Oh. Well I hope so.

BOB: Bruce is really a very conflicted person. I really suffer a lot dealing with him.

PRUDENCE: Oh I'm sorry.

BOB: And now this latest thing of having women traipse through here at all hours.

PRUDENCE: Ah.

BOB: Did you ever see the movie *Sunday Bloody Sunday?*

PRUDENCE: No I didn't. I meant to.

BOB: Well I sure wish Bruce had never seen it. It had a big effect on him. It's all about this guy played by Murray Head who's having an affair with Peter Finch *and* with Glenda Jackson.

PRUDENCE: Oh. Good actors.

BOB: Yes, well the point is it's a very silly movie because I don't think bisexuality exists, do you?

PRUDENCE: Well it's hard to know really.

BOB: I mean, I think that Bruce is just trying to prove something with all these ads in the paper for women. That's what my mother says about Bruce. She tells me I should just be patient and understanding and that it's just a phase Bruce is going through. I've put a lot of work into this relationship. And it's so difficult meeting new people, it's just thoroughly intimidating.

PRUDENCE: It is hard to meet people.

BOB: I think everyone is basically gay, don't you?

PRUDENCE: Well, no, not really.

BOB: You just say that because you haven't come out yet. I know lots of lesbians who'd like you a lot. I'd be happy to give them your number.

PRUDENCE: Thank you, but no.

(Enter Bruce.)

BRUCE: Well I burned the rice. Sorry. We'll just have more salad.

PRUDENCE: Oh that's alright.

BRUCE: So have you two been getting to know one another?

PRUDENCE: Yes.

BOB: *(Truly being conversational, not trying to be rude. To Bruce.)* Don't you think Prudence would be a big hit in a lesbian bar?

BRUCE: Yes, I guess she would.

BOB: I know Liz Skinner would certainly like her.

BRUCE: Yes, she is Liz's type.

PRUDENCE: Bruce, could I speak to you for a moment please? *(To Bob.)* I'm sorry, excuse me.

(Bruce and Prudence cross to side of room.)

PRUDENCE: Bruce, I'm getting very uncomfortable. Now you told me that Bob wasn't going to be here and that he wasn't jealous about your seeing women, and I don't want to be told which lesbians would like me, so I think maybe I should forget the whole thing and go home.

BRUCE: No please, don't go. Bob needs help to get over his feelings about this, and I'm sure he'll go to his mother's in a little while. So please just be nice to him for a little longer. For our sake.

PRUDENCE: I don't know.

BRUCE: Really, it'll be fine.

PRUDENCE: *(Deciding to try.)* All right. All right.

(They return to Bob.)

PRUDENCE: *(On returning, to Bob.)* Sorry.

BOB: Don't be sorry. I realize I make you uncomfortable.

PRUDENCE: No, no, really it's not that.

BRUCE: Prudence likes you, Bob. She isn't like the other women you know.

PRUDENCE: Yes, I do…I like lots of men. *(Laughs nervously.)*

BOB: We have that in common.

PRUDENCE: Yes… *(Laughs, very uncomfortable.)*

BRUCE: *(Making big transition into "conversation".)* So, Prudence, did you finish writing your interview with Joyce De Witt?

BOB: Who's Joyce De Witt?

PRUDENCE: *(Trying to be very friendly.)* Oh, she's the brunette actress on the TV show *Three's a Crowd*. *(Pause; looks mortified.)* I mean, *Three's Company*. *(Long pause. They all feel awful.)*

BRUCE: So, did you finish the article?

PRUDENCE: Yes, I did. Right on time. *(Pause; to Bob.)* Bruce tells me your mother is like Auntie Mame.

(Bob glares at Bruce.)

PRUDENCE: Oh, I'm sorry. Was that a bad thing to say?

BOB: It depends on what you mean by Auntie Mame.

PRUDENCE: I don't know. Bruce said it.

BOB: My mother has a certain flair, if that's what he means.

BRUCE: Your mother acts like a transvestite. I'm sorry, she does.

BOB: Just because my mother has a sense of humor is no reason to accuse her of not being feminine. *(To Prudence.)* Don't you agree that women *theoretically* can have senses of humor?

PRUDENCE: Yes indeed.

BRUCE: Sense of humor isn't the issue.

PRUDENCE: *(Trying to help conversation.)* I've always hated transvestites. It's such a repugnant image of women.

(Bob looks disapproving.)

PRUDENCE: I'm sorry, I don't mean to imply anything about your mother. I...I liked Jack Lemmon as a woman in *Some Like It Hot.*

BOB: My mother does not resemble Jack Lemmon in *Some Like It Hot.*

PRUDENCE: I'm sure she doesn't. I didn't mean to imply...

BRUCE: Change the subject, Prudence. This is getting us nowhere.

PRUDENCE: Oh, alright. *(Thinks.)* What does Bob do for a living?

BOB: I'm still in the room.

PRUDENCE: Oh I'm sorry, I know you are. *(Pause.)* What do you do for a living, Bob?

BOB: I'm a pharmacist.

PRUDENCE: Oh really?

BOB: Do you need any pills?

PRUDENCE: No thank you. *(Pause.)* Maybe later.

BRUCE: *(To Prudence.)* Can I freshen your Poland water?

PRUDENCE: No thank you. I'm fine. *(Pause.)* So you're a pharmacist.

BOB: Yes.

BRUCE: I wish I hadn't burned the rice. *(Whispers to Prudence.)* Say something to him, he's starting to sulk.

PRUDENCE: Ummmm...What exactly is in Tylenol, I wonder.

BOB: That's alright. I realize I'm making everyone uncomfortable. Excuse me. *(Exits.)*

PRUDENCE: Really, Bruce, this isn't very fair to me. This is a problem the two of you should work out together.

BRUCE: Well you're right actually. You're always right. That's why I like you so much. *(Moves closer, puts arm around her.)*

PRUDENCE: Maybe I should go.

BRUCE: Oh you're too sensitive. Besides, he'll be leaving soon.

(Bob re-enters.)

BOB: My mother's on the phone.

BRUCE: I didn't hear it ring.

BOB: I called her. *(To Prudence.)* She wants to speak to you.

PRUDENCE: I don't understand. I…

BOB: *(Hands her the phone.)* Here.

PRUDENCE: *(It's happening too fast to stop.)* Hello. Who is this? Oh, hello. Yes. *(Laughs uncomfortably.)* Yes, thank you. What? No, I don't want to ruin your son's life. What? No, really, I'm not trying to…

BRUCE: *(Takes phone away from Prudence; talks into it.)* Now, look, Sadie, I've told you not to meddle in my life. It doesn't do anybody any good when you do, including Bob. Don't sing when I'm talking to you, that's not communication to sing when someone is talking to you. Sadie…Sadie! *(Hands phone to Bob.)* She's singing "Rose's Turn" from *Gypsy*, it's utterly terrifying.

BOB: Hello, mother.

BRUCE: *(To Prudence.)* She's an insane woman.

BOB: Mother, it's me, you can stop singing now. Okay, well, just finish the phrase. *(Listens.)*

PRUDENCE: Where's Bob's father?

BRUCE: She killed him.

BOB: That's not funny, Bruce. Okay, mother, wrap the song up now. Yes, I'm alright. Yes, I'll tell them. *(To the two of them.)* My mother thinks you're both very immature. *(Back to phone.)* Yes, I think she's a lesbian too.

PRUDENCE: I'm going to go home now.

BRUCE: No, no, I'll fix this. *(Takes phone away from Bob.)* Finish this conversation in the other room, Bob. Then please get out of here, as we agreed you would do earlier, so Prudence and I can have our dinner. I mean, we agreed upon this, Bob.

BOB: You mean you agreed upon it.

BRUCE: I've finished with this conversation, Bob. Go in the other room and talk to your mother. *(Listens to phone.)* What's she singing now, I don't recognize it? *(Bob and Bruce both listen to phone.)*

BOB: That's "Welcome to Kanagawa" from *Pacific Overtures*.

BRUCE: Keep singing, Sadie. Bob is changing phones. It was good hearing from you.

BRUCE: I just don't understand your behavior. I just don't. *(Exits.)*

PRUDENCE: Bruce, I can't tell you how uncomfortable I am. Really I must go home, and then the two of you should go to a marriage counselor or something.

BRUCE: I am sorry. I should have protected you from this. *(Listens to phone, hangs it up.)*

PRUDENCE: I mean we're only seeing one another casually, and you and Bob have been living together and his mother calls up and she sings...

BRUCE: Prudence, I'm not feeling all that casual anymore. Are you?

PRUDENCE: Well I don't know. I mean, probably yes, it's still casual.

BRUCE: It needn't be.

PRUDENCE: Bruce, I just don't think your life is in order.

BRUCE: Of course it's not. How can life be in order? Life by its very nature is disordered, terrifying. That's why people come together, to face the terrors hand in hand.

PRUDENCE: You're giving me my rash again.

BRUCE: You're so afraid of feeling.

PRUDENCE: Oh, just put the lamb chops on.

BRUCE: I feel very close to you.

(Enter Bob with suitcase. Phone rings.)

BOB: Don't answer it. It's just my mother again. I told her I was checking into a hotel and then jumping out the window. There's just no point in continuing. *(To Prudence, sincerely.)* I hope you're both very happy... Really.

PRUDENCE: *(Startled, confused.)* Thank you.

BRUCE: Bob, come back here. *(Answers phone.)* Sadie, we'll call you back. *(Hangs up.)* Bob.

BOB: No, go back to your evening. I don't want to stand in your way.

BRUCE: You're just trying to get attention.

BOB: There's just no point in continuing.

(Phone rings; Bruce answers it.)

BRUCE: It's all right, Sadie, I'll handle this. *(Hangs up.)* Bob, people who announce their suicide are just asking for help, isn't that so, Prudence?

PRUDENCE: I really don't know. I think I should leave.

BOB: No, please, I don't want to spoil your dinner.

BRUCE: You're just asking for help. *(Phone rings.)* Let's let it ring. Bob, look at me. I want you to get help. Can you hear me? I want you to see my therapist.

BOB: I have my own group therapy.

BRUCE: You need better help than that. Doesn't he, Prudence? *(Answers phone.)* It's all right, Sadie, I'm going to call up my therapist right away. *(Hangs up.)* Now you just sit down here, Bob, and we're going to call Mrs. Wallace right up. *(To Prudence.)* Unless you think your therapist is better.

PRUDENCE: No! Yours would have to be better.

BOB: I don't know what you have against my group therapy. It's been very helpful to me.

BRUCE: Bob, you're trying to kill yourself. That proves to me that group therapy is a failure.

BOB: Suicide is an innate human right.

(Phone rings.)

BRUCE: *(To Prudence; hands her phone.)* Will you tell her to stop calling?

PRUDENCE: Hello?

BRUCE: You're not acting logically.

PRUDENCE: No, I don't want to see him dead.

BOB: I simply think I should end my life now. That's logical.

PRUDENCE: Please don't shout at me, Mrs. Lansky.

BRUCE: We have to talk this through.

PRUDENCE: Bruce.

BOB: I don't want to talk it through. *(Sings.)* Frere Jacques, Frere Jacques, dormez-vous? dormez-vous? *(Etc., continues on.)*

PRUDENCE: Bruce.

BRUCE: Don't sing when I'm talking to you.

PRUDENCE: Bruce.

BRUCE: What is it, Prudence?

PRUDENCE: Please, Mrs. Lansky is yelling at me.

BRUCE: Well she can't hurt you. Yell back.

BOB: *(Takes phone.)* Mother, it's alright, I want to die. *(Hands phone back to Prudence, goes back to song.)* Ding dong ding ding dong ding. Frere Jacques... *(Continues.)*

BRUCE: Bob, you're acting like a baby.

PRUDENCE: No, he's still alive, Mrs. Lansky.

BRUCE: *(Irritated, starts to sing at Bob.)* Seventy-six trombones led the big parade, with one hundred ten cornets close behind... *(Continues.)*

PRUDENCE: Mrs. Lansky, I'm going to hang up now. Good-bye. Stop yelling. *(Hangs up.)*

BOB: *(Stops singing.)* Did you hang up on my mother? *(Bruce stops too.)*

PRUDENCE: *(Really letting him have it.)* Oh why don't you just go kill yourself? *(Bob sits down, stunned. Phone rings.)*

PRUDENCE: *(Answers it.)* Oh shut up! *(Hangs up.)* I am very uninterested in being involved in this nonsense. You're both just making a big overdramatic mess out of everything, and I don't want to watch it anymore.

BRUCE: You're right. Bob, she's right.

BOB: *(Looks up.)* She is?

BRUCE: Yes, she is. We're really acting stupid. *(Phone rings. Bruce picks it up, and hangs up immediately. Then he dials.)* I'm calling Mrs. Wallace now. I think we really need help.

PRUDENCE: You have her home number?

BRUCE: Yes. She's a really wonderful woman. She gave me her home number after our second session.

PRUDENCE: I slept with my therapist after our second session.

BRUCE: Hello? Uh, is Mrs. Wallace there? Thank you. *(To them.)* I think that was her husband.

BOB: *(Not defiantly; just for something to do, sings softly.)* Frere Jacques, frere Jacques, dormez-vous…*(Etc.)*

BRUCE: *(Suddenly hearing it.)* What do you mean you slept with your therapist?

PRUDENCE: I don't know, I…

BRUCE: *(To Bob suddenly, as Mrs. Wallace is now on the phone.)* Sssssh. *(Into phone.)* Hello. Mrs. Wallace? Mrs. Wallace, this is Bruce, we have a bit of an emergency, I wonder if you can help…we're in desperate need of some therapy here…

END ACT I

ACT II

Scene 1

Act I. Mrs. Wallace's office, twenty minutes after the end of Act I. Mrs. Wallace present, enter Bruce and Bob.

BRUCE: Hi, it's us.

CHARLOTTE: Hello.

BRUCE: Really, it's so nice of you to see us right away.

CHARLOTTE: That's alright.

BRUCE: Mrs. Wallace, this is Bob Lansky.

CHARLOTTE: Hello.

BOB: Hello.

BRUCE: Well I'm going to leave you two and go have dinner with Prudence.

BOB: You're not going to stay?

BRUCE: Bob, you're the one who's not handling this situation well. Now I haven't eaten all day, and this hasn't been fair to Prudence. *(To Mrs. Wallace.)* Now if he gets totally out of control, we're going to be at the Restaurant. I mean that's the name of the restaurant. I mean I could be paged. Otherwise, I'll just see you back at the apartment.

BOB: I thought you wanted her to talk to us together.

BRUCE: Not for the first session. Now you listen to what Mrs. Wallace has to say, and I'll see you later tonight. *(Gives Bob an affectionate hug, then exits. Bob and Mrs. Wallace stare at one another for a while.)*

BOB: Should I sit down?

CHARLOTTE: Would you like to sit down?

(He sits. She sits, holds her Snoopy doll.)

BOB: Why are you holding that doll?

CHARLOTTE: Does it bother you that I hold the doll?

BOB: I don't know.

CHARLOTTE: Were you allowed to have dolls as a child?

BOB: Yes I was. It was trucks I wasn't allowed to have.

CHARLOTTE: *(Confused.)* Great big trucks?

BOB: Toy trucks.

(Silence.)

CHARLOTTE: Now, what seems to be the matter?

BOB: Bruce seems to be trying to end our relationship.

CHARLOTTE: What do you mean?

BOB: He's been putting these ads in the paper for women. And now he seems a little serious about this new one.

CHARLOTTE: Women?

BOB: Women.

CHARLOTTE: And why does this bother you?

BOB: Well, Bruce and I have been living together for a year. A little more.

CHARLOTTE: Living together?

BOB: Yes.

CHARLOTTE: As roommates?

BOB: Well, if that's the euphemism you prefer.

CHARLOTTE: I prefer nothing. I'm here to help you.

BOB: But you can see the problem.

CHARLOTTE: Well if Bruce should move out, surely you can find another roommate. They advertise in the paper. As a matter of fact, my son is looking for a roommate, he doesn't get on with the present Mr. Wallace. Maybe you could room with him.

BOB: I don't think you've understood. Bruce and I aren't just roommates, you know. I mean, doesn't he talk to you about me in his own therapy?

CHARLOTTE: Let me get his file. *(Looks through her drawers, takes out rope, binoculars, orange juice carton, folders, miscellaneous mess. Laughs.)* No, it's not here. Maybe my dirigible knows where it is. *(Pushes button.)* Marcia. Oh that's right, she's not in the office now. *(To intercom.)* Never mind. Well, I'll have to rely on memory.

BOB: Dirigible?

CHARLOTTE: I'm sorry, did I say dirigible? Now what word did I want?

BOB: Blimp?

CHARLOTTE: *(Not understanding.)* Blimp?

BOB: Is the word blimp?

CHARLOTTE: *(Irritated.)* No, it's nothing like blimp. Now you've made me forget what I was saying. *(Holds her head.)* Something about apartments. Oh yes. Did you want to meet my son as a possible roommate?

BOB: I don't understand what you're talking about. Why do you want me to meet your son? Is he gay?

CHARLOTTE: *(Offended.)* No, he's not gay. What an awful thing to suggest. He just wants to share an apartment with someone. Isn't that what you want?

BOB: No it isn't. I have not come to you for real estate advice. I've come to you because my lover and I are in danger of breaking up.

CHARLOTTE: Lover?

BOB: Your patient, Bruce! The person who was just here. He and I are lovers, don't you know that?

CHARLOTTE: Good God, no!

BOB: What do you mean, Good God no!

CHARLOTTE: But he doesn't seem homosexual. He doesn't lisp.

BOB: Are you kidding?

CHARLOTTE: Well, he doesn't lisp, does he? Now what was I thinking of? Be quiet for a moment. *(Holds her head.)* Secretary. The word I was looking for was secretary.

BOB: I mean doesn't Bruce talk about us? Am I that unimportant to him?

CHARLOTTE: I really can't remember without access to the files. Let's talk about something else.

BOB: Something else?

CHARLOTTE: Oh, tell me about your childhood. At what age did you masturbate?

BOB: I don't want to talk about my childhood.

CHARLOTTE: Very well. We'll just sit in silence. New patients are difficult, aren't they, Snoopy? *(She nods Snoopy's head, glares at Bob significantly.)*

BOB: May I see your accreditation, please?

(Charlotte starts to empty her drawer of junk again.)

BOB: Never mind.

CHARLOTTE: So you and Bruce are an item, eh? Odd that I didn't pick that up.

BOB: Well, we may be an item no longer.

CHARLOTTE: Well, the path of true love never doth run smoothly.

BOB: I mean, suddenly there are all these women.

CHARLOTTE: Well if you're homosexual, I guess you don't find me attractive then, do you?

BOB: What?

CHARLOTTE: I guess you don't find me attractive, do you?

BOB: I don't see what that has to do with anything.

CHARLOTTE: Very well. We'll drop the subject. *(Pause.)* Not even a teensy weensy bit? Well, no matter. *(Pause.)* Tell me. What do you and Bruce do exactly?

BOB: What do you mean?

CHARLOTTE: You know what I mean. Physically.

BOB: I don't care to discuss it.

CHARLOTTE: Tell me.

BOB: Why do you want to know?

CHARLOTTE: Patients act out many of their deepest conflicts through the sexual act. Women who get on top may wish to feel dominant. Men who prefer oral sex with women may wish to return to the womb. Couples who prefer the missionary position may wish to do anthropological work in Ghana Everything people do is a clue to a trained psychotherapist. *(Pause.)* Tell me! Tell me!

BOB: I don't care to talk about it.

CHARLOTTE: Very well. We'll move on to something else. *(Sulks.)* I'm sure I can guess what goes on anyway. *(Sulks.)* I wasn't born yesterday. *(Pause; then:)* Cocksucker.

BOB: What?

CHARLOTTE: Oh, I'm sorry. It was just this terrible urge I had. I'm terribly sorry. *(Gleefully.)* COCKSUCKER! *(Screams with laughter, rocks back and forth.)* Oh my goodness, I'm sorry, I'm sorry. COCKSUCKER! Whoops! Sorry. Oh God, it's my blood sugar. Help, I need a cookie. Help, a cookie! COCKSUCKER! Wait, don't leave, I think I have a cookie in one of the drawers. Oh, I'm going to say it again, oh God! *(Screams the word as she stuffs cookie into her mouth, the word is muffled. Her body shakes with laughter and pleasure.)* Mmmm, cookie, cookie. Oh God. Oh God. *(Lies on floor, laughs slightly.)* Oh, that was wonderful.

BOB: *(Stands, takes out a gun.)* It's people like you who've oppressed gay people for centuries. *(Shoots her several times.)*

CHARLOTTE: *(Startled; then:)* Good for you! Bravo! I like that. You're expressing your feelings, people have got to express their feelings. Am I bleeding? I can't find any blood.

BOB: It's a starting pistol. I bought it a couple of days ago, to threaten Bruce with.

CHARLOTTE: Good for you!

BOB: I don't want to go to prison. That's the only reason it's not a real gun.

CHARLOTTE: Good reason. You know what you want and what you don't want. Oh, I like this directness, I feel I'm starting to help you. I mean, don't you see the similarity? Now why don't I have ulcers? Do you know?

(Bob sits on floor next to her.)

BOB: I don't know what you're talking about.

CHARLOTTE: I don't have ulcers because I don't repress things. I admit to all my feelings. Now a few minutes ago when I wanted to hurl anti-homosexual epithets at you, I didn't repress myself, I just let 'em rip. And that's why I'm happy. And when you were mad at me, you took out your toy gun and you shot me. And *that's* the beginning of mental health. I mean, do you understand what I'm saying?

BOB: Well, I follow you.

CHARLOTTE: Oh, we're making progress. Don't you see? And you said it yourself. You didn't buy the gun to shoot me, you bought it to shoot Bruce and that floozie of his. Right?

BOB: Yes.

CHARLOTTE: So you see what I'm getting at?

BOB: You mean, I should follow through on my impulse and go shoot Bruce and Prudence.

CHARLOTTE: *(Stands, staggers to her desk, overwhelmed with how well the session is going.)* Oh I've never had such a productive first session!

BOB: *(Stands.)* But should I get a real gun, or just use this one?

CHARLOTTE: That would be up to you. You have to ask yourself what you *really* want.

BOB: Well, I don't want to go to jail, I just want to punish them.

CHARLOTTE: Good! Punish them! Act it out!

BOB: I mean, I could go to that restaurant right now.

CHARLOTTE: Oh yes! Oh good!

BOB: Will you come with me? I mean, in case someone tries to stop me you can explain it's part of my therapy.

CHARLOTTE: *(Agreeably.)* Okay. Let me just get another cookie. Oh, I'm so glad you came to me. Now, should I bring Snoopy with me, or leave him here?

BOB: Well, which do you really *want*?

CHARLOTTE: Oh you're right. That's the issue, good for you. Okay, now...I don't know which I want. Let me sit here for a moment and figure it out. *(She sits and thinks, weighing pro-and-con-Snoopy ideas in her head.)* *(Lights dim.)*

ACT II
Scene 2
The restaurant again. Bruce, Prudence.

PRUDENCE: Why have we come back to this restaurant? We've been here twice before and never got any service.

BRUCE: You're upset about Bob, aren't you?

PRUDENCE: No. I understand. It's all difficult.

BRUCE: Bob will get used to the idea of us, I just tried to make it happen too soon. He's innately very flexible.

PRUDENCE: Then maybe the two of you should stay together.

BRUCE: Will you marry me?

PRUDENCE: Bruce, this is inappropriate.

BRUCE: Prudence, I believe one should just *act*—without thought, without reason, act on instinct. Look at the natives in Samoa, look at Margaret Mead. Did they think about what they were doing?

PRUDENCE: Important life decisions can't be made that way.

BRUCE: But they can, they must. Think of people who become heroes during emergencies and terrible disasters—they don't stop to fret and pick things apart, they just *move,* on sheer adrenaline. Why don't we think of our lives as some sort of uncontrollable disaster, like *The Towering Inferno* or *Tora! Tora! Tora!,* and then why don't we just act on instinct and adrenaline? I mean, put that way, doesn't that make you just want to go out and get married?

PRUDENCE: But shouldn't I marry someone *specific?*

BRUCE: I'm specific.

PRUDENCE: Well, of course. But, what about the gas man? I mean, do I want the children saying I saw Daddy kissing the gas man?

BRUCE: We'd get electric heat.

PRUDENCE: Oh, Bruce!

BRUCE: Besides, I don't want lots and lots of people—I want you, and children, and occasionally Bob. Is that so bad?

PRUDENCE: Well it's not the traditional set-up.

BRUCE: Aren't you afraid of being lonely?

PRUDENCE: Well, I guess I am.

BRUCE: And aren't all your girlfriends from college married by now?

PRUDENCE: Well, many of them.

BRUCE: And you know you should really have children *now,* particularly if you may want more than one. I mean, soon you'll be at the end of your child-bearing years. I don't mean to be mean bringing that up, but it is a reality.

PRUDENCE: Can we talk about something else?

BRUCE: I mean, time is running out for you. And me too. We're not twenty anymore. We're not even twenty-six anymore. Do you remember how old thirty used to seem?

PRUDENCE: Please don't go on, you're making me hysterical.

BRUCE: No, but these are realities, Prudence. I may be your last chance, maybe no one else will want to marry you until you're forty. And it's hard to meet people. You already said that Shaun Cassidy was too young. I mean, we have so little time left to ourselves, we've got to grab it before it's gone.

(Stuart enters, sees them, hides behind a table or large plant.)

PRUDENCE: Oh, stop talking about time please. I mean, I know I'm thirty, it doesn't mean I'm dead.

BRUCE: I didn't say dead. I just said that our time on this earth is limited.

PRUDENCE: Stop talking, stop talking. *(Covers her ears.)*

BRUCE: Prudence, I think you and I can make each other happy. *(Sees Stuart.)* Do you see someone over there? Is that a waiter *hiding?*

PRUDENCE: *(Looks.)* Oh, for God's sake.

BRUCE: What is it?

PRUDENCE: It's my therapist.

BRUCE: Here?

PRUDENCE: I thought we were being followed. *(Calling.)* Dr. Framingham, we see you.

BRUCE: What's he doing here?

(Stuart comes over to them.)

STUART: I want you to leave here with me this instant.

PRUDENCE: Why are you following me?

STUART: I'm going to give you a prescription for a sedative, and then I'm going to drive you home.

PRUDENCE: I can't believe that you've been following me.

STUART: I care about my patients. *(To Bruce.)* She's really *very* sick. The work we have to do together will take years.

PRUDENCE: Dr. Framingham, I've been meaning to call you since our last session. I'm discontinuing my therapy with you.

STUART: That would be very self-destructive. You'd be in Bellevue in a week.

PRUDENCE: I really don't want to see you ever again. Please go away now.

STUART: You don't mean what you say.

BRUCE: Do you want me to hit him?

PRUDENCE: No, I just want him to go away.

BRUCE: *(Stands.)* The lady wants you to leave, mister.

STUART: *(To Prudence.)* So this is the degenerate you told me about?

BRUCE: What did she tell you about me?

PRUDENCE: Bruce, don't talk to him, please. Stuart, leave the restaurant. I'm tired of this.

STUART: Not until we set up our next appointment.

PRUDENCE: But, Stuart, I *told* you I'm discontinuing our therapy.

STUART: You haven't explained why to me.

PRUDENCE: Then I will. BECAUSE YOU ARE A PREMATURE EJACULATOR AND A LOUSY THERAPIST. NOW BEAT IT!

STUART: *(Very hurt, very mad.)* Okay, Miss Sensuous Woman. But do you know what's going to happen to you without therapy? You're going to become a very pathetic, very lonely old maid. You know what's going to happen to you? You're going to break off with this clown in a few days, and then you're not going to go out with men anymore at all. Your emotional life is going to be tied up with your cats. *(To Bruce.)* Do you know what she does in her apartment? She keeps cats! Some guy she almost married last year wanted to marry her but he was allergic to cats and so *she* chose the cats!

PRUDENCE: That's not why we broke up at all!

STUART: You're gonna end up taking little boat cruises to Bermuda with your *cats* and with spinster librarians when you're fifty unless you decide to kill yourself before then! And all because you were too cowardly and self-destructive and stupid to keep yourself from being an old maid by sticking with your therapy!

PRUDENCE: You are talking utter gibberish. Michael was only *slightly* allergic to cats and we didn't get married because we decided we weren't really in love. And I'm not going to end up an old maid, I'm going to get married. In fact, I may even marry Bruce here. And if I do, Bruce and I will send you a picture of our children every Christmas to the mental institution where you'll be locked up!

STUART: *(Hysterical.)* You're a terrible, terrible patient!

PRUDENCE: And you're a hideous doctor! I hate you!

(They throw water at each other. Enter Bob and Mrs. Wallace.)

CHARLOTTE: Hello, everybody!

STUART: Who are these people?

CHARLOTTE: Go ahead, Bob, tell them.

BOB: I want to tell you how you've made me feel. I feel *very* angry.

(He takes out his gun; Prudence, Bruce, and Stuart look terrified. He fires the gun at them six or seven times. They are terribly shocked, stunned; are trying to figure out if they've been hit and are dying. Enter a young Waiter.)

WAITER: I'm sorry. We're going to have to ask you people to leave.

BRUCE: But we haven't even seen menus.

WAITER: I'm sorry. We can't have shootings in here.

STUART: Oh my God. Oh my God. *(Feels himself all over for wounds, just coming out of his fear.)*

PRUDENCE: *(Taking the gun from Bob.)* Give me that. *(Points the gun at the Waiter; Waiter puts hands up.)* Now look here, you. I am sick of the service in this restaurant. *I am very hungry.* Now I want you to bring me a steak, medium rare, no potato, two vegetables, a small salad with oil and vinegar, and a glass of red wine. *(Angry, grouchy, waves gun toward the others.)* Anyone else want to order?

CHARLOTTE: *(Raises hand.)* I'd like to see a menu.

PRUDENCE: *(Waving the gun.)* And bring these other people menus. And make it snappy.

WAITER: Yes, ma'am. *(Exits in a hurry.)*

CHARLOTTE: *(To Prudence.)* Oh I *like* your directness. Bravo!

STUART: *(Feeling for bullet holes.)* I don't understand. Did he miss all of us?

PRUDENCE: Shut up and sit down. I'm going to eat some dinner, and I want everyone to shut up.

CHARLOTTE: Oh, I think she's marvelous.

PRUDENCE: *(Aims the gun at her.)* Shut up.

CHARLOTTE: Sorry.

(Everyone sits quietly. Waiter brings menus which people look at except for Prudence, who glares, and Stuart, who's shaken.)

WAITER: Our specials today are chicken marsala cooked in a garlic and white wine sauce; roast Long Island duck with orange sauce...

(Lights dim to black.)

ACT II
Scene 3

The restaurant still. They've finished their dinners: Prudence, Bruce, Bob, Mrs. Wallace, Stuart. The Waiter is clearing the dishes.

CHARLOTTE: Mmmmm, that chocolate mousse was delicious. I really shouldn't have had two.

WAITER: *(To Prudence.)* Will there be anything else?

PRUDENCE: Just the check please.

(Waiter exits.)

STUART: *(Who's still in a sort of shock; to Bob.)* I thought you'd killed us all. You should be locked up.

BOB: Well, all's well that ends well.

CHARLOTTE: Please, I thought we'd exhausted the whole topic of the shooting. No harm was done.

STUART: What if I'd had a heart condition?

CHARLOTTE: That would have been your responsibility. We must all take responsibility for our own lives.

STUART: I think you're a terrible therapist.

CHARLOTTE: Sounds like professional jealousy to me.

PRUDENCE: *(To Stuart.)* I would not bring up the subject of who's a terrible therapist, if I were you.

CHARLOTTE: *(To Bruce.)* Oh, she's *so* direct, I just find her wonderful. Congratulations, Bruce.

PRUDENCE: What are you congratulating him on?

CHARLOTTE: Aren't you getting married?

(Simultaneously.)

BRUCE: Yes.

PRUDENCE: No.

(Re-enter Waiter.)

WAITER: Here's the check. *(Mrs. Wallace calls for the check.)* The second chocolate mousse was on the house, Mrs. Wallace.

CHARLOTTE: Thank you, honey. *(Kisses him on the cheek.)*

(Waiter exits.)

CHARLOTTE: He's one of my patients too.

BOB: He's quite attractive.

BRUCE: I thought you were going to kill yourself.

BOB: Mrs. Wallace helped me express my anger and now I don't feel like it anymore.

STUART: If one runs around shooting off guns, blank or otherwise, just because one is angry, then we'll have anarchy.

BOB: No one is interested in your opinion.

BRUCE: I think Prudence and I are a good match. I think we should get married as soon as possible.

PRUDENCE: I never want to get married, ever. I'm going to quit my job, and stay in my apartment until they evict me. Then I'm going to become a bag lady and live in the tunnels under Grand Central Station.

(They all stare at her.)

BRUCE: *(To Prudence.)* If you marry me, I'll help you want to live again.

BOB: What am I supposed to do?

BRUCE: You seemed too busy with the waiter a minute ago.

BOB: For God's sake, I just looked at him. You're trying to go off and marry this woman. Really, you're just impossible. I thought after I shot at you, you'd get over this silly thing about women.

BRUCE: I need the stability of a woman.

BOB: You think she's stable? She just said she was going to become a bag woman.

BRUCE: She was speaking metaphorically.

BOB: What kind of metaphor is becoming a bag woman?

BRUCE: She meant she was depressed.

BOB: So I'm depressed too. Why don't you marry me? We'll go find some crackpot Episcopal minister somewhere, and then we'll adopt children together.

BRUCE: And that's another thing. I want to have my own children. I want to reproduce. She can give me children.

PRUDENCE: Please stop talking about me that way. I don't want to have your children. I want to be left alone. I want to become a lesbian and move in with Kate Millett.

BOB: Now she's making sense.

BRUCE: Don't make fun of her. She's upset.

BOB: I'm upset. No one worries about me.

BRUCE: Prudence, don't cry. We'll live in Connecticut. Everything will be fine.

STUART: Why doesn't she marry me? I make a good living. Prudence, as your therapist, I think you should marry me.

BRUCE: Prudence would never marry a man who didn't cry.

STUART: What?

BRUCE: You're too macho. Prudence doesn't want to marry you.

STUART: There's no such thing as macho. There's male and female, and then there's whatever you are.

(Bruce cries.)

STUART: Oh, I'm sorry. Was it what I said?

CHARLOTTE: Bruce cries all the time. I encourage him to.

BRUCE: *(Having stopped crying; to Prudence.)* Why won't you marry me?

STUART: She should marry me.

PRUDENCE: No. I don't want to marry either of you. You're both crazy. I'm going to marry someone sane.

BOB: There's just me left.

PRUDENCE: No. I'll marry the waiter. Waiter!

CHARLOTTE: Oh dear, poor thing. Fear of intimacy leading to faulty reality testing. Prudence, dear, you don't know the waiter.

PRUDENCE: That doesn't matter. Bruce said it's better to know nothing about people when you get married.

BRUCE: But I meant you should marry me.

PRUDENCE: But I know too much about you and I know nothing about the waiter. Waiter!

(Enter Waiter.)

WAITER: Is something the matter?

PRUDENCE: Yes. I want you to marry me.

WAITER: I don't understand. Did I add the check wrong?

PRUDENCE: No. I want you to marry me. I only have a few more years in which it's safe to have children.

WAITER: I don't understand.

CHARLOTTE: It's alright, Andrew. She's in therapy with me now.

PRUDENCE: *(Takes out the blank gun. Aims it at him.)* Marry me! Marry me! *(Starts to giggle.)* Marry me!

CHARLOTTE: It's alright, Prudence; you're my patient now. Everything's going to be alright.

PRUDENCE: I don't want any more therapy! I want tennis lessons!

CHARLOTTE: Now, dear, you're not ready for tennis yet. You must let me help you.

STUART: She's my patient.

CHARLOTTE: I think you've already failed her. I think I shall have to take her on.

PRUDENCE: *(Screams.)* I don't want either of you! I've been to see several therapists and I'm sick of talking about myself!

(Charlotte throws a glass of water at Prudence.)

CHARLOTTE: Enough of this self-destructive behavior, young woman!

(Prudence, furious, picks up another glass of water to throw back at Charlotte, hesitates momentarily, and throws it in Stuart's face.)

CHARLOTTE: Bravo, good for you!

STUART: Why did she do that?

CHARLOTTE: She's getting in touch with her instincts. Prudence, you're making progress in my care already.

PRUDENCE: I HATE THIS RESTAURANT!

CHARLOTTE: The restaurant isn't the problem. You're looking for perfection. Prudence, you know the song "Someday My Prince Will Come"? Well, it's shit. There is no prince. Everyone in this world is limited; and depending on one's perspective is either horrible or "okay." Don't you agree, Dr. Framingham?

STUART: *(Just noticing.)* I'm all wet.

CHARLOTTE: Ah, the beginnings of self-awareness, bravo, ruff ruff ruff! Oh that's right, I left Snoopy home. Well that was a wrong decision. Prudence, I'm making a point here. We're all alone, everyone's crazy and you have no choice but to be alone or to be with someone in what will be a highly imperfect and probably eventually unsatisfactory relationship.

PRUDENCE: I don't believe that's true.

CHARLOTTE: But you do. That's exactly why you act the way you do, because you believe that.

PRUDENCE: I believe there's more chance for happiness than that.

CHARLOTTE: You don't! And why should you? Look at Chekhov. Masha loves Konstantin, but Konstantin only loves Nina. Nina doesn't love Konstantin, but falls in love with Trigorin. Trigorin doesn't love Nina but sort of loves Madame Arkadina, who doesn't love anyone but herself. And Medviedenko loves Masha, but she only loves Konstantin, which is where we started out. And then at the end of the play, Konstantin kills himself. Don't you see?

PRUDENCE: What's your point?

CHARLOTTE: I've forgotten. Oh damn. Oh yes! My point is that everyone thinks Chekhov's plays are tragedies, but he called them comedies! It's all how you look at it. If you take psychological suffering in the right frame of mind, you can find the humor in it. And so that's how you should approach your relationship with Bruce.

BRUCE: This is getting too complicated.

PRUDENCE: My stomach feels queasy.

BRUCE: Never mind that. Prudence, remember what I said about acting on instinct, like you do in a crisis?

CHARLOTTE: *(Happily.)* Like when I threw the water!

BRUCE: Right.

PRUDENCE: Yes I remember.

BRUCE: Okay. I want you to answer quickly now, on instinct, don't think about it, alright?

PRUDENCE: Alright.

BRUCE: Does your stomach feel queasy?

PRUDENCE: Yes.

BRUCE: Is your name Prudence?

PRUDENCE: Yes.

BRUCE: Is your dress wet?

PRUDENCE: Yes.

BRUCE: Will you marry me?

PRUDENCE: Yes.

(There is a pause.)

CHARLOTTE: Well, I'm glad that's settled.

STUART: You're not going to say yes like that, are you?

PRUDENCE: I guess so. All the other answers were yes. I have to go to the ladies room to throw up. Excuse me. *(Exits.)*

BRUCE: I'm so happy. Not that she's sick, but that we're getting married.

BOB: *(Discontent.)* Well, everyone's happy then.

STUART: All my patients leave their therapy. It's very upsetting.

CHARLOTTE: Would you like to talk about it?

BOB: *(To Andrew the waiter.)* Hi. I don't think we've actually met yet. My name is Bob.

ANDREW: Hi, I'm Andrew.

BOB: You look awfully familiar.

ANDREW: You've probably just seen my type.

BOB: Ah, well…

ANDREW: I get off in five minutes.

BOB: Need any help?

(Everyone looks a bit aghast. Especially Bruce.)

ANDREW: Could be. *(Exits.)*

BRUCE: What are you doing?

BOB: Well if you expect me to live over the garage and let you carry on with that woman whenever you feel like it, then I'm allowed an occasional waiter.

STUART: Good God, he's not really going to live over the garage, is he?

CHARLOTTE: Well it depends on the zoning laws, I guess. *(Holds both sides of her head.)* Uh, I'm getting a rush from all that mousse. Anyone feel like going to a disco?

BOB: I'm game. Bruce?

BRUCE: Not particularly. *(Nasty.)* Maybe the waiter will want to go.

CHARLOTTE: Oh, Andrew is an excellent dancer! He's been to reform school.

BOB: Oh, he's sulking now.

BRUCE: I feel jealous about you and the waiter.

BOB: That's not very fair. What about you and Prudence?

BRUCE: You're right. But I still feel the emotion. And that's alright, isn't it, Mrs. Wallace?

CHARLOTTE: It's alright with me.

BRUCE: I feel happy about Prudence, and unhappy about the waiter. And I think I may want to cry. *(Tries.)* No. False alarm.

(Enter Andrew in leather jacket.)

STUART: He certainly cries a lot.

CHARLOTTE: Don't you ever cry, Dr. Framingham?

STUART: Only when things fall on me.

CHARLOTTE: Oh yes! Do you all remember Skylab—that space thing that fell from the sky? That upset my porpoises very much.

STUART: You have porpoises?

CHARLOTTE: I'm sorry. Did I say porpoises? Andrew, what word do I want?

ANDREW: Patients.

CHARLOTTE: Yes, thank you. Patients.

ANDREW: We had this guy in reform school that we didn't like much. So we took this big heavy metal bird bath, and we dropped it on him. *He* didn't cry.

CHARLOTTE: That's interesting, Andrew.

ANDREW: He went into a coma.

CHARLOTTE: *(Stern.)* Andrew, I've told you, I want you to have empathy for other people.

ANDREW: Oh right. I forgot. We felt real bad for him.

CHARLOTTE: Andrew has a real sensitivity in him; we just haven't seen any of it yet.

BOB: How long were you in reform school?

ANDREW: About three years. *(Grins.)* Til it burned down.

BOB: Ah. *(Starting to think Andrew may be a bad idea.)* Great.

BRUCE: I hope Prudence isn't ill.

CHARLOTTE: Oh who cares? Let's go dancing!

BOB: Bruce, would you prefer I didn't go?

BRUCE: No, it's okay. I guess you're allowed waiters. We'll talk later. Have a nice time.

BOB: Thanks.

BRUCE: I think I better go check on Prudence. Good night, everybody. *(Gives Bob and Charlotte hugs, exits.)*

CHARLOTTE: He's so nice. Well, the music is calling all of us, I think.

ANDREW: *(To Bob.)* My motorcycle's out this way.

BOB: My mother doesn't like me to ride motorcycles.

ANDREW: *(Shrugged off.)* Fuck her.

STUART: *(To Charlotte.)* I don't think I want to go. I don't like discos.

CHARLOTTE: Nonsense. You must learn to like them.

STUART: There'll be too many women. I shouldn't tell you this, but I have troubles relating to women.

CHARLOTTE: Not to me. I think you're delightful.

STUART: You do?

CHARLOTTE: You know what I think? I think I could help you. I think you should come into therapy with me. I don't mean therapy, I mean thermidor.

ANDREW: No you mean therapy.

CHARLOTTE: Do I? It doesn't sound right. Thermidor. Thorazene. Thermometer.

BOB: No, he's right, you mean therapy.

CHARLOTTE: Therapy. Therapy? Thackery. Thespian. The second Mrs. Tanqueray. Ftatateeta. Finickulee, finickula. Well let's just go. It'll come to me. *(She starts to go; then:)* Ovaltine. Orca, the killer whale. Abba dabba dabba dabba dabba dabba dabba…Oh, now I've really lost it.

(Charlotte, Stuart, and Andrew exit. Enter Bruce and Prudence.)

PRUDENCE: Please, don't ever come into the ladies room after me again, alright? It's very disconcerting.

BRUCE: I was worried.

PRUDENCE: Where is everybody?

BRUCE: They went to a disco.

PRUDENCE: Why?

BRUCE: Something about the mousse Mrs. Wallace ate.

PRUDENCE: Never mind. I don't want to know.

BRUCE: Okay, now, answer on instinct again. Where in Connecticut do you think we should live? Quick, instinct!

PRUDENCE: Bridgeport.

BRUCE: Oh, God, have you ever been to Bridgeport?

PRUDENCE: No, I meant Westport.

BRUCE: No, you said Bridgeport. There may be some psychic reason it's right we live in Bridgeport.

PRUDENCE: No, please, we can't keep making decisions like this.

BRUCE: There are probably some lovely parts of Bridgeport.

PRUDENCE: Please, I don't want to live in Bridgeport. Bruce, why do you want to marry me. Answer on instinct.

BRUCE: I wrote it down earlier. *(He takes out typed piece of paper; reads:)* "I want to marry Prudence because all my life I keep fluctuating between being traditional and being insane. For instance, marrying Sally was my trying to be traditional; while sleeping with the gas man or that time I took my clothes off in the dentist's office were my going to the opposite extreme. But I'm not *happy* at either extreme. And that's where Prudence fits in. I feel she's very traditional, like Sally, but Sally has no imagination, she's too stable. And I think that even though Prudence is very traditional, she's very *uns*ta-ble and because of that I think we could be very happy together." Do you understand what I'm saying?

PRUDENCE: I don't understand what happened at the dentist's office.

BRUCE: Well, I needed root canal…

PRUDENCE: *(Getting upset.)* And that wasn't on instinct. You'd written that down.

BRUCE: Well, I know. But it was an instinct to *read* it.

PRUDENCE: How can I marry someone who takes his clothes off at the dentist's office?

BRUCE: I don't take them off as a general rule. It just happened once.

PRUDENCE: *(Very upset.)* I must be out of my mind.

BRUCE: Oh God, you're changing your mind, aren't you? Oh my God, oh my God. *(Sits down, weeps.)*

(Prudence sits down, calm at first, then she too starts to cry. Then she starts to sob. Bruce stops crying, looks up.)

BRUCE: Prudence, you're crying. Don't cry. *(Holds her.)* What's the matter?

PRUDENCE: *(Through weeping.)* I don't know. I'm upset you took your clothes off at the dentist's office because that means you must be insane, and I thought maybe you weren't insane but just sort of, lively. *(Cries some more.)*

BRUCE: I'm lively.

PRUDENCE: No, you're too lively. I wouldn't be able to cope.

BRUCE: *(Desperate to please her, keep her, comfort her.)* Mrs. Wallace could give me lithium, she could give you speed. We might meet in the middle.

PRUDENCE: I don't want speed. I want an Alka-Seltzer. Do you think the waiter could get me one?

BRUCE: The waiter went to the disco with Bob.

PRUDENCE: Well there must be another waiter, don't you think?

BRUCE: Well, it is a restaurant. *(Calls.)* Oh waiter! Waiter! I don't see anybody.

PRUDENCE: I don't either. *(Calls.)* Waiter!

BRUCE: I'm really honored you cried in front of me. Thank you.

PRUDENCE: You're welcome. Waiter!

BRUCE: I bet you don't cry very frequently.

PRUDENCE: No. Not in front of anyone at least.

BRUCE: I'm really honored.

PRUDENCE: I'll try to cry for you again sometime. Waiter!

BRUCE: Thank you. Waiter.

PRUDENCE: Waiter. Waiter.

BRUCE: Waiter. Waiter. This is a very existential restaurant.

PRUDENCE: *(A little woozy, a little sad, a little cheerful.)* Yes, that's why I like it here so much.

BRUCE: You like it here?

PRUDENCE: Yes. Sort of. It's very comforting. They leave you alone here. It's conducive to conversation.

BRUCE: *(Very friendly, a basis for hope again.)* Yes, it's a great place to talk.

PRUDENCE: *(Smiles, then futilely calls again.)* Waiter. Waiter.

BRUCE: *(Makes a joke, sings:)* There's a waiter that I'm longing to see, duh duh duh duh…

BRUCE & PRUDENCE: *(Sing together, dreamily, a little rueful.)* Duh duh duh duh, Dum dum dum dum, over me.

BRUCE: *(Smiles at her.)* Silly song.

PRUDENCE: *(Smiles at him.)* Very silly.

(Curtain)

END OF PLAY

Baby with
the Bathwater

INTRODUCTION

I wrote the first act of *Baby with the Bathwater* as a self-contained one act sometime in late 1981. Then in late 1982 Robert Brustein told me he wanted to do the one-act *Baby* at his American Repertory Theatre in Cambridge, Massachusetts, on a double bill with a Beckett one act. I had been toying with the notion of expanding *Baby*, wondering what would happen if I followed subsequent years in Baby's life; so I asked Brustein if he'd be interested in doing a full-length *Baby with the Bathwater*, were I to come up with one. He said yes.

He then went on to schedule the full-length version before I had written it, which flattered me. However, when I heard the due dates, I became momentarily alarmed—I had to write Act II in six weeks or something in order to be ready for the scheduled first rehearsal. That wasn't much time, and what if I got stuck in the writing?

But then I shifted back to being flattered at his faith in me and what I'd come up with, and I also knew that in many instances I could (and did) write very, very fast. So I decided just to accept the shortness of time, and write.

I had a really good time writing Act II, and think it's clearly better than Act I (which makes the play, I'm afraid, a bit lopsided in performance).

The A.R.T. production was directed by Mark-Linn Baker, and featured a terrific cast, including Cherry Jones as the mother (who later went on to win the Tony for Lincoln Center Theatre's revival of *The Heiress*) and Tony Shalhoub as the father (an inventive actor who found TV fame on *Wings*). This was a very good production, but I worked more closely with the second one, the New York premiere at Playwrights Horizons, directed by Jerry Zaks.

I have a few more things I'd like to say about the play, but some of them make more sense when you've read it. So I'm going to stop here and show up again in an afterword.

ORIGINAL PRODUCTION

Baby With The Bathwater had its world premiere at the American Repertory Theatre in Cambridge, Massachusetts on March 31, 1983, Robert Brustein, artistic director, Rob Orchard, managing director. The production was directed by Mark Linn-Baker; sets designed by Don Soule; costumes designed by Liz Perlman; lighting designed by Thom Palm; sound designed by Randolph Head. Production stage manager was John Grant-Phillips. The cast was as follows:

HELEN . . . . Cherry Jones
JOHN . . . . Tony Shalhoub
NANNY/WOMAN IN THE PARK/PRINCIPAL . . . . Marianne Owen

Baby With The Bathwater was presented off-Broadway on November 9, 1983, by Playwrights Horizons in New York City, Andre Bishop, artistic director, Paul Daniels, managing director. The production was directed by Jerry Zaks; sets designed by Loren Sherman; costumes designed by Rita Ryack; lighting designed by Jennifer Tipton; sound designed by Jonathan Vall. Production stage manager was Esther Cohen; stage manager was Diane Ward. The cast was as follows:

In the subsequent run of the play, the role of Nanny/Woman in the Park/ Principal was taken over by Kate McGregor-Stewart, then by Mary Louise Wilson, then by Cynthia Darlow. The understudies were Melodie Somers and William Kux. During the play's final week Ms. Somers played the part of Helen.

CHARACTERS

HELEN, the mother

JOHN, the father

NANNY, the nanny

CYNTHIA

A WOMAN IN THE PARK

ANOTHER WOMAN IN THE PARK

MRS. WILLOUGHBY, the principal

MISS PRINGLE, a teacher

YOUNG MAN

SUSAN

The parts of Nanny, Woman in the Park, and Mrs. Willoughby may be played by the same actress. The parts of Cynthia, Another Woman in the Park, Miss Pringle, and Susan may be played by the same actress.

Baby with the Bathwater

ACT I

Scene 1

The home of John and Helen, a couple in their late 20s or early 30s. They are standing over a bassinet.

HELEN: Hello, baby. Hello.

JOHN: It looks just like me.

HELEN: Yes it does. Smaller.

JOHN: Well, yes.

HELEN: And it looks just like me. It has my hair.

JOHN: Yes it does.

HELEN: *(Slightly worried.)* I wonder if it would have been better off having your hair?

JOHN: *(Reassuringly.)* Your hair is lovely.

HELEN: *(Touched.)* Thank you.

JOHN: You're welcome.

(They smile at one another warmly.)

JOHN: *(Back to the bassinet.)* Hello, baby. Hello. Cooooo.

HELEN: Cooooooo. Cummmmm-quat. Cummmmm-quat!

JOHN: Hee haw. Hee haw. Daddy's little baked potato.

HELEN: Don't call the child a baked potato.

JOHN: It's a term of affection.

HELEN: It isn't. It's a *food*. No one wants to be called a baked potato.

JOHN: Well, it doesn't speak English.

HELEN: The various books say that you should presume your child can understand you. We don't want it to have problems in kindergarten or marriage because you called it a baked potato.

JOHN: It seems to me you're losing your sense of humor.

HELEN: *(Firmly.)* I just don't want to make the child insane—that's all. Bringing up a child is a delicate thing.

JOHN: Alright, you're not a baked potato, sweet pea.

(She looks at him in horror; he senses her look.)

JOHN: And you're not a sweet pea either. You're a baby. Bay-bee. Bay-bee.

HELEN: I want a divorce.

JOHN: What?

HELEN: You heard me. I want a divorce.

JOHN: Are you crazy? You've read the statistics on children from broken homes. Do you want to do that to our child?

HELEN: I don't feel ready for marriage, I didn't when we got married, I should have said no.

JOHN: But we love each other.

HELEN: You have blond hair. I don't like men with blond hair. I like men with dark hair, but I'm afraid of them. I'm not afraid of you. I hate you.

JOHN: What? Is this postpartum depression?

HELEN: Don't talk about postpartum depression, you know nothing about it. *(To baby.)* Men just don't understand things, do they, sweetie pie?

JOHN: If I can't call it a potato, you can't call it a pie.

HELEN: I didn't call it a pie.

JOHN: You did. You said sweetie pie.

HELEN: Sweetie pie is an expression, it isn't a pie. You don't go into a restaurant and order sweetie pie.

JOHN: Why do you insist on winning every argument?

HELEN: If I'm right, I'm right. It has nothing to do with winning. *(To baby.)* Men don't know how to argue. That's why they always end up hitting people.

JOHN: I don't hit people.

HELEN: Boys and men hit one another constantly. They attack one another on the street, they play football, they wrestle on television, they rape one another in prison, they rape women and children in back alleys. *(To baby.)* Beware of men, darling. Be glad you're not ever going to be a man.

JOHN: That's an awful thing to say. And is it a girl? I thought it was a boy.

HELEN: We don't know what sex it is. It's too young. The doctor said we could decide later.

JOHN: You don't decide later. Gender is a fact, it's not a decision.

HELEN: That's not what the doctor said to me. He said something about the DNA molecule. They're splitting it differently now. He said if the DNA combined one way, the child would have testosterone and then we could either have it circumcised or not, depending. Or else the DNA combines with estrogen, in which case it would be a girl. Or in some cases, the DNA combines with cobalt molecules, and then the child would be radioactive for 5000 years and we'd have to send it out into orbit.

JOHN: What are you talking about?

HELEN: Can't you speak English? I'm married to an idiot. *(To baby.)* Your father is an idiot. Oh God, please let me meet a dark-haired man who's smarter than I am. *(To John.)* Oh why don't you go away? I don't like you.

JOHN: I don't understand. We were very happy yesterday.

HELEN: What are you talking about? Happy? Who was happy?

JOHN: We were. We were making plans. The child's schooling, what playground to take it to, whether to let it play with toy guns, how to toilet train it.

HELEN: Oh God, toilet training. I can't face it. We'll have to hire someone.

JOHN: We don't have money to hire anyone.

HELEN: Well, we'll have to earn the money.

JOHN: But we can't earn money. I was let go from work.

HELEN: Well, you can find another job.

JOHN: I need rest, I really don't feel able to work right now.

HELEN: John, that's not practical.

JOHN: I want to go back to bed.

HELEN: But, John, you wanted to be responsible, don't you remember? Right after that week you stayed behind the refrigerator, you came to me and said, "The immaturities of my youth are over now, Helen. Let's make a baby." And then we did. Don't you remember?

JOHN: I need professional help. I want to go to McLains in Massachusetts. That's the institution James Taylor was in for a time. He seems so tranquil and calm when he gives his concerts. And he has a summer house on Martha's Vineyard. Maybe, when the doctor says I'm well enough, I could go to Mar…

HELEN: JOHN, LIVE UP TO YOUR RESPONSIBILITIES! *(Baby cries.)* Oh, God, it's crying. What should we do?

JOHN: Sing to it.

HELEN: *(Sings to baby sweetly, softly.)* There's no business like show business, like no business…

JOHN: A lullaby, sweetheart.

HELEN: I don't know any lullabies.

JOHN: *(Sings.)*
Hush little baby, don't you cry,
Mama's gonna give you a big black eye…

HELEN: Good heavens, those aren't the lyrics.

JOHN: I know they're not. I can't remember the right ones.

HELEN: Oh God. You're going to teach baby all the wrong lyrics to everything. It's going to have trouble with its peer group.

JOHN: Maybe we should hold it to stop it crying.

HELEN: We might drop it. I had a cocktail for breakfast. I'm not steady.

JOHN: Why did you have a cocktail?

HELEN: You're always picking on me! I'm sorry I married you. I'm sorry I gave birth to baby. I wish I were back at the Spence School.

JOHN: We love the baby.

HELEN: How can we love the baby? It won't stop that noise. *(To baby.)* Shut up, baby. Shut up. Oh God, please help us. Please make the baby stop.

(Enter Nanny, dressed in tweeds, wearing a ladylike hat and carrying a large cloth handbag.)

NANNY: Hello. I'm Nanny.

HELEN: Oh thank goodness you've come. Please make it stop crying.

NANNY: *(Goes over to crib; in a high, soothing if odd voice.)* Helloooooooo, baby. Hellllloooooo. Yeeeeeeeeees. Yeeeeeees. It's Nanny. Yesssssssssssss. *(Baby stops making noise.)* That's right. That's right. I've brought you a present.

(Takes out a jar; opens it—it's a trick jar—and a large snake pops out. Baby screams in terror. John and Helen are fairly startled also. Nanny laughs.)

NANNY: Ha haha haha! That surprised you, didn't it?

JOHN: See here, who are you?

HELEN: Oh my God, it's crying again. *Please* make it stop crying.

NANNY: What? I can't hear you. Child's making so much racket.

HELEN: Please. Make it stop that awful noise.

NANNY: *(High voice again.)* Quiet, little baby. Be quiet. *(No effect; then she yells stridently.)* SHUT UP!

(Baby is abruptly quiet; Nanny is pleased.)

JOHN: *(Looking at the baby.)* I think you've given it a heart attack.

NANNY: No, no, it's just resting.

HELEN: Oh thank goodness it stopped.

JOHN: Who are you?

NANNY: I am the ghost of Christmas Past. Hahahahaha. No just making a joke. I get a list of all the new parents from the hospital, and then I just *descend* upon them. Now, I need Wednesday evenings off, and I'm allergic to asparagus and lobster...

HELEN: We never have lobster.

NANNY: And I like chunky peanut butter better than the smooth kind, but if you already have the smooth kind, we'll finish that off before you buy a new jar.

JOHN: I can't afford you.

NANNY: And I don't do windows, and I don't do floors, and I don't do laundry, but I make salmon salad and tuna salad and salad niçoise and chef salad and chunky peanut butter sandwiches, and I make my own yogurt in a great big vat.

JOHN: You can't stay here.

HELEN: But I need help. I can't cope by myself. Please, John.

JOHN: But I'm on unemployment.

NANNY: Well, we'll just get you another job.

JOHN: But what can I do?

NANNY: Why don't you become an astronaut? That pays very well. Or a football player. Or a newscaster. *(To baby.)* Wouldn't you like to see your Daddy on television, baby? Baby? *(Looks into the silent bassinet.)* I think the snake scared it. *(To baby.)* WAKE UP! *(Baby cries.)* There, that's better. *(Smiles, pleased.)*

HELEN: Please don't shout at it. It's not good for it.

JOHN: Maybe I should hold it to comfort it.

HELEN: That would be very responsible, John. That's a good boy. Good boy.

JOHN: Thank you. *(Holds baby, which stops crying.)*

HELEN: John's been fired from his job, you see.

NANNY: Well, that won't put food on the table.

HELEN: I could get a job, I suppose. But what would I do?

NANNY: Well, why don't you write a novel? *The World According to Garp* sold very well recently. Why don't you write something like that?

HELEN: Oh, that's a good idea. But I need a pencil and paper.

NANNY: Oh. Well, here's a dollar. Now you go to the store and buy some paper and a nice felt tip pen.

HELEN: Now?

NANNY: No time like the present. Right, baby?

HELEN: Oh, John, please put the baby down. I'm afraid one of us might drop it. *(To Nanny.)* I had a cocktail for breakfast, and John took some Nyquil and quaaludes.

JOHN: I get tense.

NANNY: Put the baby down, John. You're spoiling it. *(Takes it from him, puts it in bassinet.)* Now, what should we call it, do you think?

HELEN: Well, John's father's name was John, and his mother's name was Joan, and my father's name was John, and my mother's name was Hillary, and my doctor's name is Dr. Arthur Hammerstein, but I really want a woman doctor who can understand me, but it's so hard to find a doctor.

NANNY: Yes, but what about a name, a name?

HELEN: Don't you get cross with me.

NANNY: All right, we won't call the baby anything.

JOHN: We could call it John after me if it's a boy, and Helen after you if it's a girl.

HELEN: No, I don't want to call it anything now. I'm going back to bed.

NANNY: I thought you were going to buy paper and pencil to start your novel.

HELEN: I don't want to. I want to sleep.

NANNY: I gave you a dollar.

HELEN: I don't care.

NANNY: Here's another dollar. Go buy yourself an ice cream soda on the way home.

HELEN: Oh, thank you nanny. I love you. *(Hugs her, runs off.)*

NANNY: We're all going to have to be very kind to her. *(To baby.)* Don't depend on mommy, baby. She's not all there. *(To John.)* So—what can I do for you?

JOHN: I really haven't hired you yet, you know.

NANNY: You want a quick one?

JOHN: Pardon?

NANNY: Us older girls have a few tricks up our sleeves, you know. I bet I know some things your wife doesn't know.

JOHN: I don't know. I had a quaalude this morning, I don't really feel up to anything.

NANNY: It's very rude to turn me down. You might hurt my feelings.

JOHN: Well, what about the baby?

NANNY: The baby doesn't have to know anything about it. Now we haven't much time, she's getting the paper and pen and the ice cream soda.

JOHN: Well, all right, but let's not do it here. I feel uncomfortable in front of the baby.

NANNY: We could distract it. We could play loud music.

JOHN: But we might hurt its eardrums. I want to be a good father.

NANNY: Well, of course you do. I have tiny little earplugs we could put in its ears.

JOHN: Well, then, what's the point of the loud music?

NANNY: *(Thinks, but can't unravel the mystery.)* I don't know.

JOHN: This is all getting too complicated.

NANNY: *(Cheerfully.)* Very well! Let's just do it in the kitchen. Come on. *(She energetically drags John off into the kitchen.)*

(After a moment, the baby starts to cry. A young woman, rather sweet-looking but dressed shabbily, enters the apartment. Her name is Cynthia. She appears to have wandered into the apartment for no apparent reason. She is very pregnant. She walks over to the bassinet and sings sweetly to the baby to comfort it. After a few lines of the song, the baby does stop crying. Cynthia keeps singing to it for a while, her voice is pleasant and soothing.)

CYNTHIA: *(Sings.)*

    Hush, little baby,

    Don't say a word,

    Momma's gonna buy you a mockingbird,

    And if that mockingbird don't sing,

    Momma's gonna buy you a golden ring,

    And if that golden ring turns brass,

    Momma's gonna buy you a looking glass,

    And if that looking glass gets broke,

    Momma's gonna buy you a billy goat.

    (Hums. Cynthia smiles that the baby has been comforted and, still humming, wanders back out of the apartment.)

    (Lights dim.)

ACT I

Scene 2

    Later that night. Dark. Baby cries. Voices of "Oh God." The lights come up. The couch has been opened up to make a bed. In the bed are Helen, Nanny, and John in nightgowns and pajamas. Nanny is sound asleep.

HELEN: Baby, we're sleeping. Now go back to sleep. John, you talk to it.

JOHN: Enough of this noise, little child. Daddy and Mommy are sleeping.

HELEN: Oh God, it won't stop. Nanny, wake up. Nanny!

JOHN: Nanny! *(They poke her.)*

NANNY: *(Coming out of a dream.)* Where am I? Help! Water to the right of me, water to the left of me. Ode to a Grecian urn. *(Lies back down.)*

HELEN: Nanny, baby's calling you.

NANNY: I'm sleepy.

HELEN: Nanny, you're the nanny.

NANNY: *(Pointing to John.)* What about Tiger here?

JOHN: Don't call me Tiger.

NANNY: Tiger. Ruff. Ruff. *(Gets up.)* All right, baby. Nanny's coming. *(Picks up baby.)* Helloooooooo, baby. Hellllloooooo, baby. That's right. Wheeeeee-eeeeeeee. Wooooooooooooooo. Waaaaaaaaaaa. *(Keeps making these odd, if soothing, sounds softly through next dialogue. Baby does stop crying.)*

HELEN: Why did she call you Tiger?

JOHN: I don't know. She was probably dreaming.

HELEN: Oh, baby's stopped. Thank goodness for Nanny. And her Salad Niçoise was so good for dinner.

JOHN: Yes it was. Helen, I don't think this is going to work out.

HELEN: What isn't?

JOHN: Nanny.

HELEN: I think it's working out fine.

JOHN: I can't sleep three in a bed.

HELEN: John, when we're rich we'll buy a big house with an extra room for Nanny. Until then, this is fine.

JOHN: Helen, I don't think Nanny is a good person.

NANNY: I heard that.

JOHN: Nanny, please, we're trying to have a private conversation.

NANNY: Don't you talk behind my back. I'll hire a lawyer. We'll slap an injunction against you.

JOHN: Please, you deal with baby, and let Helen and me figure this out.

NANNY: I've finished comforting baby. *(Brusquely.)* Go to sleep, baby. *(Tosses it back into the bassinet.)* Now you say to my face that I'm not a good person.

JOHN: Well maybe that's too strong. But I think you're too rough with baby. I mean, you just threw it into the bassinet.

NANNY: Do you hear it crying?

JOHN: No, but maybe it's fainted or something.

NANNY: It's just resting.

JOHN: You keep saying that, but I think you have it fainting. And it has this look of panic on its face.

NANNY: Look, don't tell me how to handle children. I got it down.

HELEN: Nanny knows best, John. And she's helping me with my novel. She liked the first chapter, John.

NANNY: I did. I thought it showed real promise.

HELEN: And then when I sell my novel, if we get a good deal for the paperback rights, then we can buy a house in the country and maybe we can have another baby.

JOHN: Helen, Nanny seduced me this afternoon when you were out buying paper.

NANNY: That's a lie.

JOHN: It's the truth. I was unfaithful to you, Helen.

(Helen looks hurt in earnest.)

JOHN: I'm sorry.

HELEN: I don't know how to cope with this.

JOHN: So you can see why I don't feel comfortable all three of us in the bed.

HELEN: *(Near tears.)* I don't know how to cope.

JOHN: I'm really sorry. It was Nanny's fault.

NANNY: He raped me!

JOHN: I didn't. That's a lie, Helen.

HELEN: I don't want to talk about this anymore! I'm going to work on my novel in the kitchen, and I'm going to pretend that I live alone. *(Exits.)*

JOHN: Well, things are in a fine mess.

NANNY: You told her, I didn't.

JOHN: What we did was wrong.

NANNY: Oh for God's sake, it didn't mean anything. It would've been fine if you hadn't told her.

JOHN: I felt guilty. It's wrong to cheat on your wife.

NANNY: You're such a dullard. There is no right or wrong, there's only *fun!*

JOHN: That can't be true. I mean, there are certain things that are intrinsically wrong, and when we figure out what these things are, then we are said to have values.

NANNY: Haven't you read *The Brothers Karamazov?* Ivan Karamazov realizes that because there is no God, everything is permitted.

JOHN: I don't understand.

NANNY: Everything is permitted. *(Hits the back of his head hard.)*

JOHN: Why did you do that?

NANNY: I *felt* like it. Everything is permitted. *(Laughs.)*
    (Re-enter Helen, in raincoat and rainhat, holding a sheaf of papers.)

HELEN: I'm taking my coat and the first chapter of my novel and the baby, and I'm leaving you.

JOHN: Helen, I'm sorry, it won't happen again.

HELEN: You obviously prefer Nanny to me, and so as far as I'm concerned, you can just go to hell.

NANNY: *(Genuinely meaning it.)* Oh, I love arguments.

JOHN: Helen, we have to stay together for the baby.

HELEN: No, I'm taking the baby and the novel, and you won't get any of the paperback rights at all. Good-bye.

JOHN: The baby's asleep.

HELEN: Or fainted, as you said, Nanny bats it around so. *(Picks up baby.)* Mommy's going to save you now, sweetie pie.

JOHN: I have rights to the baby too.

HELEN: Baby will thank me later.

JOHN: But where will you go at this hour?

HELEN: *(At a loss.)* We'll go to…Marriott's Essex House.

JOHN: Our credit cards have been canceled.

HELEN: All right. We'll sleep in the park, I don't care, I just have to leave here! Don't touch me!

JOHN: But it's freezing out. Baby will catch pneumonia.

HELEN: Well, I can't help it. You don't *die* from pneumonia.

JOHN: But you do, you do die from pneumonia!

HELEN: Don't tell me what to do. I KNOW WHAT I'M DOING! *(Exits with baby.)*

JOHN: Helen!

NANNY: Let her go, she'll be back in a few minutes. I know these hysterical mothers.

JOHN: They're going to get very ill, it's very cold outside.

NANNY: It's bad to fuss too much as a parent, your child will grow up afraid. Let baby discover some things for itself. You want a quick one?

JOHN: What?

NANNY: You heard me.

JOHN: But it's wrong. Sexual infidelity is *wrong.*

NANNY: Wrong, right, I don't know where you pick up these phrases. Didn't they teach you about Darwin in public school? The fish came out of the water, covered with a viscous substance, and then bones and vertebrae were evolved, and then male and female, and then the egg and the ovum and the testicles and the semen, and then reproduction, and then dinosaurs, or maybe dinosaurs before that, and then local governments, and then the space program, and then nuclear power plants and now cable television and Home Box Office. *Where* do you find right and wrong in all that??? Tell me.

(Re-enter Helen, wet, with baby, wet.)

HELEN: I fell in a puddle. I'm all wet.

NANNY: Well, if it isn't Nora five minutes after the end of *A Doll's House.*

HELEN: I thought you were going to help me, and now all you do is pick on me.

JOHN: Good God, the baby's soaking wet.

HELEN: Of course, it's wet. I told you, I fell in a puddle.

NANNY: Helen is the worst mother, isn't she, baby?

HELEN: Don't you say that. John, hit her for me.

JOHN: *(Very forceful suddenly.)* Now enough of all this arguing! We're going to get baby in some dry clothes, and Helen in some dry clothes, and then we're going to take Nyquil and quaaludes and get some sleep! And we will discuss all these problems in the morning. Is that clear?

HELEN: Yes, John.

NANNY: Yes, John.

JOHN: Very well. Now no more talking. *(John puts baby in bassinet and changes its clothes.)*

(Helen starts to take off her things, sneezing occasionally. Nanny exits, re-enters.)

NANNY: I've got the Nyquil.

JOHN: Thank God.

NANNY: You have its feet in the armholes.

JOHN: The point is that it's dry, right?

NANNY: The point is to do things right.

HELEN: You said no more talking. I want to go to sleep.

JOHN: All right. But in the morning, we're going to kill Nanny.

(Nanny looks at John with suspicion.)

HELEN: Let's just have our Nyquil and not argue anymore.

JOHN: Should we give baby Nyquil?

HELEN: Oh I don't know. What does it say on the label?

JOHN: I don't know. I can't read the small print. I need glasses.

HELEN: Well if you can't read, then there's no solution, is there?

NANNY: Why don't we just ask baby? Do you want some Nyquil, honey? Do you? Huh? *(Pause.)* It won't say. It's just staring back, hostilely.

HELEN: Oh why can't it be a happy baby? *(Notices.)* John, you've dressed it all wrong. It can barely move that way.

JOHN: I'm going to sleep now. I don't want to hear any more complaints!

(John, Helen, and Nanny get into bed.)

NANNY: Good night everybody.

HELEN: Good night, Nanny. *(Kisses her.)* I love you. *(To John.)* I hate you.

JOHN: Good night, Helen.

(They lie down to sleep. After a moment Cynthia enters. She goes to the bassinet.)

CYNTHIA: Hello, baby. Hellooooooo.

(The three in bed sit up and stare at her.)

HELEN: Who are you?

CYNTHIA: I'm just so upset. I'm very poor, and I gave birth in the hospital to a darling little boy, or girl, and when I came home from the hospital, there's no heat in my apartment and there's no furniture, there's just my German shepherd. And, of course, I hadn't fed it in about a week, since I went into the hospital, so I went out to buy some baby food and some dog food. But there's no furniture, so I left the baby on the floor, and when I came back, the dog had eaten the baby. And now I don't know what to do.

NANNY: Have you told this story to the *New York Post?*

CYNTHIA: No.

NANNY: Well, I'd start out by doing that.

CYNTHIA: But I'm so tired now.

JOHN: What is the matter with you? Why did you leave your baby on the floor?

CYNTHIA: Please don't yell at me. I don't have any furniture!

NANNY: There, there, you poor thing. We'll get you another baby. You'll adopt.

CYNTHIA: But I'm not a fit mother.

NANNY: Everyone's allowed one mistake.

HELEN: *(Suspiciously.)* Where's the dog?

CYNTHIA: I have it right outside in the hallway. Would you like to keep it? *(She goes to the door.)*

(John springs up and blocks the door.)

JOHN: Don't you bring that dog in here!

NANNY: Now there's no reason to hold this woman's stupidity against her dog. That's unfair. *(To Cynthia.)* Of course, we want the dog. It sounds like a good watchdog.

CYNTHIA: Well actually it's always been vicious, but you see normally I feed it. It's just that when I was in the hospital, they wouldn't let me leave.

NANNY: Administrative red tape. It's really behind so much evil and suffering in the world.

HELEN: I don't know. I think she's a terrible woman.

CYNTHIA: Oh, please, I feel so guilty. Don't hate me. I really just don't know any better. I didn't listen to anything they taught me in school. Something about equal sides of an isosceles triangle. And I don't have any furniture at home. And you have lovely furniture. Do you mind if I lie down and sleep for a moment. I'm really exhausted. *(She lies down on the sofa bed and falls asleep immediately.)*

NANNY: Poor child.

HELEN: Why is she here? We don't want her here.

NANNY: Where is your charity? The poor child is going to have to live with her stupidity all the rest of her life. Maybe she'll even have to go to prison when the police hear of it all. Surely you wouldn't begrudge her one night's sleep of safety and peace?

HELEN: Well, maybe not. But can we make her go in the morning?

NANNY: We'll see. Come, John, come to bed. Tomorrow's going to be a busy day.

(Nanny, Helen, and John lie down next to the sleeping Cynthia. Lights dim.)

ACT I

Scene 3

Sound of dog barking viciously; baby crying. Lights up on the four of them in the sofa bed.

HELEN: Someone make that noise stop.

JOHN: Be quiet, baby.

HELEN: Is baby barking?

JOHN: Oh God, that dog. *(To Cynthia.)* Hey, you, wake up. Shut up your dog somehow.

CYNTHIA: I was having such a pleasant dream.

JOHN: Make your dog be quiet.

CYNTHIA: What dog?

JOHN: Your dog is barking.

CYNTHIA: *(Pleasantly.)* Oh yes, I hear it now. It must smell baby.

HELEN: Oh, dear God.

CYNTHIA: Don't be alarmed. It's just hungry. Do you have any red meat?

JOHN: Maybe there's some red meat in the refrigerator.

CYNTHIA: Well, go give it some, and then it'll stop barking. *(Smiles.)* Don't let it get your hand though.
    (John exits to kitchen.)

HELEN: Where did you get the dog?

CYNTHIA: Oh, some terrible people were beating it in the park, and I felt sorry for it, so I asked them if I could have it.

HELEN: And so they gave it to you?

CYNTHIA: Yes. They beat me up for quite a while. Twenty minutes, it seemed, maybe it was shorter, it's hard to judge time that way. And then the dog and I crawled to my apartment, and we've just been together ever since.
    (John returns from the kitchen with package of chopped meat, goes into the hall to the barking dog. Barking gets worse, then ferocious eating noises occur; John comes back.)

JOHN: It took the meat.

CYNTHIA: It really *loves* meat. I'm a vegetarian myself. I tried to make the dog eat bean sprouts and broccoli once for a while, but it didn't work.

JOHN: Someone should really change baby. I think it's made a mess.

HELEN: Oh, I don't want to. Let Nanny do it.

NANNY: *(Not moving.)* I'm sleeping.

CYNTHIA: Oh, I'll do it. I love babies. *(Goes to baby.)* I had the most wonderful dream last night. I dreamt that I kidnapped your baby, and that the dog, baby and myself took a bus to Florida and had a wonderful time on the beach. *(On the word "kidnapped," the three in bed sit up and look at her with varying degrees of concern.)* I'm afraid we all got seriously sunburned in the dream, but I don't know if we died from it or not because then I woke up with the dog barking. Oh, your baby's so grumpy looking. What's the matter, baby? Don't you like me?

HELEN: It's a very grouchy baby. We're not very happy with it.

CYNTHIA: I know. I have a little toy it will like. The nurses gave it to me at the hospital. *(Holds up little red toy that jingles when she shakes it.)* Hey? It's a little red thingamajig. Isn't it cute? I don't think baby likes me. Why don't you like me, baby?

NANNY: *(With great disinterest.)* Why don't you read to it then? Baby loves to be read to. *(Exits to get into her Nanny clothes.)*

CYNTHIA: Oh all right. *(Meanders about, looking for a book.)*

HELEN: John, you better get up and go look for work.

JOHN: I just want to sleep. Leave me alone. *(Hides under pillow.)*

HELEN: John, you have responsibilities. Look at me.

CYNTHIA: Here's a book. Now if I read to you, will you promise to smile at me, baby?

JOHN: Let's get a divorce. You wanted one yesterday. Let's get one now.

HELEN: It's not practical now. Baby needs a father, and I need financial support until I finish my novel.

CYNTHIA: Chapter Seven. Shortly after Mommie Dearest won her Oscar for *Mildred Pierce,* she would burst into Christopher and my room at three in the morning screaming, "Fire drill! Fire drill!"

(John and Helen look at Cynthia for a moment, then return to their argument.)

JOHN: Helen, this novel idea is a pipe dream. Don't you know that?

HELEN: It is not. Nanny said my first chapter was brilliant.

NANNY: *(Offstage.)* Well, not brilliant perhaps. But quite commercial, I'd say.

CYNTHIA: Then she'd pour gasoline on the curtains and set them on fire, while we'd scream and scream. *(Makes playful scream noises.)* Aaaaggh! Aaaaggh!

JOHN: But you can't write, don't you know that?

HELEN: What do you know? I can too!

(Nanny re-enters with Helen's still soggy sheaf of papers.)

NANNY: Read him your first chapter then, that'll show him.

CYNTHIA: I would try to untie Christopher from his bed, but Mommie wouldn't let me.

HELEN: *(Proudly.)* Chapter One. I am born. I was born in a workhouse in London in 1853.

(Cynthia returns to reading to the baby as Helen continues to read from her novel. Nanny and John do their best to give Helen their attention, but find their focus hopelessly caught between the two novel readings. Eventually John and Nanny begin to look discouraged and disoriented by how difficult it is to follow either story.)

HELEN: My mother, whoever she may have been, had left me at the doorstep of a wealthy man named Mr. Squire of Squireford Manor. However, wicked traveling gypsies came by the Squire's doorstep and snatched me up and left me at the workhouse. My first conscious memory is of little Nell, the cobbler's daughter, being run over by a coach and four.

CYNTHIA: As the burning curtains came closer and closer to Christopher's bed, he cried aloud, "God in heaven, save me from Mommie!" Then Mommie took out a fire extinguisher and sprayed the curtains as well as Christopher and myself. And then with tears streaming down her cheeks, Mommie screamed, "Clean up your rooms! Bad Christina! Bad Christopher! Look at this dirt!"

HELEN: *(Unable to stand it anymore.)* WILL YOU BE QUIET???? I am *trying* to read from my novel.

CYNTHIA: I am reading to baby.

HELEN: I don't care what you're doing. You're a guest in this house.

CYNTHIA: Baby will grow up with no love of literature if you don't read to it.

HELEN: It's my baby, and I'll raise it as I see fit.

CYNTHIA: No, it's my baby! *(Snatches it up.)* I can see that my dream was a sign I should have it!

HELEN: Give it back to me at once!

CYNTHIA: No, I won't! You're not fit parents. I know I'm guilty of negligence with my baby, but it was an honest mistake. And I love babies. But you three are heartless. You don't hold the baby when it cries, you dress it wrong so it can't move in its pajamas, and you're both so inconsistent as people changing from one mood to another that you'll obviously make it crazy. That's why it never smiles. I may be forgetful, but baby has a chance with me!

HELEN: Give it back to me! *(Runs toward her.)*

CYNTHIA: Don't come near me, or I'll throw it out the window!

JOHN: Good Lord, she's insane.

(Everyone stands very still. Cynthia starts to move slowly to the door.)

CYNTHIA: Now I'm going to leave here with baby and with the dog, and we're going to go to Florida, and you're not to follow us.

NANNY: Now let the dream be a warning. Don't stay in the sun too long. Babies have light skin.

CYNTHIA: I know what I'm doing. Come on, baby, you'll be safe with me. *(Runs out door, dog barks.)* Come on, doggie, it's just me and baby.

(Sound of dog barking, baby crying.)

HELEN: John, what should we do?

NANNY: You could have another baby.

HELEN: John, we have to go after her.

JOHN: I need amphetamines.

HELEN: John, we haven't time.

JOHN: I told you we shouldn't have let her stay here.

HELEN: You said no such thing. And that's not the point now anyway. We've got to run after her.

JOHN: We're not dressed.

HELEN: Oh, you're impossible. *(She runs out.)*

JOHN: You're right. I'm coming. *(He runs out too.)*

NANNY: *(To audience, friendly.)* Well, time to move on here, I think. I've done all I can do here. So I'll just pack. *(Notices something.)* Oh, she forgot her little red toy. Oh, too bad. *(Picks toy up, reads something on it.)* "Caution. Keep away from children. Contains lead, asbestos, and red dye #2." *(Laughs.)* Well, I guess it isn't meant as a child's toy at all then. *(Looks at it with utter bafflement.)* But what would it be meant as, I wonder? *(Energized by an idea:)* Maybe it *is* a toy, and the cautionary warning is *satiric!* *(Tosses the toy into bassinet.)* Hard to tell. So many mysteries. But children can survive it all, they are sturdy creatures. They ebb and flow, children do; they have great resiliency. *(Warmly.)* They abide and they endure.

(Re-enter John and Helen, holding baby. They are giddy with relief.)

JOHN: We got it.

NANNY: Oh, did you?

HELEN: Yes, the stupid girl ran right in front of a bus, it ran right over her.

JOHN: Squashed her.

HELEN: Baby was just lucky and fell between the wheels.

NANNY: Oh, that was lucky. Children are sturdy creatures, they ebb and flow.

HELEN: The dog was still living, so John pushed it in front of an oncoming car, and now it's dead too.

JOHN: The motorist was *real* angry. But it seemed too complicated to explain, so we just grabbed baby and ran.

HELEN: Thank goodness. *(Looks at baby.)* Baby looks so startled. It's been a busy day, hasn't it? Yessss.

JOHN: Nanny, Helen and I were talking while we ran back here, and things are going to be different now. The immaturities of my youth are over and I'm going to take the responsibility of being a father, and Helen is going to be a mother. And we're not letting anymore crackpots into our home.

HELEN: That's right, John.

JOHN: And so, Nanny, I'm going to have to ask you to leave now. Helen and I have both decided that you're insane.

NANNY: *(Crosses to them.)* When it cries, you hold it. You should feed it regularly. You should keep it clean. Be consistent with it. Don't coo one minute and shout the next.

HELEN: I'm giving up my career as a novelist to care for baby. And any resentment I feel I won't ever show.

NANNY: Well, that all sounds excellent. Good-bye, Helen. Good-bye, Tiger.

HELEN: Good-bye, Nanny. We love you.

JOHN: Good-bye.

(Nanny smiles fondly and waves. Then exits.)

HELEN: *(After a moment.)* Oh, John. I feel so lonely now.

JOHN: We have each other. And baby.

HELEN: That's true. I wish I didn't have a baby and that I had written *Scruples* instead.

JOHN: Well, I wish I were in McLains, but I thought we were going to be positive about things from now on.

HELEN: You're right. I was just kidding. Let's be parents now. Hellooo, baby.

(They put baby back into bassinet.)

JOHN: *(To baby.)* Helllooo. Baby looks so startled.

HELEN: Well, of course, it's been a terrifying day. Baby had never even seen a bus before, let alone been under one. *(Lovingly, to the baby.)* Don't worry, sweetie pie. Mommy'll protect you from now on. She'll protect you from buses, and from dogs, and from crazy people; and from everything and anything that goes bump in the night.

JOHN: *(Playfully.)* Bump, bump, bump.

HELEN: *(Fondly.)* That's right, John.

JOHN: And Daddy loves you too, my little baked potato.

HELEN: *(Suddenly absolutely furious.)* I TOLD YOU NOT TO CALL IT A BAKED POTATO!!!

JOHN: I'm sorry, I'm sorry. Jesus. You mustn't raise your voice that way around baby. You'll make it deaf or something.

HELEN: I'm sorry. I feel better now.

JOHN: Okay, we'll forget it. *(To baby.)* All over, baby. You're safe now, my little bak-...baby. No more shouting. Everything's fine. Can you smile for daddy?

HELEN: Or mommy?

JOHN: Can you smile for mommy and daddy? Here's a nice little red toy. *(Holds up the red toy.)* Won't that make you smile? Huh? Oh why won't it smile? SMILE, damn it, SMILE!

HELEN: Smile, baby!

BOTH: *(Angry.)* SMILE! SMILE! SMILE! SMILE!

HELEN: *(Pleased.)* Oh, John, look, it's smiling.

JOHN: That's right, baby.

HELEN: Do you think it's just pretending to smile to humor us?

JOHN: I think it's too young to be that complicated.

HELEN: Yes, but why would it smile at us when we shouted at it?

JOHN: I don't know. Maybe it's insane.

HELEN: I wonder which it is. Insane, or humoring us?

JOHN: Look, it's still smiling. Maybe it likes the toy. Do you like the toy, baby? Here, you play with it a while, baby. It makes a funny noise, doesn't it? Tingle tangle. Tingle tangle.

(The baby throws the toy out of the bassinet.)

JOHN: Oh, it doesn't like the toy.

HELEN: What a fussy baby. *(Playfully.)* Fussy baby. Fussy baby.

JOHN: *(Happy.)* Oh, it's still smiling.

HELEN: Fussy baby.

JOHN: Fussy wussy wussy.

BOTH: *(Fondly.)* Fussy wussy wussy baby. Fussy wussy wussy baby.

(Lights dim.)

END ACT I

ACT II

Scene 1

A park bench. Three women in park playground. The sounds of children play-ing. On the bench are: Helen, the mother from the previous scenes; she is look-ing straight ahead, smoking a cigarette, and seems unhappy, hostile. Next to her, and presently not paying attention to her, are Angela, a sweet, drably dressed woman (can be played by same actress who played Cynthia in first part, though try to make her plain) and Kate, a bright, sharp-tongued woman with a scarf tied around her head (she can be played by same actress who played Nanny, but try to make her look noticeably different). Angela and Kate are looking straight out, watching their children, who are placed (in their and our imaginations) out in the audience. Kate is knitting.

KATE: Be careful, Billy!

ANGELA: That's your son?

KATE: Yes. Billy. He has my eyes and mouth, and his father's nose.

ANGELA: *(Looking, squinting.)* Yes, I can see that. Of course, I've never seen your husband's nose, but he does have your mouth and eyes.

KATE: Don't hang upside down, Billy! You'll crack your head open. *(To Angela.)* He's reckless, just like his uncle Fred.

ANGELA: Oh. Is that his favorite uncle?

KATE: No. He's never met Fred. Fred is dead. Is that your little girl?

ANGELA: Yes. Susie. Watch your head, Susie! It's such a full-time job looking after children.

KATE: Yes it is. Susie's a pretty child. *(Stares at Angela; suspiciously.)* Is her father very handsome?

ANGELA: Yes. His whole family is very nice looking.

KATE: Oh that's nice. Nobody in our family is particularly good looking. Except for Fred, sort of, though you'd never know it from the way he ended up, all squashed that way.

ANGELA: How did he die?

KATE: Part of the roller skating craze. He didn't know how, and he skated right under a crosstown bus. *(Calls out.)* Be careful, Billy! *(Back to conversation.)* I don't think there's such a thing as a homely child, do you? I mean Billy may well grow up to be *quite* homely, but right now he's really very cute. And your daughter is downright pretty.

ANGELA: Thank you. *(Calls.)* Be careful of your face, Susie. Don't fall down on it.

HELEN: I have a child too, you know.

KATE: What?

HELEN: No one has asked me about my child.

KATE: Well, no one was talking to you.

HELEN: Well, I'm a human being. I deserve courtesy.

KATE: Where is your child?

HELEN: That's her lying on the ground. *(Calls.)* Get up, Daisy! Stop acting like a lump.

KATE: What's the matter with her?

HELEN: She's very depressed. She falls asleep all the time. You put her in the bathtub, she falls asleep. You put her on the toilet, she falls asleep. She's a depressing child. Get up, Daisy! Maybe one of the boys would poke her for me.

ANGELA: Maybe she has narcolepsy.

HELEN: You get that from a venereal disease, don't you? You're trying to say something nasty about me, aren't you?

ANGELA: Narcolepsy is a disease. Where people fall asleep. You should take your daughter to a doctor.

HELEN: All diseases are psychological. I'm not going to waste money on some dumb doctor who can't do anything about anything. She sleeps because she doesn't want to be awake. She has no "joie de vivre." GET UP, DAISY! Hey, you, boy, the one with the stick…can you get my daughter up?

KATE: *(Staring; after a bit.)* Billy, don't put the stick there, that's nasty.

ANGELA: Why isn't she moving?

HELEN: She's willful. GET UP, YOU LUMP OF CLAY! *(To boy.)* Tug her hair a little.

KATE: Billy, leave the little girl alone and go play on the jungle gym. *(To Helen.)* I don't want you encouraging my son to pick on women. That's not a very good thing to teach.

ANGELA: She still hasn't moved. Maybe she's fainted.

HELEN: She just does this to annoy me. It's very successful. *(Calls.)* YOU'RE VERY SUCCESSFUL, DAISY. YOU'RE GETTING THROUGH. *(Back to them.)* It's passive aggression. I do it with my husband. He says to me, did you make dinner, I lie down on the rug and don't move. He says, get up, I don't move a muscle. He gets on top of me and starts to screw me, I pretend it isn't happening. She gets it from me. *(Yells.)* DO AS I SAY NOT AS I DO, DAISY, I'VE TOLD YOU THAT!

KATE: That's no way to bring up a child.

HELEN: What do you know? Do you want a fat lip? Don't cross me, I could do something terrible to your child.

KATE: What did you say?

HELEN: *(Suddenly coy and girlish.)* Oh nothing. My bark's worse than my bite. *(Calls viciously.)* Get up, Daisy! *(Sings, to Daisy, rather sweetly.)*

Daisy, Daisy,

Give me your answer, do,

I'm half crazy,

All for the love of you...

(Hostile, to Kate and Angela.) Sing. *(They hesitate.)* SING!

ALL THREE: *(Kate and Angela, uncomfortable.)*

It won't be a stylish marriage,

I can't afford a carriage,

But you'll look sweet...

HELEN: *(Echoing.)* Sweet.

ALL THREE: Upon the seat...

HELEN: *(Echoing.)* Seat.

ALL THREE: Of a bicycle built for two.

HELEN: Did she move?

ANGELA: I think her arm twitched a little.

HELEN: Oh, I bet she heard it. She loves that song, don't you Daisy? Well, I have to go home now. *(Sweetly.)* Good-bye. *(Calls out to Daisy.)* Get up, Daisy, we're going home, mother can't stand the park another minute. Get up! *(Getting wild.)* Get up, damn you, get up! All right, Daisy, I'll give you til five and then I'm gonna step on your back. You listening? One... two... three...

ANGELA: Get up, Daisy.

HELEN: ...four...four and a half...four and three-quarters...Oh, look, there she goes.

(They turn their heads in unison quickly, watching Daisy run out of sight.)

KATE: My God, she's running *fast*.

HELEN: She's like that. Very inconsistent. One minute catatonic, the next minute she *moves* like a comet.

ANGELA: My God, she's running right toward that bus!

HELEN: Yes, she's always been drawn to buses. She's always running right out in front of them. Usually the driver stops in time.

KATE: My God, it's going to hit her!

HELEN: Well, it'll probably be fine.

(Kate and Angela watch horrified, then there's a shriek of brakes, and they relax, horrified but relieved.)

KATE: Thank God.

ANGELA: It came so close.

HELEN: This happens all the time. I get quite used to it. (*Suddenly switches to real maternal feelings, gets very upset.*) Oh my God, Daisy. Oh my God, she was almost killed. Oh God. Oh God. (*Weeps.*) Daisy, I'm coming, darling, don't move, honey, mommy's coming. (*Runs off, very upset.*)

KATE: Good grief.

ANGELA: Well, at least the child's safe.

KATE: Do you think we should do something?

ANGELA: What do you mean?

KATE: I don't know. Contact social welfare or something.

ANGELA: I don't know. Maybe it's not her child. Maybe she's only baby-sitting.

KATE: I don't think so.

ANGELA: I don't think we should get involved.

KATE: Alright, we won't do anything about her. We'll wait until we read about the child *dead* in the newspaper.

ANGELA: I read about that child they found dismembered in the garbage cans outside the 21 Club. CBS is going to make a TV movie about it.

KATE: I don't think television should exploit the sufferings of real people like that.

ANGELA: But they've got all those hours of programming to do. They've got to fill it up with something.

KATE: I suppose.

ANGELA: I wouldn't like to be a television executive. You'd have to have ideas all the time, and then after a while if people don't like your ideas, they fire you.

KATE: This is really off the point of what we should do about that poor child.

ANGELA: I don't like to think about it.

KATE: Well, that won't help the child.

ANGELA: I don't like to concentrate on one thing for too long a period of time. It makes my brain hurt.

KATE: I don't think either the mother or the child are mentally well.

ANGELA: No, they're probably not, but who is nowadays? Everything's so outside our control. Chemical explosions in Elizabeth, New Jersey. Somebody killed Karen Silkwood. There are all these maniacs stalking Dolly Parton, the poor woman doesn't feel like *singing* anymore. John Hinkley, David Berkowitz, Ronald Reagan. It's so difficult to maintain "joie de vivre" in the face of such universal discouragement. (*Looks glum for a moment.*) I have to take a mood elevator. (*Takes a pill.*) I have this pharmacist friend, he gives me all sorts of things. I should be cheerful in a few minutes. *(Waits for pill to take effect.)*

KATE: *(Edging away.)* Well, fine. We'll do nothing then. I'll look forward to the CBS movie about the child under the bus. *(Calls.)* Come on, Billy, we're going home. *Billy!* Don't put the stick there, that's rude. Leave Susie alone. *(Shocked.)* Billy! Don't put *that* there either, that's *very* rude. Now put that back. *(To Angela.)* I'm sorry. He's just that age now.

ANGELA: Oh that's all right. He probably meant it affectionately. I always think sex and affection are somehow connected, don't you?

KATE: Well, no, not really.

ANGELA: Oh, I do. People need affection, you know. Susie, come give mommy a hug.

(Lights dim.)

ACT II

Scene 2

Back in the home of Helen and John. The room, though, is filled with many toys, some of them broken. There is also a pile of what seems to be laundry in clear audience view. Two little legs with red sneakers are partially visible, sticking out of the laundry pile. John and Helen are talking.

JOHN: Well, I'm very upset. That's all I can say.

HELEN: I know. You've said that, you've said that. Get on with it.

JOHN: I mean, I just don't think we're good parents.

HELEN: Why do you say that? Did the bus run over the child? No. Did a bus run over her last week? No.

JOHN: Why does she keep running to buses? What's the matter with her?

HELEN: Nothing is the matter with her. She's just depressed. We have to cheer her up. *(Crosses to pile of laundry, speaks to it.)* Cheer up, Daisy! You're depressing us.

JOHN: And why does she lie in this pile of laundry all the time? Do you think that's normal?

HELEN: Daisy is just going through a phase. She thinks she's an inanimate object. She thinks she's a baked potato because of what you said to her when she was a baby. *(To pile of laundry.)* You're not a baked potato, sweet pea. You're mommy's little darling. Mommy loves you. Mommy doesn't mind that she's not a novelist or that she's stayed in a bad marriage just for your sake. She's willing to make that sacrifice. *(Stares at laundry.)* Uh, you see how unresponsive she is. It's enough to make you want to shake and bake her.

JOHN: Helen, we can't talk about the child that way. Did you hear what you just said?

HELEN: I was making a point, John. I'm not talking about actually cooking her. You have no sense of irony. *(To Daisy.)* We're not going to eat you, Daisy. Mommy was speaking figuratively.

JOHN: Speaking of shake and bake, have you made dinner yet?

HELEN: Have I made *dinner* yet? *(Very nasty, utterly furious.)* Well, now, let me see. I can't remember. You were at unemployment, and then I was at the playground, and then Daisy tried to run in front of a bus—now I remember all these events…but as to dinner. I'm going to have to lie down and think. *(She lies down on the floor and won't move.)*

JOHN: Helen, don't do this again. You know it makes me furious. Helen, stop staring at the ceiling. Helen! HELEN! *(Stares; has quick fit.)* GODDAM IT! *(Takes one of Daisy's toys, smashes it.)* I've smashed one of Daisy's toys, Helen, do you want me to smash another one? Helen, get up! Look at me. All right, Helen, I'm going to smash another one of her toys… *(Hears himself.)* Good God, listen to me. What's happened to us? Helen, we're ruining that poor child. I'm going to take her and leave you. We've got to get away from you. *(Goes to pile of laundry.)* Get up, Daisy, Daddy loves you. Daisy, get up. *(Sings sweetly.)* Daisy, Daisy…GODDAM IT, GET UP! *(Starts to tie laundry and Daisy into a manageable bundle.)* Okay, Daisy, I'll just have to carry you. Helen, I'm taking Daisy and the laundry and we're leaving you. *(Slings laundry over his shoulder.)* I don't know where we're going, but we've got to get away. Helen, can you hear me? Helen, we're leaving you. Good-bye.

HELEN: *(Sits up.)* And you'll never get any of the paperback rights! *(Lies down again.)*

JOHN: There aren't any paperback rights, Helen! You live in a fool's paradise. We're leaving now. *(Starts to leave.)* I don't know where we're going, but we're going somewhere. *(Stops.)* I just need a drink first, though. Where's the vodka, Helen? Helen? *(Puts laundry down.)* Daisy, do you know where the vodka is? Daisy? Helen? Daisy? Helen? GODDAM IT, I'M TALKING TO YOU PEOPLE, ARE YOU DEAF? *(Sits on floor.)* Oh God, how did I get in this position? Where is the vodka?

HELEN: *(Sits up.)* It's in the toy duck. *(Does speech exercise.)* Toy duck, toy duck, toy duck. *(Lies down again.)*

JOHN: Oh right. Thank you. *(Goes to toy duck, reaches into it, takes out bottle of vodka.)* Why can't we have a liquor cabinet like normal people? *(Takes a big couple of swallows from the vodka.)* Want some, Helen? *(No response.)* Daisy? Daisy? *(Bitter.)* She's not a baked potato, she's a twenty percent cotton, eighty percent polyester pile of... *(At a loss.)* pooka-poo.

HELEN: *(Sits up.)* Pooka-poo, pooka-poo. Toy duck. Toy duck. Polly wolly windbag! Polly wolly windbag! Mee, mae, mah, moh, moo. Mee, mae, mah, moh, moo.

JOHN: Oh, Helen, you're talking again. I'm sorry I asked you about dinner. Want a cocktail?

HELEN: Thanks I'm too tired. *(Lies down.)*

JOHN: *(Sings.)*

Daisy, daisy, give me your answer, do...

(Next song.)

Hush, little baby, don't you cry,

Mamma's gonna give you a big black eye...

HELEN: *(Lying down, but calm.)* John, those aren't the lyrics.

JOHN: I know. I just don't know the lyrics. *(Sings.)*

And if that big black eye turns purple...

Mama's gonna give you a...

(Spoken.)

What rhymes with purple?

HELEN: *(Sits up.)* I don't know. I'm not a rhyming dictionary. Ask Daisy.

JOHN: Daisy, honey, what rhymes with purple? Daisy? Daisy, what rhymes with purple? Daisy? *(Listens; apparently hears an answer.)* She says she doesn't know.

HELEN: *(Slightly hopeful.)* Well at least she spoke today. That's something.

JOHN: *(Cheered.)* Yes, that is something. *(Drinks.)*

(Lights fade.)

ACT II
Scene 3

A desk and chair. The Principal is seated. She is dressed handsomely, but looks somewhat severe.

PRINCIPAL: *(To intercom.)* You can send Miss Pringle in now, Henry. *(Enter Miss Pringle, a sympathetic-looking teacher.)* I love having a male secretary. It makes it all worthwhile. *(Into intercom.)* Sharpen all the pencils please, Henry. Then check the coffeepot. Hello, Miss Pringle, how are you?

MISS PRINGLE: I'm fine, Mrs. Willoughby, but I wanted to talk to you about Daisy Dingleberry.

PRINCIPAL: Oh yes, that peculiar child who's doing so well on the track team.

MISS PRINGLE: Yes, she runs very quickly, but I felt I should...

PRINCIPAL: Wait a moment, would you? *(Into intercom.)* Oh, Henry, check if we have enough nondairy creamer for the coffee, would you? Then I want you to go out and buy my husband a birthday present for me, I don't have time. Thank you, sweetie. *(Back to Pringle.)* Now, I'm sorry, what were you saying?

MISS PRINGLE: Well, I'm worried about Daisy. She's doing very well in track, and some days she does well in her classes, and then some days she just stares, and then she's absent a lot.

PRINCIPAL: Yes. Uh huh. Uh huh. Yes, I see. Uh huh. Uh huh. Go on.

MISS PRINGLE: Well, it's her summer essay, you know..."What I Did Last Summer"?

PRINCIPAL: *(With great interest.)* What did you do?

MISS PRINGLE: No, no, no, it's the *topic* of the essay: what you did last summer.

PRINCIPAL: Mr. Willoughby and I went to the New Jersey seashore. He was brought up there. It brings back fond memories of his childhood. Bouncing on his mother's knee. Being hugged, being kissed. Mmmmmm. Mmmmmm. *(Makes kissing sounds, hugs herself; into intercom.)* Henry, sweetie, I want you to buy my husband underwear. Pink. The bikini kind. Calvin Klein, or something like that. Or you could use your "Ah Men" catalog if it wouldn't take too long. Mr. Willoughby is a medium. Thank you, Henry. *(To Pringle.)* I'm sorry, what were you saying?

MISS PRINGLE: About Daisy's essay.

PRINCIPAL: What about it?

MISS PRINGLE: Well...

PRINCIPAL: Wait a moment, would you? *(To intercom.)* Henry, I mean Mr.

Willoughby is a medium *size,* I don't mean he holds seances. *(Laughs; to Pringle.)* I didn't want there to be any misunderstanding. I don't think there was, but just in case. I myself am into black magic. *(Takes out a black candle. To intercom.)* Henry, I have taken out a black candle and I am thinking of you. *(To Pringle.)* Do you have a match?

MISS PRINGLE: No, I'm sorry. About Daisy's essay.

PRINCIPAL: I'm all ears.

MISS PRINGLE: Well…

PRINCIPAL: Which is a figure of speech. As you can indeed see, I am a great deal more than just ears. I have a head, a neck, a trunk, a lower body, legs and feet. *(To intercom.)* I have legs and feet, Henry. I hope you're working quickly.

MISS PRINGLE: Pay attention to me! Focus your mind on what I'm saying! I do not have all day.

PRINCIPAL: Yes, I'm sorry, I will. You're right. Oh, I admire strong women. I've always been afraid I might actually be a lesbian, but I've never had any opportunity to experiment with that side of myself. You're not interested, are you? You're single. Perhaps you *are* a lesbian.

MISS PRINGLE: I'm not a lesbian, thank you, anyway.

PRINCIPAL: Neither am I. I just thought maybe I was. *(Into intercom.)* Henry, you don't think I'm a lesbian, do you? *(Listens.)* The intercom only works one way, it needs to be repaired. Of course, Henry's a mute anyway.

MISS PRINGLE: Mrs. Willoughby, please, put your hand over your mouth for a moment and don't say anything.

PRINCIPAL: I'm all ears. *(Puts her hand over her mouth.)*

MISS PRINGLE: Good, thank you. I was disturbed by Daisy's essay. I want you to listen to it. "What I Did For My Summer Vacation." By Daisy Dingleberry. "Dark, dank rags. Wet, fetid towels. A large German shepherd, its innards splashed across the windshield of a car. Is this a memory? Is it a dream? I am trapped, I am trapped, how to escape. I try to kill myself, but the buses always stop. Old people and children get discounts on buses, but still no one will ever kill me. How did I even learn to speak, it's amazing. I am a baked potato. I am a summer squash. I am a vegetable. I am an inanimate object who from time to time can run very quickly, but I am not really alive. Help, help, help. I am drowning, I am drowning, my lungs fill with the summer ocean, but still I do not die, this awful life goes on and on, can no one rescue me." *(Miss Pringle and Principal stare at one another.)* What do you think I should do?

PRINCIPAL: I'd give her an A. I think it's very good. The style is good, it rambles a bit, but it's unexpected. It's sort of an intriguing combination of Donald Barthelme and *Sesame Street*. All that "I am a baked potato" stuff. I liked it.

MISS PRINGLE: Yes, but don't you think the child needs help?

PRINCIPAL: Well, a good editor would give her some pointers, granted, but I think she's a long way from publishing yet. I feel she should stay in school, keep working on her essays, the school track team needs her, there's no one who runs as fast. I think this is all premature, Miss Pringle.

MISS PRINGLE: I feel she should see the school psychologist.

PRINCIPAL: I am the school psychologist.

MISS PRINGLE: What happened to Mr. Byers?

PRINCIPAL: I fired him. I thought a woman would be better suited for the job.

MISS PRINGLE: But do you have a degree in psychology?

PRINCIPAL: I imagine I do. I can have Henry check if you insist. Are you sure you're not a lesbian? I think you're too forceful, it's unfeminine. And I think you're picking on this poor child. She shows signs of promising creativity, and first you try to force her into premature publishing, and now you want to send her to some awful headshrinker who'll rob her of all her creativity in the name of some awful God of normalcy. Well, Miss Pringle, here's what I have to say to you: I will not let you rob Daisy Dingleberry of her creativity, she will not see a psychologist as long as she is in this school, and you are hereby fired from your position as teacher in this school. Good day! *(To intercom.)* Henry, come remove Miss Pringle bodily from my office, sweetie, would you?

MISS PRINGLE: No need to do that. I can see myself out. Let me just say that I think you are insane, and I am sorry you are in a position of power.

PRINCIPAL: Yes, but I *am* in a position of power! *(To intercom.)* Aren't I, Henry? Now get out of here before I start to become violent.

MISS PRINGLE: I am sorry you will not let me help this child.

PRINCIPAL: Help this child! She may be the next Virginia Woolf, the next Sylvia Plath.

MISS PRINGLE: Dead, you mean.

PRINCIPAL: *(Screams.)* Who cares if she's dead as long as she publishes? Now, get out of here!

(Blackout.)

ACT II

Scene 4

A blank stage, a simple white spot. From a loudspeaker at the back of the auditorium we hear a male voice—serious, sympathetic in a detached, businesslike manner.

VOICE: Come in please.

(Enter a young man in a simple, modest dress. His haircut, shoes and socks, though, are traditionally masculine. He looks out to the back of the auditorium to where the voice is originating from. The young man seems shy, polite, tentative.)

VOICE: State your name please.

YOUNG MAN: Daisy.

VOICE: How old are you?

DAISY: I'm seventeen.

VOICE: I wish I had gotten your case earlier. Why are you wearing a dress?

DAISY: Oh, I'm sorry, am I? *(Looks, is embarrassed.)* I didn't realize. I know I'm a boy...young man. It's just I was so used to wearing dresses for so long that some mornings I wake up and I just forget. *(Thoughtfully, somewhat to himself)* I should really just clear all the dresses out of my closet.

VOICE: Why did you used to wear dresses?

DAISY: Well that's how my parents dressed me. They said they didn't know what sex I was, but it had to be one of two, so they made a guess, and they just guessed wrong.

VOICE: Are your genitals in any way misleading?

DAISY: No, I don't believe so. I don't think my parents ever really looked. They didn't want to intrude. It was a kind of politeness on their part. My mother is sort of delicate, and my father rests a lot.

VOICE: Did you think they acted out of politeness?

DAISY: Well, probably. It all got straightened out eventually. When I was eleven, I came across this medical book that had pictures in it, and I realized I looked more like a boy than a girl, but my mother had always wanted a girl or a best-seller, and I didn't want to disappoint her. But then somedays, I don't know what gets into me, I would just feel like striking out at them. So I'd wait til she was having one of her crying fits, and I took the book to her—I was twelve now—and I said, "Have you ever seen this book? Are you totally insane? Why have you named me Daisy? Everyone else has always said I was a boy, what's the *matter* with you?" And she kept crying and she said something about Judith Krantz and something about being out of Shake-n-Bake chicken, and then she said, "I want to die"; and then she said, "*Perhaps* you're a boy, but we don't want to jump to any hasty conclusions," so why don't we just wait, and we'd see if I menstruated or not. And I asked her what that word meant, and she slapped me and washed my mouth out with soap. Then she apologized and hugged me, and said she was a bad mother. Then she washed *her* mouth out with soap. Then she tied me to the kitchen table and turned on all the gas jets, and said it would be just a little while longer for the both of us. Then my father came home and he turned off the gas jets and untied me. Then when he asked if dinner was ready, she lay on the kitchen floor and wouldn't move, and he said, I guess not, and then he sort of crouched next to the refrigerator and tried to read a book, but I don't think he was really reading, because he never turned any of the pages. And then eventually, since nothing else seemed to be happening, I just went to bed.

(Fairly long pause.)

VOICE: How did you feel about this?

DAISY: Well I knew something was wrong with them. But then they meant well, and I felt that somewhere in all that, they actually cared for me—after all, she washed *her* mouth with soap too, and he untied me. And so I forgave them because they meant well. I tried to understand them. I felt sorry for them. I considered suicide.

VOICE: That's the end of the first session.

(Lights change. In view of the audience, Daisy removes his girl's clothing and changes into men's clothing—pants and a shirt, maybe a sweater. As he changes we hear the "Hush little baby" theme played rather quickly, as on a speeded-up music box. The change should be as fast and as simple as possible. Lights come up and focus on Daisy again.)

VOICE: This is your second session. How old are you?

DAISY: I'm nineteen now.

VOICE: Why have you waited two years between your first and second sessions? And you never called to cancel them. I've been waiting here for two years.

DAISY: I'm sorry. I should have called. I was just too depressed to get here. And I'm in college now, and I've owed this paper on Jonathan Swift and *Gulliver's Travels* for one-and-a-half *years*. I keep trying to write it, but I just have this terrible problem *beginning* it.

VOICE: In problems of this sort, it's best to begin at the beginning, follow through to the middle, and continue on until the ending.

DAISY: Ah, well, I've tried that. But I don't seem to get very far. I'm still on the first sentence. "Jonathan Swift's *Gulliver's Travels* is a biting, bitter work that…" I keep getting stuck on the "That."

VOICE: I see you're wearing men's clothing today.

DAISY: *(With a sense of decisiveness.)* I threw all my dresses away. And I'm going to change my name from Daisy. I'm considering Francis or Hillary or Marion.

VOICE: Any other names?

DAISY: Rocky.

VOICE: Have you seen your parents lately?

DAISY: I try not to. They call me and they cry and so on, but I hold the receiver away from my ear. And then I go next to the refrigerator and I crouch for several days.

VOICE: How are you doing in school?

DAISY: I'm not even sure I'm *registered*. It's not just the Jonathan Swift paper I owe. I owe a paper comparing a George Herbert poem with a Shakespeare sonnet; I owe a paper on characterization in *The Canterbury Tales*, and an essay on the American character as seen in Henry James's *Daisy Miller*.

(Daisy looks off into the distance, and sings softly.)

Daisy, Daisy,

Give me your answer, do,

I'm half-crazy…

(He looks grave, sad, repeats the line:)

I'm half-crazy…

(His sadness increases, he speaks slowly:)

"'I am half-sick of shadows,' said the Lady of Shallot."

VOICE: You sound like an English major.

DAISY: *(His attention returns to the voice.)* Yes. I learned a certain love of literature from my parents. My mother is a writer. She is the author of the Cliff Notes to *Scruples* and *Princess Daisy*. And my father liked reading. When he was next to the refrigerator, he would often read. I like reading. I have this eerie dream, though, sometimes that I'm a baby in my crib and somebody is reading aloud to me from what I think is *Mommie Dearest*, and then this great big dog keeps snarling at me, and then this enormous truck or bus or something drops down from the sky, and it kills me. *(With a half-joking, half-serious disappointment he's not dead.)* Then I always wake up.

VOICE: That's the end of our second session.

(The lights change abruptly. From now on, these abrupt light changes—prob-

ably a center spot with side lighting that switches side to side on each change—
will represent time passing and finding Daisy in the midst of other sessions.
There should not be blackouts, and though Daisy should speak only once the
lighting shift has completed, these changes should happen quickly.)

DAISY: Doctor, I'm so depressed I can hardly talk on the phone. It's like I can only function two hours a day at maximum. I have this enormous desire to feel absolutely nothing.

VOICE: That's the end of our third session.

(Lights change abruptly.)

DAISY: You know, when I *do* get up, I sleep with people obsessively. I'm always checking people out on the street to see who I can sleep with.

VOICE: Eventually you'll get a lot of venereal diseases.

DAISY: I know, I already have. It's just that during the sex, there's always ten or twenty seconds during which I forget *who I am* and *where I am.* And that's why I'm so obsessive. But it's ridiculous to spend hours and hours seeking sex just really in order to find those ten or twenty seconds. It's so *time-consuming!* I mean, no wonder I never get that paper on *Gulliver's Travels* done.

VOICE: Oh, you still haven't done that paper?

DAISY: No. I've been a freshman for five years now. I'm never going to graduate. At registration every fall, people just laugh at me.

VOICE: That's the end of our fifty-third session. See you Tuesday.

(Lights change.)

DAISY: *(Incensed.)* I mean it's the *inconsistency* I hate them most for! One minute they're cooing and cuddling and feeding me Nyquil, and the next minute they're turning on the gas jets, or lying on the floor, or threatening to step on my back. How dare they treat me like that? What's the matter with them! I didn't ask to be brought into the world. If they didn't know how to raise a child, they should have gotten a dog, or a kitten—they're more independent—or a *gerbil!* But left me *unborn.*

VOICE: That's the end of our two-hundred-fifteenth session.

(Lights change.)

DAISY: I passed this couple on the street yesterday, and they had this four year old walking between them, and the two parents were fighting and you could just *tell* that they were insane. And I wanted to snatch that child from them and…

VOICE: And what?

DAISY: I don't know. Hurl it in front of a car, I guess. It was too late to save it. But at least it would be dead.

VOICE: That's the end of our three-hundred-seventy-seventh session.

(Lights change.)

DAISY: *(Worn out by years of talking.)* Look, I suppose my parents aren't actually evil, and maybe my plan of hiring a hit person to kill them is going too far. They're not evil, they're just disturbed. And they mean well. *But meaning well is not enough.*

VOICE: How's your *Gulliver's Travels* paper going?

DAISY: I'm too depressed.

VOICE: I'm afraid I'm going to be on vacation next week.

DAISY: *(Unwilling to discuss this.)* I'm not happy with my present name.

VOICE: I'll just be gone a week.

DAISY: I wore a dress last week.

VOICE: I won't be gone that long.

DAISY: And I slept with thirty people.

VOICE: I hope you enjoyed it.

DAISY: And I can't be responsible for what I might do next week.

VOICE: Please, *please*, I need a vacation.

DAISY: All right, all right, take your stupid vacation. I just hope it rains.

VOICE: You're trying to manipulate me.

DAISY: Yes, but I mean well.

(Lights change.)

DAISY: *(Very dark, a very pessimistic anger.)* Doctor. I've been in therapy with you for *ten* years now. I have been a college freshman for six years, and a college sophomore for four years. The National Defense loan I have taken to pay for this idiotic education will take me a *lifetime* to repay. *(His voice sounds lost.)* I don't know. I just feel sort of, well, stuck.

VOICE: Yes?

DAISY: Oh. And I had another memory I'd forgotten, something else my parents did to me. It was during that period I stayed in the laundry pile.

VOICE: *(His voice betraying a tiny touch of having had enough.)* Yes?

DAISY: My mother had promised me I could have ice cream if I would just stand up for ten minutes and not lie in the laundry, and then when I did stand up for ten minutes, it turned out she had forgotten she was defrosting the refrigerator and the ice cream was all melted. *(Sighs.)* I mean, it was so typical of her. *(Suddenly starts to get heated up.)* She had a college education. *Who could forget they were defrosting the refrigerator???* I mean, don't you just hate her?

VOICE: How old are you?

DAISY: Twenty-seven.

VOICE: Don't you think it's about time you let go of all this?

DAISY: What?

VOICE: Don't you think you should move on with your life? Yes, your parents were impossible, but that's already happened. It's time to move on. Why don't you do your damn *Gulliver's Travels* paper? Why don't you decide on a name? My secretary has writer's cramp from changing your records from Rocky to Butch to Cain to Abel to Tootsie to Raincloud to Elizabeth the First to Elizabeth the Second to PONCHITTA PEARCE TO MARY BAKER EDDY! I mean, we know you had a rough start, but PULL YOURSELF TOGETHER! You're smart, you have resources, you can't blame them forever. MOVE ON WITH IT!

(Daisy has listened to the above embarrassed and uncomfortable, not certain how to respond. Then:)

DAISY: FUCK YOU!

(Blackout.)

ACT II

Scene 5

The home of John and Helen. A big box with a bow on it; on top of it a smaller box with a bow on it. A large banner that says, "Happy Birthday, Ponchitta." John has two bottles of vodka, Helen is using a Vicks inhaler.

HELEN: *(Inhaling.)* Mmmmmmm, I love this aroma. It almost makes me wish I had a cold. *(Inhales.)* Mmmmmm, delicious. Oh, there are pleasurable things in life. *(Calls offstage.)* Daisy, dear, are you almost ready? We want to see how you look in your present.

JOHN: I thought his name was Ponchitta.

(Pronounced: Pon-cheat-a.)

HELEN: John, we've been telling you all day, he called himself Ponchitta only for the month of March several years ago. He's been calling himself Charles Kuralt for the last several years, and now that he's turned thirty, as a gift to me, he's decided to go back to the name of Daisy. *(Calls.)* Daisy! We're waiting for you.

JOHN: I wish someone would've told me. I would've changed the banner.

HELEN: The banner's a lovely gesture, John. We all appreciate it. No one gives a fuck what's on it. I'm sorry, I don't mean to swear. No one gives a shit what's on it. Daisy, dear! Mommy and Daddy want to see you in your present. *(Enter Daisy, wearing a Scottish kilt; he looks somewhat pained, but has decided to be polite and not make waves. He holds his pants.)*

HELEN: *(Admiring the kilt.)* Ohhhhh. Do you like it, dear?

DAISY: I'm not certain.

HELEN: Now it's not a dress, I want to make that very clear. It's a Scottish *kilt.* Scottish *men* wear them in the highlands, and all that air is wonderful for your potency if you're wearing boxer shorts rather than those awful jockey shorts that destroy your semen. Isn't that so, John?

JOHN: I wasn't listening.

HELEN: *(Making the best of things.)* That's right, you weren't listening. None of us were. All our heads were elsewhere. *(To Daisy.)* Your father's become a Christian Scientist, and we're all so pleased. Now when he cuts himself, we don't even put a Band-aid on him, we just watch him bleed.

JOHN: *(Cheerful, telling a fun anecdote.)* Cut myself this morning. Shaving. A nasty slice on the bottom of my foot. Between the vodka and the dalmane and then the weight of the razor, I fell right over. *(Laughs.)* Then trying to get up, I sliced my foot. Mother wouldn't let me put a Band-aid on because she thinks I've become a Christian Scientist.

HELEN: *(Firmly.)* That's right. That's what I do think. Ponchitta, dear, I'm sorry, I mean Daisy, you're so silent. Do you like your birthday present?

DAISY: Did you give this to me because you thought I'd like it because you're insane, or did you give it to me as a sort of nasty barb to remind me that you dressed me as a girl the first fifteen years of my life?

HELEN: *(Sincerely.)* I gave it to you because I thought you'd like it. Because I'm insane. I'm insane because I stayed in a bad marriage and didn't do what I was supposed to do with my life. But I'm not bitter. And now that your father's become a Christian Scientist, I'm going to become a Jehovah's Witness and go to the supermarket *forcing* people to take copies of *The Watchtower.* Perhaps *The Watchtower* will publish me. Certainly somebody has to, someday.

JOHN: Your mother's going through a religious phase. Cocktail, anyone? *(Offers one of the bottles.)*

HELEN: Your father calls drinking from a bottle a cocktail. It's sort of adorable really. No, dear, but you have one. Oh, I'm enjoying life so much today. And you've turned thirty, and that means I'm getting nearer to death and have wasted my youth—oh, it cheers me up. Happy birthday, dear. *(Kisses Daisy.)*

JOHN: He hasn't opened up his other presents.

HELEN: Yes, Daisy dear, we have other presents. Here's one.

(Daisy puts his pants down on the couch and opens small box. It's a can, which when opened a large "snake" pops out of, just as happened to baby in first scene. Daisy is startled. Helen and John laugh in delight.)

HELEN: Daisy always loved surprises. And now open the bigger box.

(Daisy opens bigger box—Nanny comes springing out of the box, shrieking, much like the snake did. Daisy falls over backward.)

NANNY: AAAAAAAAAAAAAAGGGGGGGHHHHH!!! Whoogie! Whoogie! Whoogie! Surprise!!!!!

HELEN: Everybody sing!

HELEN, JOHN & NANNY: *(Sing, to the tune of "Frere Jacques.")*

Happy birthday, happy birthday,

Daisy dear, Daisy dear,

Happy, happy birthday,

Happy, happy birthday,

Happy birthday, happy birthday.

DAISY: *Who is this???*

NANNY: I'm your Auntie Mame! *(Laughs.)* No, just kidding. I'm the ANTI-CHRIST! *(Laughs.)* No, just kidding. *(Fondly.)* I'm your Auntie Nanny. *(Helen brings Daisy over to Nanny, who remains in the box.)*

HELEN: This is Nanny. Don't you remember Nanny?

DAISY: I remember something. God knows what. Why did you sing "Happy Birthday" to the wrong melody?

HELEN: Well, Nanny told us you have to pay a royalty to sing the real "Happy Birthday" melody. The selfish people who wrote the stupid melody don't have to lift a finger for the rest of their fucking lives, while I have to sweat and slave over the Cliff Notes to *The Thorn Birds*. *(Pause.)* And all because your father has never been able to earn a living. *(Looks at John; says with total, grim sincerity:)* Oh why don't you just keel over and die? *(Laughs.)* Ha, ha, just kidding, I'm fine.

NANNY: *(To Daisy, in baby-talk voice.)* Helllloooooo. Helllloooooo. What pwetty bwue eyes oo have. Cooooo. Cooooo. *(Suddenly.)* SHUT UP! Comin' back to you, honey?

DAISY: Slightly. I try not to remember too much. It doesn't get me anywhere.

JOHN: *(Sings drunkenly, to the correct melody.)* Happy birthday to you, ha-…

HELEN: SHUSH! There are spies from ASCAP everywhere.

(John turns his head with some trepidation, looking for the spies.)

NANNY: It's so nice to see one of my babies grown up. And what a pretty dress. The plaid matches your eyes.

HELEN: It's not a dress, Nanny. It's a *kilt.*

NANNY: Well, whatever it is, it's very becoming.

JOHN: *(Sings.)* Happy birthday…

HELEN: Please, John, please. *(Starts to get tears in her voice.)* We can't afford to pay the royalty. *(Starts to cry.)*

NANNY: *(To Helen, soothingly.)* There, there. SHUT UP! Ha, ha.

(Helen looks startled; then she and Nanny laugh and embrace.)

NANNY: Oh, all my babies grow up so strong and healthy, I'm so pleased. What does baby do for a living?

HELEN: He goes to college. He was a freshman for six years, and he's been in sophomore slump for seven years.

NANNY: Thirteen years of college. Baby must be very smart.

HELEN: He's been having trouble writing his freshman expository writing paper on *Gulliver's Travels.* How's that going, Rocky, I'm sorry, I mean Daisy?

DAISY: I finished it. I thought I'd read it to you.

HELEN: Oh, this will be a treat. John, are you still there? John? Daisy is going to read to us.

NANNY: Let me just put on my glasses. *(Puts on her glasses, listens attentively.)*

DAISY: *(Reads from a sheet of paper.)* "*Gulliver's Travels* is a biting, bitter work that…depresses me greatly."

HELEN: Oh, I like it so far.

DAISY: "By the end of the book, Gulliver has come to agree with the King of Brobdingnag's assessment that mankind is the quote 'most pernicious race of little odious vermin that nature ever suffered to crawl upon the surface of the earth,' unquote. At the end of the book, Gulliver rejects mankind and decides he prefers the company of horses to humans. We are meant to find Gulliver's disgust with humanity understandable, but also to see that he has by now gone mad. However, I find that I do not wish to write papers analyzing these things anymore as I agree with Gulliver and find most of the world, including teachers, to be less worthwhile to speak to than horses. However, I don't like horses either, so I have decided after thirteen years of schooling that I am not meant to go to college and so I am withdrawing. Fuck your degree, I am going to become a bus driver."

HELEN: Oh I think that's excellent, I think you'll get a very good grade. John, wasn't that good? And how interesting you're going to become a bus driver. You've always been drawn to buses.

NANNY: I love buses too! I adore *all* public transportation. The danger of derailing, the closeness of the people, the smells, the dirt. I'm sort of like a bacteria!—wherever I am, I thrive. *(Smiles at Daisy.)*

DAISY: I'm glad you like the paper. I should also tell you that I'm getting married.

HELEN: *(Taken aback.)* Married? How fascinating. John, I feel you're not participating in this conversation.

JOHN: How do you spell dipsomaniac, I wonder?

HELEN: John, you're too young to write your memoirs. Besides, I'm the writer in the family.

DAISY: I wasn't really intending to get married, but she's pregnant.

HELEN: *(More taken aback.)* Pregnant, how lovely.

JOHN: D-I-P...

HELEN: John, participate in your life now. This isn't a spelling bee, this is a parent-child discussion.

DAISY: She's the 1,756th person I've slept with, although only the 877th woman.

HELEN: *(Slight pause.)* This conversation is just so interesting I don't know what to do with it.

DAISY: I don't think I love her, but then I don't use that word; and I do think I like her. And her getting pregnant just seemed sort of a sign that we should go ahead and get married. That, and the fact that I had taken her phone number.

JOHN: S-O-M...

NANNY: *(Sings.)* K-E-Y, M-O-U-S-E.

JOHN: Yes, thank you.

NANNY: Well, I think it's marvelous. Congratulations, Daisy.

HELEN: Well, your father and I will have lots of advice to give you. Don't give the baby Nyquil until it's about three. We made a mistake with you.

DAISY: I don't really wish to hear your advice.

HELEN: Well, we listened to your awful paper. You can at least do us the courtesy of listening to whatever garbage we have to say.

JOHN: *(Looks out.)* Oh, dear, here comes that owl again. *(Ducks, bats at air.)*

HELEN: Oh, your father's having problems again. John, dear, try to spell delirium tremens. That's a fun word.

JOHN: Z-B-X...

HELEN: No, dear, that's *way* off. Oh, God, he's going to be spelling all night long now. He's impossible to talk to when he's spelling. But, Daisy, you're here, and we'll talk, won't we? I've made you a delicious dinner. I've ordered up Chinese.

DAISY: I don't really think I can stay for dinner.

HELEN: But it's your birthday. I don't like Chinese food. What should I do with it?

DAISY: I hesitate to say.

HELEN: Pardon?

DAISY: I feel I must tell you that I've decided I don't think I should speak to you or father for a few years and see if I become less angry.

HELEN: Angry? Why are you angry?

DAISY: Let me see if I can answer that. *(Thinks.)* No, I don't think I can. Sorry. So, thank you for the kilt, and I better be going.

HELEN: Going?

NANNY: Baby, dear, let me give you some advice before you go. Get a *lot* of medical check-ups. Aside from your promiscuity, your parents exposed you to lead, asbestos, and red dye #2 from this little toy you had. Also, avoid acid rain, dioxin contamination, and any capsule tablets that might have cyanide in them. Try to avoid radiation and third degree burns after the atomic explosions come. And, finally, work on having a sense of humor. Medically, humor and laughter have been shown to physically help people to cope with the tensions of modern life that can be otherwise internalized, leading to cancer, high blood pressure, and spastic colon. *(Smiles.)* Well! It was very nice to see you, best of luck in the future; and Helen, if you'd just mail me back to Eureeka, California, at your earliest convenience, I'd much appreciate it. *(Nanny disappears back into her box.)*

DAISY: What toy was she talking about?

HELEN: Oh, who knows? Nanny's memory is probably starting to go. She must be about 103 or so by now. Resilient woman.

JOHN: D-E-L...

HELEN: Oh, delirium. Better start, darling.

JOHN: E-R-I...

DAISY: Well, I must be going now.

HELEN: Oh. Oh, stay a little longer, Daisy dear.

DAISY: *(Trying to be kind.)* Very well. *(Sits for about a count of three.)* Well, that's about it. *(Stands again.)* I think I'll just give you this kilt back, and I'll call you in a few years if I feel less hostile.

HELEN: That would be lovely, thank you, Daisy.

(He gives her back the kilt. He picks up his trousers from the couch, but does not take the time to put them on, he just heads for the door. At the door he stops

and looks at his mother. She looks hurt and bewildered. He looks at her with regret, and some awful combination of dislike and tenderness.)

DAISY: *(Softly.)* Good-bye. *(Daisy leaves.)*

HELEN: *(Recites, a great sense of loss in her voice.)*
"How sharper than a serpent's tooth
It is to have an ungrateful child."
John, what's that from?

JOHN: D-E-L...

HELEN: What's that *from,* John?

JOHN: E-R-I, M-O-U-S-E. There! But what's delirimouse?

HELEN: God only knows, John.

(John sees the kilt Helen is holding.)

JOHN: Oh, another kilt.

HELEN: No, dear. Daisy gave it back. He said some very rude things, and then he left.

JOHN: Oh. Maybe he was angry about the banner.

HELEN: *(Sarcastically.)* Yes. Maybe that's it. Nonetheless, "To err is human, to forgive, divine." What's that from?

JOHN: *Bartlett's Famous Quotations.*

HELEN: Oh, you're just *useless.* Nanny, what's that from? Also, "How sharper than a serpent's tongue"—"tooth!"—what's that from?

NANNY: *(From within box; irritated.)* I have nothing more to say. Send me to the post office.

HELEN: Send me to the post office. What an orderly life Nanny leads. How I envy that.

JOHN: Uh oh. *(Ducks another owl.)*

HELEN: They're low-flying little beasts, aren't they, John? John, I wonder if I'm too old to have another baby? We could try again.

(John ducks again.)

HELEN: But perhaps you're not in the mood tonight. Well, we can talk about it tomorrow. *(Looks sadly out, feels alone.)* "Tomorrow and tomorrow and tomorrow." *(Very sad.)* John, what's that from? Nanny? *(No response from either; she sighs.)* One loses one's classics. *(Stares out.)*

(Lights dim.)

ACT II
Scene 6

The bassinet from the first scene of the play in a spot. Daisy, dressed normally in men's clothing, enters with a young woman named Susan. Susan is pretty and soft and sympathetic. They stand over the bassinet.

SUSAN: Hello, baby, hello. Coooo. Coooo. It's such a cute baby. Isn't it amazing how immediately one loves them?

DAISY: Yes, I guess so.

SUSAN: Say hello to the baby, Alexander.

DAISY: *(Somewhat stiffly.)* Hello.

SUSAN: Alexander, you're so stiff. Be more friendly to the child.

DAISY: Hello. *(He's better at it.)* Now we do know its sex, right?

SUSAN: Yes, it's a boy. Remember we sent out that card that said Alexander and Susan Nevsky are proud to announce the birth of their son, Alexander Nevsky, Jr.?

DAISY: Yes. *I* remember. I was just testing to check that you weren't insane and suddenly saying it was a girl.

SUSAN: No, I'm not insane. Hello, Alexander, Jr. *(To Daisy.)* How odd that you're called Alexander Nevsky. Do you have Russian ancestors?

DAISY: No, truthfully. I took the name myself. I liked the musical score to the movie. I've always had trouble with names.

SUSAN: Well, it's a very nice name.

(Baby starts to cry.)

DAISY: Oh, my God, it's crying.

SUSAN: Oh dear. What should we do, I wonder?

DAISY: I'm not certain. *(They pause for a while.)* Probably we should hold it.

(Susan picks the baby up.)

SUSAN: Instinctively that feels right. There, there. It's all right. It's all right.

(Baby stops crying.)

DAISY: Goodness, how did you do that?

SUSAN: Here, you try. *(Hands him the baby.)*

(Daisy holds the baby rather awkwardly; the baby starts to cry.)

DAISY: He doesn't like me.

SUSAN: Well, bounce him a little.

(Daisy does.)

DAISY: There, there.

(Baby stops crying.)

SUSAN: Sing to him, why don't you?

DAISY: *(Sings.)*

> Hush, little baby, don't you cry,
>
> Mama's gonna give you a big black....
>
> *(Daisy thinks, stares out quietly for a moment, changes the word.)*
>
> ...poodle.

SUSAN: Are those the lyrics?

DAISY: I don't know the lyrics. *(Sings.)*

> And if that big black poodle should attack,
>
> Mama's gonna step on your little...
>
> *(Catches himself again, redoes the whole line, making up the lyric as he goes:)*
>
> Mama's...gonna...teach you...to bite it back,
>
> And when baby grows up, big and strong,
>
> Baby...can help mama...rewrite this song.

SUSAN: That's very sweet, Alexander.

> *(Daisy looks at Susan, smiles a little. They both sing to the baby.)*

BOTH: Hush, little baby, don't you cry,

> Mama's gonna give you a big black poodle,
>
> And if that big black poodle should attack,
>
> Mama's gonna teach you to bite it back,
>
> And when baby grows up, big and strong,
>
> Baby can help mama rewrite this song...
>
> *(They keep humming to the baby as the lights dim to black.)*

END OF PLAY

AFTERWORD

Act I of *Baby...*was originally a self-contained one act; and I considered using it as the curtain-raiser to *Sister Mary.* But my actor-director friend Walter Bobbie correctly pointed out that the one-act version, ending with the parents waving a toxic toy at their traumatized baby, was much more of a "curtain downer." So I put the play aside for a while.

And, then as I said, I started to get ideas about expanding it and following the story of Daisy, but without ever seeing him (until he could be played by an adult; although I loved the sequence of little boys who played in *Sister Mary...*, the intricacies of finding them and kind of having baby-sitters for them back-stage was not something I thought wise to do again).

Act I was written in a bit of a throwback to the absurdist style of my first plays *(The Nature and Purpose of the Universe, Titanic, 'dentity Crisis*—a style not unlike that of Ionesco or Edward Albee's *The American Dream).*

Sister Mary Ignatius... and *Beyond Therapy,* the two plays that preceded this one, had their own comic exaggerations (especially the end of *Sister*), but they both had a kind of reality going—Sister, for instance, walks to her lectern, she doesn't pop out of a big box the way Nanny does; Bruce in *Beyond Therapy* may cry unexpectedly but he doesn't, say, show psychological upset by crouching next to the refrigerator or lying in a pile of laundry the way John and Daisy do in *Bathwater.*

Act I skips through time as we follow the child Daisy's growth without ever seeing him. I enjoyed bringing back the absurdist details of Act I in semi-real-istic form in Act II: Having the child Daisy write an essay, for instance, in which the infant's fears of the German shepherd, and of buses, and of being called a baked potato, all come back to haunt him. I also got an enormous kick out of writing the Woman Principal in that essay scene, and kept laughing out loud as I wrote her.

Then I liked switching tone in Daisy's monologue, where we realize that a) he's male, not female; and b) that for all the absurdist trappings, he's in a lot of pain.

Taking Daisy's pain (and for that matter, his parents' pain) seriously at the same time that I expect the audience to find humor in it has become for me the definition of my style, or at least what I intend it to be: Absurdist comedy mar-ried to real feelings.

The ending of the play was, for me, my first genuinely "hopeful" ending. I had been criticized for not ending my plays well, and most of the previous plays had what I call "dot dot dot" (...) endings, in which the audience sees the characters once more doing the same damn thing they've been doing all their lives, and now we see they're just going to keep on doing it forever, as the lights dim (…).

It's the opposite of plays in which characters change; the whole point of these endings tends to be that people *don't* change. I felt there was no intrinsic reason why endings *had* to have big character changes or big revelations that huff and puff, trying to explain everything.

The challenge, though, with the (…) ending is to restate the problem in a way that is dramatically satisfying and amusing to an audience (such as, I think, the sex-change couple mock-explaining the play's meaning in *'dentity Crisis* and then conjugating the word "identity": "I dentity, you dentity, he she or it dentities"…).

When I approached the ending of *Bathwater*, I surprised myself by not wanting to show Daisy repeating the exact patterns his parents had, as I might have in an earlier play; it felt falsely cynical. And although the statistics of abused children who grow up to be abusing parents is sadly high, I realized that in this instance Daisy's intelligence and introspection counted for me in a positive way.

I used to believe that intelligence was of little help in escaping the psychological patterns that had been inbred in one. I based this depressing belief on how overwhelming my own personal depressions were in my early twenties, and on how my mother and some other family members, smart people too, nonetheless seemed to make the same sorts of mistakes over and over in their lives, causing themselves the same kind of pain; there wasn't even *variety* in their pain. And other people I met seemed similarily stuck in repetition. So life seemed hopeless to me, and without progress.

As I left my early twenties behind, my life kept getting better, partially because I made some smart choices. I lost that sense of feeling like a child at the mercy of his parents; and though I'm not totally free of the subtle and buried kinds of psychological traps that all of us have, I found I was choosing to avoid being around or working with difficult or chaotic people. I think I'm oversensitive to tempestuous people—those for whom throwing a temper tantrum is just a way of releasing steam, but who terrify me—but by my consciously choosing to avoid those people, I did myself a great favor, I gave myself the right to protect myself. And as I felt more protected, I felt less a victim, and then happier. (Plus there are so many talented people out there who aren't tempestuous, that indeed, why not choose someone easy and supportive over someone unpredictable and enraging?)

Anyway, I've been rather personal in analyzing why I felt more optimistic at this point in my life, but in terms of the play it was simpler. I just "knew" that Daisy would be less unpredictable to his child than his parents were to him because, through introspection and analysis, he had been so sensitized to what it had done to him; and he was smart enough to have sought help to get "better." It meant his mistakes would not be as blatant, and that actually is progress, isn't it? I had never, to my knowledge, written an ending that was "hopeful" before. And it wasn't false to me; it was what I meant, and felt. So I was excited by this ending.

Andre Bishop at Playwrights Horizons offered to do the play at his theatre in New York for November of 1983. Jerry Zaks agreed to direct.

I love working with Jerry, who's extremely kind and smart, and who also loves actors, which makes them happy, which makes me happy. Jerry has gone on to become justly famous as a director, winning Obies (for my play *Marriage of Bette and Boo*), and many Tony awards, for his work on John Guare's wonderful plays, and his work on musicals, including the acclaimed revival of *Guys and Dolls* with Faith Prince and Nathan Lane.

Our cast at Playwrights was very gifted: Christine Estabrook and W.H. Macy as the parents, Dana Ivey as Nanny and the Principal, Leslie Geraci as Cynthia, and playwright-actor Keith Reddin as Daisy.

Christine took over the part of Helen in previews, and heroically did the first two nights holding the book, but so skillfully that one immediately forgot that she was reading. She's a fabulous actress, extremely funny, extremely touching, and we were lucky to have her.

The play was done upstairs at Playwrights' Studio Theatre, which has seventy seats. Younger audiences found the play a laugh riot. As the play went on, though, the seventy seats were often filled by the Playwrights Horizons subscription audience. Subscriber audiences tend to be older, and they have agreed to come to all the plays, on a certain date, having no idea what they are to see. And they didn't like it much.

Or rather, something happened to them in Act I. They became afraid I was going to make jokes about physical abuse of infants, while, as you know from reading it, I'm just making merry about psychological abuse, which is what I know about. So some nights, the subscriber audience would not laugh once. In the entire first act. Not once. This drove the poor actors crazy. (And I didn't love it either.)

In Act II, this same audience, though, would start to laugh. And I realized it was maybe because in the first scene of Act II, I finally had some "voices of reason" on the stage: Kate and Angela clearly loved their children, and were alarmed by Helen's behavior. And this gave the conservative audience a reference point; they suddenly breathed easier, and felt I wasn't actually in *favor* of child abuse.

In terms of my work, I also remembered that some of my early plays (especially *The Nature and Purpose of the Universe*) really upset some audiences because the characters' suffering was presented comically (and in great, hideous exaggeration), without there ever being a spokesperson in the play for normal decency or compassion. When I'd meet audience members who only knew my early plays, they would often express surprise that I didn't look and sound like the Wild Man of Borneo.

Looking back, I'm extremely fond of my early works that are so anarchic and horrifying; they do make me laugh, as was true of some of the audiences too. But starting with Diane's serious speech in *Sister Mary* where she straightforwardly expresses her upset with Sister and the Church, I started to drop the manic-ness from time to time and to talk seriously. And I realized that the subscriber audience at *Bathwater* missed this greatly in Act I; they felt they were trapped in a seventy-seat subway car with a lunatic.

However, luckily, we extended the run of *Bathwater* a bit; and as the subscriber audience thinned out and as a more general audience came (who came to see this *specific* play), the play fell into better balance, and we got laughs throughout again.

The play almost moved to an off-Broadway run, the way *Sister Mary...* did; but then the producers got cold feet or lost the money or something.

For the next two years, I worked on a steamer that crossed the Atlantic from Hoboken to Burma. No, I'm kidding. I don't remember what I did. Then in 1985, Jerry Zaks directed what I think is my best play to date, *The Marriage of Bette and Boo* at the Public Theatre.

The Marriage of
Bette and Boo

INTRODUCTION

Of all the plays I've written, I feel the closest to *The Marriage of Bette and Boo.* It is the one play I have written that is based directly on my experience as a child, and on my parents' marriage.

I have many thoughts on the play; and I share some of them in an afterword.

ORIGINAL PRODUCTION

The Marriage of Bette and Boo was first presented by the New York Shakespeare Festival (Joseph Papp, President) at the Public/Newman Theater in New York City on May 16, 1985. It was directed by Jerry Zaks; the scenery was by Loren Sherman; the costumes were by William Ivey Long; the lighting was by Paul Gallo; the original music was by Richard Peaslee; the hair was designed by Ron Frederick; the associate producer was Jason Steven Cohen. The cast was as follows:

BETTE BRENNAN . . . . Joan Allen

MARGARET BRENNAN, her mother . . . . Patricia Falkenhain

PAUL BRENNAN, her father . . . . Bill McCutcheon

JOAN BRENNAN, her sister. . . . . Mercedes Ruehl

EMILY BRENNAN, her sister . . . . Kathryn Grody

BOO HUDLOCKE . . . . Graham Beckel

KARL HUDLOCKE, his father. Bill Moor

SOOT HUDLOCKE, his mother . . . . Olympia Dukakis

FATHER DONNALLY/DOCTOR . . . . Richard B. Shull

MATT . . . . Christopher Durang

Understudies: Dalton Dearborn, Patrick Garner, Lizbeth Mackay, Rose Arrick, Ann Hillary. During the final week, Mr. Dearborn and Ms. Hillary played Karl and Soot.

CHARACTERS

BETTE BRENNAN

MARGARET BRENNAN, her mother

PAUL BRENNAN, her father

JOAN BRENNAN, her sister

EMILY BRENNAN, her sister

BOO HUDLOCKE

KARL HUDLOCKE, his father

SOOT HUDLOCKE, his mother

FATHER DONNALLY/DOCTOR

MATT

LIST OF SCENES

ACT I

ACT II

The Marriage of Bette and Boo

ACT I
Scene 1

> *All the characters, in various wedding apparel, stand together to sing: the Brennan family, the Hudlocke family. Matthew stands apart from them.*

ALL: *(Sing.)*
> God bless Bette and Boo and Skippy,
> Emily and Boo,
> Margaret, Matt and Betsy Booey,
> Mommy, Tommy too,
>
> Betty Betsy Booey Boozey,
> Soot, Karl, Matt, and Paul,
> Margaret Booey, Joanie Phooey,
> God bless us one and all. One and all.
>
> *(The characters now call out to one another.)*

BETTE: Booey? Booey? Skippy?

BOO: Pop?

MARGARET: Emily, dear?

BETTE: Booey?

BOO: Bette?

KARL: Is that Bore?

SOOT: Karl? Are you there?

JOAN: Nikkos!

BETTE: Skippy! Skippy!

EMILY: Are you all right, Mom?

BETTE: Booey, I'm calling you!

MARGARET: Paul? Where are you?

JOAN: Nikkos!

BOO: Bette? Betsy?

BETTE: Boo? Boo?

(Flash of light on the characters, as if their picture is being taken. Lights off the Brennans and Hudlockes. Light on Matt, late twenties or so. He speaks to the audience.)

MATT: If one looks hard enough, one can usually see the order that lies beneath the surface. Just as dreams must be put in order and perspective in order to understand them, so must the endless details of waking life be ordered and then carefully considered. Once these details have been considered, generalizations about them must be made. These generalizations should be written down legibly, and studied. The Marriage of Bette and Boo. *(Matt exits.)*

(Characters assume their places for photographs before the wedding. Boo stands to the side with his parents, Karl and Soot. Bette, in a wedding gown, poses for pictures with her family: Margaret, her mother; Emily, her sister, holding a cello; Joan, another sister, who is pregnant and is using nose spray; and Paul, her father. Bette, Margaret, Emily smile, looking out. Paul looks serious, fatherly. Joan looks sort of grouchy. Lights flash. They change positions.)

MARGARET: You look lovely, Bette.

EMILY: You do. Lovely.

MARGARET: A lovely bride. Smile for the camera, girls. *(Speaking out to either audience or to unseen photographer.)* Bette was always the most beautiful of my children. We used to say that Joanie was the most striking, but Bette was the one who looked beautiful all the time. And about Emily we used to say her health wasn't good.

EMILY: That's kind of you to worry, Mom, but I'm feeling much better. My asthma is hardly bothering me at all today. *(Coughs lightly.)*

MARGARET: Boo seems a lovely boy. Betsy, dear, why do they call him Boo?

BETTE: It's a nickname.

MARGARET: Don't you think Bette looks lovely, Joanie?

JOAN: *(Without enthusiasm.)* She does. You look lovely, Bette.

MARGARET: Where is Nikkos, dear?

JOAN: He's not feeling well. He's in the bathroom.

EMILY: Do you think we should ask Nikkos to play his saxophone with us, Joan dear?

JOAN: A saxophone would sound ridiculous with your cello, Emily.

EMILY: But Nikkos might feel left out.

JOAN: He'll probably stay in the bathroom anyway.

BETTE: Nikkos seems crazy. *(Joan glares at her.)* I wish you and Nikkos could've had a big wedding, Joanie.

MARGARET: Well, your father didn't much like Nikkos. It just didn't seem appropriate. *(Emily coughs softly.)* Are you all right, Emily?

EMILY: It's nothing, Mom.

JOAN: You're not going to get sick, are you?

EMILY: No. I'm sure I won't.

MARGARET: Emily, dear, please put away your cello. It's too large.

EMILY: I can't find the case.

(Joan uses her nose spray.)

BETTE: I can't wait to have a baby, Joanie.

JOAN: Oh yes?

MARGARET: *(Out to front again.)* Betsy was always the mother of the family, we'd say. She and her brother Tom. Played with dolls all day long, they did. Now Joanie hated dolls. If you gave Joanie a doll, she put it in the oven.

JOAN: I don't remember that, Mom.

BETTE: I love dolls.

EMILY: Best of luck, Bette. *(Kisses her; to Joan.)* Do you think Nikkos will be offended if we don't ask him to play with us?

JOAN: Emily, don't go on about it.

EMILY: Nikkos is a wonderful musician.

BETTE: So are you, Emily.

MARGARET: I just hope he's a good husband. Booey seems very nice, Betsy.

BETTE: I think I'll have a large family.

(Lights flash, taking a photo of the Brennans. Lights dim on them. Lights now pick up Boo, Karl, and Soot, who now pose for pictures.)

KARL: It's almost time, Bore.

BOO: Almost, Pop.

SOOT: Betsy's very pretty, Booey. Don't you think Betsy's pretty, Karl?

KARL: She's pretty. You're mighty old to be getting married, Bore. How old are you?

BOO: Thirty-two, Pop.

SOOT: That's not old, Karl.

KARL: Nearly over the hill, Bore.

SOOT: Don't call Booey Bore today, Karl. Someone might misunderstand.

KARL: Nobody will misunderstand.

(Photo flash. Enter Father Donnally. The families take their place on either side of him. Bette and Boo come together, and stand before him.)

FATHER DONNALLY: We are gathered here in the sight of God to join this man and this woman in the sacrament of holy matrimony. Do you, Bette…?

BETTE: I do.

FATHER DONNALLY: *And do you, Boo…?*

BOO: I do.

FATHER DONNALLY: *(Sort of to himself)* Take this woman to be your lawfully wedded…I do, I do. *(Back to formal sounding.)* I pronounce you man and wife.

(Bette and Boo kiss. Karl throws a handful of rice at them, somewhat hostilely. This bothers no one.)

JOAN: Come on, Emily.

(Emily and Joan step forward. Paul gets Emily a chair to sit in when she plays her cello. He carries a flute.)

EMILY: And now, in honor of our dear Bette's wedding, I will play the cello and my father will play the flute, and my wonderful sister Joanie will sing the Schubert lied, *Lachen und Weinen*, which translates as Laughing and Crying. *(Joan gets in position to sing. Paul holds his flute to his mouth. Emily sits in her chair, puts the cello between her legs, and raises her bow. Long pause.)*

EMILY: I can't remember it.

JOAN: *(Very annoyed.)* It starts on A, Emily.

EMILY: *(Tries again; stops.)* I'm sorry. I'm sorry, Bette. I can't remember it.

(Everyone looks a little disappointed and disgruntled with Emily. Photo flash. Lights change. Spot on Matt.)

ACT I

Scene 2

Matt addresses the audience.

MATT: When ordering reality, it is necessary to accumulate all the facts pertaining to the matter at hand. When all the facts are not immediately available, one must try to reconstruct them by considering oral history—hearsay, gossip and apocryphal stories. And then with perseverance and intelligence, the analysis of these facts should bring about understanding. The honeymoon of Bette and Boo. *(Matt exits.)*

(Enter Bette, still in her wedding dress. In the following speech, and much of the time, Bette talks cheerfully and quickly, making no visible connections between her statements.)

BETTE: Hurry up, Boo. I want to use the shower. *(Speaks to audience, who seem to her a great friend.)* First I was a tomboy. I used to climb trees and beat up my brother, Tom. Then I used to try to break my sister Joanie's voice box because she liked to sing. She always scratched me though, so instead I tried to play Emily's cello. Except I don't have a lot of musical talent, but I'm very popular. And I know more about the cello than people who don't know anything. I don't like the cello, it's too much work and besides, keeping my legs open that way made me feel funny. I asked Emily if it made her feel funny and she didn't know what I meant; and then when I told her she cried for two whole hours and then went to confession twice, just in case the priest didn't understand her the first time. Dopey Emily. She means well. *(Calls offstage.)* Booey! I'm pregnant! *(To audience.)* Actually I couldn't be, because I'm a virgin. A married man tried to have an affair with me, but he was married and so it would have been pointless. I didn't know he was married until two months ago. Then I met Booey, sort of on the rebound. He seems fine though. *(Calls out.)* Booey! *(To audience.)* I went to confession about the cello practicing, but I don't think the priest heard me. He didn't say anything. He didn't even give me a penance. I wonder if nobody was in there. But as long as your conscience is all right, then so is your soul. *(Calls, giddy, happy.)* Booey, come on! *(Bette runs off.)* *(Lights change. Spot on Matt.)*

ACT I
Scene 3
Matt addresses the audience.

MATT: Margaret gives Emily advice. *(Matt exits.)*
  (Enter Margaret, Emily, holding her cello.)
EMILY: Mom, I'm so upset that I forgot the piece at the wedding. Bette looked angry. When I write an apology, should I send it to Bette, or to Bette *and* Boo?
MARGARET: Emily, dear, don't go on about it.
  (Lights change. Spot on Matt.)

ACT I
Scene 4
Matt addresses the audience.

MATT: The honeymoon of Bette and Boo, continued. *(Exits.)*

(Enter Bette and Boo, wrapped in a large sheet and looking happy. They stand smiling for a moment. They should still be in their wedding clothes—Bette minus her veil, Boo minus his tie and jacket.)

BETTE: That was better than a cello, Boo.

BOO: You're mighty good looking, gorgeous.

BETTE: Do you think I'm prettier than Polly Lydstone?

BOO: Who?

BETTE: I guess you don't know her. I want to have lots of children, Boo. Eight. Twelve. Did you read *Cheaper by the Dozen*?

BOO: I have to call my father about a new insurance deal we're handling. *(Takes phone from beneath the sheets; talks quietly into it.)* Hello, Pop...

BETTE: *(To audience.)* Lots and lots of children. I loved the movie *Skippy* with Jackie Cooper. I cried and cried. I always loved little boys. Where is my pocketbook? Find it for me, Boo. *(The pocketbook is in full sight, but Bette doesn't seem to notice it.)*

BOO: I'm talking to Pop, Bette. What is it, Pop?

BETTE: *(To audience.)* When I was a little girl, I used to love to mind Jimmy Winkler. "Do you want me to watch Jimmy?" I'd say to Mrs. Winkler. He was five years old and had short stubby legs. I used to dress him up as a lamp shade and walk him to town. I put tassels on his toes and taped doilies on his knees, and he'd scream and scream. My mother said, "Betsy, why are you crying about *Skippy*, it's only a movie, it's not real." But I didn't believe her. Bonnie Wilson was my best friend and she got tar all over her feet. Boo, where are you?

BOO: I'm here, angel. No, not you, Pop. No, I was talking to Bette. Here, why don't you speak to her? *(Hands Bette the phone.)* Here, Bette, it's Pop.

BETTE: Hello there, Mr. Hudlocke. How are you? And Mrs. Hudlocke? I cried and cried at the movie *Skippy* because I thought it was real. Bonnie Wilson and I were the two stupidest in the class. Mrs. Sullivan used to say, "The two stupidest in math are Bonnie and Betsy. Bonnie, your grade is eight, and Betsy, your grade is five." Hello? Hello? *(To Boo.)* We must have been cut off, Boo. Where is my pocketbook?

BOO: Here it is, beautiful. *(He gives her the pocketbook that has been in full sight all along.)*

BETTE: I love you, Boo.

ACT I

Scene 5

Emily sits at her cello.

EMILY: I can't remember it. *(She gets up and addresses her chair.)* It starts on A, Emily. *(She sits down, tries to play.)* I'm sorry. I'm sorry, Bette. I can't remember it.

(Enter Joan with scissors.)

JOAN: It may start on A, Emily. But it ends now.

(She raises scissors up, threatening to cut the strings. Freeze and/or lights change.)

ACT I

Scene 6

Matt addresses the audience.

MATT: At the suggestion of *Redbook*, Bette refashions her wedding gown into a cocktail dress. Then she and Boo visit their in-laws. Bette is pregnant for the first time. *(Exits.)*

(Bette, Boo, Soot, Karl. Bette's dress is now a normal length.)

SOOT: How nice that you're going to have a baby.

KARL: Have another drink, Bore.

BETTE: *(To Soot.)* I think Booey drinks too much. Does Mr. Hudlocke drink too much?

SOOT: I never think about it.

KARL: Soot, get me and Bore another drink.

(Boo and Karl are looking over papers, presumably insurance.)

BETTE: Don't have another one, Boo.

SOOT: *(Smiles, whispers.)* I think Karl drinks too much, but when he's sober he's really very nice.

BETTE: I don't think Boo should drink if I'm going to have a baby.

SOOT: If it's a boy, you can name him Boo, and if it's a girl you can call her Soot after me.

BETTE: How did you get the name "Soot"?

SOOT: Oh, you know. The old saying, "She fell down the chimney and got covered with soot."

BETTE: What saying?

SOOT: Something about that. Karl might remember. Karl, how did I get the name "Soot"?

KARL: Get the drinks, Soot.

SOOT: All right.

KARL: *(To Bette.)* Soot is the dumbest white woman alive.

SOOT: Oh, Karl. *(Laughs, exits.)*

BETTE: I don't want you to get drunk again, Boo. Joanie's husband Nikkos may lock himself in the bathroom, but he doesn't drink.

BOO: Bette, Pop and I are looking over these papers.

BETTE: I'm your wife.

BOO: Bette, you're making a scene.

KARL: Your baby's going to be all mouth if you keep talking so much. You want to give birth to a mouth, Bette?

BETTE: All right. I'm leaving.

BOO: Bette. Can't you take a joke?

BETTE: It's not funny.

KARL: I can tell another one. There was this drunken airline stewardess who got caught in the propeller...

BETTE: I'm leaving now, Boo. *(Exits.)*

BOO: Bette. I better go after her. *(Starts to exit.)*

KARL: Where are you going, Bore?

BOO: Bette's a little upset, Pop. I'll see you later. *(Exits.)*
(Enter Soot with drinks.)

SOOT: Where's Booey, Karl?

KARL: He isn't here.

SOOT: I know. Where did he go?

KARL: Out the door.

SOOT: Did you say something to Bette, Karl?

KARL: Let's have the drinks, Soot.

SOOT: You know, I really can't remember how everyone started calling me Soot. Can you, Karl?

KARL: Go into your dance, Soot.

SOOT: Oh, Karl. *(Laughs.)*

KARL: Go get the veils and start in. The shades are down.

SOOT: Karl, I don't know what you're talking about.

KARL: You're the dumbest white woman alive. I rest my case.
(Soot laughs. Lights change.)

ACT I

Scene 7

Matt addresses the audience.

MATT: Bette goes to Margaret, her mother, for advice. *(Exits.)*

(Bette, Margaret. Emily on the floor, writing a note. Paul, the father, is also present.)

BETTE: Mom, Boo drinks. And his father insulted me.

MARGARET: Betsy, dear, marriage is no bed of roses.

EMILY: Mom, is the phrase "my own stupidity" hyphenated?

MARGARET: No, Emily. She's apologizing to Joanie again about forgetting the piece at the wedding. Joanie *was* very embarrassed.

BETTE: How can I make Boo stop drinking?

MARGARET: I'm sure it's not a serious problem, Betsy.

BETTE: Poppa, what should I do?

PAUL: W##hh, ah enntgh oo sh#$w auns$$dr ehvg### ing ahm.

(Note to reader and/or actor. Paul is meant to be the victim of a stroke. His mind is still functioning well, but his ability to speak is greatly impaired. Along these lines, I give him specific lines to say and be motivated by, but the audience and the other characters in the play should genuinely be unable to make out almost anything that he says—though they can certainly follow any emotional colorings he gives. I have found it useful for actors who read the part of Paul to say the lines written in the brackets, but to drop almost all of the consonants and to make the tongue go slack, so that poor Paul's speech is almost all vowels, mixed in with an occasional, inexplicable group of consonants. Paul's first line up above—emphasizing that no one should be able to make out almost any of it—would be: "Well, I think you should consider giving things time.")

BETTE: *What* should I do?

PAUL: *(Angry that he can't be understood)* On####t ump oo onoosns#$s. Eggh ing ahm#S. [Don't jump to conclusions. Give things time.]

MARGARET: Paul, I've asked you not to speak. We can't understand you.

EMILY: Mom, how do you spell "mea culpa"?

MARGARET: Emily, Latin is pretentious in an informal letter. Joanie will think you're silly.

EMILY: This one is to Father Donnally.

MARGARET: M-E-A C-U-L-P-A.

BETTE: Boo's father has given him a very bad example.

(Enter Joan, carrying a piece of paper.)

BETTE: Oh, Joan, quick—do you think when I have my baby, it will make Boo stop...

JOAN: Wait a minute. *(To Emily.)* Emily, I got your note. Now listen to me closely. *(With vehemence.)* I *forgive* you, I *forgive* you, I *forgive* you.

EMILY: *(A bit startled.)* Oh. Thank you.

JOAN: *(To Bette.)* Now, what did you want?

BETTE: Do you think when I have my baby, it will make Boo stop drinking and bring him and me closer together?

JOAN: I have no idea.

BETTE: Well, but hasn't your having little Mary Frances made things better between you and Nikkos? He isn't still disappearing for days, is he?

JOAN: Are you trying to make me feel bad about my marriage?

EMILY: I'm sorry, Joanie.

JOAN: What?

EMILY: If I made you feel bad about your marriage.

JOAN: Oh shut up. *(Exits.)*

BETTE: *(To Margaret.)* She's so nasty. Did you punish her enough when she was little?

MARGARET: She's just tired because little Mary Frances cries all the time. She really is a dreadful child.

BETTE: I love babies. Poppa, don't you think my baby will bring Boo and me closer together?

PAUL: Aszzs&* ot uh er#ry owowd# eeah oo ah uh ayee, ehtte. [That's not a very good reason to have a baby, Bette.]

(Bette looks at Paul blankly. Lights change.)

ACT I
Scene 8

Matt addresses the audience.

MATT: Twenty years later, Boo has dinner with his son.

(Boo and Matt sit at a table.)

BOO: Well, how are things up at Dartmouth, Skip? People in the office ask me how my Ivy League son is doing.

MATT: It's all right.

BOO: Are there any pretty girls up there?

MATT: Uh huh.

BOO: So what are you learning up there?

MATT: Tess of the d'Urbervilles is a masochist.

BOO: What?

MATT: It's a novel we're reading. *(Mumbles.) Tess of the d'Urbervilles.*

BOO: *(Laughs.)* A man needs a woman, son. I miss your mother. I'd go back
with her in a minute if she wanted. She's not in love with her family anymore, and I think she knows that drinking wasn't that much of a problem.
I think your old man's going to get teary for a second. I'm just an old softie. *(Boo blinks his eyes, wipes them.)*
*(Matt exits, embarrassed. Boo doesn't notice but addresses the chair as if Matt
were still there.)*

BOO: I miss your mother, Skip. Nobody should be alone. Do you have any
problems, son, you want to talk over? Your old man could help you out.
(Boo waits for an answer.)
(Lights change.)

ACT I
Scene 9
Matt addresses the audience.

MATT: The first child of Bette and Boo. *(Exits.)*
*(Enter Boo, Karl, Soot, Margaret, Emily with her cello, Joan, Paul. They all
stand in a line and wait expectantly. Enter the Doctor, who is played by the
same actor who plays Father Donnally.)*

DOCTOR: She's doing well. Just a few more minutes. *(Exits.)*

EMILY: Oh, God, make her pain small. Give me the pain rather than her.
(Winces in pain.)

MARGARET: Emily, behave, this is a hospital.

BOO: Pop, I hope it's a son.

KARL: This calls for a drink. Soot, get Bore and me a drink.

SOOT: Where would I go?

KARL: A drink, Soot.

SOOT: Karl, you're teasing me again.

KARL: All right, I won't talk to you.

SOOT: Oh please. Please talk to me. Booey, talk to your father.

BOO: Come on, Pop. We'll have a drink afterwards.

SOOT: Karl, I'll get you a drink. *(To Margaret.)* Where would I go? *(To Karl.)* Karl?

KARL: This doctor know what he's doing, Bore?

SOOT: Karl? Wouldn't you like a drink?

EMILY: It's almost here. *(Having an experience of some sort.)* Oh no, no, no no no no.

MARGARET: Emily!

KARL: This Betsy's sister, Bore?

BOO: Pop, I hope it's a boy.

KARL: You were a boy, Bore.

(Enter the doctor, holding a bundle in a blue blanket.)

KARL: This is it, Bore.

EMILY: In the name of the Father, and of the Son, and of the Holy Ghost.

DOCTOR: It's dead. The baby's dead. *(He drops it on the floor.)*

EMILY: *(Near collapse.)* Oh no!

JOAN: I win the bet.

MARGARET: I'm here, Betsy, it's all right. *(Paul picks up the baby.)* Paul, put the baby down. That's disrespectful.

PAUL: Buh uh ayee ah#S# ehh#! [But the baby's not dead.]

MARGARET: Don't shout. I can understand you.

PAUL: *(To doctor.)* Uh ayee ah#$# ehh#! Yrr uh ahherr, ann oo ee, uh ayee ah#S# ehh#! [The baby's not dead. You're a doctor, can't you see, the baby's not dead.]

DOCTOR: *(Takes the baby.)* Oh, you're right. It's not dead. Mr. Hudlocke, you have a son.

KARL: Congratulations, Bore.

EMILY: Thank you, God.

(Enter Bette, radiant. She takes the baby.)

BETTE: *(To audience.)* We'll call the baby Skippy.

EMILY: It has to be a saint's name, Bette.

BETTE: Mind your business, Emily.

MARGARET: Betsy, dear, Emily's right. Catholics have to be named after saints. Otherwise they can't be baptized.

BOO: Boo.

MARGARET: There is no Saint Boo.

EMILY: We should call it Margaret in honor of Mom.

BETTE: It's a boy.

EMILY: We should call him Paul in honor of Dad.

MARGARET: Too common.

SOOT: I always liked Clarence.

JOAN: I vote for Boo.

MARGARET: *(Telling her to behave.)* Joanie.

KARL: Why not name it after a household appliance?

SOOT: Karl. *(Laughs.)*

KARL: Egg beater. Waffle iron. Bath mat.

BETTE: *(To audience.)* Matt. I remember a little boy named Matt who looked just like a wind-up toy. We'll call him Matt.

BOO: It's a boy, Pop.

EMILY: Is Matt a saint's name, Bette?

BETTE: Matt*hew*, Emily. Maybe if you'd finally join the convent, you'd learn the apostles' names.

EMILY: Do you think I should join a convent?

BETTE: *(To audience.)* But his nickname's going to be Skippy. My very favorite movie.

(Lights change.)

ACT I

Scene 10

Matt addresses the audience.

MATT: *My Very Favorite Movie*, an essay by Matthew Hudlocke. My very favorite movie…are…*Nights of Cabiria, 8½, Citizen Kane, L'Avventura, The Seventh Seal, Persona, The Parent Trap, The Song of Bernadette, Potemkin, The Fire Within, The Bells of St. Mary's, The Singing Nun, The Dancing Nun, The Nun on the Fire Escape Outside My Window, The Nun That Caused the Chicago Fire, The Nun Also Rises, The Nun Who Came to Dinner, The Caucasian Chalk Nun, Long Day's Journey into Nun, None But the Lonely Heart,* and *The Nun Who Shot Liberty Valance.*

Page two. In the novels of Thomas Hardy, we find a deep and unrelieved pessimism. Hardy's novels, set in his hometown of Wessex, contrast nature outside of man with the human nature inside of man, coming together inexorably to cause human catastrophe. The sadness in Hardy—his lack of belief that a benevolent God watches over human destiny, his sense of the waste and frustration of the average human life, his forceful irony in the face of moral and metaphysical questions—is part of the late Victorian mood. We can see something like it in A.E. Housman, or in

Emily's life. Shortly after Skippy's birth, Emily enters a convent, but then leaves the convent due to nerves. Bette becomes pregnant for the second time. Boo continues to drink. If psychiatrists had existed in nineteenth century Wessex, Hardy might suggest Bette and Boo seek counseling. Instead he has no advice to give them, and in 1886 he writes *The Mayor of Casterbridge*. This novel is one of Hardy's greatest successes, and Skippy studies it in college. When he is little, he studies *The Wind in the Willows* with Emily. And when he is very little, he studies drawing with Emily.

(Emily, Matt. Emily has brightly colored construction paper and crayons.)

EMILY: Hello, Skippy, dear. I thought we could do some nice arts and crafts today. Do you want to draw a cat or a dog?

MATT: A dog.

EMILY: All right, then I'll do a cat.

(They begin to draw.)

EMILY: Here's the head, and here's the whiskers. Oh dear, it looks more like a clock. Oh, Skippy, yours is very good. I can tell it's a dog. Those are the ears, and that's the tail, right?

MATT: Yes.

EMILY: That's very good. And you draw much better than Mary Frances. I tried to interest her in drawing Babar the elephant the other day, but she doesn't like arts and crafts, and she scribbled all over the paper, and then she had a crying fit. *(Sits back.)* Oh dear. I shouldn't say she doesn't draw well, it sounds like a criticism of Joanie.

MATT: I won't tell.

EMILY: Yes, but it would be on my conscience. I better write Joanie a note apologizing. And really Mary Frances draws *very* well, I didn't mean it when I said she didn't. She probably had a headache. I think I'll use this nice pink piece of construction paper to apologize to Joanie, and I'll apologize about forgetting the piece at your mother's wedding too. I've never been sure Joanie's forgiven me, even though she says she has. I don't know what else I can do except apologize. I don't have any money.

MATT: Your cat looks very good. It doesn't look like a clock.

EMILY: You're such a comfort, Skippy. I'll be right back. Why don't you pretend your dog is real, and you can teach it tricks while I'm gone. *(Exits.)*

(Matt makes "roll over" gesture to drawing, expectantly. Lights change. Matt exits.)

ACT I

Scene 11

Bette enters, carrying a chair. She sits on the chair.

BETTE: *(To audience and/or herself.)* I'm going to pretend that I'm sitting in this chair. Then I'm going to pretend that I'm going to have another baby. And then I'm going to have another and another and another. I'm going to pretend to have a big family. There'll be Skippy. And then all the A.A. Milne characters. Boo should join A.A. There'll be Eeyore and Pooh Bear and Christopher Robin and Tigger…My family is going to be like an enormous orphanage. I'll be their mother. Kanga and six hundred Baby Roos. Baby Roo is Kanga's baby, but she's a mother to them all. Roo and Tigger and Pooh and Christopher Robin and Eeyore and Owl, owl, ow, ow, ow, ow, ow, ow, ow, ow! I'm giving birth, Mom. Roo and Tigger and Boo and Pooh and Soot and Eeyore and Karl and Betsy and Owl…

   (Enter quickly: Boo, Karl, Soot, Margaret, Paul, Emily, Joan. They stand in their same hospital positions. Enter the doctor with the baby in a blue blanket.)

DOCTOR: The baby's dead. *(Drops it on the floor.)*

MARGARET: Nonsense. That's what he said about the last one, didn't he, Paul?

DOCTOR: This time it's true. It *is* dead.

BETTE: Why?

DOCTOR: The reason the baby is dead is this: Mr. Hudlocke has Rh positive blood.

KARL: Good for you, Bore!

DOCTOR: Mrs. Hudlocke has Rh negative blood.

BETTE: Like Kanga.

DOCTOR: And so the mother's Rh negative blood fights the baby's Rh positive blood and so: The mother kills the baby.

EMILY: *(Rather horrified.)* Who did this??? The mother did this???

KARL: You married a winner, Bore.

BOO: The baby came. And it was dead. *(Picks up baby.)*

SOOT: Poor Booey.

BETTE: But I'll have other babies.

DOCTOR: The danger for your health if you do and the likelihood of stillbirth are overwhelming considerations.

BOO: The baby came. And it was dead.

BETTE: Mama, tell him to go away.

MARGARET: There, there. Say something to her, Paul.

   (Paul says nothing. Lights change.)

ACT I

Scene 12

Matt addresses the audience.

MATT: Bette and Margaret visit Emily, who is in a rest home due to nerves. *(Exits.)* *(Emily with her cello. Bette, Margaret. Bette seems very depressed, and keeps looking at the floor or looking off.)*

EMILY: Oh, Mom, Bette. It's so good to see you. How are you feeling, Bette, after your tragedy?

MARGARET: Emily, don't talk about it. Change the subject.

EMILY: *(Trying desperately to oblige.)* Um...um...uh...

MARGARET: *(Looking around slightly.)* This is a very nice room for an institution. Bette, look up. Do you like the doctors, Emily?

EMILY: Yes, they're very good to me.

MARGARET: They should be. They're very expensive. I was going to ask your brother, Tom, for some money for your stay here, but he's really not...Oh, I didn't mean to mention Tom. Forget I said anything.

EMILY: Oh, what is it? Is he all right?

MARGARET: I shouldn't have mentioned it. Forget it, Emily.

EMILY: But what's the matter with him? Is he ill? Oh, Mom...

MARGARET: Now, Emily, don't go on about it. That's a fault of yours. If you had stayed in the convent, maybe you could have corrected that fault. Oh, I'm sorry. I didn't mean to bring up the convent.

EMILY: That's all right, Mom.

(Silence.)

MARGARET: Besides, whatever happens, happens. Don't look that way, Emily. Change the subject.

EMILY: Um...uh...

MARGARET: There are many pleasant things in the world, think of them.

EMILY: *(Trying hard to think of something; then:)* How is Skippy, Bette?

BETTE: Who?

EMILY: Skippy.

BETTE: *(To Margaret.)* Who?

MARGARET: She means Baby Roo, dear.

BETTE: Oh, Roo. Yes. *(Stares off in distance blankly.)*

EMILY: Is he well?

MARGARET: *(Telling Emily to stop.)* He's fine, dear. Looks just like his mother.

EMILY: He's a lovely child. I look forward to seeing him when I finally leave here and get to go… *(Gets teary.)*

MARGARET: Emily, the doctors told me they're sure you're not here for life. Isn't that right, Bette? *(Whispers to Emily.)* The doctors say Bette shouldn't have any more babies.

EMILY: Oh, dear. And Bette's a wonderful mother. Bette, dear, don't feel bad, you have the one wonderful child, and maybe someday God will make a miracle so you can have more children.

BETTE: *(The first sentence she's heard.)* I can have more children?

EMILY: Well, maybe God will make a *miracle* so you can.

BETTE: I can have a miracle?

EMILY: Well you pray and ask for one.

MARGARET: Emily, miracles are very fine…

EMILY: Oh, I didn't think, I shouldn't have…

MARGARET: But now you've raised Betsy's hopes…

EMILY: Oh, Bette, listen to Mom…I'm so sorry…

BETTE: I CAN HAVE MORE CHILDREN!

MARGARET: That's right, Betsy. Emily, I know you didn't mean to bring this up…

EMILY: I'm so stupid…

MARGARET: But first you start in on your brother Tom who has a spastic colon and is drinking too much…

EMILY: OH NO!

BETTE: *(Very excited; overlapping with Margaret.)* I CAN HAVE MORE CHILDREN, I CAN HAVE MORE CHILDREN, I CAN HAVE MORE CHILDREN… *(etc.)*

MARGARET: *(Overlapping with Bette.)* …and has been fired and there's some crazy talk about him and some boy in high school, which I'm sure isn't true, and even if it is…

EMILY: Tom's all right, isn't he, it isn't true…

BETTE: …I CAN HAVE MORE CHILDREN!… *(etc.)*

MARGARET: I didn't mean to tell you, Emily, but you talk and talk…

BETTE: …I CAN HAVE MORE CHILDREN, I CAN HAVE MORE CHILDREN…

EMILY: Oh, Mom, I'm so sorry, I…

MARGARET: and *talk* about a thing until you think your head is going to explode…

EMILY: *(Overlapping still.)* I'm so sorry, I…WAIT! *(Silence. Emily sits at her cello with great concentration, picks up the bow.)* I think I remember it. *(Listens,*

tries to remember the piece from the wedding, keeps trying out different open-
ing notes. Margaret looks between the two girls.)

MARGARET: I wish you two could see yourselves. *(Laughs merrily.)* You're both
acting very funny. *(Laughs again.)* Come on, Betsy.

(Margaret and Bette exit, cheerful. Emily keeps tying to remember. Lights
change.)

ACT I
Scene 13

Matt addresses the audience.

MATT: Bette seeks definition of the word "miracle" from Father Donnally. *(Exits.)*

(Bette, Father Donnally. She kneels to him in the confessional, blesses herself.)

FATHER DONNALLY: Hello, Bette, how are you?

BETTE: I'm feeling much better after my tragedy.

FATHER DONNALLY: It's a cross to bear.

BETTE: Have you ever read *Winnie the Pooh*, Father? Most people think it's for
children, but I never read it until I was an adult. The humor is very sophis-
ticated.

FATHER DONNALLY: I'll have to read it sometime.

BETTE: Do you believe in miracles, Father?

FATHER DONNALLY: Miracles rarely happen, Bette.

BETTE: I do too! Thank you, Father. You've helped me make a decision.

(Lights change.)

ACT I
Scene 14

Matt addresses the audience.

MATT: Soot gives Bette some advice. *(Exits.)*

(Bette, pregnant, Boo, Soot, Karl.)

BETTE: And then Father Donnally said that I should just keep trying and that
even if this baby died, there would be at least one more baby that would
live, and then I would be a mother as God meant me to be. Do you agree,
Soot?

SOOT: I've never met this Father Donnally. Karl, Pauline has a retarded daughter, doesn't she? LaLa is retarded, isn't she? I mean, she isn't just slow, is she?

BETTE: I don't care if the child's retarded. Then that's God's will. I love retarded children. I like children more than I like people. Boo, you're drinking too much, it's not fair to me. If this baby dies, it's going to be your fault.

BOO: I don't think Father Donnally should have encouraged you about this. That's what I think.

BETTE: He's a priest. *(To Soot.)* Did you ever see Jackie Cooper as a child? I thought he was much cuter than Shirley Temple, what do you think, Soot?

KARL: Bore, my wife Soot hasn't said one sensible thing in thirty years of marriage...

SOOT: Oh, Karl... *(Laughs, flattered.)*

KARL: But your little wife has just said more senseless things in one ten-minute period than Soot here has said in thirty years of bondage.

SOOT: Oh, Karl. I never was one for talking.

BETTE: *(To Karl.)* Look here, you. I'm not afraid of you. I'm not going to let Boo push me to a breakdown the way you've pushed Soot. I'm stronger than that.

SOOT: Oh, my. *(Laughs.)* Sit down, dear.

KARL: Tell the baby-maker to turn it down, Bore.

BOO: Bette, sit down.

BETTE: I want a marriage and a family and a home, and I'm going to have them, and if you won't help me, Boo, I'll have them without you. *(Exits.)*

KARL: Well, Bore, I don't know about you and your wife. Whatever one can say against your mother, and it's most everything, *(Soot laughs.)* at least she didn't go around dropping dead children at every step of the way like some goddamned giddy farm animal.

SOOT: Karl, you shouldn't tease everyone so.

KARL: I don't like the way you're behaving today, Soot. *(Exits.)*

SOOT: *(Looks back to where Bette was.)* Bette, dear, let me give you some advice. Oh, that's right. She left. *(A moment of disorientation; looks at Boo.)* Boo, Karl's a lovely man most of the time, and I've had a very happy life with him, but I hope you'll be a little kinder than he was. Just a little. Anything is an improvement. I wish I had dead children. I wish I had two hundred dead children. I'd stuff them down Karl's throat. *(Laughs.)* Of course, I'm only kidding. *(Laughs some more.)*

(Lights change.)

ACT I

Scene 15

Matt addresses the audience.

MATT: Now the Mayor of Casterbridge, when drunk, sells his wife and child to someone he meets in a bar. Now Boo is considerably better behaved than this. Now the fact of the matter is that Boo isn't really an alcoholic at all, but drinks simply because Bette is such a terrible, unending nag. Or, perhaps Boo *is* an alcoholic, and Bette is a terrible, unending nag in *reaction* to his drinking so much, and also because he just isn't "there" for her, anymore than Clym Yeobright is really there for Eustacia Vye in *The Return of the Native,* although admittedly Eustacia Vye is very neurotic, but then so is Bette also.

Or perhaps it's the fault of the past history of stillbirths and the pressures that that history puts on their physical relationship. Perhaps blame can be assigned totally to the Catholic Church. Certainly Emily's guilt about leaving the convent and about everything else in the world can be blamed largely on the Catholic Church. *(Pleased.)* James Joyce can be blamed on the Catholic Church, but not really Thomas Hardy. And then in 1896 Hardy writes *Jude the Obscure.* And when Skippy is nine, Bette goes to the hospital for the third time. The third child of Bette and Boo. *(Exits.) (Lights change.)*

ACT I

Scene 16

Everyone assembles, except for Bette: Boo, Karl, Soot, Margaret, Paul, Joan, Emily. They wait. Enter the doctor. He drops the baby on the floor, exits. Pause. Lights change.

ACT I

Scene 17

Bette on the telephone, late at night.

BETTE: Hello, Bonnie? This is Betsy. Betsy. *(To remind her.)* Bonnie, your grade is eight, and Betsy, your grade is five. Yes, it's me. How are you? Oh, I'm sorry, I woke you? Well, what time is it? Oh I'm sorry. But isn't Florida in a different time zone than we are? Oh. I thought it was. Oh well.

Bonnie, are you married? How many children do you have? Two. That's nice. Are you going to have any more? Oh, I think you should. Yes, I'm married. To Boo. I wrote you. Oh, I never wrote you? How many years since we've spoken? Since we were fifteen. Well, I'm not a very good correspondent. Oh, dear, you're yawning, I guess it's too late to have called. Bonnie, do you remember the beach and little Jimmy Winkler? I used to dress him up as a lamp shade, it was so cute. Oh. Well, do you remember when Miss Willis had me stand in the corner, and you stand in the wastebasket, and then your grandmother came to class that day? I thought you'd remember that. Oh, you want to go back to sleep?

Oh, I'm sorry. Bonnie, before you hang up, I've lost two babies. No, I don't mean misplaced, stupid, they died. I go through the whole ninemonth period of carrying them, and then when it's over, they just take them away. I don't even see the bodies. Hello? Oh, I thought you weren't there. I'm sorry, I didn't realize it was so late. I thought Florida was Central Time or something. Yes, I got twelve in geography or something, you remember? Betsy, your grade is twelve and Bonnie, your grade is…what did you get in geography? Well, it's not important anyway. What? No, Boo's not home. Well, sometimes he just goes to a bar and then he doesn't come home until the bar closes, and some of them don't close at all and so he gets confused what time it is. Does your husband drink? Oh, that's good. What's his name? Scooter? Like bicycle? I like the name Scooter. I love cute things. Do you remember Jackie Cooper in *Skippy* and his best friend Sukey? I cried and cried. Hello, are you still there? I'm sorry, I guess I better let you go back to sleep. Good-bye, Bonnie, it was good to hear your voice. *(Hangs up.)*
(Lights change.)

ACT I
Scene 18
Matt addresses the audience.

MATT: Several months later, Bette and Boo have the two families over to celebrate Thanksgiving.
(Bette, Matt. Bette is on the warpath.)

BETTE: *(Calling off, nasty.)* Come *up* from the cellar, Boo. I'm not going to say it again. They're going to be here. *(To Matt.)* He's hidden a bottle behind the furnace.

MATT: Please stop shouting.

BETTE: Did you smell something on his breath?

MATT: I don't know. I didn't get that close.

BETTE: Can't you go up and kiss him?

MATT: I can't go up and kiss him for no reason.

BETTE: You're so unaffectionate. There's nothing wrong with a ten-year-old boy kissing his father.

MATT: I don't want to kiss him.

BETTE: Well, I think I smelled something.

(Enter Boo.)

BOO: What are you talking about?

BETTE: You're always picking on me. I wasn't talking about anything. Set the table, Skippy.

(Matt exits.)

BOO: When are they all coming?

BETTE: When do you think they're coming? Let me smell your breath.

BOO: Leave my breath alone.

BETTE: You've been drinking. You've got a funny look in your eye.

(Enter Matt, holding some silverware.)

MATT: Something's burning in the oven.

BETTE: Why can't you stop drinking? You don't care enough about me and Skippy to stop drinking, do you?

MATT: It's going to burn.

BETTE: You don't give me anything to be grateful for. You're just like your father. You're a terrible example to Skippy. He's going to grow up neurotic because of you.

MATT: I'll turn the oven off. *(Exits.)*

BOO: Why don't you go live with your mother, you're both so perfect.

BETTE: Don't criticize my mother.

(Enter Joan and Emily. Joan has a serving dish with candied sweet potatoes; Emily has a large gravy boat.)

EMILY: Happy Thanksgiving, Bette.

BETTE: Hush, Emily. You're weak, Boo. It's probably just as well the other babies have died.

EMILY: I brought the gravy.

BETTE: We don't care about the gravy, Emily. I want you to see a priest, Boo.

BOO: Stop talking. I want you to stop talking.

(Enter Margaret and Paul. Paul is holding a large cake.)

MARGARET: Hello, Betsy, dear.

BETTE: He's been drinking.

MARGARET: Let's not talk about it. Hello, Boo, Happy Thanksgiving.

BOO: Hello.

(Enter Soot and Karl. Soot is carrying a candelabra.)

SOOT: Hello, Margaret.

MARGARET: How nice to see you. Paul, you remember Mrs. Hudlocke?

PAUL: Icse oo ee oo, issizzse uhoch##. Iht oo ab uhulll ineing uh arreeng ace?

[Nice to see you, Mrs. Hudlocke. Did you have trouble finding a parking place?]

SOOT: I guess so. *(To everybody.)* I brought a candelabra.

BETTE: *(To Soot.)* You're his mother, I want you to smell his breath.

BOO: SHUT UP ABOUT MY BREATH!

(Boo accidentally knocks into Emily, who drops the gravy on the floor.)

BETTE: You've spilled the gravy all over the rug!

EMILY: I'm sorry.

BETTE: Boo did it!

BOO: I'll clean it up, I'll clean it up. *(Exits.)*

BETTE: I think he's hidden a bottle in the cellar.

EMILY: Joanie didn't drop the sweet potatoes.

SOOT: Are we early? *(Laughs.)*

KARL: Pipe down, Soot.

(Boo enters with a vacuum cleaner. All watch him as he starts to vacuum up the gravy.)

BETTE: What are you doing? Boo!

BOO: I can do it!

BETTE: You don't vacuum gravy!

BOO: I can do it!

BETTE: Stop it! You're ruining the vacuum!

SOOT: Oh, dear. Let's go. *(Laughs.)* Good-bye, Booey.

(Karl and Soot exit.)

JOAN: I knew we shouldn't have had it here.

MARGARET: Come on, Betsy. Why don't you and Skippy stay with us tonight?

BETTE: YOU DON'T VACUUM GRAVY!

MARGARET: Let it alone, Betsy.

BETTE: You don't vacuum gravy. You don't vacuum gravy. You don't vacuum gravy.

BOO: *(Hysterical.)* WHAT DO YOU DO WITH IT THEN? TELL ME! WHAT DO YOU DO WITH IT?

BETTE: *(Quieter, but very upset.)* You get warm water, and a sponge, and you sponge it up.

(Bette and Boo stare at one another, spent.)

EMILY: Should we put the sweet potatoes in the oven?

(Exit Matt.)

JOAN: Come on,

EMILY: Let's go home.

MARGARET: Betsy, if you and Skippy want to stay at our house tonight, just come over. Good-bye, Boo.

EMILY: *(Calls.)* Good-bye, Skippy.

(Margaret, Joan, Emily, and Paul exit. Enter Matt with a pan of water and two sponges. He hands them to Bette. Bette and Boo methodically sponge up the gravy. Music to the "Bette and Boo" round in the background.)

BOO: *(Quietly.)* Okay, we'll soak it up with the sponge. That's what we're doing. We're soaking it up.

(They more or less finish with it.)

BOO: I'm going to take a nap. *(Boo lies down where he is, and falls asleep.)*

BETTE: Boo? Boo? Booey? Boo?

(Enter Soot.)

SOOT: Did I lose an earring in here? Oh, dear. He's just asleep, isn't he?

BETTE: Boo? Boo.

SOOT: He must have gotten tired. *(Holds up earring, to Matt.)* If you should see it, it looks just like this one. *(Laughs.)* Booey? *(Laughs.)* I think he's asleep. Good-bye, Booey. *(Exits.)*

BETTE: Boo? Booey?

MATT: Please don't try to wake him up. You'll just argue.

BETTE: All right. I won't try to wake him. *(Pause.)* Boo. Booey. *(She pushes his shoulder slightly.)* Boo. *(To Matt.)* I just want to get through to him about the gravy. *(To Boo.)* Boo. You don't vacuum gravy. Are you awake, Boo? Boo? I wonder if he's going to sleep through the night. I can wait. Boo. Booey.

(Bette looks at Matt, then back at Boo. Matt looks at both of them, then out to audience, exhausted and trapped, but with little actual expression on his face. Lights dim.)

END ACT I

ACT II

Scene 19

> *Bette, Boo, Father Donnally down center. Matt to the side. All the others stand together as they did in the beginning to sing the "Bette and Boo" round. Music introduction to the round is heard.*

ALL: *(Except Bette, Boo, Father Donnally, Matt sing:)*
> Ninety-nine bottles of beer on the wall,
> Ninety-nine bottles of beer,
> Take one down, pass it around,
> Ninety-eight bottles of beer on the wall,
> Ninety-eight bottles of beer on the wall,
> Ninety-eight bottles of beer... *(etc.)*
> *(They keep singing this softly under the following scene.)*

BOO: *(Holding up a piece of paper.)* I pledge, in front of Father Donnally, to give up drinking in order to save my marriage and to make my wife and son happy.

FATHER DONNALLY: Now sign it, Boo. *(Boo signs it.)*

BETTE: *(Happy.)* Thank you, Boo. *(Kisses him; to Father Donnally.)* Should you bless him or something?

FATHER DONNALLY: Oh, I don't know. Sure. *(Blesses them.)* In the name of the Father, Son and Holy Ghost. Amen.

BETTE: Thank you, Father.

FATHER DONNALLY: All problems can be worked out, can't they?

BETTE: Yes, they can.

FATHER DONNALLY: Through faith.

BETTE: And will power. Boo, let's have another baby.

THOSE SINGING: *(Finishing.)*
> Take one down, pass it around,
> God bless us one and all!
> *(Lights change.)*

ACT II

Scene 20

> *Bette and Boo dance. Perhaps no music in the background.*

BETTE: This is fun to go dancing, Boo. We haven't gone since before our honeymoon.

BOO: You're mighty pretty tonight, gorgeous.

BETTE: I wonder if Bonnie Wilson grew up to be pretty. We were the two stupidest in the class. I don't think Joanie's marriage is working out. Nikkos is a louse.

BOO: I think the waiter thought I was odd just ordering ginger ale.

BETTE: The waiter didn't think anything about it. You think everyone's looking at you. They're not. Emily said she's going to pray every day that this baby lives. I wonder what's the matter with Emily.

BOO: Your family's crazy.

BETTE: Don't criticize my family, Boo. I'll get angry. Do you think I'm prettier than Polly Lydstone?

BOO: Who?

BETTE: You're going to have to make more money when this baby comes. I think Father Donnally is very nice, don't you? Your father is terrible to your mother. My father was always sweet to my mother.

BOO: I think the waiter thinks I'm odd.

BETTE: What is it with you and the waiter? Stop talking about the waiter. Let's just have a nice time.

(They dance in silence.)

BETTE: Are you having a nice time?

BOO: You're lookin' mighty pretty tonight, Bette.

BETTE: Me too, Boo.

(They dance, cheered up. Lights change.)

ACT II
Scene 21
Matt addresses the audience.

MATT: *Holidays,* an essay by Matthew Hudlocke. Holidays were invented in 1203 by Sir Ethelbert Holiday, a sadistic Englishman. It was Sir Ethelbert's hope that by setting aside specific days on which to celebrate things—the birth of Christ, the death of Christ, Beowulf's defeat over Grendel—that the population at large would fall into a collective *deep* depression. Holidays would regulate joy so that anyone who didn't feel joyful on those days would feel bad. Single people would be sad they were single. Married people would be sad they were married. Everyone would feel disappointment that their lives had fallen so far short of their expectations.

A small percentage of people, sensing the sadism in Sir Ethelbert's plan, did indeed pretend to be joyful at these appointed times; everyone else felt intimidated by this small group's excessive delight, and so never owned up to being miserable. And so, as time went on, the habit of celebrating holidays became more and more ingrained into society.

Eventually humorists like Robert Benchley wrote mildly amusing essays poking fun at the impossibility of enjoying holidays, but no one actually spoke up and attempted to abolish them.

And so, at this time, the Thanksgiving with the gravy having been such fun, Bette and Boo decide to celebrate the holiday of Christmas by visiting the Hudlocke's.

(Maybe a bit of Christmas music. Emily sits near Karl and Soot. Boo is off to one side, drinking something. Bette is off to another side, looking grim; she is also looking pregnant. Matt sits on floor near Emily or Soot.)

EMILY: I think Christmas is becoming too commercial. We should never forget whose birthday we are celebrating.

SOOT: That's right. Whose birthday are we celebrating?

EMILY: Our Lord Saviour.

SOOT: Oh yes, of course. I thought she meant some relative.

EMILY: Jesus.

SOOT: It's so nice of you to visit us today, Emily. I don't think I've seen you since you were away at that…well, away. *(Laughs.)*

EMILY: Skippy asked me to come along, but I'm enjoying it.

KARL: Soot, get Bore and me another drink.

BETTE: IF BOO HAS ANOTHER DRINK, I AM GOING TO SCREAM AND SCREAM UNTIL THE WINDOWS BREAK! I WARN YOU!
(Pause.)

KARL: *(Looks at Bette.)* You're having another baby, woman?

BOO: I told you, Pop. Betsy has a lot of courage.

KARL: You trying to kill Betsy, Bore?

BETTE: I'm going to lie down in the other room. *(To Boo.)* Skippy will tell me if you have another drink. *(Exits.)*

KARL: You sound like quite a scout, Skip. Is Skip a scout, Bore?

BOO: What, Pop?

KARL: Is Skip a scout, Bore?

SOOT: I was a brownie. *(Re-enter Bette.)*

BETTE: Boo upsets Skippy's stomach. *(Sits down.)* I'm not leaving the room.
(Pause.)

SOOT: *(To Emily.)* My friend Lottie always comes out to visit at Christmas time…

KARL: Her friend Lottie looks like an onion.

SOOT: Karl always says she looks like an onion. *(Doing her best.)* But this year Lottie won't be out till after New Year's.

KARL: She may look like an onion, but she smells like a garbage disposal.

SOOT: Oh, Karl. Because this year Lottie slipped on her driveway and broke her hip because of all the ice.

KARL: And she tastes like a septic tank.

SOOT: So, when Lottie gets here she's going to have a cast on her_____…Karl, where would they put the cast if you broke your hip?

KARL: Lottie doesn't have hips. She has pieces of raw whale skin wrapped around a septic tank in the middle.

SOOT: Karl doesn't like Lottie.

KARL: That's right.

SOOT: Karl thinks Lottie smells, but I think he's just kidding.

BETTE: HOW CAN YOU SMELL HER WITH ALCOHOL ON YOUR BREATH?

BOO: Oh God.

KARL: What did you say, woman?

BETTE: You're too drunk to smell anything.

BOO: Will you lay off all this drinking talk?

KARL: *(Holds up his drink.)* I think it's time your next stillborn was baptized, don't you, Soot?

SOOT: Karl…

(Karl pours his drink on Bette's lap. Bette has hysterics. Lights change.)

ACT II
Scene 22

Matt addresses the audience.

MATT: Twenty years later, Boo has dinner with his son.
(Boo, Matt.)

BOO: Well, how are things up at Dartmouth, Skip? People in the office ask me how my Ivy League son is doing.

MATT: It's all right.

BOO: Are there any pretty girls up there?

MATT: Uh huh.

BOO: So what are you learning up there?

MATT: Tess of the d'Urbervilles is a...I'm not up at Dartmouth anymore. I'm at Columbia in graduate school.

BOO: I know that. I meant Columbia. How is it?

MATT: Fine.

BOO: Why are you still going to school?

MATT: I don't know. What do you want me to do?

BOO: I don't know. Your mother and I got divorced, you know.

MATT: Yes, I know. We have discussed this, you know.

BOO: I don't understand why she wanted a divorce. I mean, we'd been separated for several years, why not just leave it at that?

MATT: She wants to feel independent, I guess.

BOO: I thought we might get back together. You know, I always found your mother very charming when she wasn't shouting. A man needs a woman, son. I think your old man's going to get teary for a second. Do you have any problems you want to talk over? *(Blinks his eyes.)* I'm just an old softie. *(Matt steps out of the scene. Boo stays in place.)*

MATT: *(To audience.)* At about the same time, Bette also has dinner with her son. *(Bette, Matt.)*

BETTE: Hello, Skippy dear. I made steak for you, and mashed potatoes and peas and cake. How many days can you stay?

MATT: I have to get back tomorrow.

BETTE: Can't you stay longer?

MATT: I really have to get back.

BETTE: You never stay long. I don't have much company, you know. And Polly Lydstone's son goes to her house for dinner twice a week, and her daughter Mary gave up her apartment and lives at home. And Judith Rankle's son moved home after college and commutes forty minutes to work.

MATT: And some boy from Pingry School came home after class and shot both his parents. So what?

BETTE: There's no need to get nasty.

MATT: I just don't want to hear about Polly Lydstone and Judith Rankle.

BETTE: You're the only one of my children that lived. You should see me more often.

(Matt looks aghast.)

MATT: That's not a fair thing to say.

BETTE: You're right. It's not fair of me to bring up the children that died; that's beside the point. I realize Boo and I must take responsibility for our own actions. Of course, the Church wasn't very helpful at the time, but nonetheless we had brains of our own, so there's no point in assigning blame. I must take responsibility for wanting children so badly that I foolishly kept trying over and over, hoping for miracles. Did you see the article in the paper, by the way, about how they've discovered a serum for people with the Rh problem that would have allowed me to have more babies if it had existed back then?

MATT: Yes I did. I wondered if you had read about that.

BETTE: Yes I did. It made me feel terribly sad for a little while; but then I thought, what's past is past. One has no choice but to accept facts. And I realized that you must live your own life, and I must live mine. My life may not have worked out as I wished, but still I feel a deep and inner serenity, and so you mustn't feel bad about me because I am totally happy and self-sufficient in my pretty sunlit apartment. And now I'm going to close my eyes, and I want you to go out into the world and live your life. Good-bye. God bless you. *(Closes her eyes.)*

MATT: *(To audience.)* I'm afraid I've made that conversation up totally.

(They start the scene over.)

BETTE: Hello, Skippy, dear. I made steak for you, and mashed potatoes and peas and cake. You know, you're the only one of my children that lived. How long can you stay?

MATT: Gee, I don't know. Uh, a couple of days. Three years. Only ten minutes, my car's double-parked. I could stay eight years if I can go away during the summer. Gee. I don't know.

(Lights change.)

ACT II

Scene 23

Matt addresses the audience.

MATT: Back in chronology, shortly after the unpleasant Christmas with the Hudlockes, Bette brings Boo back to Father Donnally. *(Exits.)*

(Bette, Boo, Father Donnally. Bette in a foul temper.)

BOO: *(Reading.)* I pledge in front of Father Donnally to give up drinking in order to save my marriage and to make my wife and son happy, and this time I mean it.

BETTE: Read the other part.

BOO: *(Reading.)* And I promise to tell my father to go to hell.

FATHER DONNALLY: Oh, I didn't see that part.

BETTE: Now sign it. *(Boo signs it. Crossly, to Father Donnally.)* Now bless us.

FATHER DONNALLY: Oh all right. In the name of the Father, Son, and Holy Ghost. Amen.

BETTE: Now let's go home.

(Bette and Boo cross to another part of the stage; Father Donnally exits.)

BETTE: Now if you give up drinking for good this time, maybe God will let this next baby live, Boo.

BOO: Uh huh.

BETTE: And I'm going to go to Mass daily. And Emily is praying.

BOO: Uh huh.

BETTE: You're not very talkative, Boo.

BOO: I don't have anything to say.

BETTE: Well you should have something to say. Marriage is a fifty-fifty proposition.

BOO: Where do you pick up these sayings? On the back of matchpacks?

BETTE: Why are you being nasty? Have you had a drink already?

BOO: No I haven't had a drink already. I just find it very humiliating to be constantly dragged in front of that priest all the time so he can hear your complaints about me.

BETTE: You have an idiotic sense of pride. Do you think he cares what you do? And if you don't want people to know you drink, then you shouldn't drink.

BOO: You are obsessed with drinking. Were you frightened at an early age by a drunk? What is the matter with you?

BETTE: What is the matter with *you?*

BOO: What is the matter with *you?*

BETTE: What is the matter with you?

BOO: What is the matter with you?

(This argument strikes them both funny, and they laugh. Lights change.)

ACT II

Scene 24

Matt addresses the audience.

MATT: Shortly after the second pledge, Bette and Skippy visit the Brennans to celebrate Joanie's birthday. Boo stays home, drunk or sulking, it's not clear. *(Margaret, Paul, Bette, Emily, Joan, and Matt. Joan looks pregnant; Bette also looks pregnant. Margaret comes downstage and addresses the audience.)*

MARGARET: All my children live home, it's so nice. Emily's here, back from the rest home. And Joanie's here because her marriage hasn't worked out and somebody has to watch all those children for her while she's working, poor thing. And Tom's here sometimes, when he gets fired or when his spastic colon is acting up really badly. Then he always goes off again, but I bet he ends up here for good eventually! *(Chuckles, pleased.)* The only one who hasn't moved back home is Betsy, because she's so stubborn, but maybe she'll end up here too someday. I just love having the children home, otherwise there'd be no one to talk to—unless I wanted to learn sign language with Paul. *(Laughs.)* Sometimes I'm afraid if I had to choose between having my children succeed in the world and live away from home, or having them fail and live home, that I'd choose the latter. But luckily, I haven't had to choose! *(Smiles, returns to the scene.)* Come on, everybody, let's celebrate Joanie's birthday, and don't anybody mention that she's pregnant with yet another baby.

BETTE: Every time I look at you, you're using nose spray.

JOAN: You just got here.

BETTE: But the last time I was here. You're going to give yourself a sinus infection.

JOAN: I already have a sinus infection.

MARGARET: *(To audience:)* The girls always fight. It's so cute. *(To Bette and Joan:)* Now, girls.

BETTE: Well, you use too much nose spray. You might hurt the baby inside you.

JOAN: Let's drop the subject of babies, shall we?

BETTE: I can't imagine why you're pregnant again.

EMILY: Happy birthday, Joan! *(Everyone looks at her.)* I made the cake. I better go get it. *(Exits.)*

MARGARET: Where's Booey, Bette?

BETTE: He's home, drunk or sulking, Skippy and I can't decide which. Where's Nikkos, Joan?

JOAN: Under a truck, I hope.

BETTE: Well, you married him. Everyone told you not to.

MARGARET: Let's change the subject. How are you doing in school, Skippy?

MATT: *(Glum.)* Fine.

MARGARET: Isn't that nice?

BETTE: Skippy always gets A's. Is little Mary Frances still getting F's? Maybe if you were home more, she'd do better.

JOAN: I can't afford to be home more. I don't have a life of leisure like you do.
(Enter Emily with the cake.)

EMILY: Happy birthday, Joan.

BETTE: Hush, Emily. If I had several children, I'd make time to spend with them.

JOAN: You have a home and a husband, and I don't have either.

BETTE: Well, it's your own fault.

EMILY: Please don't argue, Bette.

BETTE: Why do you say "Bette"? Why not "Joanie"? She's the one arguing.

EMILY: Don't anybody argue.

MARGARET: Don't excite yourself, Emily.

JOAN: You see what your talking has done? You're going to give Emily another breakdown.

EMILY: That's sweet of you to worry, Joanie, but I'm all right.

BETTE: *(To Joan.)* You're just a neurotic mess. You're going to ruin your children.

JOAN: Well, it's lucky you only have one to ruin, or else the mental ward wouldn't just have Emily in it.
(Emily has an asthma attack.)

MARGARET: This cake looks very nice, Emily. Why don't we all have some. I bet Skippy would like a piece. *(Margaret cuts the cake and passes it around.)*

EMILY: We forgot to have Joanie blow out the candles.

JOAN: There aren't any candles on the cake.

EMILY: Oh, I forgot them. I'm sorry, Joanie.

JOAN: Why should I have candles? I don't have anything else.

MARGARET: Poor Joanie.

BETTE: The dough's wet. Don't eat it, Skippy, it'll make you sick.

EMILY: It isn't cooked right?

BETTE: It's wet, it's wet. You didn't cook it enough.

JOAN: I don't like cake anyway.

MARGARET: Poor Joanie.

BETTE: Everything's always poor Joanie. But her baby's going to live.

EMILY: Oh, Bette.

JOAN: Well maybe we'll both have a miracle. Maybe yours'll live and mine'll die.

EMILY: Oh, Joanie.

BETTE: Stop saying that, Emily.

MARGARET: Girls, girls. This isn't conversation for the living room. Or for young ears.

PAUL: *(Choking on cake.)* #%#%#%GHGHR#%#%#******-***#@#@#*****.

MARGARET: Paul, stop it. Stop it.

> *(Paul falls over dead. Lights change.)*

ACT II
Scene 25

> *Matt puts a sheet over Paul and addresses the audience.*

MATT: The funeral of Paul Brennan.

> *(Paul in a chair with a sheet over him. Present are Matt, Bette, Boo, Margaret, Emily, Joan.)*

MARGARET: Paul was a fine husband. Good-bye, Paul. *(Teary.)*

BETTE: Boo, thank you for being sober today. *(Kisses him.)* Look how happy it makes Skippy.

BOO: Skippy's drunk.

BETTE: That's not funny.

> *(Enter Father Donnally.)*

FATHER DONNALLY: Dearly bereaved, Paul Brennan was a fine man, and now he's dead. I didn't know Paul very well, but I imagine he was a very nice man and everyone spoke well of him. Though he wasn't too able to speak well of them. *(Laughs.)*

> *(During the above, various characters look quizzically at Fr. Donnally's comments, wondering at their relevance and also finding his comments on colored people embarrasing and inappropriate. Especially Matt, Boo, and Joan.)*

FATHER DONNALLY: It's going to be hard not to miss him, but God put his children on this earth to adapt to circumstances, to do His will.

I was reminded of this fact the other morning, when I saw my colored garbageman collecting the refuse as I was on my way to say Mass. "Good morning, Father," he said, "Nice day." "And what's your name?" I said. "Percival Pretty, Father," he said. I smiled a little more and then I said, "And how are you—Percival?" And he said, "I'm doing the will of God, Father. God saw fit to take my little Buttermilk to Him, and now I'm emptying the garbage." "And who is little Buttermilk?" I said, and he said, "Why, Buttermilk was my daughter who broke her neck playing on the swings." And then he smiled. Colored folk have funny ideas for names. I knew one colored woman who named her daughter "January 22nd." It wasn't easy to forget her birthday!

(*Everyone looks appalled again.*)

FATHER DONNALLY: But I think Percival Pretty's smile is a lesson for us all, and so now when I think of Paul Brennan, I'm going to smile. (*Smiles.*) And then nothing can touch you. (*Shakes hands with Margaret.*) Be strong, dear.

EMILY: Thank you, Father, for your talk.

JOAN: (*To Paul's dead body.*) I've turned against Greeks after Nikkos. You were right, Dad, you were right!

MARGARET: Thank you, Joanie. That was a nice gesture.

FATHER DONNALLY: Hello, Bette. Hello, Boo. You're putting on weight, Bette.

BETTE: It's nothing. (*Sadly.*) I mean, it will be nothing.

(*Lights change.*)

ACT II
Scene 26

Matt addresses the audience.

MATT: Bette goes to the hospital for the fourth time, etcetera, etcetera. (*Exits.*)

(*Karl, Soot, Boo in their hospital "waiting" positions.*)

BOO: Pop. Eventually there's menopause, right? I mean, something happens, and then it stops, and…

KARL: Where are the Brennans? Have they lost the playing spirit?

BOO: Bette wasn't that way when I married her, was she?

SOOT: Karl, is there still a space between my eyes?

KARL: What did you say, Soot?

SOOT: Nothing. I'll wait till I get home. (*Smiles, feels between her eyebrows.*) Lottie always said when your eyebrows start to kiss, you better watch it.

KARL: Your mother's eyebrows are kissing, Bore.

SOOT: You make everything sound so dirty, Karl. I wish I hadn't said that.

KARL: You want to hear a dirty story? Bore, are you listening? Once there was a traveling salesman, Soot, who met a girl in a barn who was more stupid than you.

SOOT: I don't know this one.

KARL: The girl was an albino. Bore, you listening. She was an albino humpback with a harelip.

BOO: I'm going to get a drink. *(Exits.)*

KARL: And this albino humpback saw the traveling salesman with his dickey hanging out...

SOOT: Karl, I have heard this one.

KARL: And she saw his dickey, and she said, "What's that?" and he said, "That's my dickey."

SOOT: Karl, you told this story to Lottie, and she didn't like it.

KARL: And she said, "Why does it swing around like that?" and he said...Soot, what's the end of the story?

SOOT: Karl, I never listen to your stories.

KARL: WHAT'S THE ANSWER TO THE JOKE?

SOOT: *(Cries.)* Karl, I don't know. Something about a dickey. Maybe Bore knows. Booey? I have to go home and take a bath. I feel awful.
(Enter the Doctor. He drops the baby on the floor, exits. Karl and Soot stare at it a moment.)

SOOT: Catholics can't use birth control, can they? *(Laughs.)* That's a joke on someone.
(Enter Boo.)

KARL: You missed it, Boo.

BOO: Did it live?

KARL: Not unless they redefined the term.

SOOT: Don't tease Booey, Karl. Let's distract him, see if he remembers the joke.

KARL: You tell it, Soot.

SOOT: No, I don't like the joke. I just thought maybe he'd remember it.

BOO: It didn't live.

KARL: Tell the joke, Soot.

BOO: Pop, I don't feel like hearing a joke.

SOOT: Poor Booey.

BOO: I should probably see Bette, but I don't think I can face her.

SOOT: Why don't you go get a drink, Booey, you look awful. I've got to go home and check my forehead.

KARL: Tell the damn joke, Soot.

BOO: Pop, I don't want to hear a joke.

SOOT: It's all right, Booey. I'll tell it. Your father seems obsessed with it.

KARL: *(Rams his cigar in his mouth.)* Here, you'll need this.

SOOT: Oh, Karl. *(Laughs.)* All right, Booey, you ready?

BOO: I don't want to hear a joke.

KARL: You'll like it, Bore.

SOOT: Now, Booey…

    (Boo starts to exit; they follow.)

SOOT: …it seems there was this poor unfortunate, stupid crippled girl, and she
    met this salesman…

BOO: Will you two shut up? I don't want to hear a joke. *(Exits.)*

SOOT: He doesn't want to hear the joke.

KARL: You told it wrong, Soot.

SOOT: I'm sorry, Karl. I'm really not myself today. *(Touches between her eyes.)* I'm
    sorry, Booey. Booey!

    (They exit.)

ACT II

Scene 27

    Bette, playing rope or some such thing.

BETTE: What is the matter with Mary Jane?
    It isn't a cramp, and it isn't a pain,
    And lovely rice pudding's for dinner again,
    What is the *matter* with Mary Jane?
    Christopher Robin had weasles and sneezles,
    They bundled him into his bed.
    (Kneels, looks at imaginary gravestones; then to audience, sadly.)
    The names of the children are: Patrick Michael, February 26th;
    Christopher Tigger, March 8th; and Pooh Bear Eeyore, March 25th. Bonnie
    Wilson and I were, were… *(Calls.)* Father Donnally! Father Donnally…
    (Father Donnally enters into Bette's space.)

BETTE: Father Donnally, can you help me?

FATHER DONNALLY: I'll try. What's on your mind, Bette?

BETTE: I know sometimes one can misunderstand the will of God. But sex is for
    having babies, right? I mean, it's not just for marriage. Well, even if it is
    somewhat, I feel that I should be a mother; and I think it would be a sin
    for me not to try again. But I don't think Boo wants me to get pregnant
    again.

FATHER DONNALLY: Have you tried the rhythm method?

BETTE: But I *want* to get pregnant.

FATHER DONNALLY: What does your doctor say?

BETTE: The problem is that all the babies die. I don't see why I have to go through all this suffering. And Boo never helps me.

FATHER DONNALLY: I give a retreat for young married couples every year in the parish. Why don't you and your husband come to that? I'm sure it will help you if you're having trouble on the marriage couch.

BETTE: All right, I'll bring Booey to the retreat. Thank you, Father.

FATHER DONNALLY: You're welcome, Bette.

(Father Donnally exits.)

BETTE: *(Crosses away; calls out.)* Boo. Boo. Booey. Booey. Booey.

(Enter Boo.)

BOO: What?

BETTE: Booey, I'm pregnant again. Do you think I'm going to die?

(Lights change.)

ACT II

Scene 28

The retreat. Present are Bette, Boo, Matt; also Margaret, Emily, Joan, the dead Paul (with sheet still over him), Karl, Soot. Enter Father Donnally.

FATHER DONNALLY: In the name of the Father, of the Son, and of the Holy Ghost, Amen. Good evening, young marrieds. *(Looks about himself for a moment.)* Am I in the right room?

EMILY: I'm not married, Father. I hope you don't mind that I'm here.

FATHER DONNALLY: On the contrary. I'm delighted. I'm not married either. *(Laughs.)* The theme of marriage in the Catholic Church and in this retreat is centered around the story of Christ and the wedding feast at Cana. Jesus Christ blessed the young wedding couple at Cana, and when they ran out of expensive wine, He performed His first miracle—He took vats of water and He changed the water into wine. *(Holds up a glass.)* I have some wine right here. *(Sips it.)*

BOO: *(To Bette.)* He drinks. Why don't you try to get him to stop drinking?

BETTE: Be quiet, Boo.

FATHER DONNALLY: *(Laughs, nervously.)* Please don't talk when I'm talking. *(Starts his speech.)* Young marrieds have many problems to get used to. For some of them this is the first person of the opposite sex the other has ever known. The husband may not be used to having a woman in his bathroom. The wife may not be used to a strong masculine odor in her boudoir. Or then the wife may not cook well enough. How many marriages have floundered on the rocks of ill-cooked bacon? *(Pause.)* I used to amuse friends by imitating bacon in a saucepan. Would anyone like to see that? *(He looks around. Joan, Karl, and Soot raise their hands. After a moment, Emily, rather confused, raises her hand also.)*

(Father Donnally falls to the ground and does a fairly good—or if not good, at least unabashedly peculiar—imitation of bacon, making sizzling noises and contorting his body to represent becoming crisp. Toward the end, he makes sputtering noises into the air. Then he stands up again. All present applaud with varying degrees of approval or incredulity.)

FATHER DONNALLY: I also do coffee percolating. *(He does this.)* Pt. Pt. Ptptptptptptptptpt. Bacon's better. But things like coffee and bacon are important in a marriage, because they represent things that the wife does to make her husband happy. Or fat. *(Laughs.)* The wife cooks the bacon, and the husband brings home the bacon. This is how St. Paul saw marriage, although they probably didn't really eat pork back then, the curing process was not very well worked out in Christ's time, which is why so many of them followed the Jewish dietary laws even though they were Christians. I know I'm glad to be living now when we have cured pork and plumbing and showers rather than back when Christ lived. Many priests say they wish they had lived in Christ's time so they could have met Him; that would, of course, have been very nice, but I'm glad I live now and that I have a shower.

(Emily bothered by what he's just said, raises her hand.)

I'm not ready for questions yet, Emily.

(Emily lowers her hand; he sips his wine.)

Man and wife, as St. Paul saw it. Now the woman should obey her husband, but that's not considered a very modern thought, so I don't even want to talk about it. All right, don't obey your husbands, but if chaos follows, don't blame me. The Tower of Babel as an image of chaos has always fascinated me—

(Emily raises her hand.)

BETTE: Put your hand down, Emily.

(Emily does.)

FATHER DONNALLY: *(To Bette.)* Thank you. Now I don't mean to get off the point. The point is husband and wife, man and woman, Adam and rib. I don't want to dwell on the inequality of the sexes because these vary from couple to couple—sometimes the man is stupid, sometimes the woman is stupid, sometimes both are stupid. The point is man and wife are joined in holy matrimony to complete each other, to populate the earth and to glorify God. That's what it's for. That's what life is for. If you're not a priest or a nun, you normally get married.

(Emily raises her hand)

Yes, I know, you're not married, Emily. Not everyone gets married. But my comments today are geared toward the *married* people here.

(Emily takes down her hand.)

Man and wife are helpmates. She helps him, he helps her. In sickness and in health. Anna Karenina should not have left her husband, nor should she have jumped in front of a train. Marriage is not a step to be taken lightly. The Church does not recognize divorce; it does permit it, if you insist for legal purposes, but in the eyes of the Church you are still married and you can never be unmarried, and that's why you can never remarry after a divorce because that would be bigamy and that's a sin and illegal as well. *(Breathes.)* So, for God's sake, if you're going to get married, pay attention to what you're doing, have conversations with the person, figure out if you *really* want to live with that person for years and years and years, because you can't change it. Priests have it easier. If I don't like my pastor, I can apply for a transfer. If I don't like a housekeeper, I can get her fired. *(Looks disgruntled.)* But a husband and wife are *stuck* together. So know what you're doing when you get married. I get so *sick* of these people coming to me after they're married, and they've just gotten to know one another *after* the ceremony, and they've discovered they have nothing in common and they hate one another. And they want me to come up with a solution. *(Throws up his hands.)* What can I do? There is no solution to a problem like that. I can't help them! It puts me in a terrible position. I can't say get a divorce, that's against God's law. I can't say go get some on the side, that's against God's law. I can't say just pretend you're happy and maybe after a while you won't know the difference because, though that's not against God's law, not that many people know how to do that, and if I suggested it to people, they'd write to the Bishop complaining about me and then he'd transfer me to some godforsaken place in Latin America without a shower, and all because these people don't know what they're doing when they get married. *(Shakes his head.)* So I mumble platitudes to these people who come to me with these insoluble problems, and I think to myself,

"Why didn't they *think* before they got married? Why does no one ever *think?* Why did God make people stupid?" *(Pause.)* Are there any questions? *(Bette raises her hand, as does Emily. Father acknowledges Bette.)*

BETTE: Father, if I have a little girl rather than a boy, do you think it might live? Should I pray for this?

FATHER DONNALLY: You mean…a little girl to clean house?

BETTE: *(Irritated.)* No. I don't mean a little girl to clean house. I mean that the doctors say that sometimes a little girl baby fights infection better than a little boy baby, and that maybe if I have a little girl baby, the fighting between the Rh positive blood in her body and the Rh negative blood in my body would not destroy her, and she might live. *(Pause.)* Should I pray for this?

FATHER DONNALLY: By all means, pray for it. Just don't get your hopes up too high though, maybe God doesn't want you to have any more babies. It certainly doesn't sound like it to me.

BETTE: But I *can* pray?

FATHER DONNALLY: Yes. You can. No one can stop you.

BETTE: That's what I thought.

(Emily raises her hand.)

FATHER DONNALLY: *(Dreading whatever she's going to say.)* Yes, Emily?

EMILY: Do you think maybe it's my fault that all of Bette's babies die? Because I left the convent?

FATHER DONNALLY: Yes, I do.

EMILY: *(Stricken.)* Oh my God.

FATHER DONNALLY: I'm sorry, Emily, I was just kidding. Are there any questions about newly married couples? *(Pause; no one stirs.)* Well I don't have time for any more questions anyway. We'll take a short break for refreshments, and then Father McNulty will talk to you about sexual problems which I'm not very good at, and then you can all go home. Thank you for your attention. In the name of the Father, and of the Son, and of the Holy Ghost. Amen. *(Starts to exit.)*

EMILY: Father…

FATHER DONNALLY: I was just kidding, Emily, I am sorry. Excuse me, I have to go to the bathroom. *(Exits in a hurry.)*

JOAN: You know, he makes a better piece of bacon than he does a priest.

EMILY: I don't think he should joke about something like that.

MARGARET: He's a priest, Emily.

EMILY: I know you're right, Mom, but everyone should want to meet Our Saviour, that's more important than having a shower…

MARGARET: Don't talk anymore, Emily.

BETTE: Did that make you feel better, Boo? Are you going to be easier to live with?

BOO: *(Sarcastic.)* Yes, it's all better now.

BETTE: Why won't you let anyone help us?

BOO: What help? He just said that we shouldn't get married, and that if we did, not to bother him with our problems.

BETTE: That's not what he said at all.

MARGARET: Bette, don't talk anymore. Hello, Mrs. Hudlocke. Did you enjoy the talk?

SOOT: I'm sorry, what?

MARGARET: Did you enjoy Father's talk?

SOOT: You know, I can't hear you. I think I'm going deaf. God, I hope so.

MARGARET: What do you mean?

SOOT: I'm sorry, I really can't hear you. *(Laughs.)* I haven't been able to hear Karl for about three days. *(Laughs.)* It's wonderful.

BETTE: You should see an ear specialist.

SOOT: What?

BETTE: Oh, never mind.

EMILY: Mom, don't you think…

MARGARET: Emily, I said not to talk.

BETTE: Well, if you don't want us to talk, what do you want us to do?

MARGARET: Don't be cranky, Betsy. We'll just all wait for Father McNulty. Maybe he'll have something useful to say.

(*They all wait. Soot smiles.*)

SOOT: *(To audience.)* Little blessings. *(Laughs.)*

(*Lights change.*)

ACT II
Scene 29

Matt addresses the audience. Bette, Boo, and the dead Paul stay onstage.

MATT: Twenty years later, or perhaps only fifteen, Bette files for a divorce from Boo. They have been separated for several years, since shortly after the death of the final child; and at the suggestion of a therapist Bette has been seeing, Bette decides to make the separation legal in order to formalize the breakup psychologically, and also to get better, and more regular, support payments. Boo, for some reason, decides to contest the divorce; and so there has to be testimony. Margaret and Joanie decide that Catholics can't testify in divorce cases, even though Bette had eventually testified in Joanie's divorce; and so they refuse to testify, frightening Emily into agreeing with them also. Blah blah blah, etcetera. So in lieu of other witnesses, I find myself sort of having to testify against Boo during my sophomore year at college. I am trying to work on a paper on Thomas Hardy, but find it difficult to concentrate. I fly home for the divorce proceedings. My mother's lawyer reminds me of my grandfather Paul.

(Bette and Boo on opposite sides. Matt, C., testifies, questioned by Paul who comes to life with no to-do. He still speaks in Paul's incomprehensible speech, but otherwise is quite lawyerly.)

PAUL: Ehl ee att, oo oou ing orr agher uz acgh acgha@@-lehc? [Tell me, Matt, do you think your father was an alcoholic?]

MATT: What?

PAUL: *(Irritated he can't be understood, as Paul used to be.)* Oo oou ing, orr agher uz acgh acgha@@lehc? [Do you think your father was an alcoholic?]

MATT: Yes, I do feel he drank a fair amount.

PAUL: Uht us ee acgh acgha@@lehc? [But was he an alcoholic?]

MATT: I'm really not in the position to say if anyone is actually an alcoholic or not.

BETTE: I have a calendar here from the twelve years of our marriage. Everytime it says HD, that stands for half-drunk. And everytime it says DD, that stands for dead drunk. I offer this as Exhibit A.

PAUL: *(Telling her it's not her turn.)* Eeez own awk enn oo aht ahn uh ann. [Please don't talk when you're not on the stand.]

BETTE: What?

BOO: I was never dead drunk. She has this thing about drunks.

MATT: *(To Bette.)* He said you shouldn't talk when you're not on the stand.

BETTE: I didn't.

PAUL: *(To Bette.)* Ssssh. *(Long question to Matt.)* Ehl ee att, ihd oo eheh ee or ah#er ah ehey ohazsn, itt or uher? [Tell me, Matt, did you ever see your father, on any occasion, hit your mother?]

MATT: Yes. Hardy wrote *Tess of the d'Urbervilles* in 1891.

PAUL: *(Irritated.)* As ott ut uh ass. [That's not what I asked.]

MATT: Oh, I'm sorry. I misheard the question.

PAUL: Ihd ee itt er? [Did he hit her?] *(Makes hitting motion.)*

MATT: Yes I did see him hit her.

PAUL: Ah!

MATT: Of course, she hit him too. They both hit each other. Especially when they were driving. It was fairly harrowing from the back seat.

BETTE: He started it.

BOO: She'd talk and talk like it was a sickness. There was no way of shutting her up.

MATT: Well I would have appreciated your not arguing when you were driving a car.

PAUL: *(To Bette and Boo.)* Ee i###et! [Be quiet!]

MATT: Or at least left me home.

PAUL: Shhh! *(Back to questioning Matt.)* Ehl ee att, oo oo ih or ohn lhahf eher agh uh ink? [Tell me, Matt, do you in your own life ever have a drink?]

MATT: No I don't know any happily married couples. Certainly not relatives.

PAUL: *(Irritated.)* As ott ut uh ass. [That's not what I asked.]

MATT: Oh, I'm sorry. I thought that's what you asked.

PAUL: Oo oo ih or ohn lhahf eher agh uh ink? [Do you in your own life ever have a drink?]

MATT: No, my paper is on whether Eustacia Vye in *The Return of the Native* is neurotic or psychotic, and how she compares to Emily. That isn't what you asked either, is it? I'm sorry. What?

PAUL: *Oo oo ink?* [Do you drink?]

MATT: Ink?

PAUL: *(Gesturing as if drinking.)* Ink! Ink!

MATT: Ohhh. No, I don't drink actually.

PAUL: Ehl ee att, urr oo uhaagee ehn or errens epyrateted? [Tell me, Matt, were you unhappy when your parents separated?]

(Matt is at a loss. Paul must repeat the word "separated" several times, with hand gestures, before Matt understands.)

MATT: No, I was glad when they separated. The arguing got on my nerves a lot. *(Pause.)* I'd hear it in my ear even when they weren't talking. When I was a child, anyway.

PAUL: Ehl ee att, oo oo ink or aher uz uh goooh aher? [Tell me, Matt, do you think your father was a good father?]

MATT: Yes, I am against the war in Vietnam. I'm sorry, is that what you asked?

PAUL: Doo oo ink ee uz a goooh ahzer? [Do you think he was a good father?]

MATT: Oh. Yes. I guess he's been a good father. *(Looks embarrassed.)*

PAUL: *(Pointing at Boo, pushing for some point.)* Buh dyoo oo ink ee ad ohme or uh inkng bahblim? [But do you think he had some sort of drinking problem?] *(Makes drinking gesture.)*

MATT: Yes, I guess he probably does have some sort of drinking problem. *(Becoming worked up.)* I mean it became such an issue it seems suspicious to me that he didn't just stop, he kept saying there was no... *(Pulls back.)* well, it was odd he didn't stop. It's really not my place to be saying this. I would prefer I wasn't here. *(Pause. Matt is uncomfortable, has been uncomfortable relating to Boo for the whole scene.)*

PAUL: Orr ehcoooz, att. [You're excused, Matt.]

MATT: What?

BETTE: He said you were excused.

MATT: Oh good.

(Paul exits, or goes back undersheet.)

BETTE: Thank you, Skippy. *(Kisses him.)*

BOO: Well, son. Have a good time back at school.

MATT: Thank you. I'm behind in this paper I'm doing. *(Pause.)* I have to get the plane.

BOO: Well, have a good trip. *(Looks embarrassed, exits.)*

MATT: Thank you.

(Bette also exits. Matt addresses the audience. He is upset and tries to use doing his essay as a means of stifling the discomfort he felt testifying. But it doesn't work.)

MATT: Eustacia Vye is definitely neurotic. Whether she is psychotic as well is...In *Return of the Native*, Hardy is dealing with some of the emotional, as well as physical, dangers in the...One has to be very careful in order to protect oneself from the physical and emotional dangers in the world. One must always be careful crossing streets in traffic. One should try not to live anywhere near a nuclear power plant. One should never walk past a building that may have a sniper on top of it. In the summer one should be on the alert against bees and wasps.

As to emotional dangers, one should always try to avoid crazy people, especially in marriage or live-in situations, but in everyday life as well. Although crazy people often mean well, meaning well is not enough. On some level Attila the Hun may have meant well.

Sometimes it is hard to decide if a person is crazy, like Eustacia Vye in *The Return of the Native*, which is the topic of this paper. Some people may seem sane at first, and then at some later point turn out to be totally crazy. If you are at dinner with someone who suddenly seems insane, make up some excuse why you must leave dinner immediately. If they don't know you well, you can say you're a doctor and pretend that you just heard your beeper. If the crazy person should call you later, either to express anger at your abrupt leave-taking or to ask for medical advice, claim the connection is bad and hang up. If they call back, I'm afraid you'll have to have your phone number changed again. When you call the phone company to arrange this, if the person on the line seems stupid, hostile, or crazy, simply hang up and call the phone company back again. This may be done as many times as necessary *until you get someone sane.* As the phone company has many employees. *(Breathes.)* It is difficult to totally protect oneself, of course, and there are many precautions that one thinks of only when it's too late. But, as Virginia Woolf pointed out in *To the Lighthouse,* admittedly in a different context, the attempt is all.

Sometime after the divorce, five years or fifteen or something, Skippy has dinner with Karl and Soot and Margaret and Paul. Karl is near eighty, Margaret is senile, and Paul and Soot are dead.

ACT II

Scene 30

Matt sits at a table with all four. Paul and Soot have their heads on the table, dead. Karl seems fairly normal and himself; Margaret is distracted and vague.

MATT: Hello. Nice to see you all.

MARGARET: Emily! Huh-huh-huh. Tom! Nurse! Huh-huh huh.

(Note: The "huh-huh-huh" sound is not like laughter, but is a nervous tic, said softly and rather continuously throughout the scene. Technically speaking, it's like a mild vocal exercise using the diaphragm, like an ongoing cough reflex with no real cough behind it. A tic.)

KARL: You're Skip, aren't you?

MATT: Yes. You remember me?

KARL: Yes I remember you.

MARGARET: Doctor. Mama. Huh-huh-huh. Huh-huh-huh.

KARL: *(To Margaret.)* Shut up.

MATT: *(To Karl, with seriousness.)* What do you think I should do with my life?

KARL: Well, don't marry Soot.

MATT: Yes, but you know—

MARGARET: Emily! Huh-huh-huh.

MATT: Everyone I know is divorced except for you and Soot, and Margaret and Paul. Of course, Soot and Paul are dead, but you all stayed married right up until death. And I wondered what mistakes you thought I could avoid based on all your experience.

KARL: Don't expect much, that's for starters. Look at Bette and Bore. She kept trying to change Bore. That's idiotic. Don't try to change anybody. If you don't like them, be mean to them if you want; try to get them committed if that amuses you, but don't ever expect to *change* them.

(Matt considers this.)

MATT: Do you agree with that, grandma?

MARGARET: *(Seeing Matt for the first time, leaning over to him.)* Go to the baperdy sun ride zone a bat.

MATT: Baperdy?

MARGARET: Lamin fortris trexin home. Emily!

KARL: It's too bad Paul's not still alive. It would be interesting to hear them talk together now.

(Matt laughs at this.)

MATT: Grandma, try to be lucid. I think Karl's advice makes sense, sort of, if you're in a bad marriage. But what if you're not in a bad marriage?

MARGARET: When the bob?

MATT: I said, do you agree with Karl? Or do you see something more optimistic?

MARGARET: I want Emily to clean the mirrors with milk of magnesia. I see people in the mirrors and they don't go away.

KARL: At least that's a complete sentence.

MATT: Emily's not here right now.

MARGARET: Everyone's so late. Dabble morning hunting back, Emily. Huh-huh-huh.

MATT: *(Gives up on Margaret; back to Karl.)* You know, I didn't know you and Soot back when you were young, or Margaret and Paul either, for that matter. Maybe your marriages were happy. I have no way of knowing.

KARL: I never expected much from life. I wanted to get my way in everything, and that's about all. What did you ask?

MARGARET: Huh-huh-huh. Joan. Emily.

MATT: Why did you marry Soot?

KARL: No reason. She was much prettier when she was younger.

MATT: But surely you didn't marry her because she was pretty.

KARL: Don't tell me what I did.

MATT: And why did everyone call her Soot? How did she get the name Soot?

KARL: I don't remember. Was her name Soot? I thought it was something else.

MATT: I think her name was Soot. Do you think I misheard it all these years?

KARL: I couldn't say.

MATT: Why were you so mean to Soot?

KARL: Why do you want to know?

MATT: Because I see all of you do the same thing over and over, for years and years, and you never change. And my fear is that I can see all of you but not see myself, and maybe I'm doing something similar, but I just can't see it. What I mean to say is: did you all *intend* to live your lives the way you did?

KARL: Go away. I don't like talking to you. You're an irritating young man.

(Matt leaves the scene. Karl, Margaret, Soot, and Paul exit or fade into darkness.)

ACT II
Scene 31

MATT: *(Trying to find his place. To audience.)* Back into chronology again. Bette had the first baby, that is, the first dead baby, in 1951 or something. And then the second one in 1953 or 4 or something, and then…
(Enter Emily.)

EMILY: Hello, Skippy, dear. How does this sound to you? *(Reads from a note.)* "Please forgive my annoying qualities. I know that I talk too much about a thing and that I make people nervous that I do so. I am praying that I improve that fault and beg that you be patient with me."

MATT: Who is that to, Emily?

EMILY: I don't know. Who do you think it should be to?

MATT: I don't know. It would be up to you.

EMILY: Do you think it's all right?

MATT: I don't think you should be so hard on yourself, but otherwise I think it's fine.

EMILY: Oh, thank you. *(Exits.)*

MATT: Okay. Just as dreams must be analyzed, so must the endless details of waking life be considered.

Having intelligence allows one to analyze problems and to make sense of one's life. This is difficult to achieve but with perseverance and persistence it is possible…not even to get out of bed in the morning. To sleep. To sleep, perchance to dream, to take the phone off the hook and simply be unreachable. This is less *dramatic* than suicide, but more *reversible.*

I can't make sense out of these things anymore. Um, Bette goes to the hospital for the third time, and there's the second dead baby, and then the fourth time, and the third dead baby, and then some time after Father Donnally's marriage retreat, Bette goes to the hospital for the fifth time. The *last* child of Bette and Boo.

ACT II

Scene 32

Enter Boo. He and Matt are in their "waiting" positions, back in the hospital.

BOO: You don't have to wait here, Skip, if you don't want.

MATT: It's all right.

BOO: Who knows, maybe it will live. The doctors say if it's a girl, girls sometimes fight harder for life. Or something. *(Pause.)* You doing well in school?

MATT: Uh huh.

(The doctor throws the baby, in a pink blanket, in from offstage.)

DOCTOR: *(Offstage.)* It was a girl.

BOO: You have any problems you want to talk over, son? Your old man could help you out.

MATT: I'll be outside a minute. *(Exits.)*

(Enter Bette.)

BOO: Bette, let's not have any more. *(Mournfully.)* I've had enough babies. They get you up in the middle of the night, dead. They dirty their cribs, dead. They need constant attention, dead. No more babies.

BETTE: I don't love you anymore, Boo.

BOO: What?

BETTE: Why do you say what? Can't you hear?

BOO: Why do they never have a bar in this hospital? Maybe there's one on another floor.

BETTE: I'm tired of feeling alone talking to you.

BOO: Maybe I'll take the elevator to another floor and check.

BETTE: They don't have bars in hospitals, Boo.

BOO: I think I'll walk down. See you later. *(Exits.)*

BETTE: I feel alone, Boo. Skippy, are you there? Skippy?

(Enter Matt.)

MATT: Yes.

BETTE: Would you move this for me?

(She indicates dead baby on floor. He gingerly places it offstage.)

BETTE: Your father's gone away. All the babies are dead. You're the only thing of value left in my life, Skippy.

MATT: *(With growing anger.)* Why do you call me Skippy? Why don't you call me Matt?

BETTE: It's my favorite movie.

MATT: My favorite movie is *Citizen Kane.* I don't call you *Citizen Kane.*

BETTE: Why are you being fresh?

MATT: I don't know.

BETTE: I don't want to put any pressure on you, Skippy dear, but you're the only reason I have left for living now.

MATT: Ah.

BETTE: You're so unresponsive.

MATT: I'm sorry. I don't know what to say.

BETTE: You're a typical Capricorn, cold and ungiving. I'm an Aries, we like fun, we do three things at once. We make life decisions by writing our options on little pieces of paper and then throwing them up in the air and going "Wheeee!" Wee wee wee, all the way home. I should have had more babies, I'm very good with babies. Babies *give* to you, then they grow up and they don't give. If I'd had more, I wouldn't mind as much. I don't mean to be critical, it's just that I'm so very... *(Looks sad, shakes her head.)* I need to go to bed. Come and read to me from A.A. Milne until I fall asleep, would you?

MATT: All right.

(Bette starts to leave.)

BETTE: *(Suddenly tearful.)* I don't want to call you Matt.

MATT: That's all right. It's fine. I'll be in to read to you in a minute, okay?

BETTE: Okay. *(Bette exits.)*

MATT: So I read her to sleep from *The House at Pooh Corner.* And then I entered high school, and then I went to college, and then they got divorced, and then I went to graduate school. I stopped studying Thomas Hardy for a while and tried Joseph Conrad. Oh the horror, the horror. I'm afraid what happened next will sound rather exaggerated, but after she divorced Boo, Bette felt very lonely and unhappy for several years, and then she married another alcoholic, and then after two years that broke up, and then she got cancer. By this time I'm thirty, and I visit her once more in the hospital.

ACT II

Scene 33

Emily pushes Bette on in a wheelchair. Bette doesn't look well.

EMILY: Doesn't Bette look well today?

MATT: Very well.

EMILY: Let's join hands. *(Holds Matt's and Bette's hands.)* In the name of the Father, and of the Son, and of the Holy Ghost, Amen. Heavenly Father, please lift this sickness from our beloved Bette. We place ourselves in Your hands. Amen. *(To Bette.)* Do you feel any better?

BETTE: The pain is a little duller.

EMILY: Well, maybe I better go to the hospital chapel and pray some more.

BETTE: That would be nice, Emily. Thank you.

(Emily exits.)

BETTE: I've spent a lot of time in hospitals.

MATT: Yes.

BETTE: I sometimes wonder if God is punishing me for making a second marriage outside the Church. But Father Ehrhart says that God forgives me, and besides the second marriage is over now anyway.

MATT: I don't think God punishes people for specific things.

BETTE: That's good.

MATT: I think He punishes people in general, for no reason.

BETTE: *(Laughs.)* You always had a good sense of humor, Skippy. The chemotherapy hasn't been making my hair fall out after all. So I haven't needed those two wigs I bought. The woman at Lord and Taylor's looked at me so funny when I said I needed them because my hair was going to fall out. Now *she* didn't have a good sense of humor. Emily brought me this book on healing, all about these cases of people who are very ill and then someone prays over them and places their hand on the place where the tumor is, and there's this feeling of heat where the tumor is, and then the patient gets completely cured. Would you pray over me, and place your hand on my hip?

MATT: I'm afraid I don't believe in any of that.

BETTE: It won't kill you to try to please me.

MATT: All right. *(Puts his hand on her hip.)*

BETTE: Now say a prayer.

MATT: *(Said quickly as befits a parochial school childhood.)* Hail Mary, full of grace, the Lord is with thee. Blessed art thou amongst women, and blessed is the fruit of thy womb, Jesus. Holy Mary, mother of God, pray for us sinners, now and at the hour of our death, amen.

BETTE: I think I feel a warmth there.

MATT: *(Noncommittal.)* That's good.

BETTE: You're so cold, you won't give anything.

MATT: If I don't believe in prayer, you shouldn't make me pray. It feels funny.

BETTE: You're just like your father—unresponsive.

MATT: Let's not argue about this.

BETTE: All right. *(On a pleasanter subject.)* Do you remember when you used to smell your father's breath to see if he'd been drinking? You were such a cute child. I saw your father last week. He came to the hospital to visit.

MATT: Oh, how is he?

BETTE: Well, he's still mad at me about my second marriage, but in some ways he's always been a sweet man. I think the years of drinking have done something to his brain though. He'll be talking and then there'll be this long pause like he's gone to sleep or something, and then finally he'll go on again, like nothing's happened.

(Enter Boo, holding flowers.)

BOO: Bette?

BETTE: Oh, Boo, I was just talking about you. Look, Skippy's here.

BOO: Oh, Skip. How are you?

MATT: I'm fine. Hi. How are you?

BOO: You look good.

MATT: Oh yes? Do you want a chair?

BOO: What?

MATT: I'll get you a chair. *(He does.)*

BOO: Skip looks good.

BETTE: Yes.

MATT: Do you want to sit?

(Boo looks uncomprehending.)

MATT: I've brought you a chair.

BOO: Oh thank you. *(Sits.)*

BETTE: The flowers are lovely.

BOO: I brought you flowers.

BETTE: Thank you.

(Boo hands them to her.)

BOO: *(To Matt.)* Your mother still looks very pretty.

MATT: Mother said you came to visit last week.

BOO: I came last week.

BETTE: He repeats himself all the time.

BOO: What?

BETTE: I said, you repeat yourself. *(Boo looks annoyed.)* But it's charming. *(To Matt.)* Your father flirted with the second-shift nurse.

BOO: Your old man still has an eye for the ladies. I was here last week and there was this… *(Long pause; he stares, blank.)*

BETTE: *(To Matt.)* See, he's doing it now. Boo, are you there? Boo? *(Sings to herself)* God bless Bette and Boo and Skippy, Emily and Boo…

BOO: *(Comes back, continues.)* …nurse, and she liked your old man, I think.

BETTE: She thought he was her grandfather.

BOO: What?

BETTE: You're too old for her.

BOO: What?

MATT: Maybe he's gone deaf.

BOO: No, I can hear. I think it's my brain.

BETTE: Do you remember when you tried to vacuum the gravy?

BOO: No.

BETTE: Well, you did. It was very funny. Not at the time, of course. And how you used to keep bottles hidden in the cellar. And all the dead babies.

BOO: *(Smiles, happy.)* Yes. We had some good times.

BETTE: Yes, we did. And do you remember that time after we got divorced when I came by your office because Mrs. Wright died?

MATT: Mrs. Wright?

BETTE: You were at college, and I didn't have her very long. She was a parakeet.

MATT: *(Suddenly comprehending.)* Ah.

BETTE: And I called her Mrs. Wright because she lived in a Frank Lloyd Wright birdcage, I think. Actually it was a male parakeet but I liked the name better. Anyway, I kept Mrs. Wright free on the screen porch, out of the cage, because she liked it that way, but she'd always try to follow me to the kitchen, so I'd have to get to the porch door before Mrs. Wright, and I always did. Except this one time, we had a tie, and I squashed Mrs. Wright in the door. Mary Roberts Rinehart wrote a novel called *The Door* but I like her *Tish* stories better. Well, I was very upset, and it almost made me wish I was still married to Boo so he could pick it up. So I went to Boo's office and I said, "Mrs. Wright is lying on the rug, squashed, come help," and he did. *(To Boo, with great affection.)* You were very good. *(To Matt.)* But then I think he went out and got drunk.

BOO: I remember that parakeet.

MATT: Why did you drink? *(To Bette.)* Why did you keep trying to have babies? Why didn't Soot leave Karl? Why was her name Soot?

BETTE: I don't know why her name was Soot. I never had a parakeet that talked. I even bought one of those records that say "Pretty blue boy, pretty blue boy," but it never picked it up. Boo picked Mrs. Wright up. As a joke, I called people up and I played the record over the phone, pretty blue boy, pretty blue boy; and people kept saying, "Who is this?" Except Emily, she tried to have a conversation with the record.

BOO: I remember that parakeet. You shut the door on it.

BETTE: We moved past that part of the story, Boo. Anyway, then I called Bonnie Wilson and I played the record for her, and she knew it was me right away, she didn't even have to ask. It's nice seeing your parents together again, isn't it, Skippy?

MATT: *(Taken aback, but then it is nice.)* Yes, very nice.

BOO: *(To Matt.)* I was just remembering when you were a little boy, Skip, and how very thrilled your mother and I were to have you. You had all this hair on your head, a lot of hair for a baby; we thought, we have a little monkey here, but we were very happy to have you, and I said to your mother... *(Pause; he has another blackout; stares...)*

BETTE: Ooops, there he goes again. Boo? Boo? *(Feels pain.)* I better ring for the nurse. I need a shot for pain.

MATT: Should I go?

BETTE: No. Wait till the nurse comes.

BOO: *(Coming back.)* ...to your mother, "Where do you think this little imp of a baby came from?"

BETTE: We finished that story, Boo.

BOO: Oh.

MATT: I do need to catch my train.

BETTE: Stay a minute. I feel pain. It'll go in a minute.

(Matt smiles, looks away, maybe for the nurse. Bette closes her eyes, and is motionless.)

BOO: Bette? Betsy?

MATT: Is she sleeping?

(Matt with some hesitation feels for a pulse in her neck.)
(Enter Emily.)

EMILY: Oh hello, Boo. It's nice to see you. Are you all right, Skippy?

MATT: She died, Emily.

EMILY: Then she's with God. Let's say a prayer over her.

(Emily and Boo pray by Bette's body. Music to "Bette and Boo" round is heard softly. Matt speaks to the audience.)

MATT: Bette passed into death, and is with God. She is in heaven where she has been reunited with the four dead babies, and where she waits for Boo, and for Bonnie Wilson, and Emily, and Pooh Bear and Eeyore, and Kanga and Roo; and for me.

(Lights dim.)

END OF PLAY

AFTERWORD

I feel particularly close to this play, because it is the only one of mine that is directly autobiographical, telling the rather sad story of my parents' marriage and a bit about my place in it.

The play has a rather long writing history.

In 1972, Albert Innaurato and I were accepted for a month's stay at the Edward Albee Writers Foundation in Montauk, Long Island. (Albee generously makes available to beginning writers a residence he has, as a place to come and work in quiet, by the seashore.)

In college, I had become one of those people who expressed the upset of their family troubles by translating them into amusing if dark anecdotes over dinner conversation. In family systems theory, this is called being the mascot.

However, watching repetitive suffering is very irritating and upsetting, and transforming one's view of it into some combination of sad and funny seems as sensible a thing to do with it as any.

So I had often told Albert stories of my family; and since I was feeling stuck in my writing at the Albee Foundation, Albert suggested I write something based directly on my family. I decided to do this, but strictly as an exercise, intending for it never to be produced. And indeed in the first draft, I used all the real names.

I showed this one act to my playwriting teacher at Yale, Howard Stein. He was very enthusiastic and, without my knowledge, showed it to one of the Drama School directors, who suddenly wanted to do it in a full-scale production.

These student productions were big deals in the world of Yale Drama School—the actors were good, you got full rehearsal (as opposed to the catch-as-catch-can rehearsals at the cabaret), you got full sets, costumes, lights.

I tried to convince the director to do another play of mine, but he wanted this one. So I changed most of the names (I'll explain which ones I didn't later), and I decided that since I was in New Haven, Connecticut, and my mother was in New Jersey, there was no reason she would have to hear about this play.

This version, which lasted about forty-five minutes, was produced on a double bill with a play by William Hauptman in spring of 1973.

The one act had the same characters and the same number of stillborn children, but otherwise was much more sketchlike, and its emotional impact was far more elliptical. For instance, the scene at Thanksgiving, Bette's phone call, Matt's dinner with the dead grandparents, the divorce scene, the final hospital scene—all these were not in this early version.

At Yale it was well directed by Bill Ludel, and featured (among others) Kate McGregor-Stewart as Bette, John Rothman as Boo, Franchelle Stewart Dorn as Emily, Walton Jones as Fr. Donnally, and Sigourney Weaver as Soot.

At Yale my work had been controversial up to this point, but *Bette and Boo* seemed to win over a far larger audience to my work and was said to have more of a sense of compassion in the midst of the dark humor.

There were subsequently four other productions (that I know of) of the one-act version. The first was at Williamstown Theatre's Second Company, directed by Peter Schifter. I didn't see this production, but heard positive reports, and was especially gratified to hear it was a big success when presented at a women's prison where the inmates apparently got into cheering on Bette and, well, booing Boo.

Then there was a summer Yale cabaret version, directed by Walton Jones, and featuring Christine Estabrook as Bette, Charles Levin as Boo, and Meryl Streep as bitter sister Joan. Then a workshop at Chicago's St. Nicholas Theatre Company (now closed, and lamented). And finally a Princeton College under-graduate production, directed by Mitchell Ivers and with actress-writer Winnie Holzman a memorable, giggling Soot.

Princeton, of course, is in New Jersey; and though it was a good hour from where my mother lived, somehow she heard about it and announced she want-ed to come.

My mother and father did have an Rh negative blood incompatibility; and my mother did have three stillbirths because of this. (I added one in the play.) And though my mother did have a sense of humor, I was worried how she would respond to my surreal and odd way of presenting what happened.

So I tried to talk her out of going, but I couldn't. Then I told her I want-ed her to read it first, so she knew what she was in for. She did read it, and then went to the production, and really liked it. She thought I got my father quite accurately; she loved the portrayal of his father (whom she hated), and she thought I got her family well. Plus, in truth, I think she liked that she was the leading role in the play.

So I always felt somewhat blessed in feeling my mother accepted the idea of this play, since the full-length version was not written or produced until six years after her death.

My father's nickname was indeed Boo. I tried to change it—to Bud, say; or Bubba—but I found it so inescapable that he was called Boo and Booey and (by his father alone) Bore. So I couldn't let go of the name Boo.

My father's mother's nickname was Mud. In the Yale version I left it as

Mud; but when Joseph Papp was eventually going to present the full length play in New York, I felt in deference to my father's siblings who were still around, I should change the name, in order to emphasize that the roles of Boo's parents and Bette's family were indeed fictionalized. They are not entirely fictionalized, of course, but partially so. So I spent a few hours making lists of really odd names—Dirt, Foote, Dust, Grime—but eventually settled on the name of Soot.

(A stray other thing about names. The name Bette is one syllable, pronounced "Bet." This contrasts better with her nickname of Betsy. Yes, I know that Bette Davis came to be called by her nickname "Betty" rather than by the one syllable Bette; people got so used to this that they assumed the name "Bette" was pronounced "Betty;" but it isn't. You don't look at "Bette Midler" and pronounce it "Betty Midler." So please call my play "The Marriage of Bette and Boo," not "The Marriage of Betty and Boo.")

Papp decided to do the play in 1983, but I suddenly got concerned about my father reading about the play in the paper. He and I were not close, unfortunately; but he was a sweet man, and I started to envision him reading reviews of this play using his real nickname, and talking about Boo's alcoholism. So I withdrew the play from Papp, who was very understanding.

A year or so later, my father had a stroke which made him go away mentally. So now he'd have no knowledge of the play, and so I felt free again to have it done.

The play had gotten to Joseph Papp by a very long route. Shortly after the Princeton production (in 1976, I think?), I decided not to let the one-act version be performed anymore, because I felt that the material could be expanded to full-length, and I wanted to hold off wider exposure of the work until I did that.

I wrote the first "expansion" of the play sometime in 1980, and had a reading of it at the Actors Studio with Sigourney as Bette. Having met Joseph Papp a few times by then, I called him up and asked him if I could arrange a reading of the play for him—which I did. From that reading, I did various rewrites, especially relating to Fr. Donnally, and to the character of Matt, which was almost nonexistent in the one-act version.

For complicated reasons, the play kept not being scheduled over the next couple years, though interest never died at the Public, thanks especially to the support of Gail Merrifield and Bill Hart in the play department, and of others there as well (Robert Blacker, Lynn Holst, John Ferraro, Morgan Jenness).

In the summer of 1984, Papp and I agreed upon Jerry Zaks as director, and the play was scheduled for the 84–85 season. Sigourney was scheduled to play

Bette, but then was no longer able to due to her movie schedule not being compatible with the availability of the Newman Theatre at the Public.

Jerry and I were very worried whom we'd find to replace the wonderful Sigourney, but on our first day's audition we found the wonderful Joan Allen; and based on the one audition knew we wanted her to be Bette.

Mr. Papp (I did call him Joe, but Catholic schoolboy manners are hard to break) was very much of the opinion that I should play the part of Matt myself. Just as Tom in *The Glass Menagerie* "feels" like an author surrogate, so does the part of Matt; and Papp, who had seen me perform a few times, felt that my doing the role was a head-on way of dealing with the "author's voice" nature of the part that might pay off.

I was fearful that it might seem self-indulgent or self-pitying to have me play Matt; but conversely I also thought it might work fine, and I had had success sometimes acting in my own plays at Yale (though never in parts that had any biographical reverberations). Plus, I thought that if I were to turn down the chance, I would always wonder what it might have been like. So, particularly since Zaks was to be at the helm, I chose to chance it. (I did tell Jerry before rehearsals that I wouldn't hate him if he decided it wasn't working and I should be replaced.)

Performing the role, particularly in previews when it was very new, sometimes struck me as a preposterously public manner in which to reveal some rather personal thoughts and feelings. And the very first preview, I was disoriented and surprised to find that I choked up on the last speech. Since I don't feel I'm easily open about emotions to begin with, it seemed terribly odd to me that I had got myself into this position.

Most of the feedback I got on my doing the part was extremely positive; and I know that the last scene in particular, as experienced from inside it (and shared with actors Joan Allen, Graham Beckel and Kathryn Grody), seemed suffused with a sense of letting go and finishing that acknowledged anger but ended, basically, with—well, I was going to say with acceptance and love but that sounds glib and rhythmically convenient. But then that probably is what I mean. I know that acting the last scene did feel extremely positive and not at all despairing (though certainly sadness was there).

Some people at the time, I'm told, dismissed this play as too angry; I don't agree with them and feel they may be denying something I've found to be true: that unless you go through all the genuine angers you feel, both justified and unjustified, the feelings of love that you do have will not have any legitimate base and will be at least partially false. Plus, eventually you will go crazy. Well, anyway, I'm glad I wrote the expanded version and that I played Matt.

The production of *The Marriage of Bette and Boo* at the Public Theatre was one of the most positive and joyful experiences I have ever had in professional theatre. The pleasure of working with Jerry Zaks again, total agreement with all three designers, the support of all the departments in Papp's excellent New York Shakespeare Festival—this made for a production experience with no drawbacks. I may sound ga-ga with praise, but it would be pointless not to acknowledge it.

As for the actors, I've usually felt fondness and admiration for all the casts I've worked with, but the *Bette and Boo* company grew to be an especially close and loving one.

The ten parts are of varying size, of course, but each part is rather meaty in its way; and a few days after our opening in early May, all ten of us shared in an Obie award for Ensemble Acting. The "Ensemble," as we grew fond of grandly calling ourselves, consisted of Joan Allen, Graham Beckel, Olympia Dukakis, Patricia Falkenhain, Kathryn Grody, Bill McCutcheon, Bill Moor, Mercedes Ruehl, Richard B. Shull, and myself. God bless us, each and every one.

I also won an Obie for playwriting, Jerry Zaks for direction (and for his direction of Larry Shue's *The Foreigner*), and Loren Sherman for his set designs over the past couple of seasons, including *Bette and Boo*. One wants to limit how important awards and critical praise seem for all the times one doesn't receive them, and for the instances when fine work of others doesn't get acknowledgment. But that said, we were pretty happy about the Obies.

The opening night was a very magical one, that started with one of those unpredictable connections one sometimes gets with an audience.

During previews I had gotten used to getting a laugh in Matt's first speech about finding order beneath the surface. The over-seriousness of Matt's desire for order usually got a laugh on the line "Once these details have been considered, generalizations about them must be made."

However, this night the audience sort of got Matt's longing for order faster, in the middle of the previous sentence; and I found them wanting to laugh when I was in the middle of a word, just about. Being interrupted that way can feel like tripping over your feet, or it can be an opportunity. And so I let the audience stop me, and I gave them a look, implying I knew why they wanted to laugh, and I understood; and then I gave them a big smile. And the moment sort of cemented a very strong rapport between me and the house for the rest of that performance.

The rest of the performance was very full, very funny, very sad. And after a wonderful response at the end, when the curtain closed, the ten-person cast went automatically into a group hug.

When the hug was finished, and I started to go off to the men's dressing room, I had a very strong feeling of my mother's spirit somewhere in the theatre, approving and sending love. I hope that that was true.

Laughing Wild

INTRODUCTION

Sometime in late 1985, I wrote the Woman's monologue part of *Laughing Wild*. I wrote it the same way I wrote *Sister Mary*, with no particular production in mind, with no theatre, just because I had an impulse to write. I wish I always could write from that impulse.

I moved to New York City in 1975, and initially loved the excitement and energy and all the things to do; but by 1985, I was starting to feel really worn down by the city—the constant noise, the relentless cement everywhere, all the mental patients walking down the street, begging for money or vomiting, or both.

New York City had gotten harder and harder to live in, and the speech was partially triggered by that.

Writing the Woman I chose to let go of the "reasonableness" of my mind; I let the Woman unleash her most random complaints, and I didn't censor them or try to balance them with being fair. (Her comments on Mother Theresa are a good example; I would hardly say any of the things she says about Mother Theresa, though critics lazily listed Mother Theresa as one of the "targets" in my play, since they like to believe I have "targets" all the time. The Woman's "targets" and mine should not be assumed to be the same.)

Early on I had a reading of the Woman's monologue, and I asked the actress-writer E. Katherine Kerr to read the part. I had been a fan of hers from having seen her at auditions (especially a hilarious interpretation of Sister Mary Ignatius); and from seeing her in Tommy Tune's production of Caryl Churchill's *Cloud 9*. Indeed, I saw her three times (and the play five times), so knocked out was I by her performance, and the play itself.

I had no idea what Katherine's presence would do to the part, but I knew she had razor-sharp comic timing and, judging from the end of *Cloud 9* in particular, an ability to be deeply (and suddenly) moving.

At this initial reading, Katherine blew the invited audience away, and I filed away in my head that I wanted to make this Woman's monologue somehow be part of a full evening.

But the project stayed on a back burner. In late 1986 I was scheduled to read from my works at the Ninety-Second Street Y (on a bill with Wallace Shawn), and I decided to write something that might go with the Woman's monologue, and to try it out with the Y's audience. Katherine had become a friend by now, and had been encouraging me to write something that I could act in myself, so that's what I did.

At the Y, reading the Man's monologue was scary, it felt very personal and naked. The Woman's voice was that of a character who thought and spoke very differently from myself (however much I might occasionally mirror her crazy upset). The Man's voice and concerns were much closer to my personal ones. The audience response, though, felt very electric, and I overcame my hesitations and decided that this Man's speech, reworked, should become the companion piece to the Woman's.

The evening needed a third piece to complete it, and in it, I wanted the Man and Woman somehow to interact, but I was stuck as to how. Then, reading Jung for inspiration, the idea came to me of their having overlapping dreams, of having images and obsessions from her unconscious impinge on his unconscious, and vice versa.

I also felt that the third piece—and the evening as a whole—should be written "intuitively" and not be reasoned out. And I guess I think I failed in this—my "intuitive" glands are just too blocked still. The third piece is rather *willfully* intuitive.

Having been, I hope, disarmingly honest about this, still I think plays are rarely perfect, and I've ended up feeling good about this play. Though I didn't for a while, because the play was mostly not liked critically. (And then lots of people didn't go see it because of that.) So I felt insecure about the play, including sometimes when I'd perform it, which was very difficult. (Of course, acting is pretending, so I was supposed to be able to put doubt aside; but I couldn't always.)

I don't mean to say it went badly at Playwrights—Katherine was wonderful, and our previews were great; and our last week was a laugh riot with the audience. The middle period of subscribers was tougher, though Katherine and I started to decide that the quieter audiences "needed" to hear the play more than the audiences who would whoop it up and were thus already on the play's wavelength.

I was getting used to Frank Rich resisting my plays, but this time many other critics did too. So I had to wonder what that meant (if anything). After the play finished its run, I started to come across people who seemed really enthusiastic about the play, even including some critics (Mel Gussow of the *Times,* Jan Stuart of *Newsday*) who, unluckily for me, had not been assigned to review it.

And then in 1990 I got a chance to perform it again, this time with Jean Smart, in L.A. at the Tiffany Theatre, directed by Dennis Erdman. It was now three years later, and I had more confidence about the play; and that performance was much more playful and fun for me. (And it went well and was extended, with Christine Ebersole taking over for Jean, and Grant Shaud [of *Murphy Brown*] taking over for me.)

One of the themes of the play, especially in the Man's monologue, is the need and search for "meaning." The play pokes fun at "New Age" stuff, at the same time the Man's character is drawn to dabble in it, without its really working for him; and that's true of me as well as him. Probably one of the sincerest lines in the monologue, for me, is "I'm *starved* for some meaning...I'm tired of being an existentialist."

Maybe it's my Catholic religious upbringing, which instilled in me as a child the belief of a Father God with intricate, involved plans for your life; with its guardian angels (like ethereal teddy bears) floating around, trying to guide you in the right direction; with its myriad of saints with special skills (like St. Anthony for "finding" lost things, and, most appropriate for the 20th century, St. Jude for magical help in "hopeless causes.")

The New Age is kind of like secular humanism married to a sense of magic...crystals (and the earth) and our own bodies have healing properties that we have "forgotten" about; there are spirit guides floating around, with advice and solace and direction; if there isn't a great big Father up there to guide and judge (and condemn) us, there's a belief in a God within that we are all a part of. The world and its chaos seem so far outside our control, it's very attractive to believe or at least entertain belief in these sorts of things in order to more easily walk around, putting one foot after another.

And because I do believe in "intuition"—which is a nonlinear kind of knowing—there is a part of me perfectly willing to think there's a whole litany of different kinds of knowledge that humankind could have access to.

So some days I'm a sort of semibeliever.

And then other days, alas, I switch back to finding life an enormous, meaningless effort. And on those days I try not to talk on the telephone, and I sit in a chair and meditate on Peggy Lee singing "Is That All There Is?" And I wait for feelings of optimism to return.

So let me go sit down and rest a while. And you can read *Laughing Wild*, if you like.

ORIGINAL PRODUCTION

Laughing Wild was presented by Playwrights Horizons (Andre Bishop, Artistic Director and Paul S. Daniels, Executive Director) on October 23, 1987. It was directed by Ron Lagomarsino; the set design was by Thomas Lynch; the costume design was by William Ivey Long; the lighting design was by Arden Fingerhut; the sound design was by Stan Metelits; the press representative was Bob Ullman; the production manager was Carl Mulert; and the production stage manager was M. A. Howard. The cast was as follows:

ACT I
1. Laughing Wild
Woman.............................. E. Katherine Kerr

2. Seeking Wild
Man .... Christopher Durang

ACT II
3. Dreaming Wild
Woman.............................. E. Katherine Kerr
Man .... Christopher Durang

AUTHOR'S NOTE REGARDING TITLE

The phrase "laughing wild" occurs in Samuel Beckett's *Happy Days,* in which Winnie, who's always trying to remember her "classics" says: "Oh, well, what does it matter, that is what I always say, so long as one…you know…what is that wonderful line…laughing wild…something something laughing wild amid severest woe."

Beckett and Winnie in turn are quoting Thomas Gray and his poem *Ode on a Distant Prospect of Eton College,* in which the "something something" is "and moody Madness laughing wild amid severest woe."

Laughing Wild

I. LAUGHING WILD

A Woman enters and addresses the audience. She should be dressed fairly normally. She sits in a chair and talks to the audience. She can get up from the chair from time to time if the spirit moves her. The backdrop behind her should be nondescript—pretty much a limbo setting.

WOMAN: Oh, it's all such a mess. Look at this mess. My hair is a mess. My clothes are a mess.

I want to talk to you about life. It's just too difficult to be alive, isn't it, and to try to function? There are all these people to deal with. I tried to buy a can of tuna fish in the supermarket, and there was this *person* standing right in front of where I wanted to reach out to get the tuna fish, and I waited a while, to see if they'd move, and they didn't—they were looking at tuna fish too, but they were taking a real long time on it, reading the ingredients on each can like they were a book, a pretty boring book, if you ask me, but nobody has; so I waited a long while, and they didn't move, and I couldn't get to the tuna fish cans; and I thought about asking them to move, but then they seemed so stupid not to have *sensed* that I needed to get by them that I had this awful fear that it would do no good, no good at all, to ask them, they'd probably say something like, "We'll move when we're goddam ready, you nagging bitch," and then what would I do? And so then I started to cry out of frustration, quietly, so as not to disturb anyone, and still, even though I was softly sobbing, this stupid person didn't *grasp* that I needed to get by them to reach the goddam tuna fish, people are so insensitive, I just hate them, and so I reached over with my fist, and I brought it down real hard on his head and I screamed: "Would you kindly, move, asshole!!!"

And the person fell to the ground, and looked totally startled, and some child nearby started to cry, and I was still crying, and I couldn't imagine making use of the tuna fish now anyway, and so I shouted at the child to stop crying—I mean, it was drawing too much attention to me—and I ran out of the supermarket, and I thought, I'll take a taxi to the Metropolitan Museum of Art, I need to be surrounded with culture right now, not tuna fish.

But you know how hard it is to hail a taxi. I waved my hand, and then this terrible man who came to the street *after* I was there waved his hand, and the taxi stopped for him because he saw him first, and the injustice of it made my eyes start to well with tears again. So I lost that taxi. So I raised my hand again, and the next *three* taxis were already full, although one of them still had his "free" light on, which made me angry, because if he had had it off, I probably wouldn't have raised my arm, which was getting tired now, I think hitting the man with the tuna fish used some muscles I wasn't used to using. And then this other taxi started to get near, and this woman with groceries came out, and she started to hail it and I went right over to her and I shouted smack into her ear: "If you take this taxi from me, I will kill you!" And she looked really startled and then the taxi stopped, and I got in, and I said, "I want to go crosstown to the Metropolitan Museum of Art, I must have culture, and quiet, and things of value around me, I have had a terrible time in the supermarket." And then the taxi driver, who was Greek or Muslim or Armenian or something, said to me, I have to go *down*town now, I'm about to get off work.

Well, I thought my head would explode. I mean, was his taxi available, or wasn't it? And wasn't it *law* that they can't refuse you, even if you want to go to Staten Island? But I just couldn't bear the thought of pressing charges against this man—it would take days and days of phone calls, and meetings, and let-ters, and all because he wouldn't bring me to the goddam Metropolitan. So I sat in his taxi and I wouldn't move. I thought for a while about going back and fol-lowing through on my initial impulse to buy a can of tuna fish—tuna fish, mixed with mayonnaise, is one of the few things I can make in the kitchen—but then I realized that probably whoever was at the cash register would give me difficulties, probably because I was a woman, or because she was a woman, or maybe it was a man who hated women, or wished he was a woman—any-way it all started to seem far too complicated; so I thought, I'll just stay in this taxi cab, and I'll be damned if I get out. And he kept saying, "Lady, please, I have to get home to my family." And I said "Where? In Staten Island?"

And then I thought, I won't even argue, I'll just sit here. And he started to shout at me, obscenities and so on, and I thought, well, at least I'm sitting down; maybe eventually he'll decide it's easier just to drive me to the Metropolitan; although I started to think maybe I didn't want to go there any-way, I was hungry, for starters, maybe a movie with popcorn and diet Coke and those chocolate-covered ice cream balls, what are they called—they're delicious, and they cost about $3.50 in the movie theatre, which is ridiculously expensive, but then what movie would I see; and then all of a sudden he pulled his cab out into traffic in a great big hurry, it made me sort of lurch in my seat, and I yelled out, "I've changed my mind, I want to see a movie"; and before I could ask him for recommendations, he said he was taking me to the police station, and I thought, yes, but isn't he in the wrong, refusing a fare? But then you know the stories you've read about police brutality and all, maybe they'd have one of those electrical devices, and they'd shock me even though I wasn't Puerto Rican— well, whatever, I didn't think going to the police was worth it as a risk, so when he stopped at a stoplight—violently, I might add, there's probably something wrong with my back, I could sue, but litigation is so complicated and here I can't even buy a can of tuna—I swung the cab door open and I shouted into his open window, "Your mother sucks cocks in hell!" Although I think my tongue slipped and I actually said "Your mother sucks *socks* in hell," which was kind of funny, but I was too angry to laugh; and he just said, "You're fuckin' nuts," and he drove off in this terrible hurry, and the tire almost went over my foot, but luckily I fell backwards into the gutter. *(Looks at the audience for a moment.)*

Are you all following this so far?

Have you ever noticed how spring is lovely, but it fills one with sad long-ing because nothing in one's life will ever live up to the sweet feelings it raises; and that fall is lovely but that it fills one with sad longing because everything is dying; and life is beautiful and awful and there's no assuagement of this awful longing inside one? Have you all noticed this? I presume it's a universal feeling, isn't it? I know I feel it's universal.

(With renewed energy.) So, there I was lying on my back in the gutter, and this street musician came over to me and he asked me if I needed help, and I said, "No, but can you play 'Melancholy Baby'?" And I thought that that was a pretty funny thing for me to say under the circumstances, and that I had a fair wit and intelligence even if I had been in mental institutions, and I thought to myself, maybe if this man laughs at my comment, which is wry and peculiar and yet oddly appropriate to the circumstance, that maybe I will have found a companion for the rest of my life, to help me find spring and fall less painful, summer's too hot, I wouldn't expect anyone to be able to help with that, and winter has gotten less cold than it was when I was a child, it's probably some-thing terrible the captains of industry have done to the atmosphere, probably some ozone layer has been thinned out beyond repair, and the sun is coming through more directly, and we'll all die from it and get skin cancers, and breathe

wrong things through our nostrils...oh God, I mustn't worry about things that may not be true and that I can't do anything about anyway. Besides which, this street musician didn't laugh at my comment about "Melancholy Baby," he looked at me very seriously and asked me if I was all right, and I said, "You don't really want to know, do you? You don't want to know how I am really, to hold me in the night, to comfort me in sickness and in health," sickness caused by the dying of the ozone layer, health caused by...well, who knows what causes health, probably sugar is killing all of us, and besides, I hadn't really even gotten a good look at him in the dark, maybe I wouldn't like his looks, he might not be the right person for me to spend the rest of my life with anyway. And then he asked me if I wanted help to stand up or if I wanted to stay seated in the gutter, and I thought to myself, I don't know the answer to this question. And so I said, with a laugh, "I don't know the answer to that question, ask me another one," which I thought was kind of a funny remark in the circumstances, this crazy lady in the gutter after she's attacked someone at the tuna fish counter and been assaulted by a taxi driver, sort of gallant and witty in the midst of unspeakable woe.

What is that line from Beckett? "Laughing wild amid severest woe."

So then I said to him, with another wry smile, "I am laughing wild amid severest woe." And he looked at me blankly, and I said, "I am laughing wild!" And since he didn't seem to get it, I threw back my head, and I let out this enormous, frightening laugh I do at parties: AHAHAHAHAHAHAHAHA-HAHAH! And he looked alarmed and then he said, if you need help getting to the ladies' shelter, I'll be over there playing my guitar. And then I knew I'd been fortune's fool, that this man was not meant to share my life with me, he was humorless, he didn't have a sense of shared existential ennui, angst, whatever, I've been to college. Although I didn't read everything they assigned me, of course. What good would it have done? *(Looks at the audience.)*

Do you follow me so far?

Do you feel a kinship, or are you looking at me like that street musician did?

You know, sometimes I love street musicians—not that particular one, of course, but sometimes if one is walking down the grubby street, like yesterday I was, and this young girl was playing a cello, all by herself, it was late, it was dark, the city was filled with horrible people—outpatients from Creedmoor, some of whom I know; horrible teenagers from New Jersey who come on dates pretending that life is *wonderful,* they'll learn, I hope they cry a hundred tears; I have this hostility toward anyone who is happy. But I do appreciate beauty, and the strains of melancholy comfort rising from this young woman's cello brought a momentary peace to my soul. I stood for a moment and listened in awe, and then I gave her a nickel. You may think that was cheap, but it was a nickel bag of coke. AHAHAHAHAHAHAHA!

No, I'm kidding, it was just a nickel, five cents. I only listened to it for a moment, I can't be expected to support the woman, she plays well, why doesn't she get a job in the state symphony and not be out and about on the streets, irritating everyone, making them feel guilty? No, but that contradicts the point I was making. I love street musicians. *(She sings for a bit, prettily; in New York, she sang a bit of "Vilia" from Franz Lehar's* The Merry Widow.*)*

You may ask, what parties has she gone to to unleash this peculiar laugh? Mostly the Warhol crowd. One of the orderlies at Creedmoor said to me, you remind me of Edie Sedgewick, I bet Andy Warhol would like you. This was before he died, of course. And so one of the times I wasn't institutionalized I went to a party that Warhol was at, supposedly, but I never met him. That's why I haven't had the film career Edie Sedgewick had. But I haven't minded really. I think film takes away a little bit of your soul each time you're photographed. That was the theme of Ibsen's *When We Dead Awaken,* only it was about sculptors, not filmmakers. I wonder if Ibsen would have liked me. I wonder if I would have liked Ibsen. I'm glad I never met Strindberg, I probably would've married him. I have a bad instinct about these sorts of things. Although who should I marry? Alan Alda? I liked him for about five minutes, but now I think he's a pill. Have you ever noticed that after you've known someone for just a little while how intolerable you find them?

And speaking of which, who is Sally Jessy Raphael, and more importantly, why is she? Does anyone know? I have a television in my apartment, I don't have a bed, but I have trouble sleeping anyway, sometimes I sleep in the bathtub; but originally she was on at three in the morning, or something; now she's on at ten or four or three, her time is always changing, that is, Sally Jessy Raphael's is; and I guess she's supposed to be a kind of female Phil Donahue. But my point is, who is she? Why does she think she's interesting, or that we should listen to her? Why does she have all this self-confidence? Why doesn't she have the humility to know she's not so special? I don't have self-confidence. I think I'm special, but I have sufficient humility to question myself, maybe I'm totally worthless. But even at my most confident, I'd never try to pass myself off as a female Phil Donahue.

Plus, of course, when you're Phil Donahue you have to have opinions on so many things. I could never be President because of this. Plus, of course, if McGovern's running mate had to drop out because of shock treatments, they'd really be able to go to town with my mental history. My mental history is something, alright. I make the Frances Farmer story look like *Laugh In*. I make *The Snake Pit* look like *The Love Bug*. I make *I Never Promised You a Rose Garden* look like *Tie A Yellow Ribbon Round the Old Oak Tree*. I make the dawn come up like thunder. Why did I say that? *(Thinks.)*

I wonder if it's because *Tie A Yellow Ribbon Round the Old Oak Tree* was sung by Tony Orlando and Dawn, ergo "dawn like thunder," in which case my unconscious mind is really active, isn't it?…Useless, but active.

I had such high hopes once. AHAHAHAHAHAHAHAHAHA! She said, throwing her head back, madly. Laughing wild amid severest woe.

But what I said about having opinions—people with opinions usually pretend they know what should be done about things. I think that's hubris. Do you all know what hubris is? That's conceit, when you think you're as good as the gods. Well, everybody in this country has hubris. I'd like to take all the unwanted children in the world who some right-to-lifer keeps from being aborted, and send them all to Mother Theresa. Let her cope with the screaming, squalling little infants; she said in some interview that people who didn't want their children should send them to her rather than have an abortion. I'd like to see her dealing with three thousand shrieking infants yelling nonstop for days on end, then I hope she'd be sorry for saying such a goody-goody, disgusting thing.

I wish I had been killed when I was a fetus. It wasn't legal then, and my mother didn't think of it, but I think she'd prefer I'd never been born. I know I'd prefer she'd never have been born, and that would have taken care of my not being born as well. Plus, I'm really sick of Mother Theresa, aren't you? I mean, what makes her such a saint? She's just like Sally Jessy Raphael, only different. Oh, God, I'm starting to ramble. But I can't help it. And what does the A.A. prayer say? God help me to accept the things I cannot change. I can't change my rambling. Plus I'm not an alcoholic anyway; I just went there because I didn't know what else to do with my life, and I thought if I told them all I was an alcoholic, they'd accept me. But it didn't help. They say if you don't believe in God, you just have to believe in a Higher Power than yourself, but that didn't help me particularly. I mean, who? Phil Donahue? Mother Theresa? The god Dionysus? And there was this woman at A.A. who came and said she had stopped drinking but her life hadn't been working out anyway, and how her parents were alcoholics too, and she seemed very intense and kind of crazy, and it was hard to look at her because she was missing a tooth right in front, it didn't make for an attractive package at all; and she talked about how the program had helped her realize she was powerless over alcohol, and this seemed to make her happy for some reason or other, although I think I'm powerless over lots of things and it doesn't make me happy; and then I shouted out real loud at the top of my lungs: WHY DON'T YOU GET YOUR TOOTH FIXED? And everyone looked at me real angry, and I looked embarrassed, and then I shouted: JUST A SUGGESTION. And everyone looked uncomfortable, and there was silence for about half an hour, and then the meeting was over, though we all said the A.A. prayer again; and then nobody would speak to me. But lots of people went to speak to the woman without the tooth, sort of like to prove that they didn't care she was missing her tooth; but then this one person came over to me, and said not to drink the punch, and he said that he agreed with me and that the woman looked awful; and that furthermore he'd been going to meetings for a long time, and that this woman had been missing her tooth for several years, and clearly had not organized herself into fixing this, and so he agreed with me wholeheartedly. And then he and I went to a hotel room and fucked, and then I tried to jump out the window, and then I went to Creedmoor for the third time. *(Looks thoughtful.)*

Have you all wondered why sexual intercourse sometimes makes you want to commit suicide? That is a universal feeling, isn't it? Or is it just me? Can I see a show of hands?

Oh, well, don't worry, I'm not one of those people who force audience participation. I'm not going to stand up here and insist you sing "Those Were the Days" and then when I've bullied you into it, complain you didn't sing loud enough, and then make you sing again. I've seen Pearl Bailey and Diana Ross do that, it's really obnoxious. I want to see them killed. Well actually Pearl Bailey is dead. I'd like to be dead.

Tell me, are you enjoying my company, or are you wishing I'd go away? I can never tell in life, it's one of my problems. Reality testing of any sort is a mystery to me, my doctors say. I have the most wonderful doctors, they're all like

Dr. Ruth Westheimer on television. Dr. Ruth Westheimer. And they wonder why I have reality testing problems. Don't you find her peculiar? Andy Warhol said everyone would be famous for fifteen minutes in the twentieth century, but she's already been famous for far longer than that, it doesn't look like she's ever going to go away. Eventually we'll see her on *Password* where no matter what word she's trying to communicate, she'll only talk sex. Say the word is "nicotine." Her first clue will be "clitoris." Then "stimulation." Then "cunnilingus." Her partner will be totally baffled, especially when the host says, "No, Marjorie, I'm sorry, the word was nicotine." Then Dr. Ruth will laugh like crazy, just like me. AHAHAHAHAHAHAHAHA!

(Suddenly angry, and for real.) But her partner will have lost the game thanks to her stupid clues. She won't receive the seven hundred dollars for the first round, she will not win the trip for two to the Caribbean, to stay at the luxurious Hyatt Regency, she will not get to move on to the Speed Round where she could win thirty thousand dollars if she can guess eight words in thirty seconds, all because this nutty, smutty doctor thinks she's cute, and thinks she knows something about something, and has hubris like every other fucking creature in this stupid, horrible universe. I WANT DR. RUTH WESTHEIMER AND MOTHER THERESA TO FIGHT TO THE DEATH IN THE COLISEUM!!!—using knives and swords and heavy metal balls with spikes on them! And then when one of them has her sword to the other one's throat, I want to raise my hand and give the "thumbs down" sign just like Siskel and Ebert dismissing a particularly dreadful movie; and then I want Jesse Helms hung upside down over sulfur emissions and made to inhale toxic waste, just like those animals who are made to smoke three million cigarettes; and then I want the world to come to a complete and total end, ka-plooey, ka-ploppy, ke-plopp! AHAHAHAHAHAHAHAHAHAHAH!

Do you get how I feel? Do you identify in some way, or are you rejecting me? Would any of you give me a job ever? I can't believe you would.

Because I have tried to improve my life, I have fought, I have called people on the phone and screamed at them, "LET ME BABY-SIT WITH YOUR CHILDREN, I PROMISE I WON'T KILL THEM," but then they don't hire me. I've called editors at Doubleday and Knopf and St. Martin's Press even, and I've said to them over the telephone, "I DON'T KNOW HOW TO TYPE AND I'M TOO UNSTABLE TO READ, BUT IF YOU HIRE ME TO BE AN ASSISTANT EDITOR I COULD TRY TO BE MORE STABLE, HUH, WHADDYA SAY?"

But do they hire me ever? What do you think? No? If you think no, raise your hand. I want to see how many of you think no. I WANT SOME AUDIENCE PARTICIPATION HERE, RAISE YOUR GODDAM HANDS! That's better. And that's right, the answer is no. Now I want everyone to hold hands and sing "Give Peace a Chance." No, I'm kidding, I said I hated audience participation and so I do.

The word is flashlight. Dr. Ruth's clues are: Clitoris. Erect nipple. Mound of Venus. Pound of penis. AHAHAHAHAHA, I didn't know I was going to say that.

But, Dr. Ruth, I can't get the word "flashlight" from those clues. You're not helping me to win the prize. I can't get the prize with those clues. *(Starts to cry.)* I can't get the prize with those cluuuuuuuuueeess. Oh God, I want to die, I want to die. *(Cries violently. Silence for a bit; her crying subsides.)*

Uh, it's quite a relief having me silent for a while, isn't it? *(Smiles or laughs a bit, and continues to be silent.)*

My favorite book is *Bleak House.* Not the book, but the title. I haven't read the book. I've read the title. The title sounds the way I feel. And my most recent accomplishment was getting up out of the gutter after I fell down leaving that crazy taxi driver. And my Scotch is Dewar's White Label.

I feel terribly sorry for my doctors. My doctors get exhausted listening to me, I can tell they feel my words are charging out of my mouth and trying to invade their brain cells, and they're frightened. Understandably. And that's why I try to practice being quiet from time to time. Let me be quiet for a second again. *(She is quiet.)*

You see, you need that rest too, don't you?

Here is the key to existence. Are you all listening? Here is the key to existence; when I tell you this you will know how to run your lives. You will know if you have been living life to the full, and if you realize you haven't been, you will know immediately how to correct that state of affairs. As soon as I tell you the key to existence. Are you ready? Are you ready for me to tell you?

Oh, dear, I've built it up too much, and it's really not all that significant. But it's what I got from the est training: *Always breathe.* That's the basis of life, breathing. That's basically the basis. If you don't breathe, you die. *(Pause.)*

Well, it seemed more impressive when you hadn't slept for two days. If you're rested, it doesn't sound so important, but I try to hold on to it.

The other major thing I have learned is... *(Sincerely.)* well, I've forgotten it, so it couldn't have been too significant.

Let me try to summarize what I've told you, and then I'll remove myself from your presence. I had trouble buying tuna fish, then I had an argument with a taxi driver, I fell in the gutter, I like street musicians sometimes, I have a startling laugh, Ahahahahaha, I don't like Sally Jessy Raphael, Mother Theresa or Dr. Ruth Westheimer, I am opposed to "hubris," I wish I had never been born, I have trouble getting a job, I haven't read *Bleak House* but I like the title, and I have learned that you should always breathe.

Oh, and I feel great hostility toward teenagers from New Jersey who seem happy. I mentioned that earlier, didn't I? I think I did.

Well, then, I've covered everything I intended to. Thank you for giving me your attention. Good-bye, I love you. Of course, that's a lie. Some of you I think are first-class fools, and I hate you. In fact, I probably don't like any of you. Curse you! I curse all of you! May your children have webbed feet, and all your house pets get mange and worms! AHAHAHAHAHA!

I'm terribly sorry. I really can't leave you that way. The management would be so cranky if I cursed the audience right at the end of my speech, so forget I said that. I do love you. M-wah! I want to be a responsible member of this society, so give me a job if you can, I'm sure I can do something. I love you, m-wah! The ushers will give you my phone number, and the box office will field any job offers you call in. Thank you. Good-bye. Good-bye. I hope your lives are better than mine. Laugh laugh laugh laugh—I'm getting too tired to do the real laugh right now. Laugh laugh laugh. Laughing is a tonic. So forget crying. Cry, and you cry alone. Laugh and you...cry alone later.

And remember—always breathe. Even if I stop, you keep breathing out there, alright? Keep breathing. In and out. In and out. In and out.

(She breathes in and out several times in a somewhat exaggerated manner, as if to show us how. She then stops the exaggerated breathing, and looks at us for a few beats. She's either holding her breath or, more likely, just breathing regularly, as the lights dim.)

II. SEEKING WILD

A space in which a talk is about to be given. It could be a lecture hall, a stage, a room, a "space." In the New York production there was a dark curtain midstage. In front of the curtain R. was a chair next to a table. On the table were a water pitcher and a glass. On L. was a column-like stand (a pedestal), on which were three crystals: a large, jagged clear crystal; a chunk of amethyst (which is purple); a piece of citrine (amber-colored).

Hanging on the curtain, Upstage Center, and rather dominating the stage was a very large hand-painted canvas poster of an Egyptian Eye. The New York poster was patterned after the Eye of Ra (or "Horus card") found in the book The Way of Cartouche. *Whatever it's based on, it should be a large eye, not realistically drawn but with a primitive, bold look to it. Beneath the eye there is a small line (sort of where "circles under your eyes" would be) off of which hang little icicles or teardrops or some such design. Again, whatever "hangs" beneath the eye should not look realistically like anything; it should be some bold, primitive design one can't quite figure out. This Egyptian Eye poster should look mysterious, otherworldly, and should give a sense that the talk the audience is about to hear may be "mind-expanding," Jungian, New Age-related, etc., etc.*

After a few beats, a Man enters. (He might briefly look at the "Eye" poster, and register slight confusion.) The Man is dressed up to give a talk, to share his new thoughts. He carries with him a few file cards that he has made notes on. He smiles at the audience, checks his first note card quickly before beginning, and then speaks with earnestness and purpose. Friendly.

MAN: I used to be a very negative person. But then I took this personality workshop that totally turned my life around. Now when something bad or negative happens, I can see the positive. Now when I have a really bad day or when someone I thought was a really good friend betrays me, or maybe when I've been hit by one of those damn people riding bicycles the opposite way on a one-way street, so, of course, one hadn't looked in that direction and there they are bearing down on you, about to kill or maim you—anyway, I look at any of these things and I say to myself: This glass is not half-full, it's half-empty.

No—I said it backwards, force of habit. This glass is not half empty, it is half-full.

Of course, if they hit you with the stupid bicycle your glass will not be half-full or half-empty, it will be shattered to pieces, and you'll be dead or in the hospital.

But really I'm trying to be positive, that's what I'm doing with my life these days.

(Reads from a note card.) I was tired of not being joyful and happy, I was sick of my personality, and I had to change it.

(Off the card; back to speaking extemporaneously.) Half-full, not half-empty. I had to say to myself: You do not have cancer—at least not today. You are not blind. You are not one of the starving children in India or China or in Africa. Look at the sunset, look at the sunrise, why don't you enjoy them, for God's sake? And now I do. *(Almost as a sidetrack to himself)* Except if it's cloudy, of course, and you can't see the sun. Or if it's cold. Or if it's too hot.

(Hearing his negativity above.) I probably need to take a few more personality workshops to complete the process. It's still not quite within my grasp, this being positive business.

(Reads from cards again.) But I'm making great strides. My friends don't recognize me. *(Smiles.)*

(Off the cards again.) And it is hard for me to be positive because I'm very sensitive to the vibrations of people around me, or maybe I'm just paranoid. But in any case, I used to find it difficult to go out of the house sometimes because of coming into contact with other people.

You've probably experienced something similar—you know, the tough on the subway who keeps staring at you and you're the only two people in the car and he keeps staring and after a while you think, does he want to kill me? Or just intimidate me? Which is annoying enough.

Or the people in movie theatres who talk endlessly during the opening credits so you can just *tell* they're going to talk through the entire movie and that it will be utterly useless to ask them not to talk.

And even if you do ask them not to talk and they ungraciously acquiesce, they're going to send out vibrations that they hate you all during the entire film, and then it will be impossible to concentrate.

You can move, but the person next to you in the new location will probably, you know, rattle candy wrappers endlessly all through the movie. Basically I don't go to the movies anymore. What's the point?

But even if you can skip going to the movies, you pretty much have to go to the supermarket.

(Steps closer to the audience.) I was in the supermarket the other day about to buy some tuna fish when I sensed this very disturbed presence right behind me. There was something about her focus that made it very clear to me that she was a disturbed person. So I thought—well, you should never look at a crazy person directly, so I thought, I'll just keep looking at these tuna fish cans, pretending to be engrossed in whether they're in oil or in water, and the person will then go away. But instead *wham!* she brings her fist down on my head and screams "Would you move, asshole!" *(Pause.)*

Now why did she do that? She hadn't even said, "Would you please move" at some initial point, so I would've known what her problem was. Admittedly I don't always tell people what I want either—like the people in the movie theatres who keep talking, you know, I just give up and resent them—but on the other hand, I don't take my fist and go wham! on their heads!

I mean, analyzing it, looking at it in a positive light, this woman probably had some really horrible life story that, you know, kind of, explained how she got to this point in time, hitting me in the supermarket. And perhaps if her life—*since birth*—had been explained to me, I could probably have made some sense out of her action and how she got there. But even with that knowledge— which I didn't have—it was *my* head she was hitting, and it's just so unfair.

It makes me want to never leave my apartment ever ever again. *(Suddenly he closes his eyes and moves his arms in a circular motion around himself, round and round, soothingly.)*

I am the predominant source of energy in my life. I let go of the pain from the past. I let go of the pain from the present. In the places in my body where pain lived previously, now there is light and love and joy. *(He opens his eyes again and looks at the audience peacefully and happily.)*

That was an affirmation.

Now the theory of affirmations is that by saying something positive about yourself in the present tense—as if the positive thing is already happening—you draw in positive energies to you. For instance, who do you think will have the easier life?—someone who goes around saying inside their head, "Everyone hates me, they try to avoid me, my job stinks, my life is miserable." Or the person who says "Everyone likes me exactly as I am, every time I turn around people offer me friendship and money, my life is delightful and effortless." *(Pause.)*

Obviously, the second person will be much happier.

There's an additional theory that by thinking negatively, you actually cause, and are thus responsible for, the bad things that happen to you. Thus I need to look at whether I maybe *caused* the woman in the tuna fish aisle to hit me on the head. Or, since that sounds rather blaming, I need to look at the incident and see how else I could have behaved so she might *not* have hit me on the head.

When I sensed her presence, rather than doing nothing and pretending I didn't *notice* that she seemed odd, maybe I could have said, "Is something the matter?" Then maybe she would have said, "Yes, you're in my way," and I would have moved. Or, if when I said "Is something the matter?" she stayed hostile and said "Why???" defensively or something, if I stayed honest and said…"Well, you seem odd." Or "I sense you're distressed," she might have felt that I was "responding" to her as another human being, and that might have relaxed her, and *then* she might have told me what was the matter.

So you see, I shouldn't feel like a victim. We have power.

(Reads from his note cards.) We can change our own thoughts, from negative to positive. *(Off the cards again; explaining.)* Say I feel bad; I can *choose* to feel good.

How do I feel right now? *(Thinks.)* I feel fine. Everything's fine. Of course, that's just on the surface, underneath there's always this gnawing residue of anxiety. But is feeling anxious just part of the human condition? Or do I feel more anxious than one should normally due to some psychological maladjustment or something? Maybe I wasn't breast-fed enough as an infant. Actually I don't even know if I was breast-fed at all. *(Thinks with concern about his lack of knowledge concerning this.)* Oh well, enough about breast-feeding.

(A surge of positive energy:) Let me try to *change* how I feel. Let me try to feel happy for a moment. *(Closes his eyes, puts his fingers to his forehead and "flicks away" negative energy; waits for happiness.)*

No, I was just thinking about Chernobyl. That's like a scream from the universe warning us, but we're not paying attention. I can't believe they don't know what to do with nuclear waste, and then they keep building these things. I'm sorry, I was trying to feel happy. Let me try again. *(Closes his eyes, tries again.)*

Sorry, I was just thinking of something else, something I read in the newspaper about this fourteen-year-old boy in Montana who shot his geometry teacher—*to death*—because the teacher was flunking him. Now that's crazy enough—but it seems that this particular teacher didn't come to school that day, and so this fourteen-year-old boy shot the substitute teacher instead. Shot her dead. I don't know how to cope with that.

I mean, positive thinking aside, how do you protect yourself from these sorts of things? *(Suddenly wants some water, goes up to table and pours himself some while he's on this tangent of upset and negativity.)*

And there's acid rain and something wrong with the ozone layer, and global warming, and destruction of the rain forests. God, it's discouraging. *(Drinks water.)*

And think about God. You know, it was nice to believe in God, and an afterlife; and I'm sometimes envious of the people who seem comfortable because they still have this belief. But I remember when everybody won Tonys for *Dreamgirls,* and they all got up there thanking God for letting them win this award, and I was thinking to myself: God is silent on the holocaust, but He involves himself in the Tony awards? It doesn't seem very likely. *(Feels a need for affirmation; does the circular arm motions again.)*

I am the predominant source of my life. I release anger from my solar plexus. It is replaced by serenity and white light and joy and...serenity. Everything in my life works. Except the plumbing, and career and relationships. *(Laughs at his joke, then talks sincerely.)*

I'm sorry, I was planning on being positive out here, and it's just not happening. But I guess whatever happens is OK. Is that right?

This personality workshop I took taught me that I judge things too much, that some things just "are," you don't have to label them. And also that you shouldn't judge feelings.

This workshop also said to forgive yourself for what you haven't achieved. For instance, I had wanted to be a university professor, maybe in New England somewhere—summers off, tutorials, sherry. I'm very verbal, and that would have been a good thing to do with it.

Instead I work for a magazine, not a bad job, but not great—it's sort of a cross between... *TV Guide* and pornography. Well, that's too strong—but I do have to interview people who are on television series, and if they're at all attractive, they have them photographed with their blouses undone or with their shirts off. Sometimes I have nightmares about the upper bodies of Sharon Stone and Marky Mark. People whose first and last names begin with the same letter. Marky Mark. Suzanne Somers. Lorenzo Lamas. Cher. *(Time for another affirmation.)*

Everything unfolds in my life exactly as it should, including my career. Abundance is my natural state of being, and I accept it now. I let go of anger and resentment. *(A sudden addition to the affirmation.)* I love the woman in the tuna fish aisle. I accept her exactly as she is. I accept myself exactly as I am. I approve of my body. *(Makes equivocal face.)* I approve of *other* people's bodies.

You know, I don't like meeting people who are too attractive, and not just TV stars at my job, but anyone who's good-looking or charismatic. I hate being attracted to people, it's exhausting. It stirs up longing.

Of course, one can just do one's best to have sex with the person, and that assuages some of the longing. But the problem is, that sexual longing has no real assuagement ever, it's like longing for the moon; you can never have the moon no matter what you do, and if you were foolish enough to take a spaceship up there—and if the people running NASA didn't see to it that you were killed— you would just find that the moon was this big chunk of nothing that had nothing to do with what you were longing for at all. Oh, Olga, let's go to Moscow, and all that. There is no Moscow, there is no moon, there is no assuagement of longing.

(Affirmation.) I let go of my need for longing. I let go of sexual interest. I become like Buddha, and want nothing. *(Abruptly stops; to audience.)* Do these affirmations sound right to you? They sound off to me.

And I've certainly never successfully acted them out. Cause as soon as sexual attraction kicks in, the zen in one's nature flies out the window. You meet someone, sometimes they really are terrific, other times they're just awful but nonetheless you find yourself attracted to them anyway, knowing you're an utter fool and will be very sorry later on. And then the pursuit begins. All those opening weeks of interested conversation, with the eyes more lively than usual, and each party finding the other's comments and insights more than usually charming and delightful. And then if you've been in therapy like me, there are the flirtatious exchanges of childhood traumas—all of my family were border-line schizophrenic, they beat me, they had terrible taste in furniture—and after a while one's mind starts to reverberate with, when will I have an orgasm with this person?

If there is a God, his design about sex is certainly humiliating. It's humiliating to want things. And sex itself people say is beautiful—but is it? Maybe you think it is. Terrible viscous discharges erupting in various openings may strike you as the equivalent of the Sistine Chapel ceiling, for all I know. It doesn't strike me that way. *(He stops. He realizes how extreme and cranklike his comments have begun to sound. He smiles at the audience, wanting to re-establish his rapport with them, and his reasonability.)*

But I am being negative again. And clearly sex isn't just disgusting. I know that, and you know that. And when I'm lucky enough to go off with someone to his or her apartment, I certainly anticipate a pleasant time. *(Now he stops dead. He had no intention of going into this area of his life with this audience, and he's suddenly uncertain how he even got into it. Or, more to the point, how he can get out of it. He thinks, can't come up with any way to camouflage or take back what he's just said. For better or for worse, he decides just to speak honestly.)*

As the "his or her" comment suggests, I am attracted to women and to men. Though more frequently to other guys, which I find rather embarrassing to admit to publicly. Why do I bring it *up* publicly then, you may well ask? Well…I don't know. Why not? All my relatives are dead, and those that aren't I'm willing not to talk to.

And things like the Supreme Court ruling that sex between consenting adult homosexuals *not* be included in what's considered the rights of privacy—this makes me think it's now important to be open about this. Look, I've even brought pictures of myself in bed with people! *(Pats his inside jacket pocket.)* At intermission the ushers will let you look at them!…although I suppose some pornography commission will run in here and try to take them away from you and then force you to watch reruns of *Lassie* on the Family Channel. God, I took some Valium before I came out here, but it hasn't calmed me down a bit.

Anyway, I didn't mean to get into this… *(Puts his note cards away in his jacket.)* …but I find the Supreme Court's ruling on this issue deeply disturbing. I mean, so much of the evil that men do to one another has at its core the inability of people to *empathize* with another person's position. Say when you're seven, you find yourself slightly more drawn to Johnny than you are to Jane. This is not a conscious decision on your part, it just happens, it's an instinct like…liking the color blue.

Now in less tolerant times, you were put to death for this attraction. As time went on, this punishment was sometimes reduced to mere castration, or just imprisonment. Until recently this attraction was considered so horrific that society pretty much expected you to lie to yourself about your sexual and emotional feelings, and if you couldn't do that, certainly expected you to *shut* up about it, and go live your life bottled up and terrified; and if you would be so kind as to never have any physical closeness with anyone *ever,* when you were buried you could know that society would feel you had handled your disgraceful situation with tact and willpower. That was one *cheery* option—nothing, and then the grave.

Or, you might make a false marriage with some woman who wouldn't know what was going on with you, and you could *both* be miserable and unfulfilled. That was *another* respectable option. Or you might kill yourself. There's not a lot of empathy evident in the people who prefer these options. *(He takes out his note cards again, starts to look at them, but then his mind isn't ready to leave this topic yet.)*

I mean, *I* certainly realize how insane it would be to ask a heterosexual to deny his or her natural sexual feelings and perform homosexual acts that went against their nature. If I can have that empathy, why can't others have the same empathy in reverse? I want some empathy here! *(Goes into an affirmation.)* I am the predominant source of…well, fuck that. *(Throws his note cards over his shoulder, drives on ahead.)*

And then, of course, there are all the religious teachings about homosexuality. The Book of Leviticus, for instance, says that homosexuals should basically be put to death. It also tells you how to sacrifice rams and bullocks, and instructs you not to sit in a chair sat in by any woman who's had her period in the last seven days or something. To me, this is not a book to look to for much modern wisdom. *(If the audience laughs, he might smile with them.)*

People's concepts of God are so odd. For instance, take the Christians—"Take them, please"—who seem to believe that God is so disgusted by the sexual activities of homosexuals that He created AIDS to punish them, apparently waiting until 1978 or so to do this, even though homosexual acts have been going on for considerably longer than that, at least since…1956.

I mean, what do they think? God sits around in a lounge chair chatting with Gabriel, planning the fall foliage in Vermont—"I think a lot of orange this year"—when suddenly he says: "Boy oh boy do I find homosexuals disgusting. I'm going to give them a really horrifying disease!"

And Gabriel says: "Oh yes?"

[God] Yes! And drug addicts and…and…hemophiliacs! *(Gabriel looks fairly appalled.)*

[Gabriel] But why hemophiliacs?

[God] Oh, no reason. I want the disease to go through the bloodstream and even though I'm all powerful and can do everything cause I'm God, I'm too tired today to figure out how to connect the disease to the bloodstream and not affect hemophiliacs. Besides, the suffering will be good for them.

[Gabriel] Really? In what way?

[God] Oh, I don't know. I'll explain it at the end of the world.

[Gabriel] I see. Tell me, what about the children of drug addicts? Will they get the disease through their mother's wombs?

[God] Oh, I hadn't thought about that. Well—why not? Serve the hophead mothers right. Boy oh boy, do I hate women drug addicts!

[Gabriel] Yes, but why punish their babies?

[God] And I hate homosexuals!

[Gabriel] Yes, yes, we got you hate homosexuals…

[God] Except for Noel Coward, he was droll.

[Gabriel] Yes, he was droll.

[God] And I hate Haitians. Anything beginning with the letter "h."

[Gabriel] Yes, but isn't it unfair to infect innocent babies in the womb with this dreadful disease?

[God] Look, homosexuals and drug addicts are very, very bad people; and if babies get it, well, don't forget I'm God, so you better just presume I have some secret reason why it's good they get it too.

[Gabriel] Yes, but what *is* this secret reason?

[God] Stop asking so many questions.

[Gabriel] Yes, but…

[God] There you go again, trying to horn in on the Tree of Knowledge just like Adam and Eve did. Boy oh boy, does that make me wrathful. Okay, Gabriel, you asked for it: I hereby sentence you to become man; I give you suffering and death; I give you psychological pain; I give you AIDS, your immune system will shut down totally, you'll die from brain tumors and diarrhea, and horrible random infections. I give you bone cancer, lymph cancer, breast cancer—lots of cancer.

(A good idea, whimsical.) Oh!…and I hereby revoke penicillin. Anyone out there who has ever been exposed to syphilis will suffer and die just like they used to—as a side issue, I love to connect sex and death, I don't know why I invented sex to begin with, it's a revolting idea, but as long as I have, I want it done *properly* in the *missionary* position with *one* person for life, or I want those who disobey me to die a horrible death from AIDS and syphilis and God knows what else. Is that clear???

(Breaks "character," talks to the audience as himself again.) Now surely that God can't exist—I mean, surely the Christ who said "Blessed are the merciful" could hardly have come from such a raging, spiteful God. *(Pause, his agitation not quite gone yet. He turns around and stares U. at the "Egyptian Eye" banner for a moment. Turns back to the audience.)*

What *is* that??? *(Looks again. Then back.)*

You know, I don't want to take *away* faith in God from anyone who has it; it's just that I don't follow it. And it's not as if living without a belief in God is so pleasant. In moments of deep despair you have absolutely nothing to fall back on. You just stay in the deep despair for a while, and then if you're lucky, you go to sleep.

But I find more and more that I'm starting to long for some sense of value in things. My mind wanders to reincarnation and karma and karmic paths and so on; in some ways I am turning into Shirley MacLaine. Now one does laugh at her, but I'm starting to really identify with the desire to find some meaning out there.

Because I'm really tired of where I've been. I've been…a pretty good "ad-hoc existentialist" for about twenty years. I've gotten up every morning, and I've carried on with my life, acting decent and getting things done, while all the time believing none of it mattered. And I'm really sick of it. I'm *starved* for some meaning. For some belief in something. I'm tired of being an existentialist. It's hard to be joyful when you're an existentialist. Albert Camus was not a laugh riot.

You know, years ago I went to the Harmonic Convergence ceremony in Central Park. You probably don't remember what that even was anymore. Well, it was this strange, New Age-connected belief, prophesied in several cultures—the Mayan, the Aztec, Hopi Indians—that said that August 16th and 17th of this one specific year represented a window in time in which the planets all lined up in some special way or other, and that, supposedly, there was an opportunity for mankind to make a spiritual shift away from pollution and destruction of the planet back to being "in alignment" with Mother Earth, and so on.

The newspapers made fun of the event at the time, and people at the magazine where I work thought I was nuts; but I found I really wanted to believe in this Harmonic Convergence. And even if it were a lot of nonsense, I *liked* the idea of people getting up in the morning all over the world to greet the sunrise and to, if nothing else, sort of hope for a better way of living. I mean, it beats a punch in the eye, doesn't it?

So a couple of friends and I—I'm starting to have more friends who think this way—set our alarms for four in the morning to head up to 83rd and Central Park West, which had been designated as a sacred site. *(Realizing that sounds a bit funny.)* Or at least as a place where people were going to gather.

We went to hail a cab, and predictably we got an absolutely *terrifying* taxi driver. He'd race up to every red light at sixty miles an hour, never slowing down at all just in case the light turned green, which it sometimes did, but you had to worry about the people coming in the other direction who might be trying to run their lights. Anyway, it was harrowing. I kept saying to myself, "All is well in my universe, everyone is calm, no one rushes;" but it didn't make him slow down. Finally I had to say, slow down, goddam it, only I didn't say goddam it, and he didn't slow down, and eventually we killed two people and a dog. Well, just kidding. But it was a disorienting beginning to the Harmonic Convergence.

Well, in any case, at the sacred site itself, it was very crowded, and there was incense and so on, and wind chimes, and we all sat in a circle. And in the center of the circle there were five women and one man who were blowing on conch shells; and one of the women explained to the crowd that we were all there to align the "horizontal plane" of our present existence with the "vertical plane" of Mother Earth and the planets or...something like that...but she seemed a very *warm* woman—she reminded me of someone I know and like named Martha Rhodes. And then the woman said we should all join in and makes sounds like the conch shell if we wanted to, and eventually most of the crowd sort of hit this one sustained note that in these circles is described as "toning." *(He takes a moment to breathe and then lets out a low, sustained note kind of like chanting "ohm." It's just a held note.)* Ahhhhhhhhhhhhhhhhhhhhhh-hhhhhhhhhhhhhhhmmmmmmmmmmmmmmmm.

I liked doing that. I'm not comfortable meditating yet, but this I could do, and it was nice to be connected to the crowd that way.

And then the sun came up, but the "sacred site chosen" had all these *trees* around it so you couldn't actually *see* the sun. I had almost gone to my friend's roof and part of me wished I were there instead. And then this sort of...loopy woman who'd been dancing around the periphery of the circle saying kind of corny things like "I dance for mother moon and sister star" and stuff like that; and whom I almost admired for having the guts to say things like that, and yet I also thought her sensibility was kind of...icky...anyway, she got up and invited everyone who wanted to, to get up and share their hopes and dreams and prayers for the future. And I realized I didn't want to hear *everyone* in the crowd verbalize their hopes, we'd be stuck for *hours,* listening to a lot of gobbledegook.

And then, of course, the first person to get up to share with the group was one of those mental patients who wander the streets of New York—she looked *demented,* and she was yellow from nicotine, and she talked on and on. And what she said wasn't wrong, exactly—something about why don't people say "I love you" rather than "I hate you"?—but it was upsetting that she was crazy—

she reminded me of the woman in the tuna fish aisle, but much more clearly crazy, the woman in the tuna fish aisle could pass for normal on a good day, but this woman really couldn't.

And then the "icky woman" gave the "demented woman" a great big hug in order to *shut her up,* and then some teenager got up to recite a song—not sing it, *recite* it. I don't remember what song it was. Maybe "Blowin' in the Wind." *(Jokes.)* Or "Bali Ha'i." Anyway, it was turning into a nightmare. I didn't want anyone else to speak, I just wanted *instant transformation* of the planet, and I didn't want to take potluck of listening to any strangers in the crowd say how we should go about it, I didn't trust that they'd know, I just *wanted the transformation.* I didn't want to have to deal with *people* about it. And the Harmonic Convergence is about people coming together, and here I was disliking everyone. So I wasn't being very transformed. And my back was sore from sitting—I need to exercise, but I guess I never will, so I asked my friends if we could *please* leave the group and go out into an open area of the park so that we could actually see the sun.

And we did that, and the Great Lawn was very pretty, but I was irritated that we hadn't been there for the actual sunrise.

Well, you can see I was quite resistant; and I did feel bad I was judging everyone there, but then it doesn't really work to pretend you're not feeling something you're feeling. But when you're judging people, you certainly don't feel a sense of unity, do you?

Maybe I shouldn't be so judgmental of people. And it was moving that everyone went there and showed up. I liked that part. And I liked the toning. But otherwise, I felt...very separate. *(He looks thoughtful and a little sad at this. He stays in the moment for a bit, and then goes into another affirmation, moving his arms in that circular motion again.)*

I am *not* separate. I am one with the universe. We are all one. We are all part of the same divine energy. *(His tone becomes slightly tongue-in-cheek.)* There are spirit guides above, waiting to guide us. They speak to us through Shirley MacLaine; they knew enough not to choose Shelley Winters. These spirit guides help us. They drive Shirley's car, they make airline reservations for her, they're just great. Bali Ha'i will call you, any night, any day. Kumbaya, kumbayae.

Well, now I've depressed myself. But I really am much more positive than I ever used to be; and I think these affirmations are a good thing. It's just that...sometimes the bottom drops out for me. And then I need to go sleep for a while, and see if tomorrow feels better.

(Looks around at banner again.) I wish I knew what that was. It's a great big eye, I see that. I don't know what those things dripping off it are. It looks Egyptian. Or like Shakti Gawain's wallpaper. I shouldn't make fun of it. Maybe it is a guide.

(Makes something up.) It's an "all-seeing eye" that represents inner know-ingness, all the wisdom we know from the collective unconscious but, alas, have forgotten. *(He looks over to the crystals, and crosses to them.)*

What about crystals? Do you think crystals work? *What works,* do you think? *(He stares at the crystals, wondering what works.)*

Let me try to feel happy again. *(Puts his fingers to his forehead, "flicks" away negativity; pause.)* Let me hold a crystal to my head and try to feel happy. *(Holds the clear crystal to his head; pause; puts the crystal down again.)* Let me give up on feeling happy for now, and just concentrate on breathing. *(He takes an intake of breath, but stops and comes closer to the audience, a little disappointed.)* I don't feel I've helped you very much. But I want you to remember what I said about affir-mations. We *can* change our thoughts. And even when we can't, just kinda...try to...*silence your mind,* and then just breathe. As the last thing between us, let's just breathe, alright? *(He breathes in an exaggerated way, so the audience can get in synch with him. On the intake of breath he moves his arms up from his diaphragm to his chin; on the outtake, his arms relax downward, the palms open in the "receiving" mode. He keeps his eyes closed.)* In, out. In, out. In, out. God, life's monotonous, isn't it? No, I keep judging things, I'm going to stop doing that. I'm going to stop talking. Just breathe.

(He returns to his exaggerated breathing again, this time without words. Intake—arms up to chin; outtake—arms down to the side. He keeps his eyes closed, except on his second full breath when he opens them to check how the audience is doing, breathing with him. On his third breath, he closes his eyes again, and the lights fade.)

III. DREAMING WILD

Scene 1

The tuna fish counter in a supermarket. The Man is staring at tuna fish cans, deciding which one to buy. The Woman comes and stands behind him, waiting for him to get out of her way. Her energy is odd, and she is already overly impatient.

He senses her odd energy, kind of half looks behind him; then decides not to meet her eye—you shouldn't look at a crazy person—and he starts studying one particular tuna fish can with intensity, hoping she will soon go away. After a few moments this becomes intolerable for the Woman and she raises up her fist and brings it down on the Man's head. The Man is so thrown off-balance that he falls to the ground.

WOMAN: Would you kindly move, asshole!

(From off R., the sound of a child crying, as if startled by the Woman's ferocity.)

MAN: What's the matter with you?!!!

WOMAN: Why didn't you move? I asked you to move!

MAN: No, you didn't!

WOMAN: Yes, I did! *(To offstage, where the crying is coming from.)* Stop crying, little girl, I didn't do anything!

MAN: You're crazy!

(The Woman herself starts to cry, and she runs out of the supermarket. The Man stares after her, rubbing his head.)

(Blackout.)

Scene 2

Lights up again on the supermarket aisle. The Man is once again looking at tuna. The Woman once again comes in, and stands behind him. The audience should see that we are replaying the same scene again, so the Man and Woman's actions should be pretty close to what they did in the previous brief scene.

The Woman's energy is odd, and she is already overly impatient. He senses her odd energy, decides not to meet her eye, and starts studying one particular tuna fish can with intensity, hoping she will soon go away. The Woman suddenly speaks with suppressed fury.

WOMAN: *(Angry, through clenched teeth so it's hard to understand her.)* You reading a book? I don't have the *time!*

MAN: *(Confused; looks at his watch.)* Um…it's about 6:30.

WOMAN: That's not what I said, *asshole!*

(Woman hits him on the top of the head, he falls. Little girl cries.)

WOMAN: Shut up, little girl! I didn't do anything!

MAN: You're crazy!

(This time the "You're crazy" remark rather than making her cry makes her livid with rage, and she grabs onto the Man's grocery cart. He grabs onto the other end—for protection—and she shakes the cart wildly, sort of growling in rage while she does so. She then runs off again, the Man staring after her.)
(Blackout.)

Scene 3

Lights up again. The Man looking at tuna. The Woman comes into the supermarket again, making a beeline for where the Man is standing. Almost before she can get there, the little girl starts to cry offstage.

WOMAN: *(To crying offstage.)* Shut up, little girl, I didn't do anything yet!

(The Woman, irritated and stopped by the little girl's response, goes offstage again. The Man looks at the Woman very confused, not understanding why the little girl cried, or what the Woman was talking about. He looks out at the audience in befuddlement.)
(Blackout.)

Scene 4

Lights up again. The Man looking at tuna. The Woman enters and makes a beeline to where the Man is standing. He senses her energy behind him, looks worried, and holds up a can of tuna to "study"—but then stops himself and decides on another tack.

MAN: *(Polite, reasonable.)* Is something the matter?

WOMAN: What?

MAN: Well, you seem…odd.

WOMAN: *(Enraged.)* Don't you talk to me that way, *asshole!*

(Hits him on the head; little girl starts crying.)

WOMAN: Shut up, little girl, I didn't do anything! *(Grabs the Man's grocery cart and says with glee:)* I'm crazy!

(The Woman chases the Man with his own grocery cart. He runs offstage in terror, she follows in shrieking pursuit.)
(Blackout.)

Scene 5

Lights up again. The Man looking at tuna. The Woman enters once again, frustrated per usual. The Man senses her presence. The Woman overcomes her enormous frustration, and asks for what she wants.

WOMAN: Would you *please* move?
MAN: Are you trying to mug me?
(Turns and aims gun, shoots her dead; the little girl cries offstage.)
MAN: Shut up, little girl! *(Aims gun offstage, shoots little girl.)*
(Blackout.)

Scene 6

The sound of waves. Lights up on a blank stage. The Woman comes down in a spot and addresses the audience.

WOMAN: There's so much violence in my dreams. I've been having this recurring dream about that stupid man in the tuna fish aisle. The other night I dreamed he shot me.
(The Man comes down in another spot and addresses the audience. The Man and the Woman are seemingly not aware of one another.)
MAN: I've been having this recurring dream about the woman in the supermarket. I dream that no matter how else I try to behave, she *always* hits me on the head. The other night, though, I dreamt I shot her. I liked that dream. Although not when I was dreaming it. It was upsetting then. *(The Man freezes during the Woman's next speech.)*
WOMAN: I dreamt I was back at Creedmoor, and one of the orderlies was saying to me, "The universe doesn't make sense, there is no order, you should be a star like Edie Sedgewick, but you're not." And then I was in the institution dining room, and all the other people at the table were being really disgusting with their food, so I didn't want to look at this, so I kept staring at my plate. And on my plate there was this baked potato. And I started to get really afraid of this baked potato, and so finally I took my knife

and fork to open it up and inside the baked potato was my father—who I didn't know very well, he left my mother and me when I was pretty young. And so I wanted to know how he was, but when I asked him he said, "Who are you, I don't know you." So I put butter on him and ate him. *(The Woman freezes during the Man's next speech.)*

MAN: The other night I dreamt my father was inside a baked potato. Isn't that strange? I was very startled to see him there, and I started to be afraid other people would see where my father was, and how small he was, so I kept trying to close the baked potato, but I guess the potato was hot, cause he'd start to cry when I'd shut the baked potato, so then I didn't know what to do. I thought of sending the whole plate back to the kitchen—tell the cook there's a person in my baked potato—but then I felt such guilt at deserting my father that I just sat there at the table and cried. He cried too. Then the waiter brought dessert, which was devil's food cake with mocha icing, and I ate that. Then I woke up, very hungry. I told my therapist about the dream, and he said that the baked potato represented either the womb or where I tried to put my father during the Oedipal conflict—"What Oedipal conflict?" I always say to him, "I won, hands down." And then my therapist said my father cried because he was unhappy, and that I dreamt about the cake because I was hungry. I think my therapist is an idiot. Maybe I should just have gurus. Or find a nutritionist. But what I'm doing now isn't working. *(Lights off the Man.)*

(The Woman is alone onstage.)

WOMAN: And then the night after my baked potato dream, I dreamt about that stupid man from the tuna fish aisle again, and in my dream I got so mad at him that I started to feel sorry for myself, but then Nazis started to chase me and I had to hide in the frozen foods counter. And then the next night I dreamt that I killed Sally Jessy Raphael.

MAN: *(From offstage.)* And now the Sally Jessy Raphael Show.

(The stage transforms itself into a talk show setting. In the New York production, a section of the supermarket aisle turned around revealing a blue carpet and a blue "interview" chair; behind it was just more of the supermarket cans, but all color-coordinated blue—blue cans of soda, blue boxes of laundry detergent, etc., etc. Thus the setting rather than being a literal talk show became a kind of crackpot "dream" talk show, mixing up the supermarket and the TV show. The Woman discovers a microphone and red-framed glasses [similar to those worn by the real Sally Jessy Raphael], which she puts on.)

WOMAN: Hello. Sally Jessy Raphael can't be here today because I killed her. My aggression finally got the better of me, but what can you expect living in New York? These *are* her red-framed glasses, however. Do you like me in them? Now when my eyes are bloodshot from weeping or from allergies, you won't be able to tell whether it's my eyes that are red or my glasses!

This isn't my first time before the camera you know. The late Andy Warhol discovered me, and he said I should be as famous as Edie Sedgewick. That isn't very famous, of course, but those of you who follow the East Village scene and take drugs know who I mean. Ahahahahaha-hahahahaa.

I hope you don't mind if I do that, but I'm hoping to make that my signature on the air rather than these fuckin' glasses. Ahahahaha.

Let's see. Sally Jessy Raphael used to say "troops" a lot, I'll try that. Hey, troops! How are you? Do you like my glasses? That way when my eyes are red, you can't tell if I'm been crying or someone's punched me! Ahahahaha. Did I tell you about my father in the baked potato? I ate him. Now, troops, I don't mean sexually, I mean I ate him cannibalistically. Ahahahaha. Just kidding about that, troops, but know that my pain is sincere.

However, our show today isn't about cannibalism and it isn't about oral sex, although Dr. Ruth *is* a friend of mine…That's a lie, I hate Dr. Ruth and I hate Mother Theresa! I want them to fight to the death with chains and nuclear-fueled revolving dildos! I'm sorry…

(Calls out to technicians in the distance or offstage.) …can I say the word "dildo" on television? What? Read off the cards? Read off what cards? *(Sees something, reads from it.)* A E I O U. *(Tries to pronounce it.)* "Aeiou"? Well, that's an eye chart, not an idiot card. No, these cards are not useful. I am not an optimist. No, that's a slip of the tongue. I am not an optometrist. I am a talk show host or hostess.

Today our show is about nuclear proliferation. *And* it's also about the destruction of the ozone layer. *And* it's about sex education in the schools—should we tell our children about condoms or just wait until they get AIDS? And it's about AIDS, and it's about society's views on homosexuality—is it disgusting or is it delightful? And it's about the electoral college in our voting system—should we change it, should we rethink it, should we charge the delegates to the electoral college a tuition fee? And it's about free speech versus pay speech. Should people be allowed to say what they think? Should we demand that people who talk more pay more taxes? And where would that leave me?

Anyway, it's about all these topics—nuclear proliferation, condoms and children, the ozone layer, AIDS, homosexuality, heterosexuality, free speech, a tax on people who talk too much, and changing the electoral college—*and* we have to cover all these topics in under thirty minutes! So I better stop talking and bring out my first guest. Won't you join me in welcoming the Infant of Prague?

(Enter the Man dressed as the Infant of Prague. Now what do I mean by this? The Infant of Prague is a 17th-Century artist's invention of what the Christ Child, triumphant, might look like. Catholics are familiar with the look of this—usually in Infant of Prague statues—found in their churches, or sometimes on dashboards. Non-Catholics usually have not heard of the Infant of Prague, but some may recognize the "look." The "look" is this: a golden-haired child (of about ten to twelve maybe), dressed ornately. The most common look has white robes, embroidered with pearls and jewels, covered with a bright red cape, with white ruffles at the neck and wrists. On the top of the child's golden curls is a great big whopping crown, of gold and red, not unlike the crown in Imperial Margarine commercials on TV. [That is, it's big and has the "ball-like" red thing at the top of it.] The Infant in his left hand always carries a large orb [usually blue, and with a gold cross on top of it], and always has his right hand raised, with his first two fingers held upright, and his thumb and other two fingers folded in on one another. Since the Infant of Prague is usually a statue or sometimes a large doll whose silhouette often spreads out like an inverted "Y" due to the fullness of his robes, the New York designer chose to make the costume resemble a statue rather than a person. The robes spread out very wide to the side [on a kind of inner tubing] so that as costumed the Infant looked rather like an enormous, walking chess piece. When the audience saw underneath the Infant's robes, they saw a smooth, stretched white covering out of which two slippered feet protruded—again, looking very much like the bottom of a statue, and not that of a human being. Anyway, that, in words, is what the Infant of Prague looks like. And that is how the Man is dressed on his entrance. The Infant's personality, by the way, as played by the Man, is sunny and beatifically unflappable.)

WOMAN: *(To herself.)* Why am I dreaming about the Infant of Prague? I don't even know what that is.

MAN: *(To audience; not in character as the Infant, and perhaps lowering his upraised right hand.)* I dreamt I was the Infant of Prague appearing on the Sally Jesse Raphael show, though I've never even heard of her. *(The Man raises his right hand, with its two upraised fingers, and resumes being the Infant.)*

WOMAN: Infant of Prague, won't you sit down?

MAN: Thank you, Sally, I only stand.

WOMAN: I'm not Sally. Sally is dead.

MAN: *(With sympathy.)* Oh. And is she in heaven with my father?

WOMAN: I really don't know. Enough chitchat. Tell me—"Infant of Prague"— is that your first name?

MAN: My name is the Infant of Prague, and I am a representation of the Christ Child.

WOMAN: Really. Where do you live?

MAN: I am housed in the Church of Our Lady of Victory in Prague, capital of Czechoslovakia.

WOMAN: *(A penetrating question.)* Where is Prague exactly?

MAN: It's in Czechoslovakia.

WOMAN: And where is Czechoslovakia?

MAN: *(Confused.)* It's in Prague.

WOMAN: Ahahahahahahahal *(To Infant.)* That's my signature. Do you like my glasses? They're red. That way you can't tell if roving street gangs beat me up or not.

MAN: What?

WOMAN: Never mind. Tell us, Infant, a little bit about yourself.
(The Infant addresses a lot of his comments directly and happily to the audience because he is a born teacher, and because he is divine.)

MAN: A statue of me was given to the Discalced Carmelites in Prague in 1628 by princess Polyxena Lobkowitz.

WOMAN: Polly who Lobka-what?

MAN: The statue was a gift from her mother, Maria Mariquez de Lara, who had brought the statue with her to Bohemia when she married the Czech nobleman, Vratsilav of Pernstyn.

WOMAN: Princeton? Princeton, New Jersey?

MAN: No, not Princeton. *Pern*-styn.

WOMAN: Uh huh. I wonder if I have any other guests that could come on. *(Calls offstage.)* Oh, Ed? Is there anybody back there? *(To herself)* Who's Ed? I don't know any Ed. Oh never mind. *(To Infant.)* Tell us, Infant, a little about what you're wearing. *(To audience.)* That's pretty wild, isn't it, troops?

MAN: I'm glad you asked me that, Sally.

WOMAN: I'm not Sally. Sally's dead.

MAN: Then she's in heaven with my father. My inner garments are similar to the priest's alb, and are made of white linen and of lace. *(Proudly shows a bit of his undergarments, or beneath a ruffle.)*

WOMAN: Ooooh, this is getting racy.

MAN: Please don't make sacrilegious remarks or I'll have to leave.

WOMAN: I always get the difficult guests. First Eartha Kitt, and now a tea cozy.

MAN: *(Turning as in a fashion show.)* Covering my inner garments is a miniature liturgical cope, made of heavy damask, richly woven with gold and embroidered with pearls.

(In the New York production, the Woman actually went out into the audience to ask her questions, rather as Phil Donahue and Sally Jessy Raphael often do.)

WOMAN: Wow, you could really feed a lot of starving people with that outfit there, couldn't you, Infant?

MAN: *(Firmly.)* Most people do not eat gold and pearls, Sally.

WOMAN: Sally's dead, how many times do I have to tell you that!

MAN: Three times, representing the Blessed Trinity. Father, Son and Holy Spirit.

WOMAN: *(Referring to the orb.)* What's that little paperweight in your hand?

MAN: This is not a paperweight. It is a miniature globe, signifying the world-wide kingship of the Christ Child.

WOMAN: Uh huh. Well, fine, let's move on, shall we? *(A glint in her eye.)* Let's talk about condoms for a bit. Your church isn't very big on condoms, is it?

MAN: When people ask me, the Infant of Prague, for advice on sexuality, I sometimes think to myself, what do I know about sex?—I'm an infant. What's more, I'm the Infant of Prague; I can't sit down, let alone have sex. *(Laughs good-naturedly at his quip.)* But what people don't realize sometimes is that God my father has a holy and blessed purpose to the mystery of sexuality, and that purpose is to create other little infants like myself to glorify God and creation. That is why condoms are wrong because anything that intercepts—or *contra*-cepts—this process is deeply wrong.

WOMAN: Now let's get real here for a second, Infant. People are always going to have sex, and now we have this deadly disease AIDS which is killing people, and one of the ways to protect oneself is to use a condom. Now don't you think we better get *practical* here, and get people to use condoms? Whaddya say, Infant of Prague???

MAN: We must instruct the people at risk to abstain from sex.

WOMAN: Oh, well, fine. And we can tell the waterfall to stop falling, but is that practical?

MAN: Moses parted the Red Sea. *(Smiles at the audience, having made an unassailable point.)*

WOMAN: Uh huh. So let's get this straight—you would prefer that adolescents die from AIDS rather than tell them about condoms?

MAN: I do not prefer this at all, Sally. Yes, I know, Sally is dead. Sorry, I keep forgetting. Sally, I would tell all the teenagers of the world to be like me, an infant without sexual urges, until they were much, much older and ready to commit to one person for life, and to glory in the sacramental beauty of sex, within marriage, where during the actual act of intercourse all you can think about is "Procreation! Procreation! I am going to have a little baby, a little infant to glorify God!"

WOMAN: Well the teenagers in New Jersey are gonna love that answer. *Come on, Infant.* Don't you think you're a *little* impractical.

MAN: The Divine *is* impractical, that's why it's divine. *(The Infant smiles delight-edly, another unassailable point.)*

(The Woman would like to kill him.)

WOMAN: *(To audience.)* We have to take a little break here but we'll be right back with more of the Infant of Prague.

(ON THE AIR sign goes off, and theme music starts. Off the air, the Woman unleashes her pent-up fury and begins to pummel the Infant.)

WOMAN: YOU JERK, YOU STUBBORN SHIT, YOU EFFEMINATE EUNUCH, YOU MAKE ME WANT TO VOMIT WITH YOUR HOLIER THAN THOU ATTITUDE! WHY SHOULD WE LISTEN TO YOU ABOUT SEX??? YOU'RE AFRAID OF SEX, YOUR IDEAS ON SEX ARE RIGID AND INSANE, AND SOMEONE SHOULD HAVE YOU KILLED! I WANT YOU *DEAD!* DIE, DIE, *DIE!*

(The Infant looks startled and alarmed during this outburst. Toward the end of her outburst, one of her hits makes him fall over backwards, and the Woman dives on top of him, continuing her pummeling. The ON-THE-AIR sign comes back on, as does the theme music. The Woman looks out, caught in the act of straddling and beating up her guest. She gets off of him, and talks to the camera. The Infant remains on the ground, unable to stand up due to the weight of his clothes and crown. He struggles from time to time, moving his slippered feet about pathetically.)

WOMAN: Well, we're back on the air now. Ahahahahaha. Let's *talk* about "air," and the ozone layer, shall we? *(Notices the Infant's struggling; explains to the camera.)* He fell down during the commercial.

MAN: Would you help me stand up please?

WOMAN: Wait a minute. Give me your opinion on the destruction of the ozone layer.

MAN: I am opposed to the destruction of the ozone layer, Sally.

WOMAN: Who did we tell you was dead?

MAN: Sally.

WOMAN: Right answer. Alright, I'll help you up now.

(The Woman helps the Infant stand up. He looks disoriented for a moment.)

WOMAN: Okay. Let's go for the "gold." What about homosexuality—is it disgusting or is it delightful?

MAN: It is a grievous sin. But I love homosexuals, I just want them to be celibate until they die.

WOMAN: Who booked this jerk on here anyway??? *(Calls offstage again.)* Ed, I'm talking to you!

MAN: Where is Sally?

WOMAN: Who is Ed?

MAN: I don't want to be interviewed by you anymore. *(Starts to wander toward offstage and to call out.)* Sally? Sally!

WOMAN: *(Takes out a gun and aims it at him.)* I killed Sally Jessy Raphael, and I can kill you! *(Shoots him several times.)*

MAN: It is not possible to kill the Infant of Prague. *(He exits happily.)*

(She is enraged.)

WOMAN: *(Calling off after him.)* I hate you, I hate you, you Infant of Prague! *(To audience.)* I hate religious bigots. And I hate people who think they know what's right. And I hate people who are filled with hate. And I hate people who are filled with love. I wish my mother had had me killed when I was a fetus. That's the kind of person I am. Do you get it? Ahahahahahahal

WOMAN'S VOICE: *(On tape.)* My next guest today is Rama Sham Rama.

WOMAN: I don't want no fucking next guest! *(Shoots her gun offstage, apparently stopping Rama Sham Rama; then calls off in the other direction.)* Ed!! You're fired! *(Shoots her gun off in Ed's direction. The theme music plays nightmarishly, and the talk show set disappears or recedes into the distance. The Woman is now back in her waking-dream state again, and addresses the audience as herself once more, out of her Sally dream.)* Why is there so much violence in my dreams? I'm always killing people or they're killing me. The other night I dreamt I killed Sally Jessy Raphael. And then I tried to kill the Infant of Prague, whoever the hell that is. Then Rama Sha Rambus somebody. I have to let go of this rage, I can't live this way anymore.

(Lights off the Woman, spot on the Man, dressed back in his normal clothes again.)

MAN: I dreamt the other night that I was in Central Park before dawn at the

Harmonic Convergence ceremony, and that the "icky woman" was talking about her hopes for mankind again, but that various mental patients kept interrupting her.

(Lights back on the Woman. The Man's spot stays on also, though he doesn't yet hear what she's saying.)

WOMAN: I dreamt that I was at the "Harmonic Convergence"—whatever the hell that is. Something is wrong with my dreams lately, I keep dreaming about things I've never heard about. Anyway, and this woman with a flower in her head kept saying things like "I dance for the Sun King," and "I dance for the Moon King"—it made me *real* hostile. So I called out at the top of my lungs, "Why don't you get your tooth fixed?"

MAN: Oh! And then I dreamt that the woman from the tuna fish aisle was there, and she shouted at the "icky woman," "Why don't you see a dentist?" or "There's something wrong with your tooth," or something like that. But it didn't make much sense, there wasn't anything wrong with the woman's tooth.

WOMAN: And then all these aging hippies were sitting with their legs crossed and their eyes closed, doing meditation…

(The Man closes his eyes and puts his arms at his sides, palms out, joining in the meditation.)

WOMAN: …and I yelled out, "WHAT DO YOU THINK THIS IS—1967???" And then someone gave me a flower, and I said "Oh, fuck you!" and I ripped the flower up, and they had this real hurt look on their face, and then everyone started to make sounds together…

MAN: *(Toning, a low, calm sound.)* Ohhhhhhhhhhhhhhhmmmmmmmmmmm-mmmmmmm… *(Continues toning.)*

WOMAN: Ohhhhhhhhhhhhmmmmmmmmmmmmmm. So then I did that for a while. But I got bored, so I thought, I know, I'll pretend to be a car alarm, so I went: eeeeeeeeeeeeeeeEEEEEEEEEEEEEEEEEEEEEEEEEEEEEEEEEE-EEEEEEEEEEEEEEEEEEEEE…

(Woman does an upsettingly successful imitation of a shrieking car alarm. The Man seems to hear it in his unconscious, and it fights with his "ohm" sound. He frowns.)

MAN: *(Continuing through above.)* …mmmmmmmmmmmmmmmmmmmmm. Then I turned *off* my alarm…

(Makes a gesture of turning off alarm; the Woman stops making her noise.)

MAN: …which was waking me, but then I went right back to sleep, and now the "icky woman" wasn't there anymore, and somehow I had been designated the person who was supposed to run the ceremony in her absence. I tried to blow on a conch shell, which I thought I had in my hand, but it was actually a ham sandwich, so, of course, when I blew on it it didn't make any noise. So then I addressed the crowd.

(Lights shift. The Man crosses center. The sound of a light wind, and of tinkling wind chimes. The Woman is seated nearby. He and she are now in a kind of joint dream about the Harmonic Convergence. In the New York production, a black backdrop moved away, and the setting was a dreamlike setting of Central Park, with bushes and shrubbery around, mixed in strangely with parts of the supermarket aisle and some of the elements of the talk show as well. It was lit like night, a bit before dawn. The man speaks to the crowd, he projects a bit loudly.)

MAN: I seem to have misplaced my conch shell. If anyone finds it, please let me know.

WOMAN: *(Disruptively loud.)* WHAT THE FUCK'S A CONCH SHELL?

MAN: *(Trying to pay no attention.)* I have been asked to lead the ceremony until dawn comes. The icky woman—that is…Vicki, her name is Vicki—has had to leave the park to take several patients back to various mental institutions.

WOMAN: Was any of them Creedmoor? I have connections at Creedmoor.

MAN: *(To Woman, patiently, but bothered.)* Please, don't just call out, I find it disorienting.

WOMAN: Why don't you get your tooth fixed?

MAN: There is nothing wrong with my tooth. *(To crowd.)* We are here to enter a new age. The planets of Mars and…Hathor are in alignment with the seventh moon of the seventh sun of the seventh seal.

WOMAN: Why don't you give me a job?

MAN: Please everyone hold a crystal to your head, and align yourself with Mother Earth. *(Holds a small clear crystal to his head, and closes his eyes to concentrate.)*

WOMAN: If you hire me at the magazine, I promise not to write "pig" on the wall with your blood!

MAN: I would not be willing to hire you under those circumstances.

WOMAN: Well, fuck you!

MAN: Can someone take this woman away? Is Vicki back?

WOMAN: Vicki's dead. She and Mother Theresa fought to the death with knives at the coliseum.

MAN: *(Closes his eyes, does his "affirmation" hands-in-a-circular-motion gestures.)* Everyone in my universe is cooperative. I am a natural leader, and no one yells out in the middle of my speaking. I let the gems of the earth empower me. *(Holds the crystal to his forehead.)*

WOMAN: Why are you holding that piece of chandelier to your forehead?

MAN: It's a crystal.

WOMAN: And my doctors think *I'm* crazy.

MAN: Would you please be quiet?

WOMAN: No! *(Sings "Vilia" operatically, to annoy the man, and to block out what he's saying.)*

MAN: *(Trying to ignore her.)* The earth is entering a *new phase* where it is going to evaluate what man has done to it over the past many centuries. And, if there are 144,000 *enlightened people* on the earth at the time of the Harmonic Convergence, it's possible we can shift away from death and destruction…

WOMAN: I dance for the sun king! *(Dances across the stage in a put-on, arty way.)*

MAN: …to a place of unity, and unconditional love and harmony…

WOMAN: I dance for the moon king! *(Dances some more.)*

MAN: …both for mankind and for the planet.

WOMAN: And when I don't dance, I laugh. Ahahahahahahahaha!

MAN: We only have a few minutes left until dawn.

WOMAN: *(Suddenly direct; to the Man.)* You're blocking my way.

MAN: We should all be silent now, until the dawn.

WOMAN: You're blocking my way.

MAN: What?

WOMAN: Why are you always blocking my way to the tuna fish?

MAN: What tuna fish? There isn't any tuna fish here. We're in Central Park.

WOMAN: Well, what's that then?

(She points upstage where, indeed, there is a section of supermarket aisle with tuna fish cans on it, mixed in with the Central Park shrubbery. The Man is very disoriented. There had been no tuna fish in his Central Park dream up till now.)

MAN: *(Very annoyed, to the crowd.)* Why is there tuna fish in Central Park??

WOMAN: It's a Gristedes. It's very convenient.

MAN: No, we all have to cooperate now, this isn't the time for tuna fish.

WOMAN: I want to get by you!

MAN: No, we have to prepare for the dawn.

WOMAN: I make the dawn come up like thunder!

MAN: No! Now go sit down and wait. Can't you do that?

WOMAN: I'm always being told to wait. When is it my turn??

MAN: NEVER! NOW SIT THE FUCK DOWN!!!

(The Woman is startled by the Man's fury. She sits. He goes into toning, some-what abruptly after his screaming.)

MAN: Ohhhhhhhhhhhhhhhmmmmmmmmmmmmmmm.

WOMAN: *(Hands over ears, hating the sound.)* Stop making that noise!

(The Man continues to tone. The Woman is driven crazy by the sound. She stands and makes her "car alarm" sound again. She crosses to him, dreamlike, raises her fist in slow motion and brings it down on his head. He falls to the ground, and she is now free to get to the tuna fish finally. All sound stops. The Woman runs over to the tuna fish aisle, thrilled.)

WOMAN: At last! I'm here now, I'm safe, I'm here, I have what I want! *(Takes a can, reads it.)* Poison. *(Throws it offstage; looks at next one.)* Poison. *(Throws it offstage; looks at next one.)* Poison! *(Throws it; looks at next one.)* Salmon. I don't want salmon. *(Throws it; looks at next one.)* Poison! *(Throws it; looks at next one.)* Tomato soup! *(Throws it.)* WHAT IS THE MATTER WITH THIS STORE??? *(Weeps.)*

(The Woman moves away from the aisle. The stage darkens. In New York, a black backdrop came in and swallowed up the whole Central Park–supermarket setting. The Man starts to come to from having been hit. He rubs his head, and notices the darkening around him.)

MAN: Oh, everything's turning black. Keep toning. Ohhhhhhhhhhhhhhhhhh-hhhhmmmmmmmm…

(The Woman's weeping continues. The sound of the little girl crying offstage is heard also, nightmarishly. The Man keeps trying to tone, to drown out the sound of crying.)

MAN: If people are going to refuse to tone, the dawn may not come up. Ohhhhhhhhhhhhhhhhmmmmmm. Ohhhhhhhhhhhhmmmmm. *(To weeping Woman.)* SHUT UP!

(The lights shift to two spotlights, one on the Man, one on the Woman. All noise stops.)

WOMAN: *(To audience.)* And then I dreamt that the man in the tuna fish aisle was suddenly empathetic with me.

MAN: *(To audience.)* And then I dreamt that the woman and I were still in Central Park and she was still weeping, but I felt this sudden wave of empathy for her.

(The lights shift back to how they were before the asides. The Woman goes back to weeping, but the scene is otherwise quiet. The Man tries to think how to speak to her.)

MAN: What's the matter?

WOMAN: I'm laughing wild amid severest woe.

MAN: But you're weeping.

WOMAN: Oh, sorry. *(Burst of crazy laughter.)* Ahahahahahahahahahaha!

MAN: Did you get the tuna fish you need?

WOMAN: Why don't you get your tooth fixed?

MAN: Ummmm…That's a good suggestion, thank you, I will.

WOMAN: The tuna fish is all mislabeled. Some of it is salmon, and some of it is poison, and some of it is tomato soup.

MAN: That's a shame. Maybe you would like to tell the people here in the park about your hopes for the Harmonic Convergence?

WOMAN: Yes, I would. *(Addresses the crowd; with a soft quality.)* I hope that the pounding in my head stops. And I hope that people will not spit on me as I pass them in the street. And I hope that someone gives me a job. And I hope that I have more good days than bad days. That I learn to say this glass is half-full, it is not half-empty. And to hell with my half-full glass— I want a *full* full glass, I want it overflowing. And I want to feel joy like I did that one summer day for ten minutes right before I decided life was horrible and I went crazy. I want to recapture the feeling of *liking* to be alive. I want to feel joy that looks like this. *(She throws her head back and spreads her arms wide in an exuberant, open, receiving position.)*
(The darkness on the stage changes to vibrant color: deep purple to deep red to a warm, rose hue. In other words, it's dawn, though not presented realistically. The Man notices the light. He stands and feels he should probably continue "leading" the crowd.)

MAN: The sun's up. Everybody, breathe. In…
(The Woman is in her exuberant, head-thrown-back posture still. Without making it a big deal, she automatically joins the Man's, and crowd's, breathing rhythms.)

WOMAN: And out…
(The Man notes her joining. Again, no big deal, but it's the first time they've had agreement on anything ever. There is relief. Breathing, dawn.)

MAN: In…

WOMAN: …and out…
(The Man and the Woman maybe look at one another on their last lines, before the lights fade.)

MAN: In…

WOMAN: …and out…

END OF PLAY

AUTHOR'S NOTES

(In the acting edition of *Laughing Wild,* in place of my usual acting and directing notes, I published the following.)

Eggs, butter, cheese. Return phone calls to Jon Denny, Jay Siem at Merrill Lynch, Nancy Quinn at the young Playwrights Festival. Answer letter from three years ago asking me to speak on Whither American Drama at the University of Rochester. Buy triple A batteries for my VCR remote control.

I went to a restaurant the other day and read David Mamet's *Writing in Restaurants.* I ordered Eggs Benedict, and spilled Hollandaise Sauce on the book. It was a sign of something, but of what?

Last year I was re-experiencing my feelings of grief and deep sorrow at feeling (or being) abandoned at age three, when my mother went into a deep depression at the death of her second child and my father was stopping up his feelings by drinking. This year I am about to relive parts of my adolescence. Along these lines, I have grown my first beard; it has bits of gray in it, which is not appropriate for a teenager, but is fine for a man of my age.

Some days I want to kill Frank Rich, the drama critic of the *New York Times.* He represents this Great Deaf Ear I must somehow get through to in order to reach a theatre-going public. The "New Age" part of me knows this perception regarding him is merely a giving away of my power to him; and, truthfully, in New York I seem to have an audience that comes to my plays regardless, more or less, of what he says.

The genuine problem I face is that the approval and hoopla of the *Times* is very important to creating an "atmosphere" around a play, a sense that one should see it soon; and this "must see" quality is what sells tickets at the beginning, and motivates a producer to move a play from a nonprofit New York theatre (like Playwrights Horizons or Manhattan Theatre Club) to a commercial run on- or off-Broadway. After a couple of months, this *Times'* support is much less important, and then word of mouth kicks in. But for that initial period, the *Times* support is awfully significant. And having your play in an open commercial run, versus a few weeks at a nonprofit theatre, is of enormous difference in terms of reaching a larger audience, and of finances. (You can make a living with royalties from a play that runs; you can pay maybe two months rent with payment from a play at a nonprofit theatre.)

Oh Lord, I really don't want to talk about the critics particularly, because I don't see a solution in sight. And yet every time I sit down to work on the notes for this play the issue comes charging up for me.

Everyone in theatre knows how crazy it is to have One Critical Voice that carries such weight, and that it's the result of having only one newspaper that most of the theatre-going public seems to read. And it's pointless to blame anyone because nobody "caused" this state of affairs. But most people in theatre suffer severely under this state of affairs.

Nothing similar exists in movies or books because they are reviewed nationally, and quickly a consensus forms. For instance, Woody Allen's film *Hannah and Her Sisters* received a very ho-hum response from Pauline Kael in the *New Yorker*. The bulk of the other reviews indicated a consensus that *Hannah* was one of his best films, and Kael's opinion quickly fit into its proper place as an idiosyncratic nay vote. If *Hannah* had been a play and the gifted Ms. Kael had been the *New York Times* theatre critic, *Hannah* would probably have closed.

The truth is I'm worn out working in this system. Of my last four plays—*Beyond Therapy, Baby with the Bathwater, The Marriage of Bette and Boo,* and *Laughing Wild*—the *Times* (in the Pontiff-like voice of Rich) only liked *Baby with the Bathwater,* and that, due to his review, was the one that came closest to being moved to a commercial run. However, it was the one that least should have been considered for a commercial run since audiences way preferred the other three, especially *Beyond Therapy,* which most people found very funny, and *Bette and Boo,* which most found funny and touching.

I've twice now had ecstatic receptions to plays on opening nights—*Bette and Boo* and *Laughing Wild*—that are impossible for me to enjoy because I know I'm waiting for the word from his Lord Chief Executioner. It's such a stupid system. If he didn't write for the major newspaper in New York, Frank Rich's opinion per se would be of zero interest to me, especially as the years have gone on and he's gotten harder and harder. It must be all that veal he eats at Orso's.

Now one can buck the system to a point. If a producer is aggressive and pours money into a campaign and gets the actors to take lower salaries and gets the writer, director, and designers to waive their royalties (and everyone is getting low salaries to begin with), you can keep a show open until it finds its audience. Jack McQuiggan, producer of Larry Shue's *The Foreigner,* did that in recent years. So did the producers of Shue's *The Nerd.* More power to these people.

In my situation I've mostly been working with the New York nonprofit theatres which have subscription seasons of plays so that a play must either be so acclaimed that it moves to a different theatre (a commercial house On- or Off-Broadway), or it must close to make room for the next play. So in those houses—Playwrights Horizons, Manhattan Theatre Club, the Public Theatre (though Joe Papp has a bit more flexibility, having more spaces)—one cannot keep a play running open-ended until an audience "finds" it. One must be acclaimed, with the accompanying hoopla causing a flurry of box office activity that pretty much demands a move to a commercial run—which is indeed what happened to my play *Sister Mary Ignatius Explains It All For You* at Playwrights Horizons in 1981. Without the critical *Times* hoopla, you most likely will close in a few weeks to make room for the next play.

Now in a "this glass is half-full, not half-empty" scenario, I must admit I get my plays produced, and I make a living. So what more do I want?

Well, the truth is, I do want more. I want to work in a theatrical arena where one man's opinion does not carry this crazy weight, where if audiences and other critics find *Beyond Therapy* funny, Mr. Rich's opinion that it is not funny will not count except as a tiny part of a larger consensus. But seemingly I can't have that. The *Times* is totally unmoving about "taking responsibility" for its power. People from the theatre community have been meeting with its editors on and off for at least twenty years, and the *Times* prides itself on being open to solving this problem, and claims to be embarrassed by its power. But the possible solutions to the problem—having more than one critic review a play at a time, running a "scorecard" of what the other critics said, even a tiny suggestion like having "opinion" written at the top of the review—are invariably overruled by the *Times*. The truth is, whether they admit it to themselves or not, the editors of the *Times* and Rich love their power. It makes them feel, well, powerful.

So, in truth, to overcome Frank Rich I have to either work with more aggressive producers (like the aforementioned McQuiggan, who bucked the critical rejection of *The Foreigner* to keep it running until audiences found it, thereby making his property very valuable, and produced all over the country), or somehow be satisfied with a four-week run at a nonprofit theatre in New York.

But right now I feel worn out by the notion. I don't want to go up in front of His Pontiff Rich again. Theatre seems an unfriendly and unaccepting arena to work in, at least in New York. I can't seem to see around this problem right now. I've recently had good times writing for camera—a half-hour episode of PBS' *Trying Times* series called "The Visit" and starring Swoosie Kurtz, and a crackpot seven-minute film for Showtime's *By-line* series that was a mock documentary of my life as a writer (with Christine Estabrook as my wife who sleeps on the kitchen floor). It was fun to make these works, and to know there was no one-man pit bull waiting to devour them. Maybe it's time to hand the theatre over to Rich—let him order it just like his veal and pasta at Orso's.

I love theatre, which is why there's anger (and sorrow) in my tone for what I perceive Rich and the *Times* to have done to New York theatre, and to my possible place in it. It's just not a good place here.

Christopher Durang
New York City
March 1988

UPDATE ON ESSAY ON CRITICS IN NEW YORK

I received many nice and encouraging letters after my essay on critics appeared at the end of *Laughing Wild*. I thank the people who wrote me.

I don't feel I have anything to take back from what I said, though the essay seemed to give rise to a rumor that I stopped writing "because" of Frank Rich. This was partially true, partially untrue. As the essay reflected accurately, I found his frequently dismissive response to my work was, indeed, making me dread presenting a play in New York, and from 1988 to 1993 I did not.

But looking back, it wasn't only that which was stopping me. I think I was in a kind of writer's block during that time. Totally disconnected to Rich, I just wasn't feeling the "impulse" to write.

So my silence for several years came about from something within my own spirit as much as from my frustration with critics.

Oddly, in 1993, I was just moving to the psychological space of re-accepting the critical situation and being willing to brave writing for New York theatre again when Rich on his own retired from the theatre page and moved to editorial writing on the Op Ed page of the *Times*.

Rich is a classmate of mine from Harvard. I didn't know him there, but I keep trying to come to peace with him in my head. I think he's a genuinely fine writer. I often agree with his liberal opinions on the Op Ed page. Most days I wish him well. I also know I feel that after he so liked and praised *Sister Mary* that he became somehow unwilling to go where my other work went. That's his right; he can't say he liked something if he didn't. But, in the pit of my stomach, I started to dread having a play open, knowing he'd review it. It's a fact of my stomach.

So what have I been doing since 1987?

Well, gosh, what. Consciously choosing to avoid theatre critics, I chose to do a crackpot cabaret act, *Chris Durang and Dawne,* in 1988 at the Criterion Center Cabaret. This musical comedy-obsessed act let me sing, which I enjoy, and perform with my talented cohorts, John Augustine and Sherry Anderson, who played my backup group "Dawne."

The act began with us singing Michael Jackson's "Bad" (current at the time), which then segued into "Bali Hai." My early patter included the lines: "I'm Chris Durang, and this is Dawne, and together we're Chris Durang and Dawne. I used to be a playwright, but it was too hard. I'm hoping being a lounge singer will be easier."

This particular patter added to the perception I had given up writing, but I did mean it mostly tongue-in-cheek. But then, on the other hand, I guess I was partially serious. So I meant two things, both contradictory.

My plans for avoiding theatre critics, by the way, turned out to be amusingly pointless: We got horrible reviews from the cabaret critics ("They shouldn't give up their day jobs," the *Post* cabaret critic wrote), but suddenly got wonderful reviews from the theatre critics (including Rich and John Simon), whom I hadn't realized had even been invited. We then became a hot ticket for a while (and quirky celebrities would show up, like the night Carol Channing and Tommy Tune came backstage, grinning and each seeming seven feet tall).

So, you see, double-guessing who's going to like you just doesn't work.

Then, unable to stand the city that doesn't sleep for another noisy minute, I rented a house in Connecticut with my friend John Augustine, ostensibly for a summer, but it became over two years. The house I rented had floor-to-ceiling glass windows and doors everywhere, and I stared out at the trees and the snow and the deer and the raccoons for hours at a time. I bought a home movie camera, and filmed the deer obsessively. I have fifteen hours of deer on tape, if you'd ever like to see them. I also have film of raccoons who would come up on the deck at dusk to eat bird seed, and would stare in at me and John having dinner. I discovered raccoons have terrible eating habits, and after a while I would give them leftovers on paper plates. They liked anything that was carbohydrate or sugar, but would ignore vegetables. One night I gave them an entire microwave devil's food cake. They liked it very much.

I guess in this country period, I was withdrawing somewhat, but it was also healing.

I supplemented my income—and had fun—by getting some supporting parts in movies. (I started to get acting auditions for films after being in *Bette and Boo.*) I played a disgruntled executive in *Secret of My Success* (and also rewrote some of the scenes, including all the scenes I was in). I played Jeff Daniel's psychiatric patient in *The Butcher's Wife;* I had a nice part in *Mr. North,* based on a Thornton Wilder book; I played a minister counseling Steve Martin and Goldie Hawn in *Housesitter.* Even though my pay was not high in Hollywood terms, it sometimes paid me more to act for two weeks in a movie than to write a play that ran for a few weeks at a New York not-for-profit theatre.

In 1990 I did *Laughing Wild* in L.A., and then was approached by Warner Bros. to write a sitcom.

For over a year, I worked on writing an original pilot, which I'm proud of, called *Dysfunction!—The TV Show,* which we then sold to the Fox Network. When I was hired, *Twin Peaks* and off-beat material were "in"; nine months later, when I finished my eighth draft (still a good script, I kept hanging in there), off-beat was no longer "in", and Fox chose not to make the pilot. NBC considered it for a minute, but felt it had another show too similar (which it didn't, but let it pass); they asked if I had any other series ideas. If I were a different personality, I would have tried to stay out there and come up with another series idea; but I felt tired, and came back to Connecticut.

In 1992 I wrote a play, *Media Amok,* that Brustein presented at A.R.T. I worked with a nice director, Les Waters, and the cast was terrific—especially Christine Estabrook, Alvin Epstein and the invaluable Anne Pitoniak as the lead, a sweet little lady who can't stand the vileness she sees on television, and one day wanders into the TV and gets stuck there. It ends with her and her husband in a tree house in the forest, more or less looking forward to death.

Lots of the play I like; but something about it didn't hold together; and I couldn't figure out how to fix it. So I chose to put it away in a drawer. Maybe some day I'll return to it and make it a one act.

In late 1992 I became concerned about my finances, and tried to bully myself into writing something light-hearted and theoretically commercial like *Beyond Therapy.* But I just didn't want to write anything. And bullying yourself is a terrible way to get in the mood to write.

So I then decided to consider giving up on writing. Just because I had been a writer since my twenties didn't mean that's what I had to do for my entire life. I decided I needed to open myself up to other options—perhaps more acting, or should I be a casting agent? Or should I live in a small town and give lessons to people on how to use the pumps at self-serve gas stations?

I'm being a bit flip, but it was important for me genuinely to entertain letting go of writing…holding on to something that isn't flowing doesn't really work, and just makes you unhappy.

The reason I tell this is that a few weeks after I decided to let go of forcing the writing, I feel the universe rewarded me with a most exciting offer. Did I want to perform in a Stephen Sondheim revue at the Manhattan Theatre Club called *Putting It Together?* Sondheim, who had seen me perform in *Das Lusitania Songspiel* and in *Chris Durang and Dawne,* thought I'd be a good idea for the singing narrator, who's meant to be playful and a bit cynical.

I'm an enormous fan of Sondheim's, and I was flattered and excited to do this. Sondheim told me they were seeking a star to do the leading lady part (in London it had been Diana Rigg); and then all of a sudden they got Julie Andrews to agree to do it, her first stage appearance since *Camelot.*

So I got to be in this five-person musical of fabulous songs with Julie Andrews (and Michael Rupert, Stephen Collins and Rachel York). The first week and a half I went into overwhelm, and I think almost got fired; but then I got much better, and wasn't fired; and basically I had the most wonderful time.

I remember when we recorded the CD, looking around the room and seeing Julie Andrews with headphones on, and me with headphones on, and thinking: How did I get in this position? And isn't it fun?

I guess why this is germane to this wrap-up essay is that being in this show challenged and excited me, and lifted my spirits; and toward the end of our three-month run, one night I suddenly had the impulse to write again...the actual impulse, not the "you should" impulse, not the "oh my God, I need money" impulse...but that genuine impulse that I hope keeps visiting me in my life.

Since then, I've had an evening of one acts called *Durang Durang* at Manhattan Theatre Club; I did *Chris Durang and Dawne* again; I moved to nearby Pennsylvania (rural and pretty and quiet; though I do go to New York a few times a week); and I recently wrote a play *Sex and Longing* that Lincoln Center Theatre presented in 1996 with Sigourney Weaver. I think the play's very good (and it's very political); however, I'm rethinking some of it before getting it published.

I keep wishing I were on a psychological plateau, where everything is balanced and makes sense, and where one knows it will all unfold successfully and without trauma. But then it wouldn't be life, would it? So I'm in movement; I'm awake; I'm okay.

Christopher Durang
February 1997